Peachtree Complete
Business Toolkit

About the Author...

John Hedtke is the award-winning author of *Peachtree Complete Accounting for Windows Made Easy, Third Edition*; *Peachtree Accounting for Windows Made Easy, Second Edition*; *Using Computer Bulletin Boards, Third Edition*; and 10 other books. A software expert with 20 years of experience, Hedtke develops and writes documentation and books for many leading software products and contributes frequent articles to computer magazines. He has also developed and documented accounting, payroll, tax preparation, and spreadsheet software. Hedtke is the President of the Puget Sound chapter of the Society for Technical Communication and can be reached through his web site at *http://www.oz.net/~jhedtke*. He lives in Seattle.

Peachtree Complete Business Toolkit

John Hedtke

Osborne/**McGraw-Hill**

Berkeley New York St. Louis San Francisco Auckland Bogotá Hamburg London Madrid Mexico City
Milan Montreal New Delhi Panama City Paris São Paulo Singapore Sydney Tokyo Toronto

Osborne/**McGraw-Hill**
2600 Tenth Street
Berkeley, California 94710
U.S.A.

For information on translations or book distributors outside the U.S.A., or to arrange bulk purchase discounts for sales promotions, premiums, or fund-raisers, please contact Osborne/**McGraw-Hill** at the above address.

Peachtree Complete Business Toolkit

1234567890 DOC DOC 901987654321098

ISBN 0-07-882373-0

Publisher
Brandon A. Nordin

Editor-in-Chief
Scott Rogers

Acquisitions Editor
Wendy Rinaldi

Technical Editor
Ian Hagemann

Project Editor
Nancy McLaughlin

Editorial Assistant
Ann Sellers

Copy Editor
Tim Barr

Proofreader
Jeff Barash

Indexers
James Minkin
Rebecca Plunkett

Computer Designer
Roberta Steele

Illustrator
Arlette Crosland

Cover Design
Elysium Design

Dedicated to Margaret Knight,
one of my oldest friends,
who makes the world a better place.

Contents at a Glance

Contents

Acknowledgments

Being an author is a lot of fun. You don't have to commute, you have a lot of flexibility when setting your working schedule, and you don't have to dress up for the office. But being an author is also a lot of work. All of the following people have helped make the process of writing this book more fun and less work than it would have been otherwise:

To my esteemed reviewers:

✦ Maryanne Tyson, who once again donated her time and effort to making this book that much better. Thanks, Maryanne; you've added enormously to the quality of this book.

✦ Brenda Winkers-Huset and her two able assistants, Craig Coleman and Jeff Schandel, the technical reviewers at Peachtree, without whom this book would not have been as good.

✦ Ian Hagemann, who was technical editor on the book. Good show, Ian.

To the contributing editors:

✦ Elisabeth Knottingham, who wrote the chapters on PeachLink and filled in with many other valuable writing services. Elisabeth, you're a heckuva writer!

✦ Lynn McManus, for Chapter 11, "Peachtree Accounting Add-ons and Other Software," as well as for valuable contributions to the CD-ROM. It's always a pleasure working with you, Lynn.

✦ Linda Bell, for providing good writing on Chapter 10. Thanks, Linda!

To a long list of great people at Peachtree: Susan Thompson, Dave Richards, Greg Grimes, Brad MacAfee, Doug Meyer, Jay Parcon, Becky Capps, Kim Wills, Diane Maxson, and Tim Waggoner, all of whom donated their time and energy to this project.

To Brian Chinn, who provided special assistance with hardware and information.

To Ronald A. Blackmore, ace service guru at MicroSupply in Bellevue, WA, for providing last-minute service replacing a dead power supply at cost. Bravo, bravo!

To Lonnie Foster, for HTML information and for the ducks.

To Constance Maytum, for more things than I can possibly list.

To the noble contributors:

+ Carol and Jim Groves, Maryanne Tyson, Richard Petro, Brian Futrell, Chris Lyon, and Jingqing Ren (all of whom contributed greatly) of Wizard Business Solutions, for providing both suggestions and software for the CD.
+ Robert Walraven of Multiware, Inc., for PAW/et.
+ Bob Berry of Canyon State Systems & Software, for CompuShow for Windows.
+ Christina Delger, Leslie Grandy, and John Bove of Visio, for the Visio 5 Standard demo.
+ Nico Mak of Nico Mak Computing, for WinZip.
+ Bill Tiede of iSBiSTER International, for Time & Chaos32.
+ Kathy Episcopo and Anita Hix of QUALCOMM, for Eudora.
+ Julie Murdoch of Forté, Inc., for Free Agent.
+ David Karp and Melissa Riccio of Ipswitch, Inc., for WS_FTP.
+ Matt Knutson and Nancy Johnson of JASC Software, Inc., for Paint Shop Pro.

To all the wonderful folks at Osborne/McGraw-Hill:

+ Brandon A. Nordin and Scott Rogers for their continued support.
+ Wendy Rinaldi, senior acquisitions editor, who is always great fun to work with.
+ Ann Sellers, editorial assistant, for coordinating the thousands of little details on this book.
+ Nancy McLaughlin, project editor; Tim Barr, copyeditor with a keen eye, Jeff Barash, proofreader, and James Minkin and Rebecca Plunkett, indexers.
+ Jani Beckwith and Roberta Steele, designers, for doing the page layout, and Lance Ravella, for the screen shots, all of whom are working under Marcela Hancik, design supervisor.

And finally, to you, the reader, for buying this book.

To all of these people and many more, my heartfelt thanks for making this book possible.

And always remember: you should avoid buying a house and moving the week before a writing deadline.

John Hedtke
Seattle, 1998

Introduction

Welcome to *Peachtree Complete Business Toolkit*. This book shows you how to use several important add-on products and features for Peachtree Accounting products:

✦ **Peachtree Report Writer** Peachtree Report Writer lets you add custom reports to the wide variety of reports that already accompany Peachtree Accounting for Windows and Peachtree Complete Accounting for Windows. You can use Peachtree Report Writer to create and modify standard reports, area, bar, and pie charts, and labels.

✦ **PeachLink** The PeachLink software lets you create a web site for your company. You can set up a web site with information from your Peachtree Accounting files, providing you with an instant interface to your product lists so you can take orders directly over the Internet.

✦ **Electronic Bill Payment** Both Peachtree Accounting for Windows and Peachtree Complete Accounting for Windows come with Electronic Bill Payment (formerly known as *e*-Check) that lets you do electronic transfers, saving yourself time mailing checks and also saving the cost of physically cutting, signing, and processing checks.

✦ **Peachtree Add-ons and Other Software** You'll be introduced to a wide variety of Peachtree add-on software, including PAW/et from Multiware, Inc., a tool that lets you import and export data directly between Peachtree and other programs, and the Utility Pack for Peachtree, a suite of programs and utilities for Peachtree Accounting from Wizard Business Solutions that augment many of the features in Peachtree Accounting. In addition, you'll also learn about a number of different programs and utilities that will make Windows 95 easier and more convenient to use. (Many of these programs are included on the CD-ROM accompanying this book.)

There are also appendixes of reference information and online resources.

Why This Book Is for You

Peachtree Complete Business Toolkit is written for anyone who wants to get the most out of Peachtree Accounting for Windows or Peachtree Complete Accounting for Windows. Readers unfamiliar with Peachtree Accounting will be able to use this book to learn how to use the features and add-ons for Peachtree Accounting, while intermediate and advanced users of Peachtree Accounting will be able to explore some of the more powerful features of the products to further increase their company's productivity and effectiveness.

NOTE: If you haven't used Peachtree before, it's a good idea to go through the Peachtree online tutorial and learn some of the basics of the Peachtree Accounting software. Only minimal accounting experience is required.

If you have already used any of the products described in this book, the process-oriented approach makes this an excellent book for easy reference or for a handy guide to a feature that you have not used before. Experienced users will find discussions on how features can be used together to integrate your accounting system with your reporting system, your web site, and your electronic check writing system.

Peachtree Complete Business Toolkit is the perfect choice for a brief, self-contained introduction to the things you can do with Peachtree add-ons.

TIP: If you're not already familiar with many of the features of Peachtree Accounting and want information on the basics, you may want to purchase *Peachtree Complete Accounting for Windows Made Easy* from Osborne/McGraw-Hill, described later in this introduction.

About This Book

This book is meant to be a fast introduction to Peachtree Report Writer, PeachLink, and Electronic Bill Payment, as well as some of the software recommended for Peachtree Accounting users.

After giving an introduction to the software, each feature is discussed by taking you through the menus and explaining how to use the feature. Experienced users will find it quite simple to look up the techniques they will need to run and adapt their system. New users will find instructions on setting up features and the options available to them.

You don't need to be familiar with Peachtree Accounting to use the programs featured in this book, but you should know some basic accounting concepts and understand how to operate your computer. You also need to have Peachtree Accounting for Windows or Peachtree Complete Accounting for Windows installed on your system.

How This Book Is Organized

This book is divided into three sections, which are outlined below.

Part 1: Peachtree Report Writer

The first section tells you how to use Peachtree Report Writer to create and print reports and labels in Peachtree Accounting.

Chapter 1, "Using Peachtree Report Writer," deals with Peachtree Report Writer basics. It shows you how to install Peachtree Report Writer and introduces you to the various general options and features in the product. You will see how to install and configure the program, learn the basics of report design, and understand the various general options and features in the product.

Chapter 2, "Creating a Procedure," introduces you to the elements of report design. You'll see how to plan a report by identifying the report requirements and lay out the information on a design form. You'll also see how to create and save a simple procedure, learn the basics of Peachtree Report Writer commands, add subtotals and totals to your reports, and print reports to the printer and to a file.

In Chapter 3, "Working with Procedures," you will continue exploring procedures. You will learn techniques such as performing calculations, creating temporary columns, adding prompts for information, and editing using commands. You'll also see how to create charts of data, such as area, pie, and bar charts, and modify the appearance of the chart information by changing colors, legends, and keys.

Chapter 4, "Designing Reports and Labels," discusses the Report Designer and Label Designer. These two tools take a graphical approach to report and label design, letting you lay out reports and labels on the screen rather than on paper, which can speed up the design process and encourage creativity.

Chapter 5, "Using Advanced Peachtree Report Writer Features," is the final chapter in the first section. It focuses on several of the more advanced features of Peachtree Report Writer, including using conditional statements to select for specific information, using matrixes to report multiple sets of information on a single report, and exporting and importing procedures, which lets you transfer procedures from one Peachtree Report Writer user to another.

Part 2: PeachLink

The second section tells you how to get online using PeachLink and Electronic Bill Payment.

Chapter 6, "Setting Up PeachLink," shows you how to install the PeachLink web page creation software on your system and register the software with Harbinger. You'll learn the basics features of the main PeachLink window. This chapter also introduces you to Netscape Navigator and shows you how to move around the Netscape Navigator window.

Once PeachLink is set up, Chapter 7, "Using PeachLink," tells you how to design and create a web site with PeachLink. The chapter steps you through the web page creation process, identifying where the information comes from in each case, and gives you options for ways to design your company's web page. You also see how to use Netscape Navigator to view the web pages you've created. Finally, you learn how to publish your web site and become a part of the World Wide Web.

In Chapter 8, "Using PeachLink Order Processor," you complete the order processing loop by taking the orders your web site generates and transferring them to Peachtree Accounting. You'll also learn how to handle credit card orders, process sales orders, and enter new web customers in Peachtree Accounting.

Chapter 9, "Using Advanced PeachLink Features," is for intermediate and advanced users who want to customize their web sites. You will see how to add clip art and backgrounds to the web site you created with PeachLink and how to change the look of your web site by using HTML. You will also learn the basic concepts behind web page creation and HTML, and how to integrate your customer's web pages into your PeachLink web site.

Chapter 10, "Electronic Bill Payment," shows you how to use Electronic Bill Payment to automate your check writing process. You start by activating Electronic Bill Payment in Peachtree Accounting and setting up vendors, and then enter vendor payments, transmit the data, maintain Electronic Bill Payment information, and print reports. The chapter also shows you some basic troubleshooting techniques and how to import Electronic Bill Payment information to and export from Peachtree Accounting and how to rebuild the data for an existing company.

Part 3: Using Peachtree Accounting with Other Products
The third section focuses on other products that you can use with Peachtree Accounting.

Chapter 11, "Peachtree Accounting Add-ons and Other Software," shows you how to further enhance the effectiveness of Peachtree Accounting software with an assortment of add-ons for Peachtree Accounting as well as other useful programs. This chapter contains information on a selection of programs and utilities, many of which appear on the CD accompanying this book.

Part 4: Appendixes
Appendix A, "Commands and Keywords in Peachtree Report Writer," describes the commands in Peachtree Report Writer and lists the available keywords. Individual commands are described in detail, with command syntax, description, and one or more examples of how to use the command.

Appendix B, "Online and Printed Resources," contains a selection of online and printed resources, including web sites, newsgroups, and books. Web sites and newsgroups are listed for HTML and web tutorials and references, web site support, search engines, shareware resources, Peachtree products, CD web sites, and other sites of interest. The appendix also lists a selection of books on Peachtree Accounting, web design, and HTML.

Conventions Used in This Book
This book has several standard conventions for presenting information.

Defined terms are in *italics*.

Keyboard names appear in SMALL CAPITALS. If you are supposed to press several keys together, the keys are joined with a hyphen. For example, "Press CTRL-F1" means to hold down the control key (CTRL) and press F1.

There are four types of notes in the text:

NOTE: A *note* is simply a comment related to the material being discussed.

TIP: A *tip* is a technique for doing things faster, easier, or better in Peachtree Complete Accounting for Windows.

 REMEMBER: This flags something you should keep in mind when performing the task on your own system.

 CAUTION: A *caution* is a warning to prevent you from doing something that could result in a loss of data or cause you problems with the way you run your business.

The screen shots in this book show you how Peachtree Complete Accounting for Windows looks on a Pentium computer using a VGA monitor with a standard 800×600×256 color display in Microsoft Windows 95. What you see on your screen may be slightly different, depending on the configuration of your hardware.

 ## Other Books by the Author

If you enjoy *Peachtree Complete Business Toolkit*, you may also enjoy some other books by John Hedtke, including the following.

Peachtree Accounting for Windows Made Easy (Osborne/McGraw-Hill, 1995). This book shows you how to install and configure Peachtree Accounting for Windows, set up charts of accounts, general ledgers, and journals, and use Peachtree Accounting for Windows. The book covers Accounts Receivable, Accounts Payable, Payroll, Inventory, customizing reports, and using management tools and procedures. Call Osborne/McGraw-Hill at 1-800-227-0900 to order directly, or simply ask your bookseller to stock it.

Peachtree Complete Accounting for Windows Made Easy, Third Edition (Osborne/McGraw-Hill, 1997). This book shows you how to install and configure Peachtree Complete Accounting for Windows using the standard and the multimedia set-up programs. In addition to describing the basic accounting features—Accounts Receivable, Accounts Payable, Payroll, and Inventory—the book shows you how to use Job Costing, Fixed Assets Management, and the new Time & Billing features. The book also describes how to create customized reports and use the management tools and procedures in Peachtree Complete Accounting for Windows. Call Osborne/McGraw-Hill at 1-800-227-0900 to order directly, or simply ask your bookseller to stock it.

Using Computer Bulletin Boards, 3rd Edition (MIS Press, 1995), is the complete guide to computer bulletin board systems (BBSes), online information services, and the Internet for the complete beginner. This multiple-award-winning book is designed to introduce novices to BBSes and basic telecommunications, and to help intermediate and advanced BBS users to use BBSes more effectively. There is also extensive information on the various online information services and how to get on to and use the Internet. For advanced users, there is also information on how to set up your own BBS for business or pleasure.

Other Books

If you aren't already familiar with Windows 95 and will be using Windows 95 with Peachtree Complete Accounting, you may want to buy *Windows 95 Made Easy*, by Tom Sheldon (Osborne/McGraw-Hill, 1995), a comprehensive guide for the reader who is not familiar with Windows 95. Another book you will enjoy is *Windows 95 Is Driving Me Crazy!*, by Kay Yarborough Nelson (Peachpit Press, 1996), a guide to the "headaches, hassles, bugs, potholes, and installation problems" of Windows 95. These two books will make you an expert on Windows 95 and how to resolve the problems you may have when using it.

For More Information...

For news and information about other products of interest to Peachtree users and on upcoming books and software, check out the author's web page, at the following address:

http://www.oz.net/~jhedtke

You'll find general information for Peachtree Accounting users, procedures for ordering other books on Peachtree and related topics, and files and software you can download. For users converting from another accounting system (particularly a manual system), you can download a complete set of forms for writing up your data before entering it in Peachtree Complete Accounting for Windows. Each form is designed to match the individual windows in which you enter data.

PART 1

Peachtree Report Writer

Peachtree Accounting for Windows and Peachtree Complete Accounting for Windows come with a wide variety of reports and procedures, but you may want to add reports that fulfill your company's unique reporting requirements. The first section of this book focuses on how to use Peachtree Report Writer: you will see how to install and configure Peachtree Report Writer, learn the basics of designing reports and procedures, perform calculations and comparisons, create graphical versions of reports, and add design elements such as borders and titles.

Using Peachtree Report Writer

This chapter shows you how to install Peachtree Report Writer and introduces you to the various general options and features in the product. You will see how to install and configure the program, learn the basics of report design, and understand the various general options and features in the product.

TIP: For detailed information on using Peachtree Complete Accounting for Windows, look at *Peachtree Complete Accounting for Windows Made Easy* (Osborne/McGraw-Hill, 1997). For detailed information on using Peachtree Complete Accounting, see *Peachtree Accounting for Windows Made Easy* (Osborne/McGraw-Hill, 1995).

What Is Peachtree Report Writer?

Peachtree Report Writer is an add-on product sold by Peachtree that expands and augments your ability to create and modify reports. (Although there are different versions of Peachtree Report Writer for use with both Peachtree Complete Accounting for Windows and Peachtree Accounting for Windows, they look and act alike.) Peachtree Report Writer comes with over 30 report and label procedures for tasks such as sales analysis, vendor analysis, job tracking, payroll, and inventory analysis. You can use Peachtree Report Writer to create new reports, labels, and forms. To order Peachtree Report Writer, contact your Peachtree Support Center or order directly from Peachtree by calling 800-247-3224.

NOTE: For simplicity, Peachtree Accounting for Windows and Peachtree Complete Accounting for Windows will be referred to as Peachtree Accounting throughout this book, unless otherwise noted.

Installing Peachtree Report Writer

Peachtree Report Writer is very easy to install and is shipped on 3.5" diskettes.

TIP: You can use Peachtree Report Writer with Peachtree Accounting for Windows or with Peachtree Complete Accounting for Windows, but be sure that you have the correct version of Peachtree Report Writer for the corresponding Peachtree product you're using.

To install Peachtree Report Writer, simply insert the first disk of the set into your computer's diskette drive. If you're installing on Windows 95, select Start and then Run, and then type **A:SETUP** (or **B:SETUP** if you're installing from diskette drive B) and click OK. Follow the instructions on the screen and insert each installation disk when prompted. If you're installing on Windows 3.1, select the Run command from the File menu in the Windows Program Manager. Type **A:SETUP** (or **B:SETUP** if you're installing from diskette drive B) and click OK, then follow the instructions on the screen, inserting each installation disk when prompted.

REMEMBER: You must install Peachtree Accounting on your system before installing Peachtree Report Writer.

Getting to Know Peachtree Report Writer

Once you install Peachtree Report Writer, you can start it from within Peachtree Accounting by clicking the Reports menu and then selecting the Peachtree Report Writer option at the bottom of the menu. You can also start Peachtree Report Writer by double-clicking the Peachtree Report Writer icon in the Peachtree Accounting program group on the Start menu.

Peachtree
Report Writer

When you open Peachtree Report Writer, the Open window is displayed, prompting you to select a company, as shown in Figure 1-1.

Open window
Figure 1-1.

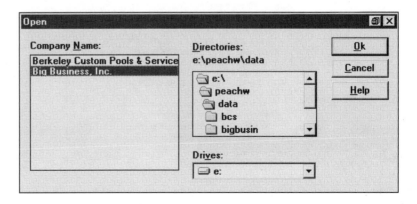

NOTE: If you start Peachtree Report Writer from within Peachtree Accounting, it will automatically use the company that is already open.

Select the company from the list and click OK. Peachtree Report Writer appears with the Open Procedure window displayed (see Figure 1-2).

NOTE: Most of the windows you'll see in Peachtree Report Writer have a "PRW" prefix. For simplicity's sake, the prefix will be omitted within the text and figure references throughout this book.

The Open Procedure window lets you select any of the procedures in Peachtree Report Writer. For right now, click Cancel. You'll see how to use this window in Chapter 2, "Creating a Procedure."

Take a moment to look at the main Peachtree Report Writer window (shown in Figure 1-3).

The Peachtree Report Writer window is somewhat different from both the main Peachtree Accounting and Peachtree Fixed Assets windows you may

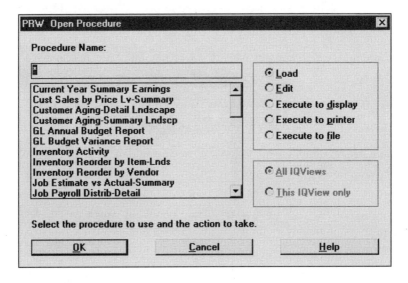

Open Procedure window
Figure 1-2.

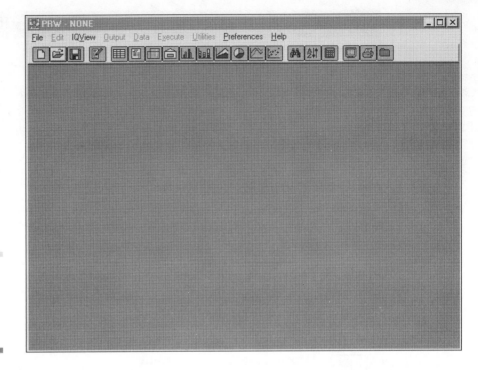

1

Main
Peachtree
Report Writer
window
Figure 1-3.

already be familiar with. Table 1-1 lists the various menus and explains
what they do.

Menu	What It Does
File	Creates, opens, saves, deletes, exports, imports, and prints procedures
Edit	Cuts, copies, and pastes information during editing of procedures
IQView	Opens IQViews (most of the options on this menu are not enabled with this release of Peachtree Report Writer)
Output	Specifies where and how the procedure should display or print the information
Data	Searches for, sorts, or manipulates the information
Execute	Generates the report and displays it on the screen, prints it on the printer, or saves it to a file

Menu
Categories
Table 1-1.

Menu	What It Does
Utilities	Sets the title and author of the procedure and specifies the format, output device, and limit (if any) on the number of rows to display
Preferences	Sets Peachtree Report Writer options
Help	Provides basic online help for Peachtree Report Writer

Menu
Categories
(*continued*)
Table 1-1.

You'll see how to use each of these menus and their options in later chapters.

Peachtree Report Writer has an extensive toolbar for selecting some of the most commonly used menu options. The icons and their descriptions are listed in Table 1-2.

Icon	What It Does
	Starts a new procedure
	Opens an existing procedure
	Saves the current procedure
	Edits the current procedure
	Displays the Columnar Output window for setting up columns
	Displays the Report Design window for laying out a report
	Displays the Matrix window for defining a matrix
	Displays the Label Design window for laying out a label

Toolbar Icons
on the Main
Peachtree
Report Writer
Window
Table 1-2.

Icon	What It Does
	Displays the Chart Bar window for specifying bar chart output
	Displays the Chart Stacked_Bar window specifying stacked bar chart output
	Displays the Chart Area window specifying area chart output
	Displays the Chart Pie window specifying pie chart output
	Displays the Chart Line window specifying line chart output
	Displays the Chart Scatter window specifying scatter chart output
	Displays the Search window for searching for information
	Displays the Sort window for sorting information
	Displays the Create Column window to create one of seven types of columns
	Generates a report and displays it on the screen
	Generates a report and prints it on the printer
	Generates a report and saves it to a file

Toolbar Icons
on the Main
Peachtree
Report Writer
Window
(*continued*)
Table 1-2.

Selecting menu options, moving and sizing windows, making selections from lists, and so on are much the same in Peachtree Report Writer as in most other Windows 95 applications. One feature that you will find useful for selecting information in some of the windows is using an asterisk (*) as a *wildcard*. For example, in the Open Procedure window (shown earlier in Figure 1-2), there is an asterisk in the Procedure Name field. This tells Peachtree Report Writer to show all of the procedures. If you wanted just the procedures starting with the letter "S," you could enter S* in the Procedure Name field and click OK. Peachtree Report Writer would display only those procedures that start with "S," as shown in Figure 1-4.

REMEMBER: This feature is case-sensitive. Entering **S*** is not the same as entering **s***.

If you had multiple procedures with names starting with "Sales," "Stock," or "Summary," you could filter even tighter by entering ST* or SU* to see only those procedures starting with "St" or "Su."

You can also look for items in the middle of a report name. For example, to find all procedures for employees, you might search for *yee*. This would turn up reports with names such as "Basic Employee List," "Employee List 2," and "Sorted Employee Labels."

While the asterisk will find any number of characters, you can use a question mark (?) as a wildcard for a single character. For example, searching for Empl?? would find procedures with names like "Empl01," "Empl23," and "EmplAA," but it would not find "Employee List" (because there are more than two characters after Empl in the name).

Using a wildcard in the Open Procedure window

Figure 1-4.

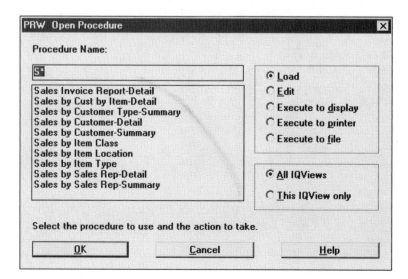

1

You can even combine asterisks and question marks to find procedures. For example, *yee List 2?? would find "Employee List 201," "Sorted Employee List 224," and "employee List 2XX," but it would not find "Employee List 100," "employee list 200," or "Employee List 20334."

Setting Default Options

There are a couple of default options that you should set before you begin: page margins and default font. To set the default page margins, select the Page Margins option from the Preferences menu. The Page Margins window appears:

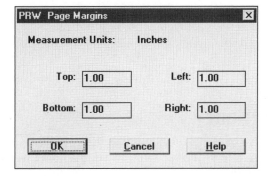

The Page Margins window lets you set the margins for the page. As with most Windows word processing programs, you set the margins from the top, bottom, left, and right edges of the page. When you subtract the margins from the total page size, you get the printable area on the page. If you try to print outside the printable area on the page, Peachtree Report Writer will print an extra page to accommodate the overlap. The defaults of one inch are probably adequate as a starting default for most contemporary printers.

TIP: If your printer has an area it can't print to, be sure to increase the top and left margins appropriately. For example, many laser printers cannot print in the half-inch from the edges of a page, so you should increase the top and left margins each by a half an inch (0.5"). Check your printer's manual if you're not sure. A quick way to test whether your printer has an area it can't print to is to set all the margins in the Page Margins window to zero and test print a procedure to see where the printer can and can't print. You can also go into many Windows word processing programs and set the margins to zero—the program will change the margins to the default minimums for that printer automatically.

When you are satisfied with the entries on the Page Margins window, click OK. Remember that you can override these options for specific procedures—these are just the default margins.

The other option you may want to set is the default font. Peachtree Report Writer uses the default font when displaying reports on the screen. To set the default font, select the Default Font option from the Preferences menu. The Default Font window appears, as shown in Figure 1-5.

The Default Font window is the standard Windows font selection dialog box. Select the default font, style, size, and other attributes. When you are satisfied with your entries, click OK.

NOTE: Peachtree Report Writer requires font sizes to be in whole points. You cannot specify a font size of 11.5, for example.

Summary

In this chapter, you have seen how to install and start Peachtree Report Writer, and you have been introduced to the menu categories and toolbar icons. You have also seen how to set default options within Peachtree Report Writer. In the next chapter, you will be introduced to the elements of report design—how to create, edit, and delete simple procedures.

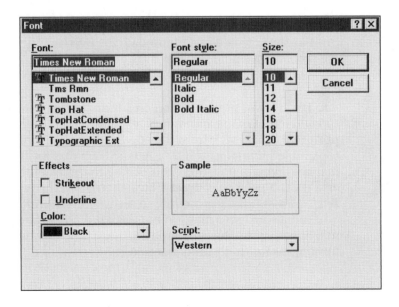

Default Font window

Figure 1-5.

2

Creating a Procedure

The previous chapter showed you how to install Peachtree Report Writer and introduced you to the various general options and features in the product. In this chapter, you'll be introduced to the elements of report design. You'll also see how to create and save a simple procedure, learn the basics of Peachtree Report Writer commands, add subtotals and totals to your reports, and print reports to the printer and to a file.

Understanding Report Design

Before you begin working with Peachtree Report Writer, you should understand some basic concepts of report design. These concepts will help you understand what you're doing when you start working with Peachtree Accounting files.

Information is stored in Peachtree Accounting in *records*. A record is a related collection of individual, but related, data items, such as a customer record or a sales order record. The individual data items are known as *fields*. Whereas records are made up of fields, fields themselves—like an employee's last name, a product ID, or a General Ledger account number—can't be subdivided.

When you print a report or a procedure, you are actually getting a specific *view* of the data fields in Peachtree Accounting. A *view* is a selection of data fields that may come from one or more records. For example, the Customer Ledgers report in Peachtree Accounting can have information from the General Ledger, Accounts Receivable, Inventory, and Job modules.

Peachtree Report Writer has predefined views of information known as IQViews. You can think of an IQView as a table of information. The records in Peachtree Report Writer are referred to as rows. The individual fields are referred to as columns.

Peachtree Report Writer stores the commands necessary to create a report, a label, a form, or a graphic in a *procedure*. The reports and forms in Peachtree Accounting are all generated by procedures. Peachtree Report Writer comes with some 30 additional report procedures, all of which you can modify or customize. You can also use Peachtree Report Writer to create new procedures as you need them.

Planning Your Report

Before you start modifying an existing procedure or creating a new one in Peachtree Report Writer, you need to plan your report requirements carefully. The following questions will help you identify some of the considerations before creating or modifying a procedure:

♦ Whom is this report for?

♦ Will anyone besides an accountant be able to understand and interpret this report?

♦ If this procedure is for a report, will it be displayed on the screen, printed, or both?

♦ If this procedure is for a form, what kind of stock or pre-printed forms (such as checks or W-2s) should be used for printing it?

2

♦ If this procedure generates printed output, what kind of printer will be used (a multi-form, tractor-feed printer or a laser printer)?

♦ How often will you need to print this report? Is this report to be produced daily, weekly, monthly, quarterly, or year-to-date? Is it an "on-demand" report or procedure?

♦ Is this report for use exclusively inside your company or will it be available for people outside the company as well? Are there data security or confidentiality issues?

♦ What will the report be called? What titles and headings should the report or procedure have?

♦ What information will the report contain?

♦ Are there any calculations or data masking that must be performed on the information in the report? Will there be calculations that use information that doesn't appear on the report, and if so, where will it come from?

♦ What kinds of information breaks, subtotals, and totals should be on the report?

♦ What final footings, instructions, legends, or keys must be on the report?

♦ What fonts and formats should you use? Do you need to include logos or use specific formatting to meet company standards for reports?

♦ Should the data be presented in text form (columns of numbers and text) or in graphic form (such as a pie or bar chart)?

Perhaps the most important question to ask is, "Do I really *need* to create a new report?" Many times, the information from an existing report will actually fit the bill without requiring you to create another report. You might also be able to add another column to an existing report and make the report more useful to everyone. Although a few custom reports may not be difficult to maintain, the number of custom reports people in your company want can multiply alarmingly, requiring someone—probably you—to catalog and maintain 20, 30, or even a 100 similar, but slightly different, reports.

TIP: Each time you create a new procedure, keep a printed copy of the procedure in a notebook along with a copy of the printed report. When you modify an existing procedure, make a note on the changes to the procedure with the date and the reason for the modification and print and save an updated version of the report. Although this may seem like time-consuming paperwork, it's a vital part of tracking the changes to the procedures, thereby avoiding the extra effort of writing similar procedures.

Laying Out Your Report

One of the most effective ways to plan a report layout is on paper. The advantage is that you can quickly sketch your report layout by hand and see what the report will look like before you build it in Peachtree Report Writer. Having a draft of the report on paper also lets you carry the report layout around and discuss it with the people who are going to use the report. Comments and changes can be written in the margins and the report will be easier to understand because you can see all of it. (Many people, frequently those who may not be very familiar with computers, have problems visualizing reports until they actually can see them laid out on paper.) Finally, laying a report out on paper is particularly useful if you are going to print the report on pre-printed stock. Report layout forms (as shown in Figure 2-1) can be purchased at any office supply store.

To lay out your report on paper, start by printing the titles and headings as you want them to appear. The columns on report layout forms are numbered so you can easily center or align titles and headings. Remember that laying a report out in *portrait* mode (8-1/2" × 11") generally allows you 80 printable characters on each line of the report, whereas a report laid out in *landscape* mode (11" × 8-1/2") can usually have 132 printable characters.

Once you've laid out your titles and headings, start mocking up the information in the locations it should appear. Enter X's for alphanumeric characters (such as employee names) and 9's for numbers (such as amounts). As you design your report, always budget the *maximum* amount of space for each item. For example, if the employee net earnings can potentially reach

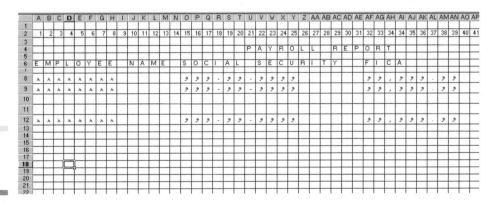

Typical report
layout form
Figure 2-1.

ten spaces, such as 100,000.00, be sure to allow enough room for the whole number. Remember to include column spaces for things like spaces, commas, decimal points, and dollar signs, too.

TIP: For purposes of report design, many numbers, such as phone numbers, social security numbers, and postal codes should be treated as alphanumeric information rather than numeric information. This is because their fields may contain special characters such as parentheses, hyphens, or letters.

2

Experiment with how the report information appears on the page. Try adjusting column widths, the order of columns, and how data is presented. For example, you may find it most useful to have the street address stacked above the city, state, and ZIP code, rather than all on the same line. Try inserting blank lines or using underlining to improve the report's readability. You can also add more headings, footers, keys, and legends. (For simple experimentation and minor changes, you probably don't need to plan extensively.)

Once you've worked up the report layout on paper, show it to the people who are going to be using it to make sure that the layout is best for what they need. Often, you'll find that a report can be much more usable by moving a column to a different location on the page or by adding additional subtotals and formatting.

CAUTION: You are strongly encouraged to follow GAAP (Generally Accepted Accounting Practices) when designing all of your reports. This means that assets should precede liabilities and equity. Although you may want reports for internal use, accountants, bankers, and auditors all expect reports in a standardized form. Check with your accountant for more information on GAAP as it applies to report design.

When you are satisfied with the report layout, you need to identify where the information on the report is going to come from. Report elements like titles, headings, and footers are *hard-coded:* the information is built into the report procedure and never changes. Accounting information—customer data, sales transactions, vendor records, purchase orders, employee payroll records, inventory and job costs, and so on—can all be obtained directly from the Peachtree Accounting files. Other information, such as the name of the requester or the report options, may come from user input gathered each time the report is generated. Still other information, such as employee sales commissions or the total discounts taken by customers, can be calculated using information from other sources. Label all the columns with the source of the information. Assembling this information may take some time, but you will find that creating your report is quicker and easier if you take the time up front to plan what you want to do.

After you have determined where each field on the report will appear and where the information comes from, you are ready to enter the report specifications. The next section shows you how to create your first procedure.

Creating Your First Procedure

In this section, you'll see how to create a simple procedure to list data from a sample client and display the results on the screen. Begin the process by starting Peachtree Report Writer either from Peachtree Accounting's Reports menu or directly from Windows. Select a client from the Open window, shown here:

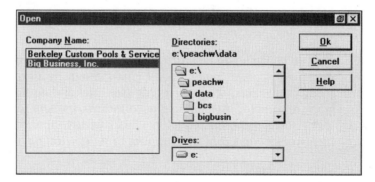

(The Open window does not appear if you are starting Peachtree Report Writer from within Peachtree Accounting.)

NOTE: In these examples, you'll be working with a company called Big Business, Inc., a firm that develops coin-operated software and personal computers.

When you have selected the company and clicked OK, Peachtree Report Writer appears with the Open Procedure window displayed, as shown in Figure 2-2.

The Open Procedure window lets you select any of the procedures in Peachtree Report Writer.

2

Procedure Name   Enter the procedure name you want to work with in this field. Alternatively, you can select one of the procedure names in the list below by clicking the name. The name then appears in this field.

Load   Click this button to load the procedure into Peachtree Report Writer without generating a report.

Edit   Click this button to load the procedure into Peachtree Report Writer for editing.

Execute to Display   Click this button to generate a report, using the procedure you have selected, and display it on the screen.

Execute to Printer   Click this button to generate a report, using the procedure you have selected, and print it on the printer.

Execute to File   Click this button to generate a report, using the procedure you have selected, and print it to a file.

Open
Procedure
window
Figure 2-2.

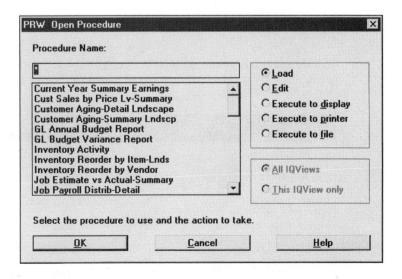

All IQViews   Show the procedures for all IQViews. When you open a procedure, Peachtree Report Writer opens the corresponding IQView if it is not already open.

This IQView Only   Show the procedures for only the IQView that's open. (This is helpful if you have a large number of procedures.)

Because you're going to create a new procedure at this point, click Cancel. From the IQView menu, select Open. The Open IQView window appears:

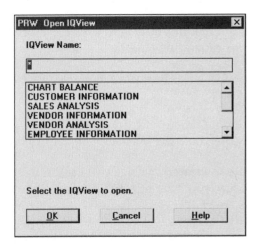

NOTE: The Open option is the only option available on the IQView menu. The other options are not available in this release of Peachtree Report Writer.

An IQView is a predefined selection of the information in your Peachtree Accounting files. Table 2-1 lists the IQViews and describes what each contains.

IQView	Contents
Chart Balance	General Ledger information
Customer Information	Customer information
Sales Analysis	Detailed sales information
Vendor Information	Vendor information
Vendor Analysis	Detailed vendor information
Employee Information	Employee information

IQViews in the Open IQView Window

Table 2-1.

IQViews in
the Open
IQView
Window
(*continued*)
Table 2-1.

IQView	Contents
Employee Analysis	Detailed employee information
Inventory Information	Inventory information
Inventory Analysis	Detailed inventory information
Job Information	Job information
Job Analysis	Detailed job information

You're going to create a procedure dealing with employee and payroll information, so select the "Employee Analysis" option from the list and click OK.

You're now ready to create your procedure. From the Output menu, select the Columnar option. The Columnar Output window appears (as shown in Figure 2-3).

Peachtree Report Writer offers you several different output formats. The most effective for displaying general information is the columnar output format in which information is displayed in columns, as in a typical spreadsheet. Peachtree Report Writer uses column names as the default headers for the columns. (You'll see how to add your own custom titles and headers later in this book.)

Columnar
Output
window
Figure 2-3.

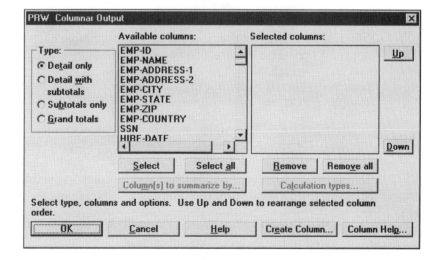

Type   Select one of four possible report types:

♦ **Detail only** Creates a procedure with just detail-level information, such as an employee name and address list, or an inventory picklist. (This report type is the default.)

♦ **Detail with subtotals** Creates a procedure with detail-level information and subtotals, such as a customer list with sales transactions subtotaled for each customer.

♦ **Subtotals only** Creates a procedure with summary-level information only, such as a list of the total purchases for each customer.

♦ **Grand totals** Creates a procedure with totals for the selected fields without any subtotals, such as a summary of the total payroll expenditures for a period or a quick reference of total sales.

Available columns   Selects the columns to include on the report. (The columns that appear in this field may differ depending on which report type you've selected.)

Selected columns   The columns you select for inclusion on the report will appear in this box. Columns are listed in the order they will appear when the report is generated.

Up   Moves the selected column up one line. (Up and Down are very convenient for experimenting with displaying columns in different orders.)

Down   Moves the selected column down one line.

Select   Selects the highlighted column(s) in the "Available columns" list for inclusion on the procedure.

Select all   Selects all the columns in the "Available columns" list for inclusion on the procedure.

Remove   Removes the highlighted column(s) in the "Selected columns" list from the procedure.

Remove all   Removes all the highlighted column(s) in the "Selected columns" list from the procedure.

Column(s) to summarize by   Changes the column used to summarize by when creating a procedure with subtotals.

Calculation types   Changes the type of calculation for the column highlighted in the "Selected columns" box.

Create Column   Creates a temporary column for calculations or manipulating information.

Column Help   This feature is not implemented for this release of Peachtree Report Writer. For your first procedure, you're going to create a simple employee list that shows employee ID, name, and SSN. Take a moment to examine the column names in the "Available columns" list. These include all the fields in the Maintain Employee windows in Peachtree Accounting as well as quarterly amounts that have accrued for the employee. Most of the column names are easy to understand, but some of them (such as QTD-1-AMT-EE-1-30) may appear a little cryptic at first. You'll see how to use these fields a little later.

Start by selecting EMP-ID from the "Available columns" list and then clicking Select. The EMP-ID column name will now appear at the top of the "Selected columns" list. (You can also double-click a column name in the "Available columns" list to add it to the "Selected columns" list.) Repeat the process with the EMP-NAME (employee name) and the SSN (social security number) columns.

Click OK. This closes the Columnar Output window. You're now ready to execute the procedure you've just created.

From the Execute menu, select the "to Display" option. Peachtree Report Writer displays the information in the Output window, as shown in Figure 2-4.

The Output window has several new buttons, which are described in Table 2-2.

Sample procedure displayed on the screen

Figure 2-4.

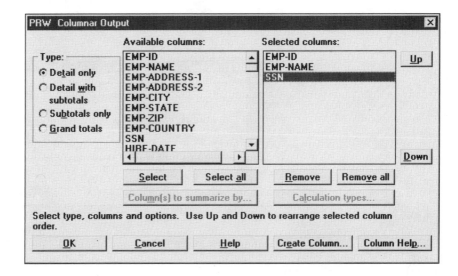

Button	Action
⏮	Moves cursor to the first page of the report
◀	Moves cursor to the previous page of the report
▶	Moves cursor to the next page of the report
⏭	Moves cursor to the last page of the report
STOP	Stops the execution of the report (useful for stopping large or complex reports that take a while to generate)
	Closes the Output window
🖨	Prints the report displayed in the Output window

Buttons on the
Output
Window
Table 2-2.

Close the Output window by clicking the Close Output Window icon on
the toolbar.

The final thing you need to do now is to save the procedure for future use.
From the File menu, select the Save Procedure option. The Save Procedure
window appears:

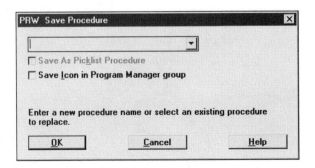

Procedure name   In the unlabeled text box, enter a name for your procedure of up to 30 characters such as "Basic Employee List." The procedure name may contain spaces, but they cannot contain the following characters: vertical bar (|), asterisk (*), question mark (?), less-than (<), greater-than (>), plus (+), comma (,), or semicolon (;). This is the name that appears on the list of procedures in the Open Procedures window so make sure that it's descriptive. In other words, don't use GL SUMMARY REPORT when you can say GL QTD FIXED ASSETS SUMMARY. A longer, more descriptive name also prevents you from accidentally overwriting an existing procedure with the same name.

2

NOTE: Procedure names are not case-sensitive. Peachtree Report Writer treats GL QTD FIXED ASSETS SUMMARY, gl qtd fixed assets summary, and GL QTD Fixed Assets Summary as the same name.

Save as Picklist Procedure   Check this box to save this procedure as a picklist. A picklist is a single-column report used for such tasks as labeling. (Peachtree Report Writer lets you select this option if your procedure only has a single column.)

Save Icon in Program Manager Group   Check this box to create a shortcut icon for the procedure so you can run it directly just by double-clicking on the icon. If you select this option, Peachtree Report Writer displays a Group Name field. You can select a group in which to enter the shortcut by clicking the down arrow to the right of the field, or create a new group entirely by typing the name of the new group in the Group Name field. Peachtree Report Writer will create the group (if necessary) and then add the shortcut icon to it.

REMEMBER: Unlike procedure names, the names of Windows 95 program groups *are* case-sensitive. Windows 95 treats PRW PROCEDURES and PRW Procedures as two different program group names.

When you are satisfied with your entries on the window, click OK. Peachtree Report Writer saves the procedure and adds the procedure name to the list. In the future, you will be able to load it from the Open Procedure window.

NOTE: You can delete a procedure by selecting Delete Procedure from the File menu, then selecting the procedure you want to delete. Peachtree Report Writer asks if you are sure that you want to delete the procedure. Click OK to delete the procedure.

Congratulations! You've written and saved a simple procedure.

Understanding Peachtree Report Writer Commands

Every procedure is stored as a text file containing commands that tell Peachtree Report Writer how to create the report. A command is a line of text that starts with a command keyword that tells Peachtree Report Writer to perform a specific action. It is followed by one or more column names or other keywords that further define the things that you want Peachtree Report Writer to do. (A complete list of Peachtree Report Writer keywords appears in Appendix A.)

When you start a procedure and select the columns, Peachtree Report Writer assembles a command to create the report. To view the commands in a procedure, select Show Procedure from the Preferences menu. The Show Procedure window appears with the command for the procedure you just created:

Take a moment to examine the information in the Show Procedure window. The first word, COLUMNAR, identifies this as a columnar report. The rest of the command is the three columns. Finally, the period tells Peachtree Report Writer that this is the end of the command. The simple command in the procedure in Figure 2-5 tells Peachtree Report Writer to start a columnar report and display the employee ID, the employee name, and the social security number (in the order these records appear in the Peachtree Accounting files). Whenever you create or modify a procedure, Peachtree Report Writer adds to or changes the commands in the procedure. (As a matter of fact, you can edit procedures directly by displaying the procedure and then typing the changes into the Show Procedure window.)

Close the Show Procedure window for now. As you go through this and subsequent chapters, you'll see how the commands in the procedure change as you modify it.

2

Modifying a Procedure

In the first part of this chapter, you saw how to create a procedure. You'll now see how to modify the procedure you just created.

Sorting Information

When you generate a report, the information comes directly from the Peachtree Accounting files as it is entered. However, this may not be in the most effective order for your needs, so you'll need to sort the data. To demonstrate this, you'll see how to add a column to the procedure you created earlier, and then sort by it.

Suppose you want to generate a report that sorts employees by their hire dates, for determining seniority. You're going to need to add the employee's hire date information to the procedure in order to sort by it. Since the Basic Employee List procedure is still open, you just need to add the hire date column. From the Output menu, select Columnar. The Columnar Output window appears with the information for the Basic Employee List procedure already displayed.

Highlight HIRE-DATE in the list of columns in the "Available columns" list and click Select. HIRE-DATE appears at the bottom of the selected columns in the "Selected columns" list. Click OK to close the Columnar Output window, then select "to Display" from the Execute menu to see what the report looks like with the HIRE-DATE column added. (The report with the HIRE-DATE column appears in Figure 2-5.)

You can see in Figure 2-5 that Peachtree Report Writer has displayed the hire date information as the fourth column in the report, but that the data is still sorted by the employee ID (the default for employee information). You now need to tell Peachtree Report Writer to sort the information by the hire date. Close the Output window then select Sort from the Data menu. The Sort window appears, as shown in Figure 2-6.

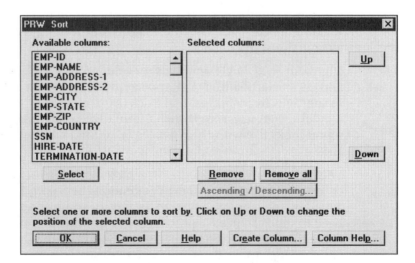

EMP-ID	EMP-NAME	SSN	HIRE-DATE
ALANJ	Jim Alan	234-23-4234	04/15/97
ALANT	Tames Alan	789-78-9789	01/01/97
ANDERSONKB	Karen B. Anderson	814-24-5220	11/13/96
BILLINGSND	Nancy D. Billings	340-13-0247	02/03/97
FITZGERALDRG	Ronda G. Fitzgerald	905-10-1147	05/09/96
FRANKLINJL	John L. Franklin	999-65-4309	07/12/95
JOHNSONPR	Pamela Johnson	021-50-2436	09/10/97
KOELLERDV	Dylan V. Koeller	098-87-7654	07/10/96
LANEJF	James F. Lane	534-50-2456	02/10/97
LINDBOMCC	Chuck Lindbom	555-66-7654	09/13/95
MARTINC	Cal Martin	887-76-6554	06/05/96
MCINTYRESD	Stephanie D. McIntyre	333-44-5555	05/23/96
NGP	Pho Ng	001-23-8642	05/08/96
OLSENCR	Catherine R. Olsen	982-32-0000	05/28/97
SCHOENINGJY	Jeremy Y. Schoening	901-09-1901	02/12/97
SIMMONDSA	Albert Simmonds	252-52-5252	06/02/93
SIMMONDSM	Mathilda Symonds	343-34-3434	07/15/96
SUNGYM	Yong Mi Sung	777-11-7777	12/02/96

Basic
Employee List
report with the
HIRE-DATE
column added
Figure 2-5.

Sort window
Figure 2-6.

Available columns   Lets you select the columns to sort the report by.

Selected columns   Shows the columns already selected for sorting the report by.

Up   Moves the selected column up one line. (Up and Down are very convenient for experimenting with sorting columns in different orders.)

Down   Moves the selected column down one line.

2

Select   Selects the highlighted column(s) in the "Available columns" list for sorting the report.

Remove   Removes the highlighted column(s) in the "Selected columns" list.

Remove all   Removes all the highlighted column(s) in the "Selected columns" list.

Ascending/Descending   Changes the sort sequence for the highlighted column in the "Selected columns" list.

Create Column   Creates a temporary column for calculations or manipulating information.

Column Help   This feature is not implemented for this release of Peachtree Report Writer.

To sort by the hire date, select HIRE-DATE from the "Available columns" list and click Select. The Sort Sequence window appears:

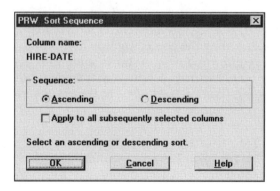

Sequence   Click Ascending or Descending to sort the column in ascending or descending order.

Apply to all subsequently selected columns   Click this box to automatically apply the sequence to all subsequent sorts. (You might do this if you wanted to sort everything in ascending order as the default sort order.)

For this example, click Ascending to sort in ascending order, then click OK on the Sort Sequence window. You can see that HIRE-DATE now appears in the "Selected columns" list. Click OK, then select the "to Display" option from the Execute menu to generate the report a second time. The new report appears in Figure 2-7.

Take a look at the commands in the procedure now. Close the Output window and then select the Show Procedure option from the Preferences menu. The Show Procedure window displays the changes to the procedure:

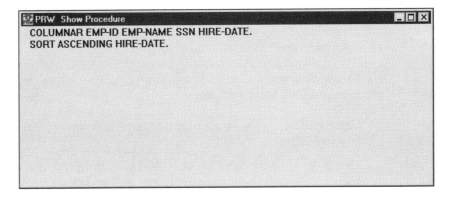

```
PRW  Show Procedure                                    _ □ X
COLUMNAR EMP-ID EMP-NAME SSN HIRE-DATE.
SORT ASCENDING HIRE-DATE.
```

You can see HIRE-DATE added to the list of columns to display on the report. The second line tells Peachtree Report Writer to sort the information generated by the preceding line in ascending order by HIRE-DATE. The Show Procedure window also shows something else that you should know about the way Peachtree Report Writer works: the first command line generates the raw information to be used in the report, then the second line sorts the information.

NOTE: You can sort by multiple columns if you want. Columns will be indented in the "Selected columns" list to show the sort order. For example, if you selected HIRE-DATE and then EMP-NAME, EMP-NAME would be indented under HIRE-DATE. Peachtree Report Writer would sort the report by EMP-NAME within HIRE-DATE.

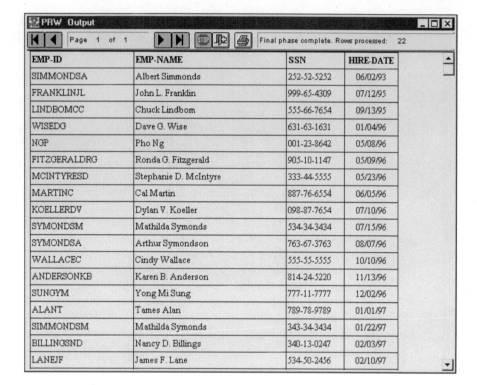

PRW Output

EMP-ID	EMP-NAME	SSN	HIRE-DATE
SIMMONDSA	Albert Simmonds	252-52-5252	06/02/93
FRANKLINJL	John L. Franklin	999-65-4309	07/12/95
LINDBOMCC	Chuck Lindbom	555-66-7654	09/13/95
WISEDG	Dave G. Wise	631-63-1631	01/04/96
NGP	Pho Ng	001-23-8642	05/08/96
FITZGERALDRG	Ronda G. Fitzgerald	905-10-1147	05/09/96
MCINTYRESD	Stephanie D. McIntyre	333-44-5555	05/23/96
MARTINC	Cal Martin	887-76-6554	06/05/96
KOELLERDV	Dylan V. Koeller	098-87-7654	07/10/96
SYMONDSM	Mathilda Symonds	534-34-3434	07/15/96
SYMONDSA	Arthur Symondson	763-67-3763	08/07/96
WALLACEC	Cindy Wallace	555-55-5555	10/10/96
ANDERSONKB	Karen B. Anderson	814-24-5220	11/13/96
SUNGYM	Yong Mi Sung	777-11-7777	12/02/96
ALANT	Tames Alan	789-78-9789	01/01/97
SIMMONDSM	Mathilda Symonds	343-34-3434	01/22/97
BILLINGSND	Nancy D. Billings	340-13-0247	02/03/97
LANEJF	James F. Lane	534-50-2456	02/10/97

Basic
Employee List
report sorted
by HIRE-DATE
Figure 2-7.

Save the changes you've just made to the procedure as "Sorted Employee List" using the Save Procedure option on the File menu as you did earlier. In the next section, you'll see how to modify the procedure to include more information and add subtotals.

Adding Subtotals

The example procedure you've created only lists text information without any amounts. Now you'll see how to use amounts and add subtotals.

Suppose you want to create a procedure that shows the employee name and their net paycheck amounts. Start by telling Peachtree Report Writer to create a new procedure. From the File menu, select the New Procedure option. Now select the Columnar option from the Output menu to display the Columnar Output window. This time, select the "Detail with subtotals" type. The Subtotal-By Column window appears:

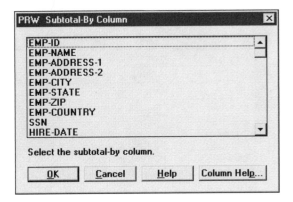

You need to tell Peachtree Report Writer where to *break*. A break occurs whenever the value of a column that you sort changes, such as when there's a different employee name. At each break, Peachtree Report Writer generates the appropriate subtotal. To summarize by the employee name, select EMP-NAME from the list and click OK. EMP-NAME appears in the "Selected columns" list. Next, scroll down the list in the "Available columns" list until you see CHECK-NUMBER. Select CHECK-NUMBER and click Select (or simply double-click CHECK-NUMBER) to move it to the "Selected columns" list.

Now select NET-CHECK-AMOUNT and click Select. Peachtree Report Writer displays the Summary Calculations window:

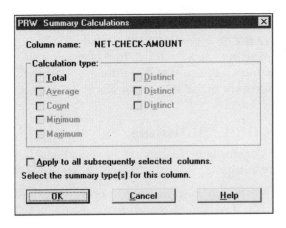

Calculation Type   Select the calculation type for the column:

♦ **Total**   Totals the amounts in the column

♦ **Average**   Takes the average of the amounts in the column

♦ **Count** Counts the number of entries in the column

♦ **Minimum** Displays the smallest value of all the values in the column

♦ **Maximum** Displays the largest value of all the values in the column

The Distinct option is not implemented for this release of Peachtree Report Writer.

Apply to all subsequently selected columns Click this box to automatically apply the calculation to all subsequent summary calculations. (You might do this if you wanted to total everything as the default summary calculation.) For this example, click Total.

When you are satisfied with your entries, click OK, then click OK on the Columnar Output window. You've selected the items you want to appear on this report, so click OK, then select the "to Display" option on the Execute menu. The report appears in the Output window shown in Figure 2-8.

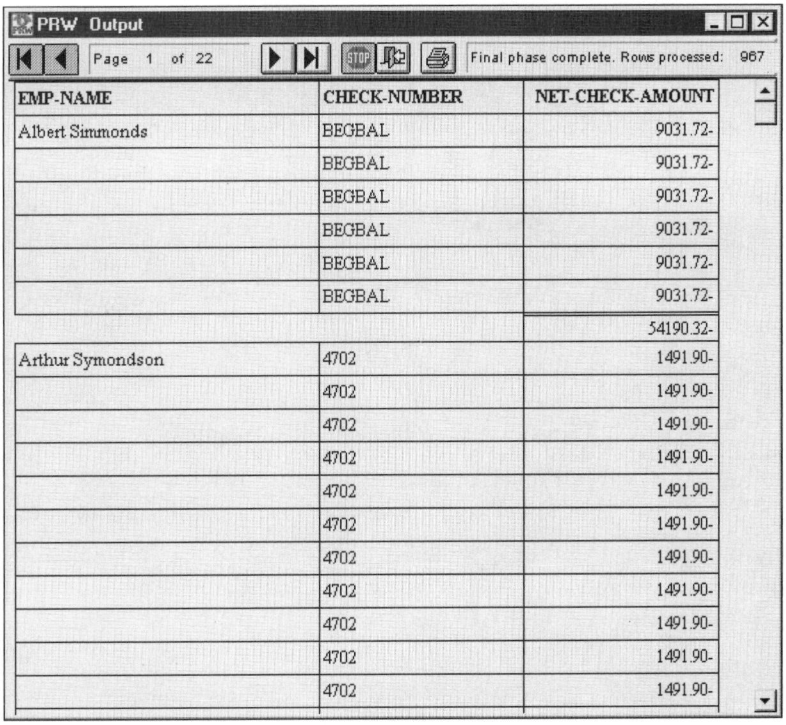

2

PRW Output		_□×
Page 1 of 22 Final phase complete. Rows processed: 967		
EMP-NAME	**CHECK-NUMBER**	**NET-CHECK-AMOUNT**
Albert Simmonds	BEGBAL	9031.72-
	BEGBAL	9031.72-
	BEGBAL	9031.72-
	BEGBAL	9031.72-
	BEGBAL	9031.72-
	BEGBAL	9031.72-
		54190.32-
Arthur Symondson	4702	1491.90-
	4702	1491.90-
	4702	1491.90-
	4702	1491.90-
	4702	1491.90-
	4702	1491.90-
	4702	1491.90-
	4702	1491.90-
	4702	1491.90-
	4702	1491.90-
	4702	1491.90-

Detail output with subtotals

Figure 2-8.

As you can see, there's something wrong with the report—there are duplicate entries for beginning balances and checks. In this example, Peachtree Report Writer has used the information in the Peachtree Accounting files for the check. Each payroll check has distributions for the employee and employer deductions, each of which triggers a new record to be displayed in the output. (If you counted the number of lines for a single check on the report, you'd see that it has the same number of lines of detail information listed for that check on the Payroll Journal report in Peachtree Accounting.)

What you need to do now is tell Peachtree Report Writer to suppress duplicate records. You do this by searching for a special field called ZIDX (which you will see how to do in the next section).

Searching for Information

You can use the search features in Peachtree Report Writer to search for specific records, perform comparisons between columns, filter information, or use Peachtree Report Writer to suppress duplicate records. To search for specific information, select Search from the Data menu (or click the Search button on the toolbar). The Search window appears, as shown in Figure 2-9.

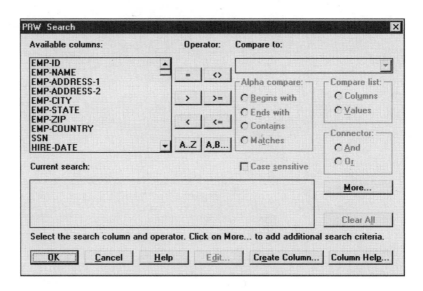

Search
window
Figure 2-9.

Available columns   Select the column to search.

Operator   Click one of the buttons (listed in Table 2-3) to specify the type of search.

Compare to   Enter the column name or value you want to compare to the selected column. You can also click the down arrow to the right of the field and select a column or a value, depending on the selection you made for the Compare list option.

2

Alpha compare   Select one of the options described in Table 2-4.

Case sensitive   Check this box to do case-sensitive searches. (Searching in Peachtree Report Writer is case-insensitive by default.)

Compare List   Click either Columns or Values to see a list of columns or values in the "Compare to" field.

Button	Action
=	Searches for something equal to the value of the column
<>	Searches for something not equal to the value of the column
>	Searches for something greater than the value of the column
>=	Searches for something greater than or equal to the value of the column
<	Searches for something less than the value of the column
<=	Searches for something less than or equal to the value of the column
A..Z	Searches for a range of values
A,B...	Searches for multiple values

Search
Operator
Buttons
Table 2-3.

Alpha Compare	Action
Begins with	Selects all entries that begin with the value in the "Compare to" field. For example, if you are searching for employee names beginning with a value of "Jo," Peachtree Report Writer will select the following employee names: "Joanna," "Joe," and "John."
Ends with	Selects all entries that end with the value in the "Compare to" field. For example, if you are searching for employee names ending with a value of "son," Peachtree Report Writer will select the following employee names: "Christenson," "Johnson," and "Olson."
Contains	Selects all entries that contain the value in the "Compare to" field. For example, if you are searching for employee names containing a value of "John," Peachtree Report Writer will select employee names such as "John Smith," "Nancy Johns," and "William St. John."
Matches	Selects all entries that exactly match the value in the "Compare to" field.

Alpha
Compare
Table 2-4.

Connector   Click And or Or to add another search criterion to the current one. (Searching with multiple criteria is discussed later in this section.)

More...   Click to enter another search criterion.

Current search   Displays the search criteria you've created.

Create Column...   Creates a temporary column for calculations or manipulating information.

Column Help...   This feature is not implemented for this release of Peachtree Report Writer.

To suppress duplicate records, select ZIDX from the "Available columns" list. (ZIDX is a special Peachtree Report Writer column that assigns a number to each transaction. Selecting the record that has a ZIDX value of zero will suppress the duplicate records.) Next, click = in the list of operators to tell Peachtree Report Writer that you want to look for something equal to the value in ZIDX. Finally, type **0** in the "Compare to" field.

One final thing to do for this procedure is to sort it by the check number as well as by employee name. From the Data menu, select Sort (or just click the

Sort icon on the toolbar). From the "Available columns" list in the Sort window, select CHECK-NUMBER, then click OK on the Sort Sequence window to accept Ascending for the sort order. CHECK-NUMBER appears indented under EMP-NAME in the "Selected columns" list, showing that Peachtree Report Writer will sort by CHECK-NUMBER within EMP-NAME. Click OK in the Sort window and then select the "to Display" option from the Execute menu. Figure 2-10 shows the revised report with the duplicate records suppressed.

As you can see, the duplicate entries on the report have been suppressed and the records are sorted by check number. Subtotals will generally appear with a single line above them. However, if the Show Grid option on the Preferences menu is checked, all the amounts will have a single line around them and the subtotals will be preceded by a double line (as you can see in Figure 2-10). When you generate subtotals in a report, Peachtree Report Writer automatically includes a grand total for each column that is subtotaled. The grand total will have a double line above it (if the Show Grid option is not selected) or a double-line box (if the Show Grid option is selected).

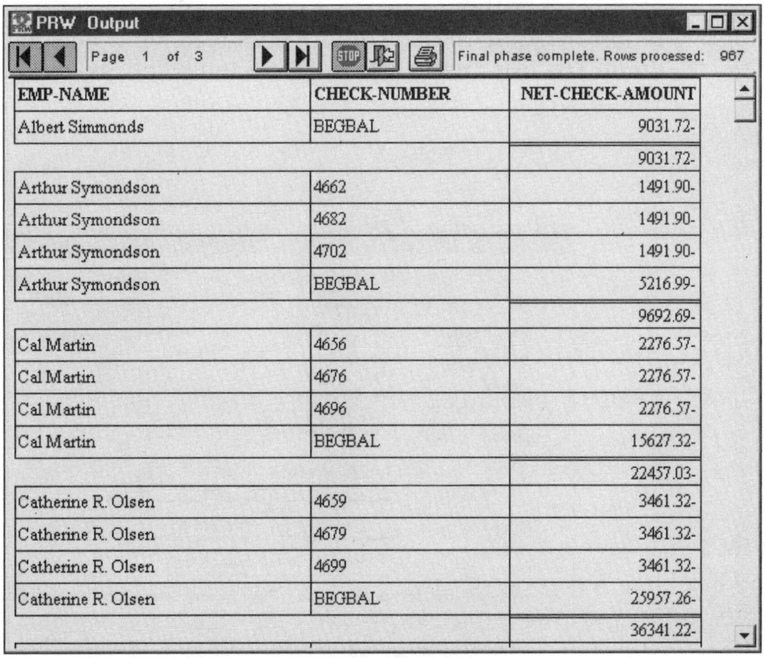

PRW Output — Page 1 of 3 — Final phase complete. Rows processed: 967

EMP-NAME	CHECK-NUMBER	NET-CHECK-AMOUNT
Albert Simmonds	BEGBAL	9031.72-
		9031.72-
Arthur Symondson	4662	1491.90-
Arthur Symondson	4682	1491.90-
Arthur Symondson	4702	1491.90-
Arthur Symondson	BEGBAL	5216.99-
		9692.69-
Cal Martin	4656	2276.57-
Cal Martin	4676	2276.57-
Cal Martin	4696	2276.57-
Cal Martin	BEGBAL	15627.32-
		22457.03-
Catherine R. Olsen	4659	3461.32-
Catherine R. Olsen	4679	3461.32-
Catherine R. Olsen	4699	3461.32-
Catherine R. Olsen	BEGBAL	25957.26-
		36341.22-

Revised report with subtotals added

Figure 2-10.

NOTE: Peachtree Report Writer sorts numbers before letters, so the BEGBAL entry appears after the numbered checks rather than before.

Searching for Multiple Criteria

You can search for more than one criterion by entering the first search condition and then clicking More. When you enter a second condition, you click And or Or to link the criteria. For example, SEARCH FOR HIRE-DATE < 5/21/93 AND EMP-TYPE = 'FIELDREP' would find all employees who have more than five years with the company and who are field representatives. Similarly, SEARCH FOR EMP-TYPE = 'FIELDREP' OR EMP-TYPE = 'SALESREP' to find employees who are either field or sales representatives. Be careful when you specify your search criteria, however, as you may inadvertently specify criteria that are too broad. For example, SEARCH FOR HIRE-DATE < 5/21/93 OR EMP-TYPE = 'FIELDREP' would find all the employees who have more than 5 years with the company (regardless of their EMP-TYPE) as well as all employees who are field representatives (regardless of how long they've been with the company).

Displaying Subtotals Only

Suppose you have dozens of employees and just want the totals paid to the employees without the check level details. You can generate a subtotals-only report by going to the Columnar Output window and clicking Subtotals Only. The information in the "Selected columns" list will change as shown in Figure 2-11.

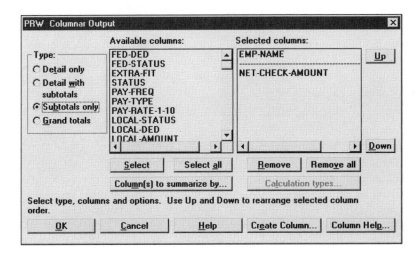

Columnar Output window for a Subtotals Only report

Figure 2-11.

Notice that Peachtree Report Writer has removed CHECK-NUMBER from the "Selected columns" list because it is detail-level information that cannot be summarized.

When you generate this report, the output only has subtotals, as shown in Figure 2-12.

A quick comparison of the report in Figure 2-12 with the report shown earlier in Figure 2-10 shows that the subtotals on the report are the same, but the details are omitted from the subtotals-only version. Be sure to check the Show Procedure window again to see the differences in the commands for the subtotals-only report:

2

```
PRW  Show Procedure                                    _ □ ×
COLUMNAR BY EMP-NAME TOTAL NET-CHECK-AMOUNT.
SORT ASCENDING EMP-NAME.
```

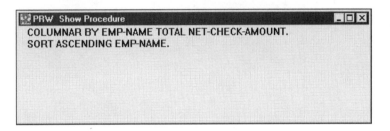

EMP-NAME	TOTAL NET-CHECK-AMOUNT
Albert Simmonds	9031.72-
Arthur Symondson	9692.69-
Cal Martin	22457.03-
Catherine R. Olsen	36341.22-
Chuck Lindbom	18475.64-
Cindy Wallace	21467.31-
Dave G. Wise	24528.07-
Dylan V. Koeller	14945.21-
James F. Lane	38086.43-
Jeremy Y. Schoening	17291.08-
Jim Alan	9798.10-
John L. Franklin	14250.53-
Karen B. Anderson	27165.81-
Mathilda Symonds	28017.40-
Nancy D. Billings	26958.23-
Pamela Johnson	14809.73-

Subtotals Only report
Figure 2-12.

Displaying Grand Totals

As you have already seen, grand totals appear at the bottom of any column that has subtotals. To create a report with nothing but a grand total, select "Grand totals" from the Columnar Output window. Only the amount to be totaled, NET-CHECK-AMOUNT, will remain in the "Selected columns" list. When you click OK and generate the report, the output will look like this:

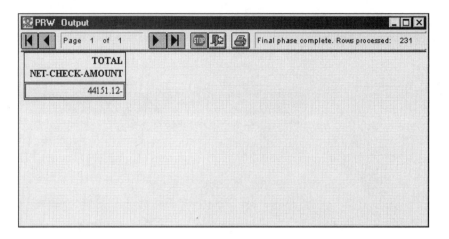

Choosing Different Printing Options

All of the procedures in this chapter have been displayed on the screen, but you can also print reports or save them to a file.

Printing Reports to the Printer

You may print reports to the printer by selecting the "to Printer" option from the Execute menu. The Execute To Printer window appears:

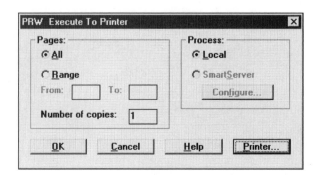

Pages   Select All (the default) or print a range of pages (as you specify in the From and To fields). You can also specify multiple copies by entering the appropriate number in the "Number of copies" field.

Process   This feature is not implemented in this release of Peachtree Report Writer.

Printer   Click this to display the standard Windows printer selection box.

When you are satisfied with your entries, click OK. Peachtree Report Writer prints the report on the specified printer.

Printing Reports to a File

You can also print a report to a file by selecting the "to File" option from the Execute menu. The Execute To File window appears:

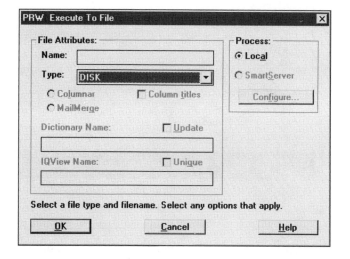

Name   Enter the filename to save the information under. If you do not enter a file extension, the default is .PRT. You can enter a pathname as well as a filename. If you leave out the pathname, Peachtree Report Writer saves the file in the \PEACHW directory.

Type   Lets you select the file type you prefer. Table 2-5 lists the file types.

Columnar   Saves the report in columnar output format.

MailMerge   Saves the report in a table format for mail-merging or other data manipulation.

Column titles   Check this box to include column titles in the file.

Dictionary Name   This feature is not implemented in this release of Peachtree Report Writer.

Update   This feature is not implemented in this release of Peachtree Report Writer.

IQView Name   This feature is not implemented in this release of Peachtree Report Writer.

Update   This feature is not implemented in this release of Peachtree Report Writer.

Process   This feature is not implemented in this release of Peachtree Report Writer.

When you are satisfied with your entries, click OK. Peachtree Report Writer saves the file to the filename in the format specified.

Output File Formats
Table 2-5.

File Type	Description
ASCII_CSV	Comma-delimited ASCII. (Almost all spreadsheets, databases, and word processors will be able to read comma-delimited ASCII files.)
ASCII_FIXED	ASCII file with fixed-length columns
DBASE_2	dBASE II format
DBASE_3	dBASE III format
DIF	Data Interchange Format, used mostly by older DOS-based programs

File Type	Description
DISK	Straight ASCII file. (This file includes titles and page numbers, where the fixed and comma-delimited ASCII files do not.)
EXCEL	Microsoft Excel version 3.0
LOTUS_123_1A	Lotus 1-2-3 version 1A
LOTUS_123_R2	Lotus 1-2-3 version 2
LOTUS_123_R3	Lotus 1-2-3 version 3
MULTIPLAN	Microsoft Multiplan symbolic file format
WORDMARC	WordMARC (can be either document or mail-merge format)
WORDPERFECT_42	WordPerfect version 4.2 (can be either document or mail-merge format)
WORDPERFECT_51	WordPerfect version 5.1 (can be either document or mail-merge format)
WORD_WIN	Word for Windows version 2.0 (can be either document or mail-merge format)

Output File Formats (*continued*)
Table 2-5.

Summary

In this chapter, you've been introduced to the elements of report design. You've also seen how to create and save a simple procedure, learned the basics of Peachtree Report Writer commands, added subtotals and totals to your reports, printed reports to the printer, and saved reports to a file. In the next chapter, you'll see how to create temporary columns, add prompts, and use matrixes and charts.

3

Working with Procedures

In the preceding chapter, you were introduced
to the elements of report design. You learned how
to create and save a simple procedure and the
basics of Peachtree Report Writer commands. You
also learned how to add subtotals and totals to
your reports, and print reports to the printer and to
a file. In this chapter, you'll see how to perform
calculations, create temporary columns, add
prompts, edit using commands, and use charts.

Performing Calculations

The procedures you created in Chapter 2 were fairly basic: there were no calculations or data manipulation other than simple totals. In this section, you'll see how to add, subtract, multiply, and divide columns, as well as how to combine columns and convert data from one format to another.

The columns that you have worked with so far are columns contained in Peachtree Accounting files. The information in these columns is static: you can't change what's in the columns through the Peachtree Report Writer. However, you can create *temporary columns* to use for calculations, comparisons, or other data manipulation. Temporary columns are report columns that are created each time you generate the report. You can use them for calculations, printing, and you can change the information in them. However, the results will not be stored as part of the Peachtree Accounting fields.

NOTE: Temporary columns are also known as variables because they contain information that may vary during the generation of the report. Actual numeric values used in computations or comparisons are known as constants because their values are constant throughout. Text (also known as alphanumeric information) is referred to as a string. Like spreadsheets and databases, Peachtree Report Writer distinguishes between a number that is a constant (which can be used in calculations) and a number that is a string (which is treated as text).

Suppose you want to see the financial impact of giving every employee a $1,000 bonus. You'll first need to create a couple of temporary columns for the calculations. To create a temporary column in a procedure, start a new procedure in Peachtree Report Writer and click the Temporary Column icon on the toolbar. The Create Column window appears, as shown in Figure 3-1.

NOTE: You can select options from the Data menu to create specific types of temporary columns—arithmetic, prompt, and so on—but there is no command within the menus that displays the Create Column window.

Type of column   Select the type of temporary column you want to create:

♦   **Arithmetic** Adds, subtracts, multiplies, or divides columns or a combination of columns and a constant.

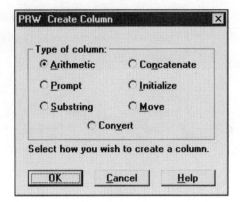

3

♦ **Prompt** Prompts for information, such as a date range, a bonus amount, or a search value, each time you generate the report.

♦ **Substring** Extracts a *substring* (a portion of a column), such as the first few letters of an employee's last name.

♦ **Concatenate** Combines two or more columns into a single column, as in combining city, state, and ZIP code information or combining an employee's first and last name for mailing labels.

♦ **Initialize** Sets a temporary column to a specified value. This *initialization* process occurs once each time you generate the report.

♦ **Move** Moves a constant, a text string, or the value of a column into the temporary column. Data is moved each time Peachtree Report Writer processes a record from the Peachtree Accounting files.

♦ **Convert** Converts numbers to dates, times, or intervals. You can also convert from one time measurement to another, such as from minutes to hours.

Initializing Temporary Columns

Whenever you create a temporary column, it's a good idea to initialize it. Select Initialize from the list of options and click OK. The Initialize window appears, as shown in Figure 3-2 (with sample data entered).

Column to create   Enter the name of the temporary column. Column names can be up to 45 characters long, so be descriptive: BONUS_AMOUNT is easier to understand than BNS_AMT. This field is not case-sensitive: temp_column, Temp_Column, and TEMP_COLUMN are treated the same.

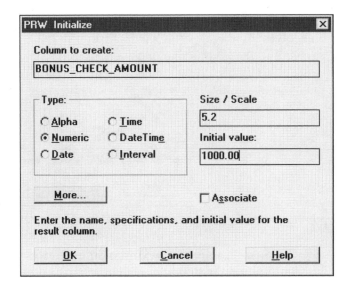

REMEMBER: You can use hyphens (-) and underscores (_) as part of the column name, but you can't have embedded spaces. Whichever you use, be consistent throughout your procedure; otherwise, you'll likely encounter problems with similar temporary column names such as BONUS_AMOUNT versus BONUS-AMOUNT.

Type   Select the type of column to create:

♦ **Alpha**   Creates an alphanumeric (text) column. If numbers are entered in this column, they will be treated as text rather than as numeric values.

♦ **Numeric**   Creates a numeric column. Numbers entered in this column will be treated only as numeric values. You cannot enter text in a numeric column.

♦ **Date**   Creates a date column. This column will contain a value representing a date, such as May 29, 1998.

♦ **Time**   Creates a time column. This column will contain a value representing a time, such as 9:30 A.M.

♦ **DateTime**   Creates a date-time column. This column will contain a value representing a date and time, such as May 29, 1998, 9:30 A.M.

♦ **Interval**   Creates an interval column. This column will contain a value representing a date or time interval, such as 15 hours or 3 days.

Size/Scale   Both Alpha and Numeric columns require a size. Alpha columns can be up to 60 characters long. Numeric columns are specified by the number of digits, a decimal point, and the number of decimals. For example, a Size/Scale specification of 4.2 for a numeric column would allow you to enter a number up to 9999.99 in the column.

REMEMBER: If you don't allow enough decimal points in this field, Peachtree Report Writer will truncate the excess decimal places and display the number to fit the format. For example, if you have a field formatted for 4.2 and you try to display a number such as 6231.89321, Peachtree Report Writer will display the number as 6231.89.

3

Initial value   Enter the initial value for the column as appropriate—an employee name or a location, a number, a date, a time, or an interval.

TIP: If you are initializing a column but you don't care what the initial value is, it's good practice to use an entry that is clearly not a normal value (such as AA_STARTVAL_ZZ for alphanumeric columns), or a "dummy" value that's unlikely to trigger an error (such as 0 or 1 for a numeric column).

Associate   This field is not implemented for the current release of Peachtree Report Writer.

More   Click to initialize another temporary column.

When you are satisfied with your entries, click OK. The temporary column has been initialized. When you generate the report, Peachtree Report Writer will use the settings you've specified to create the temporary column and set it to the initialized value. You'll also want to use the Initialize window to set up BONUS_AMOUNT_CHECK with a size/scale of 5.2 and an initial value of 0.00. If you don't initialize the BONUS_AMOUNT_CHECK, you'll have too many zeroes after the decimal point for BONUS_AMOUNT_CHECK when you generate the report.

Creating Arithmetic Temporary Columns

You are now ready to perform calculations with the BONUS_AMOUNT temporary column. Click the Temporary Columns icon on the toolbar, select Arithmetic, and click OK to display the Arithmetic window. (You can also just select the Arithmetic option from the Data menu). The Arithmetic window is shown in Figure 3-3 with the Multiply option selected and sample data entered.

Operator   Click one of the four radio buttons to add, subtract, multiply, or divide in this calculation.

Operands   For the first and second operands, select a column name from the drop-down list or enter a numeric value. (You will not see column names for text items in the drop-down list.) Temporary columns that you've already created will appear near the end of the list in alphabetic order.

Equals   Enter a new temporary column name or select from the temporary columns in the drop-down list. Peachtree Report Writer will put the value created by the calculation of the first two operands in this temporary column.

Numeric   If you are creating a new temporary column in the Equals field, select Numeric to specify that the temporary column will be numeric. (Used only if the operator is Multiply or Divide.)

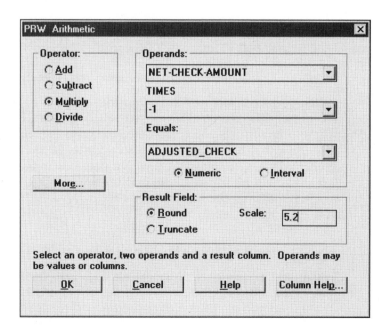

Arithmetic
window
Figure 3-3.

Interval   If you are creating a new temporary column in the Equals field, select Interval to specify that the temporary column will be an interval. (Used only if the operator is Multiply or Divide.)

Result Field   Select either Round (the default option) or Truncate. (This field is used only if the operator is Multiply or Divide.) Selecting Round tells Peachtree Report Writer to round up the first decimal past the limit set in the Scale field if it is greater than or equal to five. Values less than five are rounded down. Selecting Truncate tells Peachtree Report Writer to simply ignore the decimals past the limit set in the Scale field. For example, if the Scale field is set up for 5.2 (up to a value of 99,999.99) and the calculation produced an actual value of 23,451.315, rounding would change this number to 23,451.32 whereas truncating would change the value to 23,451.31.

3

More   Click this button to enter another arithmetic calculation.

Column Help   This feature is not implemented for the current release of Peachtree Report Writer.

The amount in NET-CHECK-AMOUNT paid to the employees is a negative amount. This is because the amount is entered as a credit against cash in the General Ledger. To switch the sign, you can multiply NET-CHECK-AMOUNT by -1. Figure 3-3 shows this calculation with the result being put into a temporary column called ADJUSTED_CHECK. Now that you have a positive amount (which is easier to read on the reports), add the temporary column BONUS_AMOUNT to the value of ADJUSTED_CHECK for the total amount with bonus. Figure 3-4 shows the result of the calculations when you generate the report.

The procedure for this report looks like this:

```
SORT ASCENDING EMP-NAME.
SEARCH FOR ZIDX = 0 .
INITIALIZE BONUS_AMOUNT TO 1000.00 NUMERIC 5.2.
INITIALIZE BONUS_AMOUNT_CHECK TO 0.00 NUMERIC 5.2.
MULTIPLY NET-CHECK-AMOUNT TIMES -1.000 GIVING ADJUSTED-CHECK SCALE 5.2.
ADD ADJUSTED-CHECK PLUS BONUS_AMOUNT GIVING BONUS_CHECK_AMOUNT.
COLUMNAR EMP-NAME ADJUSTED-CHECK BONUS_CHECK_AMOUNT ON EMP-NAME
CHANGE SUBTOTAL ADJUSTED-CHECK BONUS_CHECK_AMOUNT.
```

Using Substrings

The most common use of substrings is to create abbreviations, but you can also select area codes and phone exchanges, or extract portions of a custom field. (Substrings are used for alpha columns only.)

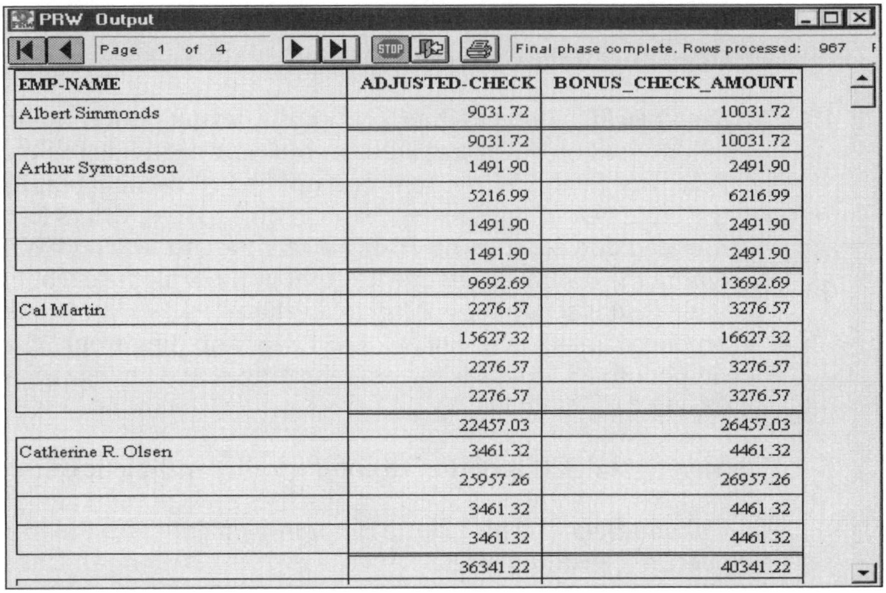

EMP-NAME	ADJUSTED-CHECK	BONUS_CHECK_AMOUNT
Albert Simmonds	9031.72	10031.72
	9031.72	10031.72
Arthur Symondson	1491.90	2491.90
	5216.99	6216.99
	1491.90	2491.90
	1491.90	2491.90
	9692.69	13692.69
Cal Martin	2276.57	3276.57
	15627.32	16627.32
	2276.57	3276.57
	2276.57	3276.57
	22457.03	26457.03
Catherine R. Olsen	3461.32	4461.32
	25957.26	26957.26
	3461.32	4461.32
	3461.32	4461.32
	36341.22	40341.22

Bonus report showing calculation results

Figure 3-4.

To create a substring temporary column, click the Temporary Columns icon on the toolbar, select Substring, and click OK to display the Substring window. You can also just select the Substring option from the Data menu. The Substring window is shown in Figure 3-5.

Source column Select the column from which the substring will be extracted.

Alpha part Enter the starting point and the size of the substring. The starting point is where to start extracting from within the column and the size is the number of characters to extract. For example, using the column string ABCDEFGHI with a starting point of 4 and a size of 3, Peachtree Report Writer would start extracting at the fourth character (D) and extract three characters. The resulting substring for this column would contain DEF.

Date/Time/Interval fields Select the date, time, or interval field you'd like to select from the drop-down list. Because Peachtree Report Writer stores

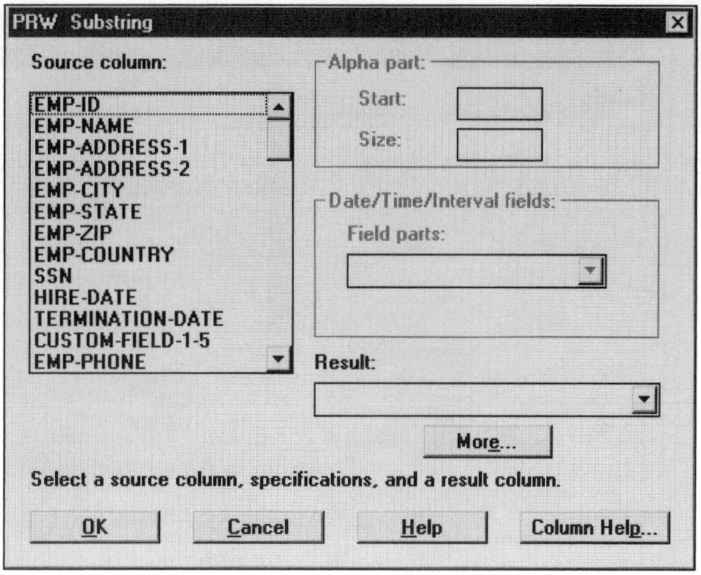

Substring
window
Figure 3-5.

dates, times, and intervals in a special numeric format, you need to tell it
which part of the information to extract and in what format it should
appear. Table 3-1 shows the results of applying the various selections in
the drop-down list against a date-time column containing a value of
04/16/98 10:25:36, as well as the type of temporary column the selection
will create.

NOTE: The type of column produced will be alpha if you check the
Alpha date format box; otherwise, Peachtree Report Writer will produce
results using the type of information noted in the table. Information must
be in alpha format if you are using this temporary column for concatenating
information (described a little later in this chapter).

Result   Enter a new temporary column name or select from the temporary
columns in the drop-down list. Peachtree Report Writer will put the value
created by the calculation of the first two operands in this temporary
column.

More   Click this button to enter another temporary substring column.

Selection	Type of Column	Result
Date	Alpha or Date	04/16/98
Time	Alpha or Time	10:25 AM
Month - 2 digit	Alpha or Numeric	04
Month - 3 char	Alpha only	APR
Day of Month	Alpha or Numeric	16
Day of Year	Alpha or Numeric	105
Year - 2 digit	Alpha or Numeric	98
Year - 4 digit	Alpha or Numeric	1998
Hours	Alpha or Numeric	10
Minutes	Alpha or Numeric	25
Seconds	Alpha or Numeric	36

Date/Time/
Interval
Selections
Table 3-1.

Column Help This feature is not implemented for the current release of Peachtree Report Writer. When you are satisfied with your entries, click OK. Figure 3-6 shows the sorted report from Figure 3-4 with a RAISE_MONTH column inserted after the employee name.

The procedure for this report looks like this:

```
SORT ASCENDING EMP-NAME.
SEARCH FOR ZIDX = 0 .
INITIALIZE BONUS_AMOUNT TO 1000.00 NUMERIC 5.2.
INITIALIZE BONUS_AMOUNT_CHECK TO 0.00 NUMERIC 5.2.
MULTIPLY NET-CHECK-AMOUNT TIMES -1.000 GIVING ADJUSTED-CHECK SCALE 5.2.
ADD ADJUSTED-CHECK PLUS BONUS_AMOUNT GIVING BONUS_CHECK_AMOUNT.
SUBSTRING LAST-RAISE-DATE FORMAT MMM TO RAISE_MONTH.
COLUMNAR EMP-NAME RAISE_MONTH ADJUSTED-CHECK BONUS_CHECK_AMOUNT ON EMP-NAME
CHANGE SUBTOTAL ADJUSTED-CHECK BONUS_CHECK_AMOUNT.
```

Concatenating Information

Combining two or more columns into a single column, as in combining city, state, and ZIP code information for a mailing label, is a process known as

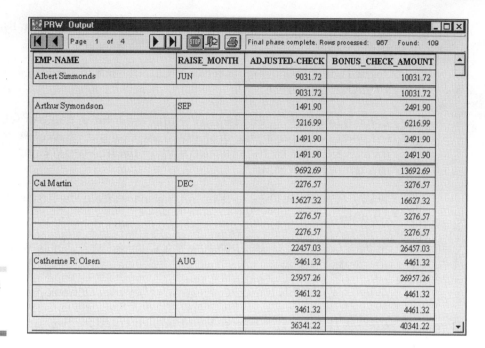

Report using a
substring
Figure 3-6.

concatenating. You will typically concatenate address or custom field
information for easier handling.

To create a concatenated temporary column, click the Temporary Columns
icon on the toolbar, select Concatenate, and click OK to display the
Concatenate window. Alternatively, you can also just select the Concatenate
option from the Data menu. The Concatenate window will appear, as
shown here:

First column or string   Select a column from the drop-down list or enter a string of text to use.

Second column or string   Select a column from the drop-down list or enter a string of text to use.

Column to create   Enter a new temporary column name or select from the temporary columns in the drop-down list. Peachtree Report Writer will put the value created by the concatenation of the first two columns or strings in this temporary column.

Trim   Check this box to trim trailing spaces from the first and second columns.

Add space   Check this box to add a space between the first and second columns or strings.

More   Click this button to create another concatenated temporary column.

Column Help   This feature is not implemented for the current release of Peachtree Report Writer. When you are satisfied with your entries, click OK. Figure 3-7 shows a report with the string "SEATTLE-" added in front of the EMP-ID to distinguish the employees on this report from employees in other divisions.

The procedure for this report looks like this:

```
SORT ASCENDING EMP-NAME.
SEARCH FOR ZIDX = 0 .
MULTIPLY NET-CHECK-AMOUNT TIMES -1.000 GIVING ADJUSTED-CHECK SCALE 5.2.
CONCATENATE 'SEATTLE-' AND EMP-ID TO SEATTLE_EMP_ID.
COLUMNAR SEATTLE_EMP_ID EMP-NAME ADJUSTED-CHECK ON EMP-NAME
CHANGE SUBTOTAL ADJUSTED-CHECK.
```

NOTE: The temporary column created by concatenating columns will be as long as the combined length of the first and second columns, plus one additional character if you select Add Space.

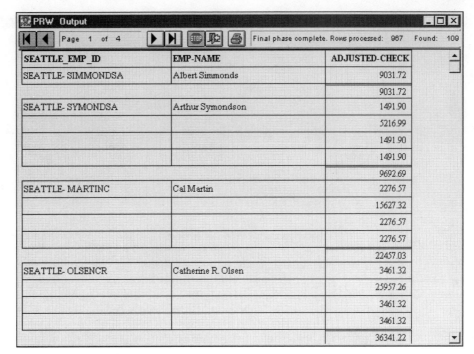

Report using a
concatenated
column
Figure 3-7.

Adding Prompts

One of the most useful custom features you can add to your reports is
prompts. When you generate a report with a procedure containing a
prompt, Peachtree Report Writer will prompt the user for input, which is
then stored in a temporary column. You can use prompts for selecting
information such as dates, names, titles, or other selection criteria.

To add a prompt, click the Temporary Columns icon on the toolbar, select
Prompt, and click OK to display the Prompt window. (You can also just
select the Prompt option from the Data menu.) The Prompt window is
shown in Figure 3-8.

Prompt message   Enter a message of up to 60 characters. Peachtree Report
Writer will display this message when you generate the report.

Column to create   Enter a new temporary column name or select from the
temporary columns in the drop-down list. Peachtree Report Writer will put
the value input by the user in this temporary column.

Column type Select the type of temporary column you want to create: Alpha, Numeric, Date, Time, Date/Time, Interval. As previously described, Numeric columns are specified by the number of digits, a decimal point, and the number of decimals. For example, a Size/Scale specification of 4.2 for a numeric column would allow you to enter a number up to 9,999.99 in the column.

PickList Type Select None to allow any entry for the prompt or Columns to have Peachtree Report Writer display a list of valid options to select from. If you select Columns, you must also select a column to display from the drop-down list. (The Procedures option is not available.) For example, if you selected EMP-ID in the drop-down list, Peachtree Report Writer would display a list of the employee IDs to choose from. You could then choose from the list or enter another response.

More Click this button to create another prompt.

When you are satisfied with your entries, click OK. When you generate the report, Peachtree Report Writer displays the User Prompt window with the list of prompts. Here is a sample procedure with a prompt for the bonus amount:

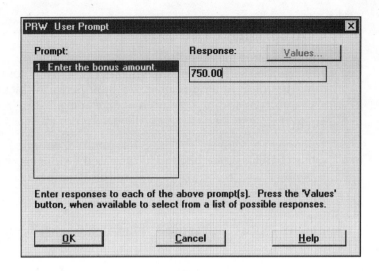

Prompt Select the prompt to respond to. Prompts are numbered in the order in which they were entered.

Response Enter the response to the prompt.

Values If the response has an associated picklist column, clicking Values adds a drop-down button to Response. You can click the drop-down button to select a value from the list.

When you are satisfied with your entries, click OK. Peachtree Report Writer uses the information you entered to generate the report (not shown).

The procedure for a report that prompts for the bonus amount looks like this:

```
SORT ASCENDING EMP-NAME.
SEARCH FOR ZIDX = 0 .
PROMPT 'Enter the bonus amount.' TO PROMPT_BONUS_AMOUNT NUMERIC 5.2 .
INITIALIZE BONUS_AMOUNT_CHECK TO 0.00 NUMERIC 5.2.
MULTIPLY NET-CHECK-AMOUNT TIMES -1.000 GIVING ADJUSTED-CHECK SCALE 5.2.
ADD ADJUSTED-CHECK PLUS PROMPT_BONUS_AMOUNT GIVING BONUS_CHECK_AMOUNT.
COLUMNAR EMP-NAME ADJUSTED-CHECK BONUS_CHECK_AMOUNT ON
EMP-NAME CHANGE SUBTOTAL ADJUSTED-CHECK BONUS_CHECK_AMOUNT.
```

Converting Columns

Some columns may require conversion from one format to another before you can use them. For example, you may want to compare a date or a time to information in a numeric column, or perform calculations using dates or times, such as adding 90 days to a date and printing the results on a report. To do this, you need to covert the data types to the same format.

To convert a column, click the Temporary Columns icon on the toolbar, select Convert, and click OK to display the Convert window. (You can also just select the Convert option from the Data menu.) The Convert window is shown here:

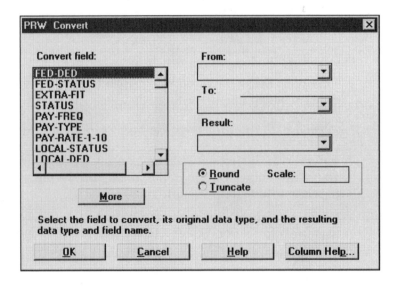

Convert field   Select the column to be converted.

From   Select the format to convert from using the drop-down list.

To   Select the format to convert to using the drop-down list.

Result   Enter a new temporary column name or select from the temporary columns in the drop-down list. Peachtree Report Writer will put the value created by the conversion into this temporary column. Select either Round (the default option) or Truncate. (See the section "Creating Arithmetic Temporary Columns" earlier in this chapter for descriptions and examples of the Round and Truncate functions.)

More   Click this button to convert another temporary column.

Column Help This feature is not implemented for the current release of Peachtree Report Writer. When you are satisfied with your entries, click OK. Peachtree Report Writer will convert the date and put the results in the temporary column you specified.

NOTE: You won't need to convert columns very often. The most common use of this feature is to add or subtract a number of hours or days from a time or date field. For example, you may need to determine the date of the next billing period by adding a number of hours or days to a Date Time column.

Editing Procedure Commands

3

So far, the changes you have made to the commands in a procedure have been through the menus and toolbar. However, sometimes it's more convenient to make changes manually. You can do this with the Procedure Editor.

From the Edit menu, select the Edit Procedure option. The Procedure Editor window appears (shown in Figure 3-9, with one of the sample procedures that comes with Peachtree Report Writer).

From the Procedure Editor window, you can type commands and use standard cut and paste features to add, modify, transpose, and delete commands. You can also edit a procedure in a text editor such as Notepad or WordPad, or in your favorite word processor, and then cut and paste the commands into the Procedure Editor window.

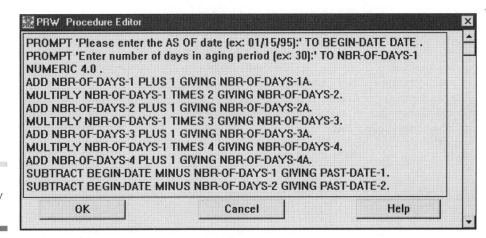

Procedure Editor window
Figure 3-9.

TIP: You can edit the procedure by selecting Edit rather than Load in the Open Procedure window.

If you prefer, you can abbreviate commands, making sure that Peachtree Report Writer can distinguish them from other commands. For example, you could abbreviate CONCATENATE to CONC, but not to CON because Peachtree Report Writer wouldn't be able to distinguish it from an abbreviation for CONVERT.

Some general tips for manually editing commands are:

◆ Don't over-abbreviate. Using the full command or most of it will make your procedure easier to read the next time you're editing it.

◆ Make sure that your commands always start on a new line and end with a period. If your command is longer than one line, make sure not to split column names or words between two lines.

◆ Put Initialize commands at the start of your procedure, followed by any other commands that create temporary columns. This keeps all the temporary columns commands in one place, making them easier to maintain, and also prevents using a command that relies on a temporary column that has not yet been defined in the procedure.

In addition, you should use comment lines to document your procedure commands. Comment lines start with a #. You may have as many comment lines in a procedure as you like. Here is a sample procedure with comments added:

```
#Bonus amount procedure, created 3/21/98 by Melvin Morsmere.
#Modified 5/29/98 to prompt for bonus amount.
SORT ASCENDING EMP-NAME.
SEARCH FOR ZIDX = 0 .
#Prompt added 5/29/98.
PROMPT 'Enter the bonus amount.' TO PROMPT_BONUS_AMOUNT NUMERIC 5.2 .
INITIALIZE BONUS_AMOUNT_CHECK TO 0.00 NUMERIC 5.2.
MULTIPLY NET-CHECK-AMOUNT TIMES -1.000 GIVING ADJUSTED-CHECK SCALE 5.2.
ADD ADJUSTED-CHECK PLUS PROMPT_BONUS_AMOUNT GIVING BONUS_CHECK_AMOUNT.
COLUMNAR EMP-NAME ADJUSTED-CHECK BONUS_CHECK_AMOUNT ON EMP-NAME
CHANGE SUBTOTAL ADJUSTED-CHECK BONUS_CHECK_AMOUNT.
```

One of the advantages of editing procedures through the Procedure Editor window is that you can manipulate special fields more easily. Special fields are described in the next section.

Understanding Special Fields

As you've seen, Peachtree Report Writer lets you access the information in Peachtree Accounting files through views that have column names. Some of these columns are special fields that require some additional explanation.

There are two types of special fields. The first type is the class of fields where Peachtree Accounting stores numbers to signify information rather than a full text description. For example, Peachtree Accounting stores a number in the FED-STATUS to signify the federal tax status for the employee: 0 for Single, 1 for Married, 2 for Head of Household, and so on. (A list of the special fields appears in Appendix G of the Peachtree Report Writer manual.)

3

The second type of special field is an *array*. Array special fields have separate but related entries known as *elements*. Arrays are generally used for information that is defined by the Peachtree user for their companies rather than as part of the standard settings for Peachtree Accounting. For example, an employee in Peachtree Accounting can have up to five different user-defined fields of custom information. If you select the CUSTOM-FIELD-1-5 column name, you must also specify which of the five custom fields you want Peachtree Report Writer to display. Similarly, to see a quarter-to-date employee pay amount, you need to tell Peachtree Report Writer which of the different employee pay classifications (there are up to 30) in this array you want to see. When you select an array in the Available columns list, Peachtree Report Writer will usually prompt you for the element in the array.

NOTE: Some options in Peachtree Report Writer, such as the temporary columns selections, do not prompt you for the array element. In these cases, you can enter the temporary columns command without specifying the element, then use the Procedure Editor window to add the element information to the command.

For example, suppose that you want to display the employee's quarter-to-date (QTD) information for the third quarter in a simple report. Start by selecting the column for the QTD information: in the Columnar Output window, scroll down the list in the Available columns list until you see QTD-3-AMT-EE-1-30. This is the column for the quarter-to-date (QTD), third quarter (3) amounts (AMT) for the employee (EE), with up to 30 elements (1-30). The order for the elements in this column is determined by how the rates are set up on the Maintain Employees/Sales Reps window in Peachtree Accounting (shown for reference in Figure 3-10).

When you select QTD-3-AMT-EE-1-30, Peachtree Report Writer displays the Array Column window:

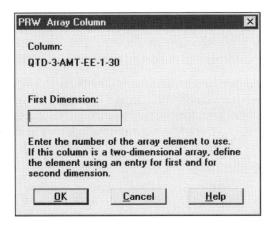

Enter the number corresponding to the element of the array you want to display. As you can see from Figure 3-10, there is only one array element that

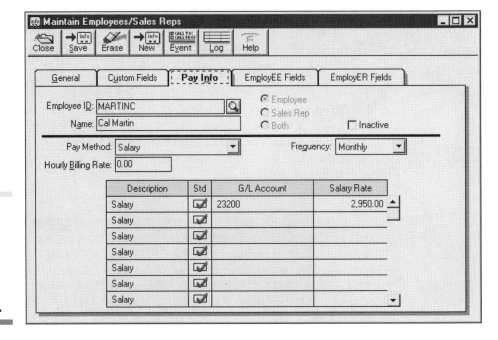

Maintain Employees/ Sales Reps window in Peachtree Accounting

Figure 3-10.

you want to look at—the first "Salary" entry—so enter 1 in this field. Figure 3-11 shows a simple report using this information.

The procedure for this report looks like this:

```
SORT ASCENDING EMP-NAME ASCENDING CHECK-NUMBER.
SEARCH FOR ZIDX = 0 .
COLUMNAR BY EMP-NAME TOTAL QTD-3-AMT-EE-1-30#1.
```

Note the #1 after the special field. This identifies the first element of the QTD-3-AMT-EE-1-30 special field. You can edit the special field information using the Procedure Editor window simply by changing the array element appropriately.

3

Using Charts

The final section of this chapter focuses on using charts. Where the columnar report format is text-based, charts are graphical representations of data. Peachtree Report Writer supports bar, stacked bar, area, pie, line, and scatter charts.

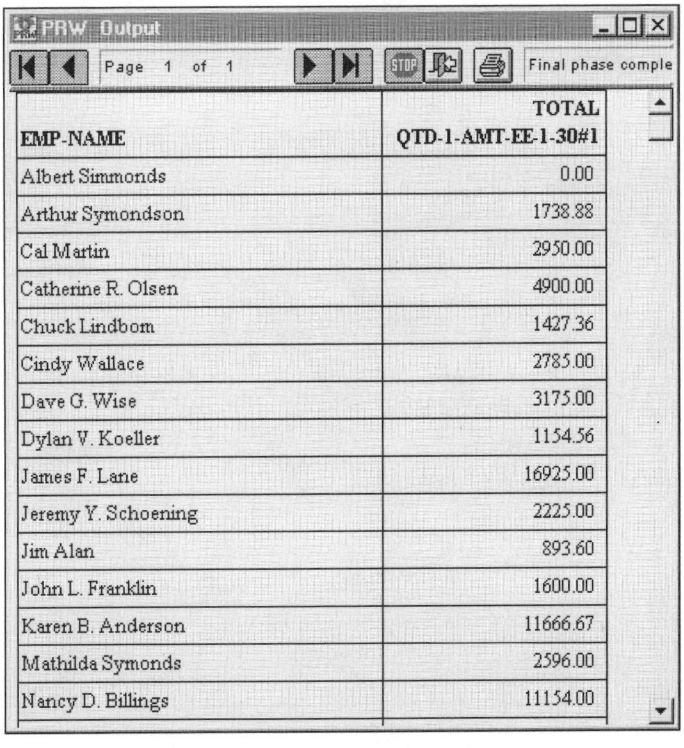

EMP-NAME	TOTAL QTD-1-AMT-EE-1-30#1
Albert Simmonds	0.00
Arthur Symondson	1738.88
Cal Martin	2950.00
Catherine R. Olsen	4900.00
Chuck Lindbom	1427.36
Cindy Wallace	2785.00
Dave G. Wise	3175.00
Dylan V. Koeller	1154.56
James F. Lane	16925.00
Jeremy Y. Schoening	2225.00
Jim Alan	893.60
John L. Franklin	1600.00
Karen B. Anderson	11666.67
Mathilda Symonds	2596.00
Nancy D. Billings	11154.00

Sample report using a special field

Figure 3-11.

To create a chart, select Chart from the Output menu, then select the option for the type of chart you wish to create from the submenu. (You can also select the type of chart directly from the toolbar by clicking the appropriate chart icon.) The chart window appears. Figure 3-12 shows the Chart BAR window with sample data already entered.

NOTE: Most of the information on the chart windows is the same as on the Chart BAR window, with only minor variations from window to window.

Vertical Axis   Select the column to be charted from the drop-down list. Also select if you want Peachtree Report Writer to total, average, or take the minimum or maximum amount in the selection.

Legend   Enter the legend for the vertical axis. The default is the column name in the Vertical Axis field.

Column to Chart   Select the column to be charted against from the drop-down list.

Group By (Optional)   Select a column to summarize (or "group") information by. If this is a bar chart, Peachtree Report Writer creates separate bars for each of the values in this column. If this is a stacked bar chart,

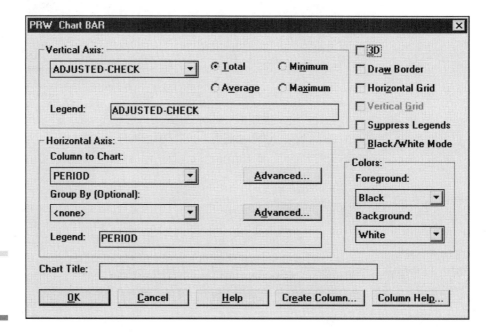

Chart Bar window

Figure 3-12.

Peachtree Report Writer will stack bars for the values in the column. For all other charts (except pie charts), Peachtree Report Writer will plot points for each of the values in the column.

Advanced   Click this button to open the Advanced Chart window (shown in Figure 3-13) to customize the appearance of the chart.

The Advanced Chart window lets you modify the ranges, legends, colors, and patterns for data.

Define By   You can define your chart using one of the three radio button choices. Choose Specific Values or Range of Values for the data you are defining. If this is a numeric data item, you can choose Number of Values to tell Peachtree Report Writer how many data items you want to appear on the chart.

3

(From) Value   Enter the starting value in the range or a single value if you are charting a single value.

To   Enter the ending value in the range or leave it blank if you are charting a single value.

Legend   Enter a legend for this data item.

Color   Select a color from the drop-down list for this data item.

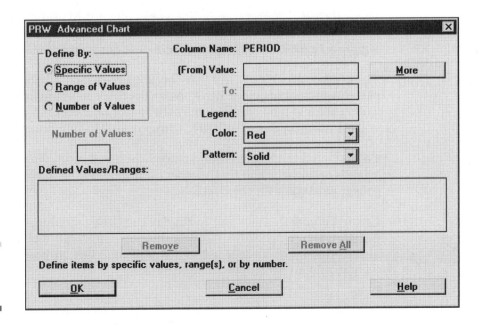

Advanced
Chart window
Figure 3-13.

Pattern   Select a pattern from the drop-down list for this data item.

Defined Values/Ranges   A list of the values and ranges you have selected will appear in this field.

Remove   Removes the highlighted entries in the Defined Values/Ranges from the chart.

Remove All   Removes all entries in the Defined Values/Ranges from the chart.

More   Click this button to modify another column on the chart.

When you are satisfied with your entries, click OK. You will return to the Chart window (Figure 3-12), where you can continue making entries.

Legend   Enter the legend for the horizontal axis. The default is the column name from the Column to Chart field.

Chart Title   Enter a title for the chart. The title will appear at the top center of the output.

3D   Select this checkbox to add 3-D effects to the chart.

Draw Border   Select this checkbox to add a border to the chart.

Horizontal Grid   Select this checkbox to add horizontal grid lines to the chart.

Vertical Grid   Select this checkbox to add vertical grid lines to the chart.

Suppress Legends   Select this checkbox to suppress the legends for data items.

Black/White Mode   Select this checkbox to display in black and white patterns instead of colors. (Any color selections you may have made in the Colors fields will be overridden by this selection.) This is a useful feature if you are using a laptop computer with a monochrome display.

Colors   Select the foreground color which will be used for the text in the legends and labels, and for the lines on the report. Also select the background color for the chart.

Create Column   Click this to display the Create Column window (shown earlier in Figure 3-1). After clicking this, you can create a temporary column. This feature is particularly useful if you need to initialize a temporary column you are creating for the report.

Column Help   This feature is not implemented for the current release of Peachtree Report Writer. When you are satisfied with your entries, click OK. When you generate the report, the results will appear as a chart rather than as a columnar report (shown in Figure 3-14).

TIP: You can see the value of any specific data item by double-clicking the item on the chart. Peachtree Report Writer displays the values for the horizontal and vertical axis for the selected data item.

Figure 3-15 shows the effects of adding 3-D, horizontal grid lines, and a border to the chart.

3

Figure 3-16 shows the same chart as in Figure 3-15, but with Black/White mode selected.

Charts can be tailored to your specific requirements. You are encouraged to experiment with the different chart types and charting options to see what best fits your needs.

At the end of the previous chapter, you saw how to output reports to the screen, your printer, or a file. You can display charts on the screen and print

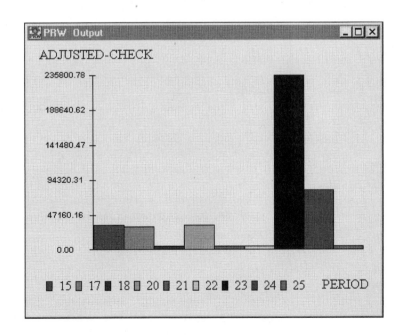

Bar chart
Figure 3-14.

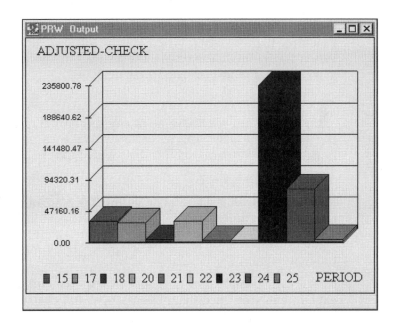

3-D bar chart
Figure 3-15.

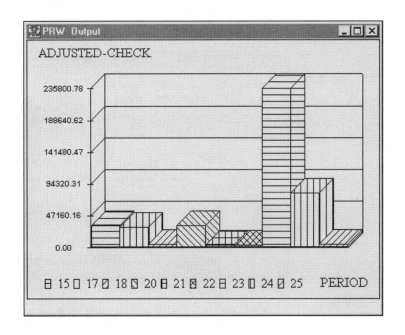

Black/White
3-D bar chart
Figure 3-16.

them to the printer, but you cannot save them to a file. If you want to save the report information online, you can display the chart on the screen, copy the report to the Windows clipboard, and then paste it into a file in another application.

Summary

In this chapter, you saw how to create temporary columns, add prompts, edit procedures manually, and use charts. In the next chapter, you'll see how to use the Report Designer and Label Designer to lay out reports on the screen.

4

Designing Reports and Labels

In the preceding chapter, you saw how to create temporary columns, add prompts, edit procedures manually, and use charts. In this chapter, you'll see how to use the Report Designer and Label Designer to lay out reports and labels on the screen.

Understanding the Report Designer

In Chapter 2, "Creating a Procedure," you saw why it's a good idea to plan your report on paper before you build it in Peachtree Report Writer. You can use the Report Designer in much the same way, to see a model of your report as you add columns and subtotals. You can also use the Report Designer to customize a columnar procedure you've already created. You can add titles and headings, change column sizes and attributes, alter the font and the character attributes, and change the report's margins.

The first decision to make when creating a report with the Report Designer is whether you want to create the report in graphical mode or character mode. Graphical-mode reports let you use the full range of fonts on your computer, add borders and drop shadows, and work in either inches or centimeters. Character-mode reports come in a single font only (10-point Courier) and cannot have borders or drop-shadows. Although the character-mode reports allow far fewer report formatting options, they are quick to create and easy to read. In addition, the Report Designer is slow when working with reports in the graphical mode. As a result, you may want to use character mode to start designing a report, then conclude with the graphical mode when the report is largely complete and needs only the final graphical formatting.

NOTE: Peachtree Report Writer can switch between graphical and character mode automatically, but all graphical formatting such as font selections and borders will be lost when you switch to character mode. You may also have to adjust the location of some columns, as they may overlap following the conversion from a proportional font, such as Times New Roman, to 10-point Courier, which is a monospaced font.

Creating a Report Using the Report Designer

To create a new procedure using the Report Designer, start by selecting New Procedure from the File menu, then selecting either the Graphical Report or the Character Report option from the Preferences menu in the main Peachtree Report Writer window. Next, start the Report Designer by clicking the Report Designer icon on the Peachtree Report Writer toolbar (or select the Report option from the Output menu). The Report Design window appears (shown in Figure 4-1).

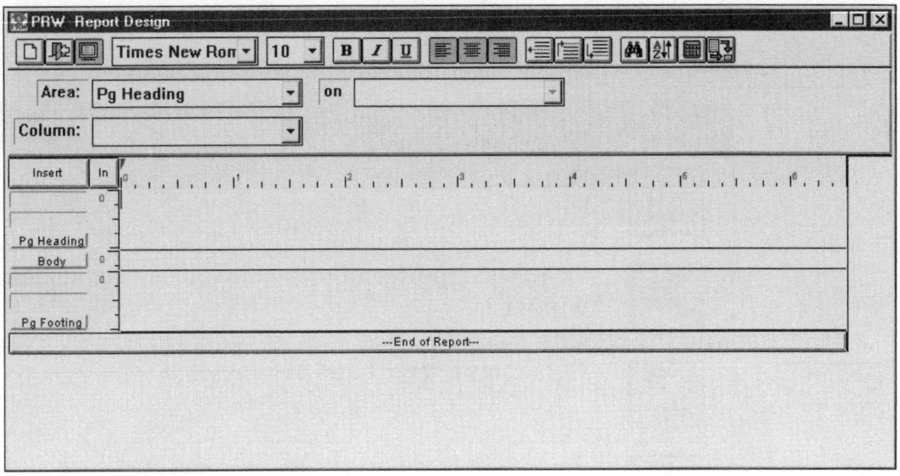

Report Design
window (in
graphical
mode)
Figure 4-1.

The Report Design window is somewhat different from the main Peachtree
Report Writer window. Table 4-1 shows the menu categories and what they do.

4

NOTE: When you first start the Report Designer, Peachtree Report
Writer sets up a default report with three lines for the page header, one line
for the body, and three lines for the page footer.

Menu	What It Does
File	Creates a new report, previews a report, saves the report and exits, or just exits without saving
Edit	Cuts, copies, and pastes information, or deletes an object, line, or area when procedures are edited in the Report Designer
Insert	Inserts a column, line, area, or page break
Format	Formats the report font, border, and other elements
Data	Searches, sorts, and limits the data that appears on the report
Preferences	Sets Report Designer options
Help	Accesses help on using Report Designer

Report
Designer
Menu
Categories
Table 4-1.

The toolbar icons found in the Report Design window are listed in Table 4-2, along with their descriptions.

Icon	What It Does
	Starts a new report
	Saves the report procedure and closes the Report Design window
	Generates a report and displays it on the screen
 **B**	Toggles bold on and off for the selected text
 *I*	Toggles italic on and off for the selected text
 U	Toggles underline on and off for the selected text
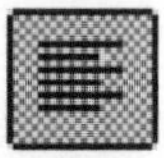	Left-justifies the selection (in graphical mode only)
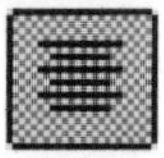	Centers the selection (in graphical mode only)
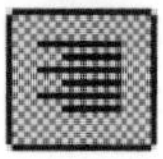	Right-justifies the selection (in graphical mode only)
	Deletes the current line
	Adds a line before the current line
	Adds a line after the current line
	Searches for information in a column (in graphical mode only)

Toolbar Icons
on the Main
Report Design
Window
Table 4-2.

Icon	What It Does
	Sorts column information (in graphical mode only)
	Creates a temporary column
	Limits the number of records on the report (in graphical mode only)
	Inserts a count of the records (in character mode only)
	Accesses column help (in character mode only; not enabled in this release of Peachtree Report Writer)

Toolbar Icons on the Main Report Design Window (*continued*)
Table 4-2.

4

Area   Select the area of the report you want to work with. From the drop-down list, select Pg Heading, Subheading, Body, Subtotal, Grand Total, or Page Footing.

on   Shows the column to break on for a subheading, subtotal, or grand total. You can modify the column break by selecting a different column from the drop-down list.

Column   Select the column to display at the break specified for the subheading, subtotal, or grand total.

Insert/Overwrite   Click this button to toggle between insert and overwrite mode.

In/CM   Click this button to toggle between inches and centimeters for the report measurements. (This button is set to "Ch" for characters in character mode.)

TIP: You can also change the report measurement option by selecting Ruler Measurements from the Preferences menu on the Report Designer window.

Understanding Report Areas

Reports in the Report Designer have *areas*, each of which has separate properties. The report areas are:

◆ **Pg Heading** Information in the Pg Heading area appears at the top of every page, such as the report title and column headings. Some information on the Insert Column submenu, such as the page number and date and time information, can only appear in the page heading or the page footing areas.

◆ **Subheading** Information in the Subheading area appears every time there is a subtotal break, such as when the employee name changes. Use subheadings as column headings for subtotals or for additional subtotal information. You can have a subheading for each subtotal in the report. (Include a page break in the subheading to force a page break when the subtotal break happens.)

◆ **Body** Information in the Body area appears once for each record. To create a double-spaced report, add a blank line after each line of text or information in the body area. The Body area is omitted for a summary report.

◆ **Subtotal** Information in the Subtotal area appears once for each subtotal break. The Subtotal area contains column subtotals and calculations.

◆ **Grand Total** Information in the Grand Total area appears once at the end of the report. The Grand Total area contains text, column totals, and calculations.

◆ **Pg Footing** Information in the Pg Footing area appears at the bottom of every report page, such as the page number and date.

Report areas are identified by the area marker on the left side of the Report Design window.

Creating a Report

In the following example, you will re-create the employee SSN report you created in Chapter 2, "Creating a Procedure," but you will be using the Report Designer in graphical mode instead of the Columnar Output window. However, because you're using the Report Designer, you'll be able to add formatting and additional information to make the report more readable. Start the example by adding a date and time to the report heading.

REMEMBER: Because the Report Designer's graphical mode is very slow, be sure to allow enough time for the Report Designer to respond to your commands and mouse actions.

Position the cursor at the top left of the Pg Heading section and click. When the blinking insertion point appears, select Column from the Insert menu, then select Datetime from the submenu. The Datetime information appears in the Report Design window. This is where the date and time information will print on the report.

To add a page number, click below the 5.5" mark on the ruler, then type **Page**. Next, select Column from the Insert menu, then select Page Number from the submenu. The Report Designer adds a page number after the word "Page." Finally, to add a title, click on the second line of the Pg Heading area at the 2.75" mark and type **Employee SSN Report**. Click the bold toolbar button to change the title to bold. Figure 4-2 shows the report so far.

You can see in Figure 4-2 that there is a gray box around the title. The squares on either side are handles you can use to expand or contract the title. Try pulling the handle out an inch or so by moving the mouse pointer to the handle (the pointer will change from an arrow to a bar with arrows on either side), and clicking and dragging the handle. The gray box will expand and show the area the Report Designer has allotted for the title. You can use the justification and centering buttons on the toolbar to change the location of the title in its box. You can also move the title on the page by clicking and dragging the title. Position the outline of the title (which appears as a

4

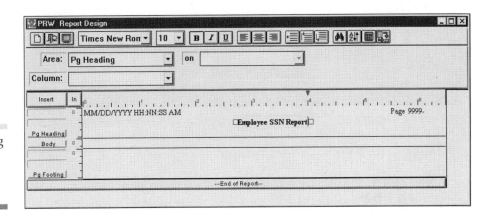

Report with Pg
Heading area
completed
Figure 4-2.

box with a dashed border) on the Pg Heading area and release the mouse button. Finally, to delete an item entirely, select the item, click the Edit menu, and select Cut or Delete Object. You can also delete an entire line or area with the Delete Line or Delete Area option on the Edit menu. If you delete the wrong item, you can undo the last delete with the Undo Last Delete option.

With the page heading completed, you can now add the body information. Select Body from the drop-down list in the Area field. Note that the cursor immediately appears at the leftmost position of the Body area. You can use this technique to position the cursor at the leftmost position of an area. Select EMP-ID from the drop-down list in the Column field. The Report Designer positions the EMP-ID item in the Body area. The Xs show the largest possible number of characters in the field. Now use the same technique to position the EMP-NAME and SSN fields. Also add custom column headings in the Pg Heading area (as you will remember from previous chapters, Peachtree Report Writer uses the column names as the default column headings).

Because this is a simple list of names and social security numbers, the report contains all the information you need. Figure 4-3 shows the finished report with some additional character formatting added.

When you generate the report, the character formatting appears on the finished report, as shown in Figure 4-4.

When you include a date or time on the report, Peachtree Report Writer uses the current system date and time when you generate the report.

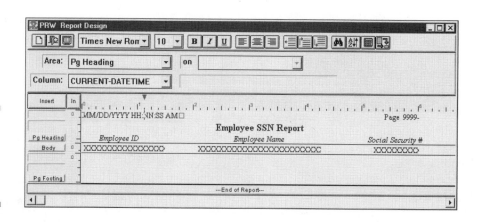

Completed report in the Report Design window

Figure 4-3.

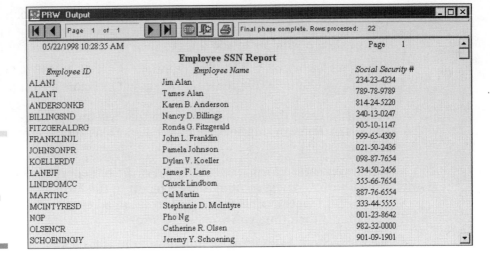

Report
generated
from the
Report Design
window
Figure 4-4.

Using Subtotals and Totals in the Report Designer   4

You can see how the Report Designer treats subtotals and grand totals by opening the BONUS_CHECK_AMOUNT procedure from the beginning of Chapter 3, "Working with Procedures." Figure 4-5 shows the Report Design window with this procedure loaded.

TIP: You can use the Report Designer to edit a procedure whenever you used the Columnar Output window in earlier chapters.

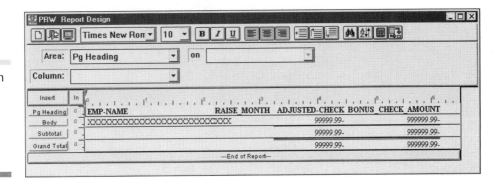

Report Design
window
showing the
bonus check
amount
Figure 4-5.

The Report Designer uses the column names as the default column headings. You can use the Insert Line Before and Insert Line After buttons in the Report Design window to add lines to the Pg Heading area as necessary.

Now double-click on the X's that represent the EMP-NAME data in the Body area. The Column Attributes window (shown in Figure 4-6) appears.

Format Enter the format for the data that will appear in this column. If there is no entry in this field, Peachtree Report Writer uses the default format.

When you enter a format in this field, Peachtree Report Writer will set the default format of the column for this report to the format you enter. If you use the field several times in a report, you can accept the default or enter a new format each time you use the column.

See the section "Formatting Columns" later in this chapter for information on how you can format the column information.

Characters Enter the number of characters to display. The default number for this field is the number of characters for the field. If you specify fewer characters to print than are in the column and there is information that won't fit in the width you specify, the remaining information is truncated. This option is useful for reducing the width on fields that are normally too wide for your company's data; for example, the employee ID may be 30 characters wide, but your company only issues employee IDs that are 6 characters.

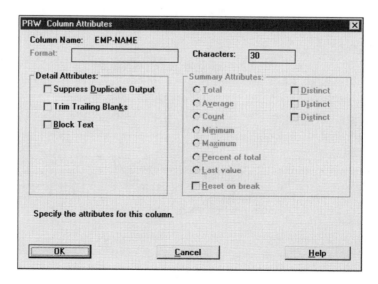

Column Attributes window

Figure 4-6.

Suppress Duplicate Output   Check this box to suppress duplicate output for the row.

NOTE: This option applies only to the item selected. If you have several different elements in the Body area, you may need to suppress the duplicate output for each one.

Trim Trailing Blanks   Check this box to suppress the trailing blanks in a field.

Block Text   Check this box to block out a text area for a column. Peachtree Report Writer formats the blocked column as a gray rectangular block. When Peachtree Report Writer displays information in a text area, it wraps the information to fit in the text area.

When you check this box, two additional fields appear for entering the number of rows and the width of your block. Enter the number of rows for the item and the width (in characters for character-mode reports or in inches or centimeters for graphical reports). Peachtree Report Writer will automatically block out an area on the report determined by the number of rows and the width specified in these fields. Use this feature for long entries (such as product descriptions or long custom fields) that might require an excessive amount of width to print on a single row.

Blocked columns cannot be larger than a page. Peachtree Report Writer always prints blocked columns on a single page rather than breaking them between two pages.

Summary Attributes   Select the calculation type for the column:

- ♦ **Total** Totals the amounts in the column
- ♦ **Average** Takes the average of the amounts in the column
- ♦ **Count** Counts the number of entries in the column
- ♦ **Minimum** Displays the smallest value of all the values in the column
- ♦ **Maximum** Displays the largest value of all the values in the column
- ♦ **Percent of total** Displays the value as a percentage of the total of the column for all rows that appear in your report
- ♦ **Last value** Displays the last value in the column before the subtotal break (that is, the value in the previous line)
- ♦ **Reset on break** Check this box to make the calculations you specify for the Summary Attributes specific to each Subtotal area rather than having running calculations for all subtotals in the report.

4

NOTE: The Distinct option is not available in this release of Peachtree Report Writer.

When you are satisfied with your entries, click OK.

You can set column attributes and formatting for each column individually. As you change the column attributes for the columns, you can display the report and see how your changes affect the finished product.

TIP: You can quickly select one field after another by pressing TAB or SHIFT-TAB.

Formatting Columns

Peachtree Report Writer offers extensive features for providing custom formatting of columns. You can let Peachtree Report Writer use the default column formats or specify your own through the Column Attributes window.

Formatting Text Columns

The formatting options for text fields such as employee names, descriptions, and so on, appear on the Column Attributes window (shown earlier in Figure 4-6).

Formatting Numeric Columns

There are three groups of numeric formatting characters. The first group of formatting characters represents single numeric digits.

- The number 9 replaces leading zeroes with spaces, although if the value of the column is zero, Peachtree Report Writer prints a single zero for the column. For example, a format of 99999 would print the value 00123 as 123 and the value 00000 as 0.

- The letter "B" also replaces leading zeroes with spaces, but if the value of the column is zero, Peachtree Report Writer prints nothing for the column. For example, a format of BBBBB would print the value 00123 as 123 and a value of 00000 would not be printed.

- The letter "Z" does not suppress leading zeroes: a format of ZZZZZ would print the value 00123 as 00123.

The second group of formatting characters can represent single digits as well as add special formatting options of their own. You can combine the formatting characters in the second group of characters with those in the first group as you wish.

♦ A minus sign (–) shows the location of the minus sign in the number. A minus sign after the format tells Peachtree Report Writer to put the minus sign after the number. For example, a format of 99999- would print the value -00123 as 123- and the value 00000 as 0. A minus sign before the format tells Peachtree Report Writer to put the minus sign and a separating space before the number; in other words, a format of -99999 would print the value -00123 as - 123. Multiple minus signs before the number suppress leading zeros, but the minus sign precedes the printed number with no separating space; therefore, a format of ---999 would print the value -00123 as - 123.

♦ A plus sign (+) works similarly to the minus sign, except that a positive number will have a plus sign and a negative number will have a minus sign. (A zero will have no sign at all.) For example, a format of +99999 would print 00123 as + 123 and -00123 as - 123.

♦ A dollar sign ($) tells Peachtree Report Writer to insert a dollar sign in the number at the location. For example, $99999 would print 00123 as $ 123. (The additional spaces between the dollar sign and number are there because the 9 character replaces leading zeros with spaces.) Similarly, $ZZZZZ would print 00123 as $00123. Multiple dollar signs put the currency symbol at the start of the number and suppress leading spaces; for example, $$$$$$ would print 00123 as $123.

♦ CR and DB tell Peachtree Report Writer to put CR or DB after a negative number. For example, 99999CR prints -00123 as 123CR, while 99999DB prints -00123 as 123DB.

4

The third group of formatting characters lets you add decimal points, separators, and other currency symbols to your formats.

♦ A period (.) tells Peachtree Report Writer where to place the decimal point. For example, 99999.99 would print 00123 as 123.00 and 00123.45 as 123.45. A format of ZZZZZ.ZZ would print 00123.45 as 00123.45.

♦ A comma (,) tells Peachtree Report Writer where to put a comma in the number. If a number has leading zeroes that have been suppressed with either the 9 or B formatting character, Peachtree Report Writer does not print the comma in the number. For example, 999,999 prints 00123 as 123 and 987654 as 987,654. A format of ZZZ,ZZZ would print 000123 as 000,123.

♦ The hyphen (-), slash (/), and colon (:) can be used as separators anywhere in the number. For example, ZZZ-ZZ-ZZZZ (the standard formatting used for social security numbers) would print a value of 123456789 as 123-45-6789.

NOTE: A hyphen is the same character as a minus sign. Peachtree Report Writer treats it as a separator rather than a minus sign when it appears in the middle of a format as a separator.

The left and right parentheses bracket the format. You can add additional left parenthesis characters to suppress leading spaces. For example, ((((999) would print 00123 as (123). Keep in mind that you must have at least one pair of parentheses in a format; you can't use a single left or right parenthesis.

♦ An asterisk (*) replaces leading zeros with asterisks. If the value is zero or there is a zero to the left of the decimal point, Peachtree Report Writer prints a zero for that digit. For example, a format of ***** would print the value 00123 as **123 and the value 00000 as ****0.

♦ DM, Lit, Yen, Fr, and other currency symbols or text information can appear at the beginning or end of a format. You can use any combination of characters except the formatting characters Peachtree Report Writer recognizes. You may also include spaces, but they must be followed by a character that is not a space. For example, a format of 999,999 Yen would print 098765 as 98,765 Yen. A format of BONUS AMT $9,999 would print 2345 as BONUS AMT $2,345.

It's a good idea to allow for the largest number possible in each field and to test your reports with the largest possible numbers you will print. When a number is larger than the space you allow for it (including currency symbols, digits, separator characters), Peachtree Report Writer will first ignore currency symbols and separator characters to increase the number of digits available. If there is still not enough room, it adds digits at the right of the column until the number will print. This may throw off the formatting on pre-printed forms or labels.

Formatting Date Columns

Date formatting characters are "D" (for the day), "M" (for the month), and "Y" (for the year). You use them as follows:

♦ A format of DD prints the date (from 01 to 31).

♦ A format of DDD prints the day of the year (from 001 to 366).

♦ A format of MM prints the month (from 01 to 12).

♦ A format of MMM prints the three-letter abbreviation for the month (JAN, FEB, and so on).

♦ A format of YY prints a two-digit year (such as 98).

♦ A format of YYYY prints a four-digit year (such as 1998).

You can format date columns with any combination of date formatting characters and a separator character. This separator character can be any character (including a space) other than a "D," "M," or "Y," but you must use the same separator character for the entire date. The default date separator character is a forward slash (/). Peachtree Report Writer will convert a lowercase separator character to uppercase.

Table 4-3 shows some examples of how various formats will print the date March 21, 1998.

Formatting Time Columns

Time formatting characters are "H" (for the hour), "N" (for the minute), and "S" (for the second). You use them as follows:

♦ A format of HH prints the hour (from 01 to 24).

♦ A format of NN prints the minute (from 01 to 60).

♦ A format of SS prints the seconds (from 01 to 60).

You can format time columns with any combination of time formatting characters and a separator character. This separator character can be any character (including a space) other than an "H," "N," or "S," but you must use the same separator character for the entire date. The default time separator character is a colon (:). Peachtree Report Writer will convert a lowercase separator character to uppercase.

Date Format	What It Prints
MM/DD/YY	03/21/98
MM/DD/YYYY	03/21/1998
DD/MM/YYYY	21/03/1998
MM-DD-YY	03-21-98
MMM DD YY	MAR 21 98
MM-DD	03-21
DDD/YY	080/98

Sample Date
Formats
Table 4-3.

The default for a time column is 24-hour time. You can force Peachtree Report Writer to use AM and PM by adding the formatting characters AM to the end of your format.

Table 4-4 shows some examples of how various formats will print the time 6:45:00 PM.

TIP: You can print columns that have dates and time by combining a valid date format and a valid time format.

Formatting Interval Columns

You can format intervals similar to time formats but you cannot include AM or PM designations. You can also add a DD to indicate the number of days (such as DD:HH:NN or DD:HH).

Changing Other Report Options

In addition to the formatting options you have seen previously, you can adjust other options to change the report size and margins, add grid snap, and add a count of the number of rows.

Changing Report Size and Margins

To change the report width, select Report Width from the Format menu. The Report Width window appears, as shown here:

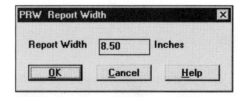

Report Width   Enter the width of the report.

Time Format	What It Prints
HH:NN:SS	18:45:00
HH:NN:SS AM	06:45:00 PM
HH:NN	18:45
NN	45

Sample Time
Formats
Table 4-4.

To change the report's margins, select Report Margins from the Format menu. The Report Margins window appears, as shown here:

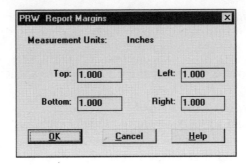

Top   Enter the distance from the top of the page.

Bottom   Enter the distance from the bottom of the page.

Left   Enter the distance from the left of the page.

Right   Enter the distance from the right of the page.

When you are satisfied with your entries, click OK.

CAUTION: Set the report width and the report margins for the printer to which you will print the report. If you print the report on a different printer, Peachtree Report Writer will continue to use the width and margins you originally specified.

Setting Grid Snap

Setting Grid Snap on lets you align columns, headings, and objects on the Report Designer window. When Grid Snap is on, Peachtree Report Writer will automatically align elements so they start at a multiple of the grid size you enter.

To set Grid Snap on, select Grid Snap from the Preferences menu on the main Report Designer window. The Grid Snap window appears, as shown here:

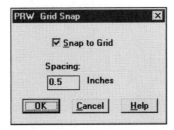

Snap to Grid   Check this box to turn Grid Snap on. (Grid Snap is off when you first start Peachtree Report Writer.)

Spacing   Enter the grid size. The default entry is 0.5 inches, so when grid snap is turned on, Peachtree Report Writer aligns report elements to start at .5", 1.0", 1.5", and so on.

When you are satisfied with your entries, click OK.

Adding a Row Count

You can add a count of the number of rows in the Subtotal or Grand Total area by clicking the icon in the Report Designer window. The Report Designer displays a standard report summary calculation window (not shown). When you generate the report, Peachtree Report Writer displays the number of rows in that group or total for the report, depending on whether you leave the "Reset on break" box checked or not.

Adding Borders

You can add a border to selected items. Start by selecting an item in the Report Design window, then select Border from the Format menu. The Borders window appears, as shown in Figure 4-7.

Box   Specifies a box with or without a border. Select the number of lines for the box from the drop-down list in Number. You can select None (for no border), Single (for a single-line border), or Double (for a double-line border). Select the style of the border from the drop-down list in Style—Solid (for a

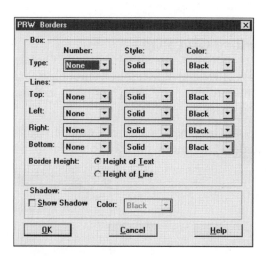

Borders
window

Figure 4-7.

solid line), Dashed (for a dashed line), and Dotted (for a dotted line). You can also select a color for the border from the drop-down list in Color—black, green, blue, cyan, magenta, yellow, red, dark gray, gray, light gray, or white.

NOTE: When you set attributes for a box, Peachtree Report Writer changes the attributes for the individual lines accordingly.

Lines Specifies individual lines around a column. You can specify individual attributes for top, left, right, and bottom border lines around a column as you did for the Box attributes.

Border Height Specify whether the border is drawn based on the height of the entire line or the height of the selected column. You will need to use this if you have information on a row with different font sizes.

Shadow Check this box to show a drop-shadow around the border. You can also select a border color from the associated drop-down list.

4

When you are satisfied with your entries, click OK.

TIP: Right-clicking on a column in the Report Design window displays a small floating menu with many of the options discussed in this section.

Changing Column Alignment

You can change the column alignment in several ways. Start by selecting the item to change the alignment of, then select Alignment from the Format menu. The Alignment window appears:

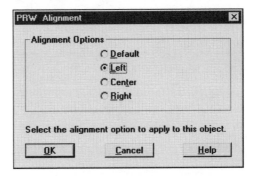

Alignment Options   Select the alignment option for the selected column. Selecting Default sets the item to the default alignment (left-justified for text, right-justified for numeric columns, and centered for dates and times).

When you are satisfied with your entries, click OK.

You can also center a single heading, such as a report title, on a line by selecting Center Line from the Format menu.

The Report Designer allows you a great deal of flexibility when planning your reports. You will find that the most effective way to use the Report Designer is to use it to experiment with your report layouts, generating sample reports periodically to see how the report looks with the specific changes you've made.

Using the Label Designer

The Label Designer is similar to the Report Designer in that it allows you to graphically create and change your labels. There are a few differences between reports and labels that make labels much easier to create.

Labels have a single body area with no headings, footings, or subtotal and total breaks. In addition, the Label Designer can create side-by-side output where the Report Designer cannot. Labels also do not have page breaks, dates, page numbers, and so on.

As with the Report Designer, the first step in creating a label using the Label Designer is to select either the Graphical Report or the Character Report option from the Preferences menu in the main Peachtree Report Writer window. Next, start the Label Designer by clicking the Label Designer icon

Label Design window (in graphical mode)
Figure 4-8.

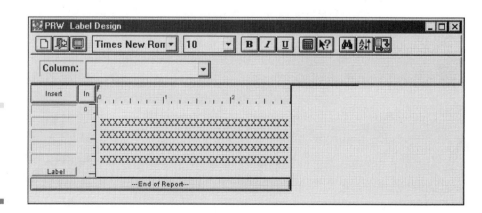

on the Peachtree Report Writer toolbar (or select the Label option from the Output menu). The Label Design window appears (shown in Figure 4-8 with sample data). The buttons appearing on the Label Designer toolbar have the same functions as those in the Report Design window.

Column   Select the column to display.

Insert/Overwrite   Click this button to toggle between insert and overwrite mode.

In/CM   Click this button to toggle between inches and centimeters for the label measurements. (This is set to "Ch" for characters in character mode.)

NOTE: You can also change the label measurement option by selecting Ruler Measurements from the Preferences menu on the Label Design window.

4

As an example, you will see how to create an employee mailing label using the Label Designer in graphical mode. Start a new procedure by selecting New Label from the File menu, or by clicking the New Label icon on the Label Designer toolbar. Next, you need to tell Peachtree Report Writer what dimensions to use for the labels. Select Label Layout from the Format menu. The window that appears depends on the mode you are using. If you are in graphical mode, the Graphical Label Layout window appears, as shown in Figure 4-9.

Pre-defined Forms   Select the type of label from the list. The measurements for the selected label appear in the fields.

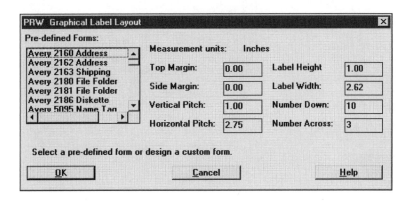

Graphical
Label Layout
window
Figure 4-9.

Top Margin   Enter the top margin. This measurement is from the top of the sheet of labels to the top of the first line of text on the first row of labels.

Side Margin   Enter the side margin. This measurement is from the left side of the sheet of labels to the left margin of the label text in the first column of labels.

Vertical Pitch   Enter the height of the printable area of the label.

Horizontal Pitch   Enter the width of the printable area of the label.

Label Height   Enter the height from the top edge of one label to the top edge of the next label. This will include any gutter space between the labels.

Label Width   Enter the width of the label from the left side of one label to the left side of the next label. This will include any gutter space between the labels.

Number Down   Enter the number of rows of labels on the sheet.

Number Across   Enter the number of labels across one row on the sheet.

When you are satisfied with your entries, click OK. Peachtree Report Writer saves the attributes for the label as part of the procedure.

If you are working in character mode, you will see the Character Label Layout window, as shown in Figure 4-10.

Character
Label Layout
window

Figure 4-10.

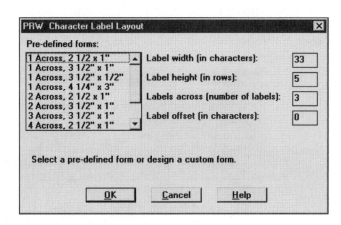

Pre-defined Forms   Select the measurements for the type of label from the list. The measurements for the selected label appear in the fields.

Label width (in characters)   Enter the width (in characters) from the start of one label to the start of the next label. Be sure to include characters for the spaces between the labels.

Label height (in rows)   Enter the distance (in lines) from the top of one label to the top of the next label. Be sure to include characters for the spaces between the labels.

Labels across (number of labels)   Enter the number of labels across the page.

Label offset (in characters)   Enter the number of characters in from the left side of the page for the first character on the first column of labels. (Peachtree Report Writer uses this offset as the left margin for the page.)

As with report sizes and margins in the Report Designer, Peachtree Report Writer stores the label dimensions you specify. If you use the label on another printer that prints a different number of characters per inch, you must change the label settings appropriately.

4

TIP: Character label settings are primarily useful for continuous feed labels.

When you are satisfied with your entries, click OK.

To add columns to the label, position the cursor at the desired insertion point in label, then select the column from the drop-down list in Column or create a temporary column by clicking the Temporary Column icon on the Label Design window toolbar. (You can also select a column by selecting Column from the Insert menu and then select Database Column from the submenu to insert a column, or Create Column to create a temporary column.)

Here are a couple of final tips for using the Label Designer:

♦ When you save label procedures, start the procedure name with the word "Label." This will make the procedures specifically for labels easy to find on the Open Procedures window. (If you also print labels in several sizes and layouts or print labels on more than one printer, you should also include information in the procedure name about the size and layout of the labels and the printer for which the procedure is designed.)

♦ When you are testing your procedures on the printer, print labels on plain paper first to see if they accurately match the layout of your label stock. You will find that this will save you a great deal of money in labels.

♦ You can right-click in the report area to get a handy floating menu of options. You can also select multiple objects (such as several column headings) by holding down the CTRL key and clicking the objects you want to select. You can then apply formats to all the selected objects at once.

♦ In addition to limiting data on previews to cut down on processing time, you can use the Data Limit option to limit the output on printed reports and labels to a single page to test your formatting and alignment. This prevents you from printing dozens or even hundreds of sheets of incorrectly formatted or misaligned reports or labels on expensive pre-printed stock.

♦ Peachtree Report Writer does not prevent you from creating more lines than will fit on a label, but you will see a warning when you exceed the size of the label.

The Label Designer, like the Report Designer, allows you a great deal of flexibility when creating labels. Experimenting with the Label Designer will prove the most effective way of using it.

Summary

In this chapter, you saw how to use the Report Designer and Label Designer to lay out reports and labels on the screen. In the next and final chapter on Peachtree Report Writer, you'll see how to use conditional statements to select for specific information, use matrixes, and export and import procedures.

5

Using Advanced Peachtree Report Writer Features

In the preceding chapter, you saw how to use the Report Designer and Label Designer to lay out reports and labels on the screen. In this final chapter on the Peachtree Report Writer, you'll see how to use conditional statements to select for specific information, use matrixes, and export and import procedures.

Using Conditionals

A *conditional* lets your procedure evaluate conditions and perform actions based on the results. Conditionals can be phrased as a statement starting with "If," followed by some condition or conditions to test for, followed by the action or actions to perform.

You're actually used to working with conditionals every day: any decision requires you to set conditions and then act based on the various outcomes. Suppose you decide to telephone Bill. You could make this a conditional statement by saying, "If Bill answers the telephone, then I'll talk to him." The condition to test for in this case is Bill answering the telephone, and the action is talking to him. Similarly, you might say, "If I complete this project, then I'll go home early." The condition to test is completing the project and the action is going home early.

You can apply conditionals to report writing in a variety of ways. The following are some examples of conditionals you might use in reports:

♦ If the customer invoice amount is more than 30 days past due, add the past-due amount to the 30-days-past-due total.

♦ If the customer's credit limit is greater than the amount owed to the customer, print the customer's name on a report for evaluating the current credit limit.

♦ If the employee hire date is greater than five years ago, print a comment on the report.

You can create a conditional test for any condition you use as a search criterion. (Search criteria operators were described previously in Table 2-3 in Chapter 2, "Creating a Procedure.")

Creating A Simple Conditional

Suppose you want to modify the bonus amount procedure you created in Chapter 3 to list a bonus amount for only those employees who make more than $5,000 in a month. The commands would look like this:

```
SORT ASCENDING EMP-NAME.
SEARCH FOR ZIDX = 0 .
INITIALIZE BONUS-AMOUNT TO 1000.00 NUMERIC 5.2.
INITIALIZE BONUS-AMOUNT-CHECK TO 0.00 NUMERIC 5.2.
MULTIPLY NET-CHECK-AMOUNT TIMES -1.000 GIVING ADJUSTED-CHECK SCALE 5.2.
MOVE ADJUSTED-CHECK TO BONUS-CHECK-AMOUNT.
IF ADJUSTED-CHECK > 5000.00 THEN
        ADD ADJUSTED-CHECK PLUS BONUS-AMOUNT GIVING BONUS-CHECK-AMOUNT.
COLUMNAR EMP-NAME ADJUSTED-CHECK BONUS-CHECK-AMOUNT ON EMP-NAME
CHANGE SUBTOTAL ADJUSTED-CHECK BONUS-CHECK-AMOUNT.
```

Take a look at the MOVE command. The MOVE command tells Peachtree Report Writer to move the value in the first field (ADJUSTED-CHECK) to the second field (BONUS-CHECK-AMOUNT). You could also use the MOVE command to assign a specific numeric value to the field. For example, the following command sets ADDITIONAL-CHECK to 750.00:

```
MOVE 750.00 TO ADDITIONAL-CHECK.
```

You can also move a text string to a temporary column as well, as in

MOVE 'HIGH PERFORMER' TO COMMENT-COLUMN.

This would print the phrase "HIGH PERFORMER" in the COMMENT-COLUMN field.

The IF command in the procedure tests for an ADJUSTED-CHECK amount of more than $5,000.00, and if the test is true, adds BONUS-AMOUNT to the amount for ADJUST-CHECK to create the BONUS-CHECK-AMOUNT. It's very important to note that, if the test is not true—that is, if the ADJUSTED-CHECK amount is $5,000.00 or less—then Peachtree Report Writer will make no change to the BONUS-CHECK-AMOUNT and the amount from the previous row will appear. This is why it's important to have the MOVE command before the IF command so that there is a value in BONUS-CHECK-AMOUNT.

5

When you generate a report using this procedure, the results will look something like Figure 5-1.

NOTE: You can only enter IF commands through the Edit Procedure window.

You can use any of the following commands as actions in an IF command:

♦ ADD
♦ CONCATENATE
♦ CONVERT
♦ DIVIDE
♦ MOVE
♦ MULTIPLY
♦ SUBSTRING
♦ SUBTRACT

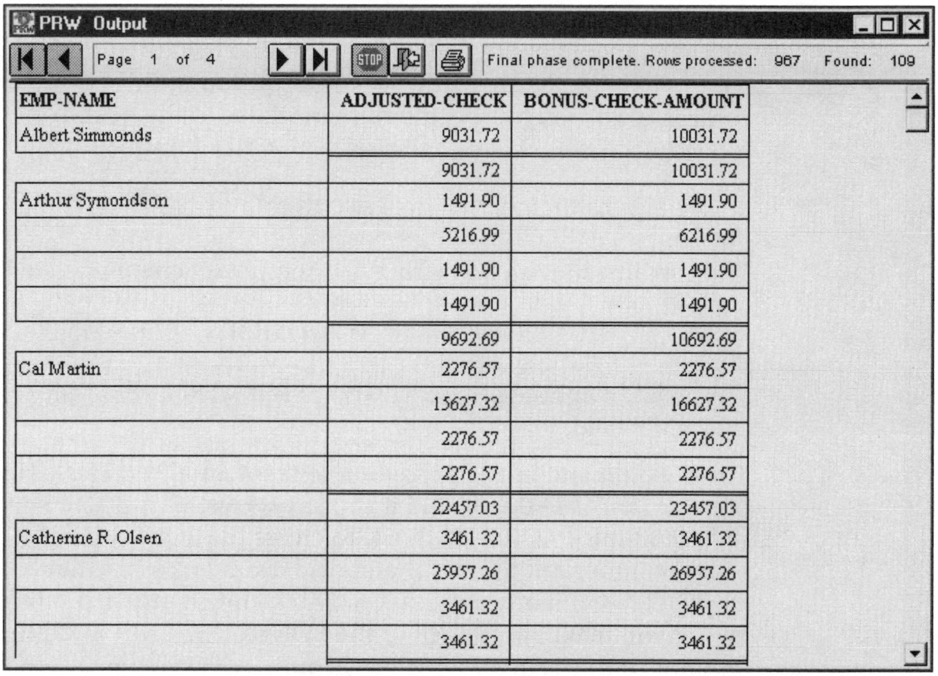

Peachtree Complete Business Toolkit

Bonus
Procedure
using a simple
IF...THEN
command
Figure 5-1.

You can create an IF command that performs multiple actions simply by
adding more actions to the THEN list. Just be sure that the period goes after
the last action only. The following is an example of an IF command that
does several different things:

```
IF ADJUSTED-CHECK > 5000.00 THEN
     MOVE 600.00 TO QUOTA-BONUS
     MOVE .005 TO BONUS-COMMISSION
     MOVE 'Sales Superstar!' TO COMMENT-COLUMN.
```

As you can see, indenting the actions to perform makes it easy to read the IF
command. It's good practice to have one command per line and indent the
subordinate lines by five spaces.

Using the ELSE Option

As you've seen so far, a simple conditional has the general format of
"IF <a condition is true> THEN <perform one or more actions>." But not all

conditionals are straight IF/THEN conditions. For example, you might say "If the weather is good, I'll walk around the lake, but if it's rainy, I'll go to a movie instead." This could be stated in terms of IF/THEN/ELSE, where if the condition is true, you do one set of actions; otherwise, you'll do another set of actions.

As an example of how you might apply this is to add an ELSE condition to the bonus procedure so that employees who didn't make $5,000 on a paycheck get a smaller bonus of $250.00, as follows:

```
SORT ASCENDING EMP-NAME.
SEARCH FOR ZIDX = 0 .
INITIALIZE BONUS-AMOUNT TO 1000.00 NUMERIC 5.2.
INITIALIZE STANDARD-BONUS-AMOUNT TO 250.00 NUMERIC 5.2.
INITIALIZE BONUS-AMOUNT-CHECK TO 0.00 NUMERIC 5.2.
MULTIPLY NET-CHECK-AMOUNT TIMES -1.000 GIVING ADJUSTED-CHECK SCALE 5.2.
IF ADJUSTED-CHECK > 5000.00 THEN
     ADD ADJUSTED-CHECK PLUS BONUS-AMOUNT GIVING BONUS-CHECK-AMOUNT
ELSE
     ADD ADJUSTED-CHECK PLUS STANDARD-BONUS-AMOUNT GIVING BONUS-CHECK-AMOUNT.
COLUMNAR EMP-NAME ADJUSTED-CHECK BONUS-CHECK-AMOUNT ON EMP-NAME CHANGE SUBTOTAL
ADJUSTED-CHECK BONUS-CHECK-AMOUNT.
```

Figure 5-2 shows the results of this procedure.

5

Note that there are no periods in the IF command until the final action to perform when the ELSE condition is true.

You can stack several IF commands to test for multiple conditions. For example, suppose you wanted to check for varying levels of sales performance and create bonuses based on levels. The following block of code shows how you might do this:

```
SORT ASCENDING EMP-NAME.
SEARCH FOR ZIDX = 0 .
INITIALIZE BONUS-AMOUNT-CHECK TO 0.00 NUMERIC 5.2.
MULTIPLY NET-CHECK-AMOUNT TIMES -1.000 GIVING ADJUSTED-CHECK SCALE 5.2.
MOVE ADJUSTED-CHECK TO BONUS-CHECK-AMOUNT.
IF ADJUSTED-CHECK > 3000.00 THEN
     ADD ADJUSTED-CHECK PLUS 500.00 GIVING BONUS-CHECK-AMOUNT.
IF ADJUSTED-CHECK > 4000.00 THEN
     ADD ADJUSTED-CHECK PLUS 750.00 GIVING BONUS-CHECK-AMOUNT.
IF ADJUSTED-CHECK > 5000.00 THEN
```

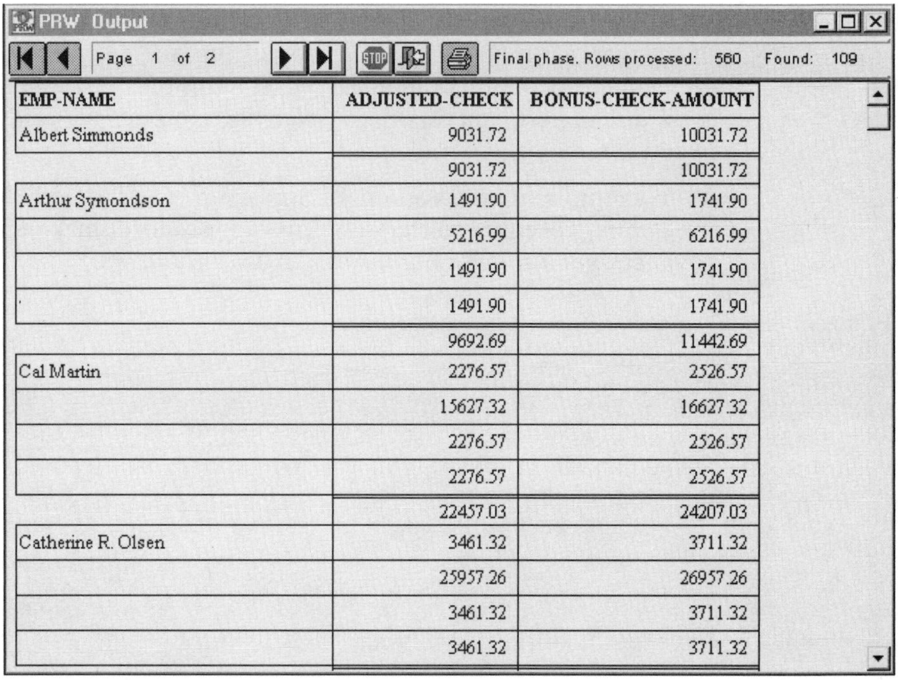

EMP-NAME	ADJUSTED-CHECK	BONUS-CHECK-AMOUNT
Albert Simmonds	9031.72	10031.72
	9031.72	10031.72
Arthur Symondson	1491.90	1741.90
	5216.99	6216.99
	1491.90	1741.90
	1491.90	1741.90
	9692.69	11442.69
Cal Martin	2276.57	2526.57
	15627.32	16627.32
	2276.57	2526.57
	2276.57	2526.57
	22457.03	24207.03
Catherine R. Olsen	3461.32	3711.32
	25957.26	26957.26
	3461.32	3711.32
	3461.32	3711.32

Bonus
Procedure
using an
IF...THEN...ELSE
command
Figure 5-2.

```
    ADD ADJUSTED-CHECK PLUS 1000.00 GIVING BONUS-CHECK-AMOUNT.
COLUMNAR EMP-NAME ADJUSTED-CHECK BONUS-CHECK-AMOUNT ON EMP-NAME
CHANGE SUBTOTAL ADJUSTED-CHECK BONUS-CHECK-AMOUNT.
```

The order in which the IF commands appear is very important. For example, if you reversed the order of the IF commands in the preceding example and first tested for an adjusted check amount of more than $5,000, then $4,000, then $3,000, Peachtree Report Writer would only assign the correct bonus amounts for employees who made more than $3,000 and less than $4,000. For an employee who made more than $5,000 and the first IF command would be true, so Peachtree Report Writer would add $1000 to the adjusted check. The next IF command would also be true, however (the employee also made more than $4000), so the results of the previous IF command would be overwritten by adding $750 to the adjusted check amount and moving that to the bonus check amount. Finally, Peachtree Report Writer would evaluate the third IF command and, because that would be true also, would add $500 to the adjusted check amount to create the bonus check amount, which would be the amount that actually appeared on the report.

CAUTION: Because of the greater complexity of IF commands, you may have unexpected results with your procedures. Test your procedures carefully with known data so that you can be sure that the information is being tested and processed correctly. If you are writing lots of procedures, you may want to create your own test company using sample data you've created or a copy of your company's data that you can make changes to for testing purposes.

Creating Multiple Conditions

In Chapter 2, "Creating a Procedure," you saw how to use AND and OR as part of your search criteria. You can also use AND and OR as part of your IF commands to test for several conditions at once. For example, the following IF command will set the commission percentage at 7.5 percent for employees who have made more than $5,000 on their adjust check amounts *and* who are classed as "SALES2" employees:

```
IF ADJUSTED-CHECK > 5000.00 AND EMP-TYPE = 'SALES2' THEN
    MOVE .075 TO COMMISSION-PERCENT.
```

In this example, Peachtree Report Writer checks to see if ADJUSTED-CHECK is more than $5,000.00. If so, Peachtree Report Writer then checks to see if the EMP-TYPE is SALES2. If both of these conditions are true, it then sets the commission percentage to 7.5 percent. If either condition is false, Peachtree Report Writer doesn't change the commission percentage.

You can also use the OR connector to create multiple conditions. For example, the following IF command would flag employees for anyone who made more than $5,000 on a paycheck or who is classed as SALES2:

```
IF ADJUSTED-CHECK > 5000.00 OR EMP-TYPE = 'SALES2' THEN
    MOVE 'ELIGIBLE FOR BONUS' TO COMMENT-COLUMN.
```

As with searches, the AND connector requires that all the conditions be met in order for the IF command to perform the actions for the THEN clause, while the OR connector requires that only one of the conditions be met. As a result, you should be very careful about using an ELSE clause when you are testing for multiple conditions, as you may have unexpected results. If any one of the conditions for an AND connector tests false, Peachtree Report Writer will perform the actions for the ELSE clause.

```
IF ADJUSTED-CHECK > 5000.00 AND EMP-TYPE = 'SALES2' THEN
    MOVE .075 TO COMMISSION-PERCENT
ELSE
    MOVE .06 to COMMISSION-PERCENT.
```

5

In this example, if either condition is not true, then Peachtree Report Writer sets the commission percentage to 6 percent. Similarly, for an OR connector, all the conditions must be false before Peachtree Report Writer will perform the conditions in the ELSE clause.

```
IF ADJUSTED-CHECK > 5000.00 OR EMP-TYPE = 'SALES2' THEN
     MOVE .075 TO COMMISSION-PERCENT
ELSE
     MOVE .06 to COMMISSION-PERCENT.
```

In this example, the employee's adjusted check must be less than $5000.00 and the EMP-TYPE must also not be SALES2 in order for Peachtree Report Writer to move the lower percentage to COMMISSION-PERCENT.

Using Counters

A *counter* is a temporary column for counting the number of rows that meet certain criteria. In its simplest form, you could have a counter for each entry on a report, as follows:

```
SORT ASCENDING EMP-NAME.
INITIALIZE EMP-COUNTER TO 0 NUMERIC 3.0.
ADD 1 TO EMP-COUNTER GIVING EMP-COUNTER.
COLUMNAR EMP-COUNTER EMP-ID EMP-NAME SSN.
```

Figure 5-3 shows the report that this procedure creates.

More frequently, however, you'd use a counter with an IF command to count the number of entries. For example, to get a quick count of the number of employees with more than five years seniority, you'd use something like this:

```
SORT ASCENDING EMP-NAME.
INITIALIZE EMP-COUNTER TO 0 NUMERIC 3.0.
IF HIRE-DATE < 5/21/93
    ADD 1 TO EMP-COUNTER GIVING EMP-COUNTER.
COLUMNAR MAXIMUM EMP-COUNTER.
```

You can use counters for a variety of applications, such as counting the number of paychecks an employee has received this year or calculating the number of bills for a customer.

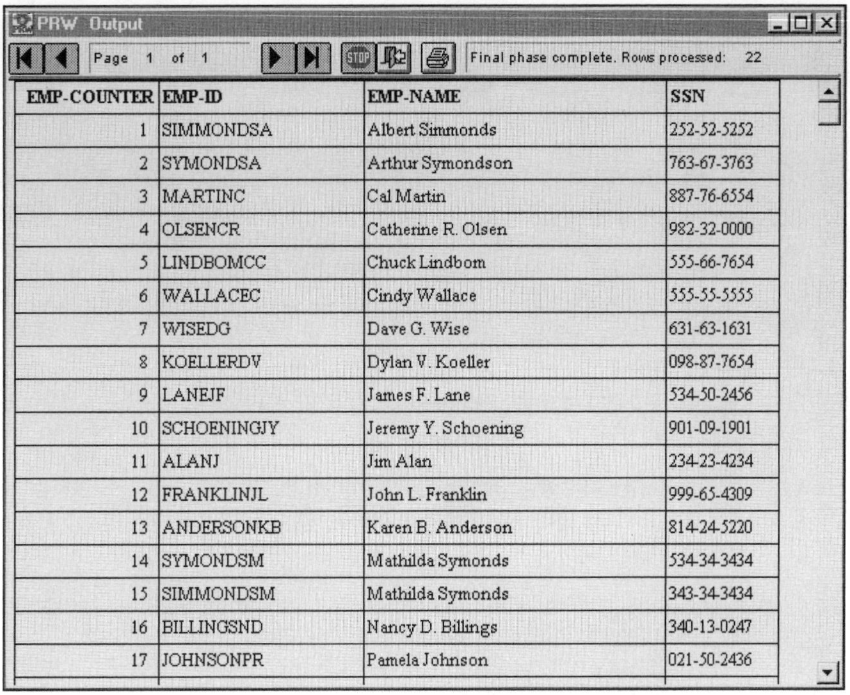

EMP-COUNTER	EMP-ID	EMP-NAME	SSN
1	SIMMONDSA	Albert Simmonds	252-52-5252
2	SYMONDSA	Arthur Symondson	763-67-3763
3	MARTINC	Cal Martin	887-76-6554
4	OLSENCR	Catherine R. Olsen	982-32-0000
5	LINDBOMCC	Chuck Lindbom	555-66-7654
6	WALLACEC	Cindy Wallace	555-55-5555
7	WISEDG	Dave G. Wise	631-63-1631
8	KOELLERDV	Dylan V. Koeller	098-87-7654
9	LANEJF	James F. Lane	534-50-2456
10	SCHOENINGJY	Jeremy Y. Schoening	901-09-1901
11	ALANJ	Jim Alan	234-23-4234
12	FRANKLINJL	John L. Franklin	999-65-4309
13	ANDERSONKB	Karen B. Anderson	814-24-5220
14	SYMONDSM	Mathilda Symonds	534-34-3434
15	SIMMONDSM	Mathilda Symonds	343-34-3434
16	BILLINGSND	Nancy D. Billings	340-13-0247
17	JOHNSONPR	Pamela Johnson	021-50-2436

Report with simple counter
Figure 5-3.

Other IF Command Techniques

There are a couple of other things you should know about using IF commands: performing case-sensitive evaluations and trapping data.

Case-Sensitive IF Commands

Peachtree Report Writer defaults to case-insensitivity; that is, "ALAN" and "Alan" are the same as far as testing in an IF command. If you want to do case-sensitive comparisons, you need to use the CASE keyword, like this:

```
IF EMP-TYPE = 'SALES2' CASE THEN
     MOVE 'ELIGIBLE FOR BONUS' TO COMMENT-COLUMN.
```

In this example, EMP-TYPE must be SALES2 but not Sales2 or sales2 in order for Peachtree Report Writer to perform the associated MOVE command.

Trapping Information

Trapping information is setting up a series of IF statements that test for the conditions you want to test for, but that also make sure that incorrect or unanticipated entries are trapped and handled. For example, suppose you want to print a list of employees with their seniority levels. However, since the field for the date hired is not a required field, it's possible that some of the employees' hiring dates won't be entered, or will be entered incorrectly. Your company has been in business since June 1, 1992, so you know that there's no employee with a valid hire date earlier than that. The following procedure will print an employee seniority list and trap employee records that have missing or incorrect information.

```
SORT ASCENDING EMP-NAME.
INITIALIZE SENIORITY TO ' ' ALPHA 20.
MOVE ' ' TO SENIORITY.
IF HIRE-DATE > 5/31/97 AND HIRE-DATE < 5/31/98 THEN
     MOVE 'LESS THAN 1 YEAR' TO SENIORITY.
IF HIRE-DATE > 5/31/96 AND HIRE-DATE < 6/1/97 THEN
     MOVE '1 YEAR' TO SENIORITY.
IF HIRE-DATE > 5/31/95 AND HIRE-DATE < 6/1/96 THEN
     MOVE '2 YEARS' TO SENIORITY.
IF HIRE-DATE > 5/31/94 AND HIRE-DATE < 6/1/95 THEN
     MOVE '3 YEARS' TO SENIORITY.
IF HIRE-DATE > 5/31/93 AND HIRE-DATE < 6/1/94 THEN
     MOVE '4 YEARS' TO SENIORITY.
IF HIRE-DATE > 5/31/92 AND HIRE-DATE < 6/1/93 THEN
     MOVE '5 YEARS' TO SENIORITY.
IF HIRE-DATE < 6/1/92 OR HIRE-DATE > 12/31/98 THEN
     MOVE '**INVALID/MISSING DATE**' TO SENIORITY.
COLUMNAR EMP-NAME HIRE-DATE SENIORITY.
```

The MOVE command resets SENIORITY to spaces each time a new column is read. This is another way of making sure that you're checking for every possible condition. Should the SENIORITY column ever be blank on the report, you'll know that there's something you're not testing for with the IF commands. The IF command tests for all the levels of seniority until the last one, which checks for dates before the company started or after the current date. Figure 5-4 shows the report this procedure generates.

Take a look at the report in Figure 5-4 for a moment. The first two invalid entries have missing hiring dates. However, the entry for Mary Simmonds is November 15, 1999, much later than the current period.

It's a good idea to devise traps in your procedures to ensure that the data you are reporting is complete and correct. You could refine your error trapping in

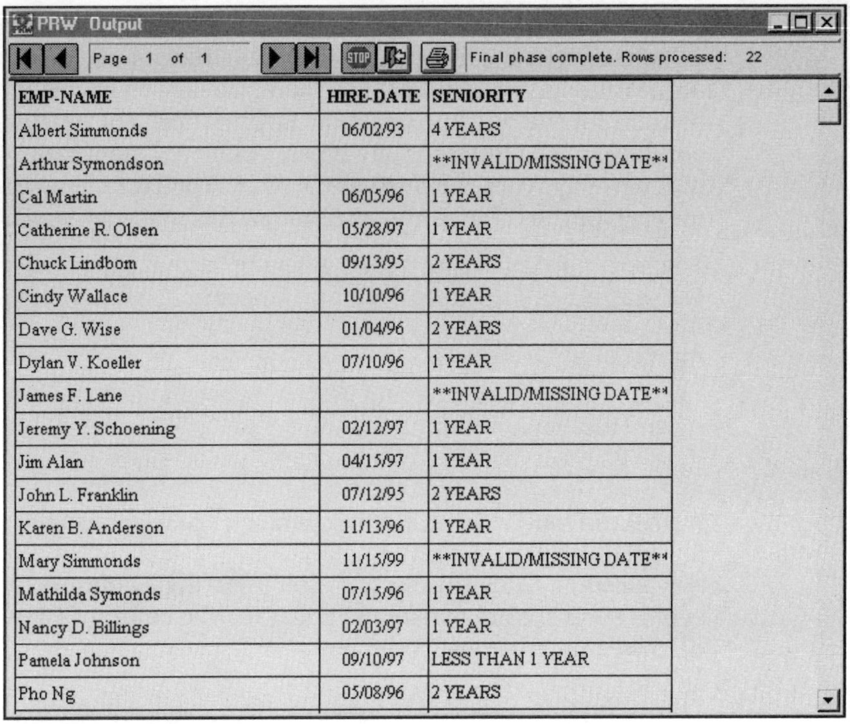

EMP-NAME	HIRE-DATE	SENIORITY
Albert Simmonds	06/02/93	4 YEARS
Arthur Symondson		**INVALID/MISSING DATE**
Cal Martin	06/05/96	1 YEAR
Catherine R. Olsen	05/28/97	1 YEAR
Chuck Lindbom	09/13/95	2 YEARS
Cindy Wallace	10/10/96	1 YEAR
Dave G. Wise	01/04/96	2 YEARS
Dylan V. Koeller	07/10/96	1 YEAR
James F. Lane		**INVALID/MISSING DATE**
Jeremy Y. Schoening	02/12/97	1 YEAR
Jim Alan	04/15/97	1 YEAR
John L. Franklin	07/12/95	2 YEARS
Karen B. Anderson	11/13/96	1 YEAR
Mary Simmonds	11/15/99	**INVALID/MISSING DATE**
Mathilda Symonds	07/15/96	1 YEAR
Nancy D. Billings	02/03/97	1 YEAR
Pamela Johnson	09/10/97	LESS THAN 1 YEAR
Pho Ng	05/08/96	2 YEARS

Report using trapping
Figure 5-4.

this example by differentiating between a date out of the range and a missing date, as shown with the following commands:

```
IF HIRE-DATE < 6/1/92 OR HIRE-DATE > 12/31/98 THEN
     MOVE '**INVALID DATE**' TO SENIORITY.
IF HIRE-DATE = ' ' THEN
     MOVE '**MISSING DATE**' TO SENIORITY.
```

Other Techniques

Another way in which you can use IF commands is to combine them with SEARCH commands. As you saw in previous chapters, the SEARCH command lets you filter the information you are processing (such as searching for all employees who are field representatives) and then performing calculations based on the information in the records.

As a final note, remember that IF commands give you a substantial amount of power to perform calculations selectively, but they can be complex. To minimize the possibility of errors, be sure to test the procedure with a carefully screened set of test records before you put any procedure into operation.

Using Matrixes

All of the reports you've seen so far have had a format of one row (or record) of information in columns. Matrix reports let you print information within a column for the possible classes of information. For example, if you have employees with different pay types, you could summarize paychecks by the different pay types for employee names. You could also print the total paid for each of the different types of purchases made by vendors.

To create a matrix report, start a new procedure, then select Matrix from the Output menu. The Matrix window appears, as shown in Figure 5-5.

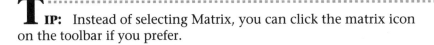 **IP:** Instead of selecting Matrix, you can click the matrix icon on the toolbar if you prefer.

Across the top   Select the column to appear across the top of the report.

Advanced   Click this button after selecting a column to display across the top to enter specific values or ranges for the column. (This feature is discussed later in this section.)

Down the side   Select the column to appear down the side of the report.

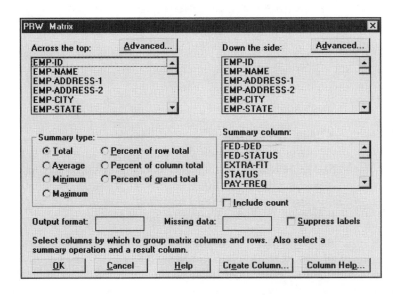

Matrix window

Figure 5-5.

Advanced   Click this button after selecting a column to display across the top to enter specific values or ranges for the column. (This feature is discussed later in this section.)

Summary Type   Select the summary type as follows:

◆ **Total** Totals the information in the selected summary column

◆ **Average** Averages the information in the selected summary column

◆ **Minimum** Displays the minimum value of the information in the selected summary column

◆ **Maximum** Displays the maximum value of the information in the selected summary column

◆ **Percent of row total** Displays the value as a percentage of the total values in the row

◆ **Percent of column total** Displays the value as a percentage of the total values in the column

◆ **Percent of grand total** Displays the value as a percentage of the grand total values

Summary column   Select the column to summarize.

Include count   Check this box to include a count of the number of values that comprise each field on the report. Peachtree Report Writer adds a second line for the number of rows in each summary line.

Output format   Enter an optional output format, such as $$$,$$$.00. (Output formats are discussed in the "Formatting Numeric Columns" section of Chapter 4, "Designing Reports and Labels.")

Missing data   Enter an optional text string to display when there is no corresponding value on the report. (The default is for Peachtree Report Writer to leave the field blank, or to display a 0 if the procedure displays a count.)

Suppress labels   Check this box to suppress column and row labels.

Create Column   Creates a temporary column for calculations or manipulating information.

Column Help   This is not implemented for this release of Peachtree Report Writer.

5

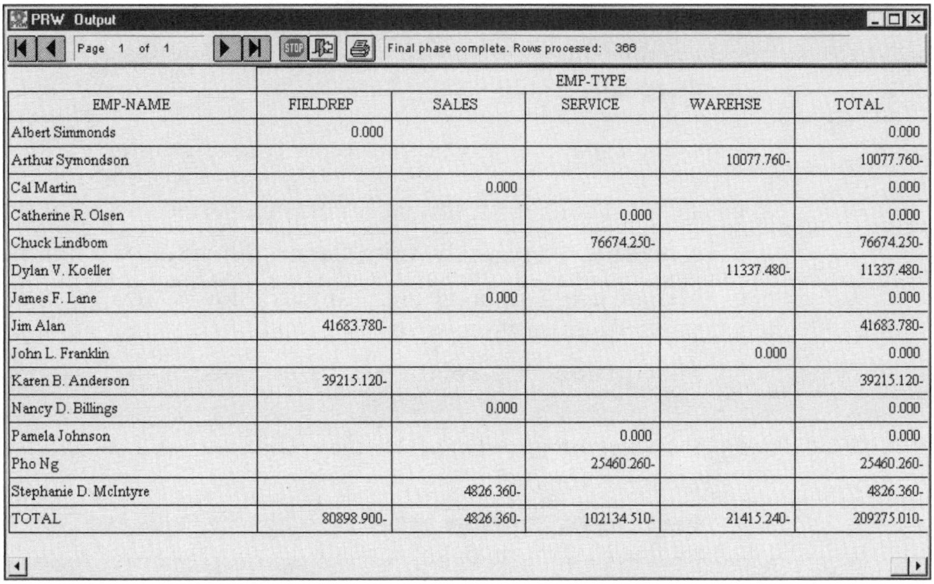

PRW Output					_ □ ×
◄◄ ◄ Page 1 of 1 ► ►► STOP 🔲 🖨 Final phase complete. Rows processed: 366					

	EMP-TYPE				
EMP-NAME	FIELDREP	SALES	SERVICE	WAREHSE	TOTAL
Albert Simmonds	0.000				0.000
Arthur Symondson				10077.760-	10077.760-
Cal Martin		0.000			0.000
Catherine R. Olsen			0.000		0.000
Chuck Lindbom			76674.250-		76674.250-
Dylan V. Koeller				11337.480-	11337.480-
James F. Lane		0.000			0.000
Jim Alan	41683.780-				41683.780-
John L. Franklin				0.000	0.000
Karen B. Anderson	39215.120-				39215.120-
Nancy D. Billings		0.000			0.000
Pamela Johnson			0.000		0.000
Pho Ng			25460.260-		25460.260-
Stephanie D. McIntyre		4826.360-			4826.360-
TOTAL	80898.900-	4826.360-	102134.510-	21415.240-	209275.010-

Sample Matrix report

Figure 5-6.

When you are satisfied with your entries, click OK. Figure 5-6 shows a sample matrix report of employee information.

Peachtree Report Writer normally displays all the rows and columns of information. You can use the Advanced Matrix window to select specific values, ranges of values, or limit the total selections in the report. To display the Advanced Matrix window, click Advanced on the Matrix window (shown earlier in Figure 5-5). The Advanced Matrix window (shown in Figure 5-7) appears.

The column name you are working with appears near the top of the window.

Define By Select one of the options as follows:

♦ **Specific Values** Look for specific values in the column

♦ **Range of Values** Look for a range of values in the column

♦ **Number of Values** Use the first *n* rows or columns, where *n* is the number you enter in the Number of Values field. (You can only specify a number of rows or columns if this is a numeric column.)

Peachtree Report Writer normally displays a row or column for each different value in the column. You can use this feature to limit the number of rows or columns that appear on the report. For example, you could

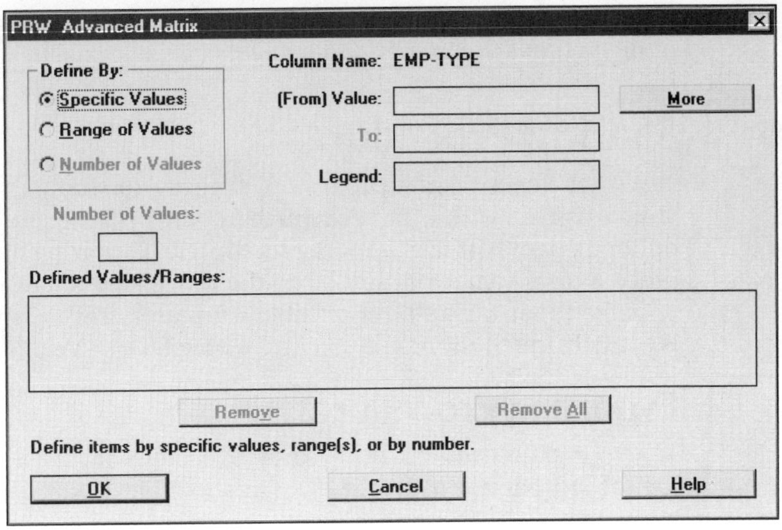

Advanced
Matrix window
Figure 5-7.

display a report of only those employees who have an EMP-TYPE of SALES1 or SALES2.

(From) Value   Enter the first value to select for (if you are looking for specific values) or the starting value for the range (if you are looking for a range of values).

To   Enter the ending value of the range (if you are looking for a range of values).

Legend   Enter an optional column title for a specified value. For example, if the codes in EMP-TYPE are unclear, you could enter an alternate column title for the specified value.

More   Click this button to add the specific value or range to the Defined Values/Ranges box and then enter another specific value or range.

Number of Values   Enter the number of values to use. (You can only make an entry in this field if you selected Number of Values in the Define By field).

Defined Values/Ranges   This display-only field shows the values or ranges you have entered for this column. To remove a value or range, highlight the line in this field and click Remove. To remove all the values and ranges, click Remove All.

5

When you are satisfied with your entries, click OK. Peachtree Report Writer returns you to the Matrix window.

Sharing Procedures

Peachtree Report Writer has several options for sharing the procedures you've written with other Peachtree Report Writer users. The most effective option is to export and import procedures. (Exporting and importing procedures is somewhat similar to the process you may already be familiar with for exporting and importing information in Peachtree Accounting, but is actually much more like copying whole files in Windows 95.)

Exporting Procedures

To export a procedure, select Export Procedure from the File menu. The Export Procedure window appears as shown in Figure 5-8.

Path Enter the drive and directory you want to export the procedures to. By default, Peachtree Report Writer enters the path for Peachtree Report Writer. Click Browse to the right of this field if you want to browse the directories.

All IQViews Select All IQViews if you want to see the procedures for all IQViews.

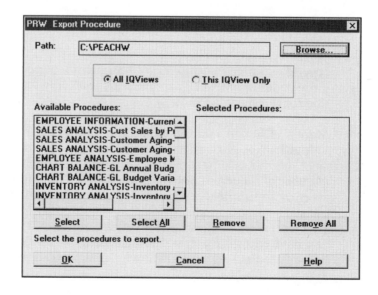

Export Procedure window

Figure 5-8.

This IQView Only   Select This IQView Only if you want to see just the procedures for this IQView.

Available Procedures   Select the procedure from this list that you want to export by highlighting the procedure and clicking Select. (You can also just double-click the procedure name to select it.) You can select all the procedures in the list by clicking Select All.

Selected Procedures   This list contains the procedures you have already selected to export. You can remove a procedure from this list by highlighting the procedure and clicking Remove. (You can also just double-click the procedure name to remove it.) You can remove all the procedures in the list by clicking Remove All.

When you are satisfied with your entries, click OK. Peachtree Report Writer exports the selected procedures, together with an IQPROCS.DAT file, to the drive and directory you specified. The IQPROCS.DAT file contains information about the exported procedures such as which IQView each procedure uses.

Importing a Procedure

Once you have exported a procedure, you will need to import the procedure into the new copy of Peachtree Report Writer. Select Import Procedure from the File menu. Figure 5-9 shows the Import Procedure window ready to select procedures from a diskette in the A: drive.

5

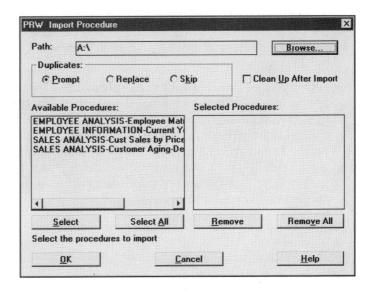

Import
Procedure
window
Figure 5-9.

Path   Enter the drive and directory you want to import the procedures from. By default, Peachtree Report Writer enters the path for Peachtree Report Writer. Click Browse to the right of this field if you want to browse the directories.

Duplicates   Select Prompt if you want Peachtree Report Writer to prompt you each time it tries to import a procedure with the same name as an existing procedure, Replace if you want Peachtree Report Writer to replace any existing procedures with the procedures being imported, or Skip if you want Peachtree Report Writer to skip the import for duplicate procedures.

Clean Up After Import   Check this box if you want Peachtree Report Writer to delete the exported procedure files and the associated IQPROCS.DAT file after completing the import process.

Caution: Don't use this feature until you're familiar with exporting and importing procedures.

Available Procedures   Select the procedure from this list that you want to import by highlighting the procedure and clicking Select. (You can also just double-click the procedure name to select it.) You can select all the procedures in the list by clicking Select All.

Selected Procedures   This list contains the procedures you have already selected to import. You can remove a procedure from this list by highlighting the procedure and clicking Remove. (You can also just double-click the procedure name to remove it.) You can remove all the procedures in the list by clicking Remove All.

When you are satisfied with your entries, click OK. Peachtree Report Writer imports the selected procedures. If you asked Peachtree Report Writer to prompt you for duplicate procedures, you will be prompted to skip importing the duplicate procedure or to replace the existing procedure with the one you're importing. When it has finished the import process, Peachtree Report Writer will display a status window showing the number of procedures it read, created, the number of duplicates found, and the number of duplicate procedures skipped and replaced.

Other Ways of Sharing Procedures

In addition to exporting and importing procedures, you can exchange procedures by storing the procedure's commands in a simple text file. To save a procedure in a text file, first open a procedure, then display the procedure in the Edit Procedure window. Highlight the whole procedure and then select Copy from the Edit menu to copy the procedure to the Windows clipboard. You can then use NotePad or WordPad to save the procedure to a text file. To bring this procedure into another copy of Peachtree Report Writer, you would reverse the process by first opening the text file, selecting the procedure and copying it to the clipboard, then opening the appropriate IQView in Peachtree Report Writer, pasting the commands into the Edit Procedure window (for a new procedure), and saving the new procedure.

Copying and pasting procedures is effective for transferring one or two procedures, but it is much more efficient to use the built-in export and import features in Peachtree Report Writer. (Copying and pasting procedures is also handy when you want to email a procedure to someone else, as you don't have to include the *.DAT and *.P* files.) Exporting and importing procedures is very simple. By contrast, cutting and pasting information is rather tedious and there are more opportunities to make mistakes that will affect the finished procedure. In addition, when you copy a procedure, you must also know which IQView the report was created in so you can set up the Edit Procedure window correctly before pasting. You can also export selected procedures or your entire library of procedures all at once rather than one at a time. Perhaps most importantly, you can export procedures from a previous version of Peachtree Report Writer and then import them into an updated version.

5

Summary

This chapter concludes the section on the Peachtree Report Writer. In this chapter, you saw how to use conditional statements to select for specific information, use matrixes, and export and import procedures. The next section of this book shows you to how to use the PeachLink software (included with the CD-ROM) to create your own web page and how to use Peachtree Accounting's Electronic Bill Payment features to automate your check processing.

PART 2

PeachLink

The second section of this book focuses on how to create a web site for your company using the PeachLink software. The PeachLink software lets you set up a web site with information from your Peachtree Accounting files. This provides an instant interface to your product lists so you can take orders directly over the Internet. You will also see how to use Electronic Bill Payment (formerly known as *e*-Check) to do electronic transfers, saving yourself time mailing checks, and also saving the cost of physically cutting, signing, and processing checks.

6

Setting Up PeachLink

The chapters in the previous section showed you how
to install and use Peachtree Report Writer. This chapter
shows you how to install the PeachLink web page
creation software on your system and register the
software with Harbinger. You'll also be introduced
to the basics of the main PeachLink window.

NOTE: For PeachLink to work, you must already have Peachtree Accounting installed on your system. For detailed information on using Peachtree Complete Accounting for Windows, look at *Peachtree Complete Accounting for Windows Made Easy* (Osborne/McGraw-Hill, 1997). For detailed information on using Peachtree Complete Accounting for Windows, see *Peachtree Accounting for Windows Made Easy* (Osborne/McGraw-Hill, 1995).

Understanding Internet Basics

The Internet grew out of a network created by the US government in the 1960s known as ARPANET, a private network started by the US Department of Defense Advanced Research Projects Agency (ARPA). The government hoped to create a system that could withstand both natural and man-made disasters, but still allow effective communications throughout the system. To this end they envisioned a network that had no central hub and would send messages from one computer to another by any route possible. The first computers on the network were at universities and a few large corporations and very quickly, e-mail became the most popular application of the new network.

International sites were added to the Internet in the early 1970s and by the early 1980s, the first commercial sites began. In the mid-1980s, companies started to use the Internet as a tool to communicate with their customers. In the early 1990s, the military and other government agencies removed their restrictions on the data allowed to flow through the network and commerce began in earnest on the Internet.

If instant and inexpensive communication brought the Internet to the public's attention, it is the World Wide Web (WWW) that has made the Internet truly popular. In 1992, the World Wide Web (or simply, the Web) was created by Tim Berners-Lee at CERN, the European Particle Physics Laboratory, when he published a set of standards that were then adopted by the Internet. The Web profoundly increased the popularity of the Internet: the graphical interface of web browsers, such as Netscape, Mosaic, and Internet Explorer, and Internet information retrieval systems have helped make the Internet approachable and easy to understand for millions of people.

The small private network has grown over the last three decades to include millions of host computers with tens of millions of users all over the world. Today, more than 150 countries are connected by more than ten million host computers (most of which are used for routing e-mail and storing information).

The ability to retrieve information from virtually any computer on the Internet, from virtually anywhere in the world has made the Internet vital to modern business. By using Internet information retrieval systems such as AltaVista, Yahoo, and WebCrawler, thousands, if not millions, of customers can find you quickly.

There are many ways to access the Internet. Traditionally, you could gain access through most universities, large companies, and government computing centers. In the last few years, however, many independent Internet service providers (ISPs) furnish access to smaller companies and individuals. For less than $100 dollars a month—frequently as little as $20 a month—you can reach your customers 24 hours a day, 7 days a week.

The Internet is a place unequaled for small companies to get national and international customers. Many companies have found that adding a web site to provide marketing, sales, and support information for their customers has enhanced their revenues. In fact, the potential for profit is so large that some companies exist solely on the Internet and have no physical storefront at all. Internet commerce topped $1 billion per year in 1995 and has continued to grow explosively ever since.

PeachLink lets you create your own virtual storefront on the Web in 60 minutes or less. The next section of this chapter will show you how to install PeachLink for use on your computer.

REMEMBER: You must have already installed Peachtree Accounting on your system before installing PeachLink.

6

What Is PeachLink?

PeachLink is an add-on product from Peachtree that helps you create and manage a web site to take orders over the Internet. It interfaces directly with Peachtree Accounting to get those orders into your accounting system. PeachLink comes with basic art and design capabilities to create your web site. It also includes PeachLink Order Processing, which allows PeachLink to work with modern versions of Peachtree Accounting to take orders over the Internet.

NOTE: Some earlier versions of Peachtree Accounting do not come with PeachLink on the Peachtree product diskettes or CD. If you do not have PeachLink already installed on your system, contact Peachtree Software to obtain a copy.

Installing PeachLink

PeachLink is not difficult to install. The whole process takes about 20 minutes.

TIP: You can use PeachLink with Peachtree Accounting for Windows 5.0 or with Peachtree Complete Accounting for Windows 4.0, but be sure that you know which version of the Peachtree product you're using.

When you have finished with the actual PeachLink installation, the setup program will ask you to modify your copy of Peachtree Accounting so the two can work together. As before, simply follow the prompts. You will need to know if you have installed Peachtree Accounting on a network or individual system. It is also important to know the location of the folder into which you installed Peachtree Accounting.

After the PeachLink modifies Peachtree Accounting, you will be asked to install TrustedLink INP. TrustedLink INP is the program that builds and maintains the web site. If you don't already have a copy of Netscape Navigator installed on your system, the installation will also install Netscape.

NOTE: You must install Netscape if you do not already have it as your web browser.

Registering PeachLink

Once you have installed the PeachLink software on your system, you need to register it. PeachLink will not become fully functional until you register it with Harbinger.

As part of the registration process, you need to tell PeachLink which Internet service provider to use. If you don't already have an ISP, you need to decide whether you want to use Harbinger or another ISP.

Paralleling the enormous growth of the Internet in general, there are hundreds of Internet service providers emerging every month. An ISP is your connection to the Internet and the World Wide Web. ISPs provide such services as:

♦ **Dial-up Internet access** This gets you access to the ISP via your computer's modem and a telephone line.

♦ **E-mail accounts** This is a unique address on the Internet, such as *jhedtke@oz.net*, that lets you send and receive e-mail. You may have one or more e-mail accounts.

♦ **Web access** This gives you the ability to "surf" the Net, browsing web pages with a browser such as Netscape.

♦ **Space for your company's web page** Your completed web page is actually stored on a computer run by the ISP. After you load the files you create with PeachLink onto the ISP's system, they host the web site for you, handling all the connections your customers make to your web site.

♦ **Usenet newsgroups** These are continuing discussions categorized into virtually any topic.

NOTE: Although newsgroups are not directly essential to your ability to create and maintain a web page, they can be a valuable source of information from other people with similar interests. (Of particular interest to Peachtree users will be the biz.comp.accounting newsgroup.)

When you set up an Internet account with Harbinger (the ISP that handles most of the business for PeachLink) or another ISP, you should receive most or all of these features as part of your monthly fee. One of the advantages of using Harbinger is that they provide active support for users of Peachtree products. (The details of Harbinger's ISP services are outlined in the paperwork that ships with the Peachtree Accounting software.) On the other hand, it's very likely that your office already has an ISP (usually e-mail and "Web surfing" connections), and almost all ISPs are capable of providing space for hosting your web site. (AOL and similar services are not able to host the web site created by PeachLink.)

6

TIP: Check with your company's system administrator—you may already have a preferred ISP or have direct Internet access.

If you are considering using an ISP in your area, you should evaluate their costs, how much technical support they provide, and the type and quantity of features available for your web site. It is important to note that many ISPs charge at a higher rate for "business" or "commercial" accounts, so be sure to check possible price differences for business accounts versus personal accounts. Since the Internet is undergoing constant change, it is a good idea to shop around to find the service that best fits your business style. Like any business decision, shopping around until you understand the market is the best idea.

CAUTION: If you are going to be taking orders over the Internet (as opposed to simply using your web site for marketing, advertising, and contact information), you must trust the ISP's security as you will be asking your customers to post their credit cards to it. Although credit card fraud is relatively rare, it is a very real concern on the World Wide Web. It is not difficult for someone to pick out a credit card number off a system that isn't secure enough. There are services like First Virtual (*http://www.fv.com/*) that can help keep your transactions secure, but these outside services may not interface well with Peachtree. The best protection is to make sure you are subscribing to a secure system.

To register PeachLink, select the Registration Wizard from the Harbinger program folder in the Start menu. (You can also run the Registration Wizard via the Windows Explorer by running REGCOMM.EXE from the \HARB folder.) The first window of the Harbinger Registration Wizard appears, as shown in Figure 6-1.

NOTE: Some versions of PeachLink have the name "TrustedLink INP" on the windows. This is Harbinger's name for the product.

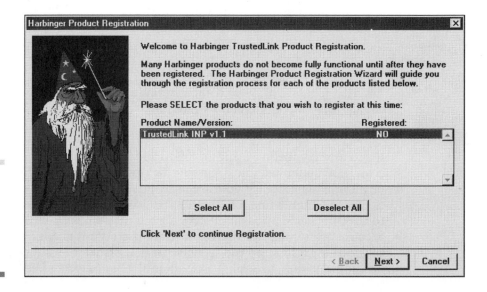

First Harbinger Registration Wizard window

Figure 6-1.

Click Select All, then click Next to continue. The Harbinger Net Access Registration window appears, as shown in Figure 6-2.

If you choose "YES, Sign me up for Harbinger Net Access!" and click Next, you will see a service agreement window (not shown). Read the license terms, and click Accept and then Next to continue with the Product Registration and Billing Information window (discussed later in this section). If you choose "NO, I already have Internet access at my site" and click Next, you will see the Third-Party Internet Service Provider window (shown in Figure 6-3).

Username   Enter the user name you want to use to log in to your web site.

Password   Enter an 8-character password. (PeachLink displays asterisks as you type for security.)

Verify Password   Enter the same 8-character password in this field. This makes sure that you typed the password in the preceding field correctly. If the two password fields aren't identical, PeachLink will prompt you to re-enter your passwords before you can continue.

E-Mail address   Enter the e-mail address where Harbinger should e-mail information from the site. Keep in mind the following tips when setting up passwords in this window:

♦   Passwords in this window must contain exactly 8 characters.

6

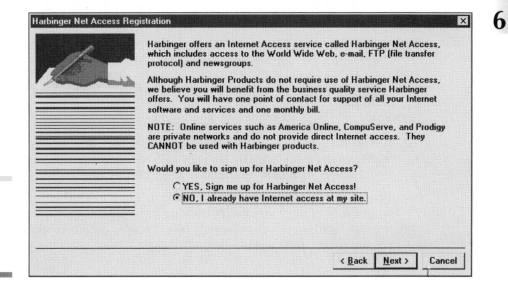

Harbinger
Net Access
Registration
window
Figure 6-2.

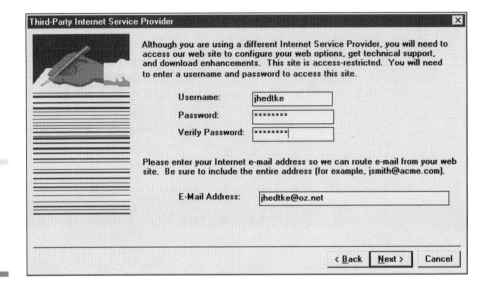

Third-Party
Internet
Service
Provider
window
Figure 6-3.

♦ Passwords are case-sensitive: *PASSWORD* is not the same as *password*.

♦ Avoid using passwords like "password," "security," your name, your
spouse's name, your children's names, birthdays, anniversaries, or
holiday dates.

♦ Mix letters and numbers, and use both upper and lowercase letters.

♦ If you write your password down, store it in a safe place. Don't write
your password down and then leave it in a desk drawer where anyone
can get to it.

When you are satisfied with your entries, click Next. The Product
Registration and Billing Information window appears, as shown in Figure 6-4.

Enter the product number for PeachLink on this window and click Next to
continue.

From this point, the registration process will vary depending on the options
you choose, but you will need to provide contact and address information.
Someone in your company will need to be responsible for your Internet site,
and it is best to decide who that is at the start.

You will also need to provide financial information either for direct
withdrawal of fees from your checking or savings account, or a credit card
number. Harbinger will withdraw fees if you're on direct withdrawal or bill
them to your credit card.

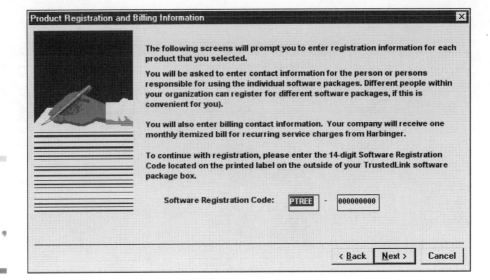

Product
Registration
and Billing
Information
window
Figure 6-4.

REMEMBER: You will need a credit card handy for the registration. You have 30 days before anything is charged to the credit card, but this step is necessary to create your web site.

When you have finished the registration process, you will receive a customer number and account number from Harbinger. It is a good idea to write these numbers down and have them ready in case you ever need technical support.

If you don't have the Windows 95 dial-up networking already set up on your system, PeachLink will set up dial-up networking for you. You may need information about your system and your ISP to complete the setup of dial-up networking.

6

Getting to Know PeachLink

Once you install and register PeachLink, you're ready to start building your web site. Take a moment first to get to know PeachLink. To start PeachLink, select TrustedLink INP from the Harbinger program group in the Start menu, or by simply click the INP icon:

The opening window for PeachLink looks like this:

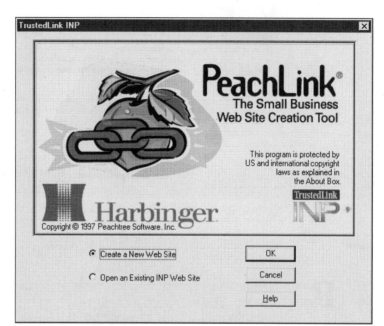

Select "Create a New Web Site" and click OK. The Select Business Type window appears:

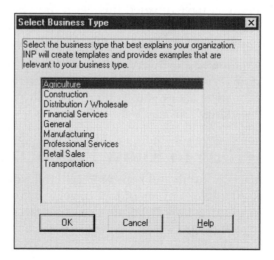

When you are creating a new web site, you select your business type from the list. For right now, just select any of the business types to continue;

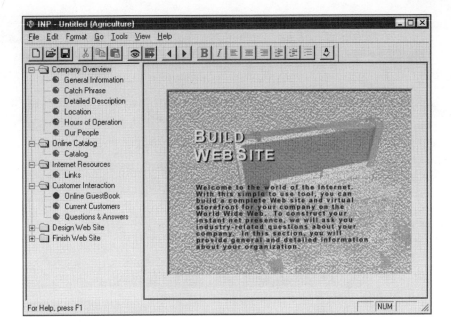

Main
PeachLink
window
Figure 6-5.

you'll see how to use this in Chapter 7, "Using PeachLink." When you click OK, the main PeachLink window appears, as shown in Figure 6-5.

As you can see, in Figure 6-5, the main PeachLink window has a split screen with the Content List on the left and the Content Worksheet on the right. The Content List shows the individual steps in the web site creation process. Each item on the Content List corresponds to a worksheet that appears on the right side of the window. To create and publish your web site, you step through the items on the Content List and fill out the Content Worksheets. PeachLink then uses this information to create your web site's files. As each worksheet is completed, the button next to it on the Content list will turn from red to blue.

The PeachLink window is somewhat different from the Peachtree Accounting windows you may already be familiar with. Table 6-1 shows the menu categories and what they do.

You'll see how to use these menus and their options in Chapter 7, "Using PeachLink," and Chapter 8, "Using the PeachLink Order Processor."

PeachLink has a toolbar for selecting some of the most commonly used menu options. The icons and their descriptions are listed in Table 6-2.

You'll see how to use these features in Chapter 7, "Using PeachLink."

6

Menu	What It Does
File	Creates, opens, saves, previews, and publishes your web site
Edit	Cuts, copies, and pastes information as you edit your text
Format	Boldfaces, italicizes, or justifies text (also allows you to insert bullets or change indents)
Go	Moves you between steps in the creation process
Tools	Accesses spell check and the option menu
View	Turns the toolbar and status bar on and off
Help	Accesses help files and can connect to on-line support

Menu
Categories on
the PeachLink
Window
Table 6-1.

Icon	What It Does
	Creates a new web site
	Opens an existing web site
	Saves the current web site
	Cuts selected text
	Copies selected text
	Pastes text from the clipboard
	Previews the web site
	Publishes the web site

Toolbar Icons
on the Main
PeachLink
Window
Table 6-2.

Icon	What It Does
◀	Returns to the last step in the building process
▶	Proceeds to the next step in the building process
B	Boldfaces the selected text
I	Italicizes the selected text
☰	Left-justifies the selected text
☰	Centers the selected text
☰	Right-justifies the selected text
☰	Indents the selected text
☰	Removes the indent on the selected text
☰	Creates a bulleted list
✓	Launches the spelling checker

Toolbar Icons
on the Main
PeachLink
Window
(*continued*)
Table 6-2.

6

Setting PeachLink Options

The final step in configuring PeachLink is to set your options. On the main
PeachLink window, select Options / Info from the Tools menu. The Options /
Info window appears with the Catalog folder already selected:

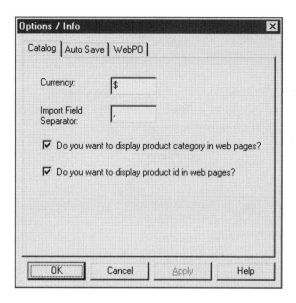

Currency   Enter the default currency symbol for your products' prices in the online catalog.

T **IP:**   If you are using a currency symbol such as $ or £ that is used by more than one country and you will be receiving orders from other countries, you may want to specify the country as part of the currency symbol, for example, US$, CAN$, AUS$, UK£, or IR£.

Import Field Separator   Enter the field separator for importing files. PeachLink looks for this separator to delimit fields in a text file you are importing.

N **OTE:**   If you are not familiar with importing and exporting files, leave this field at its default value.

Do you want to display product category in web pages?   Check the box to display the product categories to appear on the catalog web page as part of the description.

Do you want to display product in web pages?   Check the box to display the product ID assigned in Peachtree Accounting to appear on the catalog web page as part of the description.

When you are satisfied with your entries, click the Auto-Save tab. The Auto-Save folder appears:

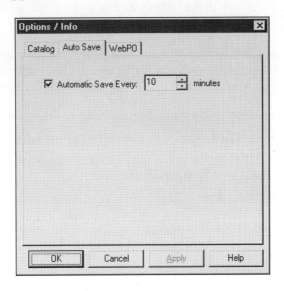

Automatic Save Every   Check this box to have PeachLink save your files automatically.

Minutes   Enter the number of minutes between auto-saves.

When you are satisfied with your entries, click the WebPO tab. The WebPO folder appears:

6

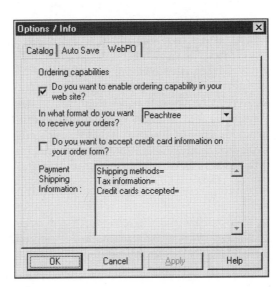

Do you want to enable ordering capability in your web site? Check this box if you want to list your products and services on your web site and take orders for them online through your online catalog web page. Orders are e-mailed to you in an electronic format.

In what format do you want to receive your orders? Select the format from the drop-down list in which the purchase orders will be e-mailed to you. Choose from one of the following formats:

- ♦ **EDI - 850** The purchase order is formatted as an ANSI EDI document.
- ♦ **E-Mail** The purchase order is formatted for manual processing.
- ♦ **HTML** The purchase order is formatted for displaying in a Web browser such as Netscape Navigator.
- ♦ **Peachtree** The purchase order is formatted for Peachtree Accounting.

Do you want to accept credit card information on your orders? Check this box if you want to accept credit card information on online purchase orders.

CAUTION: For security reasons, you may not want to accept credit card information on online purchase orders.

Payment Shipping Information Enter the payment and shipping information.

When you are satisfied with your entries, click OK. Your PeachLink software has been configured and is now ready to create a web page.

Using Netscape Navigator

As you create your web page, you will need to preview what PeachLink is doing so you can make changes and corrections. You will also need to access your web site when it is finished. To do this, you need a browser. A *browser* lets you view web pages graphically. There are several popular Windows browsers. One of the best is Netscape Navigator. A version of Netscape Navigator comes with PeachLink. It was installed on your system as part of the PeachLink installation process.

Take a moment to acquaint yourself with Netscape Navigator.

NOTE: You must already be connected to your (ISP) via dial-up networking to use Netscape.

Once you have a connection, select Netscape Navigator from the Programs in your Windows 95 Start menu. The Netscape Navigator main window appears, as shown in Figure 6-6.

The Netscape window is somewhat different from the Peachtree Accounting window or other standard windows you may already be familiar with.

The Location box is the most important part of the Netscape window because it shows the address of a web page. The address of a web page is called a Uniform Resource Locator, or URL. The Location box displays the URL address for the page you are currently looking at. To move to another page, simply highlight and delete the URL currently in the Location box and type a new URL and press Enter. Web URLs always start with *http://*.

The bottom portion of the Netscape Window displays the web page corresponding to the address in the Location box. Table 6-3 explains the Netscape Navigator menus.

Netscape Navigator has a toolbar for selecting some of the most commonly used menu options. The icons and their descriptions are listed in Table 6-4.

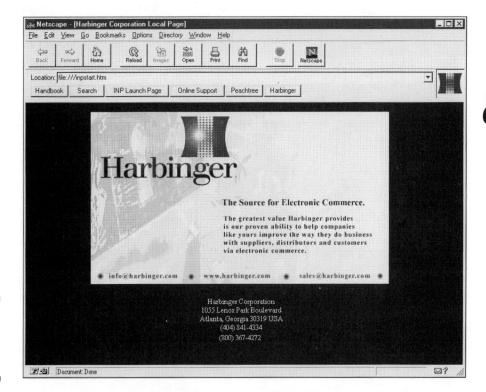

6

Netscape
Navigator
main window
Figure 6-6.

Menu	What It Does
File	Opens a new browser window, saves a copy of a web page, creates a new e-mail message
Edit	Cuts, copies, and pastes information
View	Refreshes, reloads, and views the document source
Go	Moves backward and forward between web pages you've visited
Bookmarks	Creates and displays a list of your favorite sites
Options	Sets preferences and turns toolbars on and off
Directory	Locates a list of predefined web sites
Window	Creates a new mail message, accesses newsgroups and the internal address book
Help	Accesses help files and connects to online support

Netscape Navigator menus
Table 6-3.

Icon	What It Does
Back	Returns to the previously viewed web page
Forward	Moves to the following page (useful only when you've gone **Back**)
Home	Takes you to your home page
Reload	Reloads the current page
Images	Inserts the graphics for the current page (useful only if you have turned images off)
Open	Displays a window in which you can enter any URL
Print	Prints the current web page

Toolbar Icons on the main Netscape Navigator window
Table 6-4.

Icon	What It Does
Find	Finds text within a web page
Stop	Stops loading a page
Netscape	Loads Netscape's home page
Handbook	Opens the Netscape help manual
Search	Takes you to a search service
INP Launch Page	Takes you to the PeachLink home page
Online Support	Takes you to the PeachLink online support page
Peachtree	Opens Peachtree Accounting
Harbinger	Takes you to the Harbinger home page

Toolbar Icons on the Main Netscape Navigator Window (*continued*)
Table 6-4.

Selecting menu options, moving and sizing windows, making selections from lists, and so on are all about the same in Netscape as in most other Windows 95 applications.

You'll learn how to use Netscape Navigator to view your web page in Chapter 7, "Using PeachLink."

6

Summary

In this chapter, you've seen how to install the PeachLink web page creation software on your system and register the software with Harbinger. You've also been introduced to the basics of the main PeachLink window. In the next chapter, you will see how to use PeachLink to create a working web page for your company.

7

Using PeachLink

In the last chapter, you saw how to install PeachLink and were introduced to the menu categories and toolbar icons. You also saw how to register with Harbinger. In this chapter, you will see how to design and create a web site with PeachLink and how to use Netscape Navigator to view the web pages you've created. You'll also see how to publish your web site and become a part of the World Wide Web.

NOTE: A web page is a single screen of information, whereas a web site comprises the individual web pages.

Designing Your Web Site

Before you begin creating your web site with PeachLink, give some thought to what you want to accomplish. Designing a web site is very different from creating other promotional materials. Unlike brochures or catalogs, your customers must download your web pages over the web. The bigger a graphics file is, the longer it will take your customers to download the web page and display it. As a general rule, most shopping on the Web is conducted through personal ISP accounts on a customer's home computer. (Even if companies are making purchases, the web sites are frequently first discovered by an employee web surfing on their own time.) This means that most of your potential customers are accessing the Internet using a 33.6K modem through their personal ISP.

To make sure your web site is the right size, keep text concise and graphics under 20K each. A good rule of thumb is that a single web page should take less than half a minute to download over a 33.6K modem connection. (An overly long download time caused by excessively large graphic files can actually cost you sales.) This constraint may mean that you need to create a smaller version of your company logo, possibly with fewer colors. It may also mean that you cannot display all the text of your marketing materials on a single page. As average access speeds through ISPs increase, it will be possible to put more material on single web pages, but for now, you should plan for a standard 33.6K modem connection as the lowest common denominator.

Another major concern in web design is accuracy. Not only must your page have complete and correct information, it must be well-written and proofread. As with software and printed promotional materials, typos, bad grammar, and poor word choices will make your web pages look amateurish and, again, may cost you sales. Double and triple-check your web site before you publish it. Being "cute" on your web page can also be a bad idea. Unless you are selling small, plush toys or baby clothes, it is unlikely that cuteness will gain you any customers on the Internet.

CAUTION: If you do not have a writer on your staff, make sure your page is proofed by the best writer and/or speller you can find. Typos can be death to a web site.

There are hundreds of thousands of truly terrible web pages on the Web today. There are even awards given for the very worst of them. You can look at examples of bad web pages on sites like Vincent Flanders' Web Pages That Suck (*http://www.webpagesthatsuck.com*) to see some of the things that you should avoid.

REMEMBER: The best way to get an idea of how to design for the Web is to look at other pages. Take a little time before you create your own web site with PeachLink and use Netscape Navigator to look at other web sites. In particular, examine your competitors' and your suppliers' web sites to see how they are selling to your potential customers. Just a few hours of "surfing" can help you understand a great deal about the Web.

Perhaps the most important question to ask is, "What do I want my customers to see?" Your web page may be the first and only contact you have with a new customer before they decide to do business with you. As a result, your web site should be an important part of your marketing strategy.

NOTE: For additional information on where the Web fits into your marketing scheme, see the "Other Resources" section at the end of this chapter for a list of excellent books on marketing and selling on the Web.

Before You Begin

Before you begin creating your web site with PeachLink, you should assemble the information and files you will need. To make the process as simple as possible, assemble as much of the following information as you can:

◆ Your company logo in JPG or GIF format (preferably a relatively small version of it)

◆ A company marketing statement or other document talking about the scope and purpose of your company

◆ An employee list (this can be exported from Peachtree Accounting)

◆ A product list (this can be exported from Peachtree Accounting—see the "On-Line Catalog" section later in this chapter for further information)

◆ A list of other web sites you would like your site to link to (you can always add to this later if you wish)

◆ A list of questions you'd like to ask your customers

7

♦ JPG or GIF graphic files of your products or other pictures you would like to display on your web site

As you'll see a little later in this chapter, these files and lists of information are used by PeachLink as part of the web site creation process. Some of the information (such as the graphics files) may be optional, depending on what you want your web site to look like.

 NOTE: If you're not familiar with how to create and manipulate graphics files, take a look at Chapter 9, "Using Advanced PeachLink Features," for information on using PaintShop Pro (which is on the CD accompanying this book).

Creating Your Web Site

In Chapter 6, "Setting Up PeachLink," you saw how to install PeachLink on your system and configure it. Once you have assembled the information in the preceding list, you are ready to start creating your web site.

To start PeachLink, select TrustedLink INP from the Harbinger program group in the Start menu, or click the INP icon. The opening PeachLink window appears (as shown in Chapter 6, "Setting Up PeachLink"). Select "Create a New Web Site" and click OK. The Select Business Type window appears:

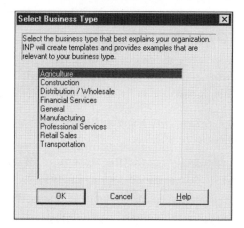

When you are creating a new web site, you select your business type from the list. Select the business type that closest resembles your type of business. If none of the other entries match, select General. When you click OK, the main PeachLink window appears, as shown in Figure 7-1.

Content List   Content Workbook

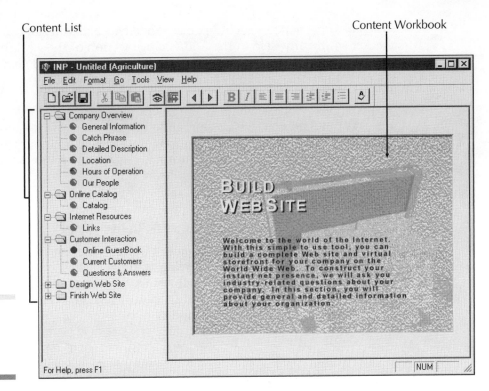

Main
PeachLink
window
Figure 7-1.

The main PeachLink window has a split screen with the Content List on the left and the Content Worksheet on the right. The Content List shows the individual steps in the web site creation process. Each item on the Content List corresponds to a worksheet that appears on the right side of the window.

To create and publish your web site, you step through the items on the Content List and fill out the Content Worksheets. When you enter information in each of the Content Worksheets, PeachLink uses the information to create web pages. PeachLink will take care of formatting, layout, and all the details to create your web site's files; all you have to do is tell PeachLink what to say. As you complete each Content Worksheet, the button next to it on the Content list will turn from red to blue.

Also, when you're in any of the Import Document windows within the PeachLink worksheets, you must delete everything currently listed for that worksheet before importing. If you do not delete the current information, PeachLink will append the new data to the old data, which can result in duplicate entries. This is particularly important in the On-Line Catalog when you are importing new inventory lists from Peachtree Accounting.

7

For your convenience, PeachLink has a spell checker. You can use the spell checker within any field in the Add/Change section of the worksheets or in a text fill-in box by highlighting the text and clicking the spell check button on the toolbar.

NOTE: When you're changing something on a worksheet and have saved the modification, PeachLink disables the delete option for that worksheet. To re-enable the delete feature, you need to go to another worksheet and then return to this worksheet.

Creating the Company Overview Web Page

The first step in creating your company's web site is to enter the company information for the Company Overview web page. The Company Overview web page is the first page your customers will see when they go to your web site. Click General Information in the Content List. The General Information worksheet (shown in Figure 7-2) appears.

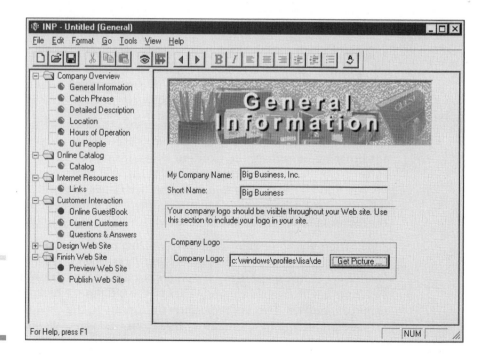

General Information worksheet
Figure 7-2.

The General Information worksheet collects your company name and logo. This information is displayed at the top of each web page.

My Company Name   Enter your company's name (up to 64 characters).

Short Name   Enter a short name for your company (up to 30 characters). For example, if your company is "Amalgamated Big Business, Inc." you might also be known as "Big Business" for short.

Company Logo   Enter the path and filename for the picture file for your company's logo. You can click the Get Picture button to the right of this field to browse your file directories.

NOTE: The picture must be in GIF or JPG format and should be no larger than 20K. If you're not familiar with how to create and manipulate graphics files, take a look at Chapter 9, "Using Advanced PeachLink Features," for information on using PaintShop Pro (which is on the CD accompanying this book). If you don't have a graphics file for your company's logo, you can leave this field blank and enter it later.

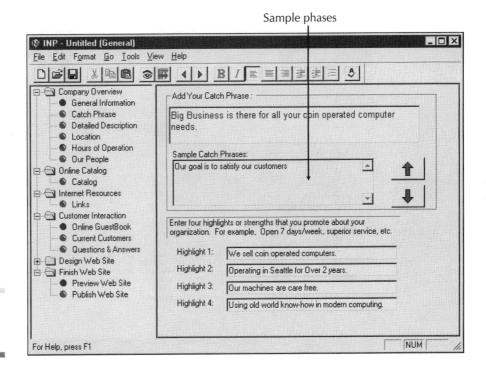

Catch Phrase
worksheet
Figure 7-3.

When you are satisfied with your entries, click Catch Phrase in the Content List. The Catch Phrase worksheet (shown in Figure 7-3) appears.

The Catch Phrase worksheet is used for collecting your company motto and up to four company highlights.

Add Your Catch Phrase   Enter a company motto or other short phrase that illustrates what your company strives to achieve. It should be less than 20 words. An example appears on the Catch Phrase worksheet in the "Sample Catch Phrases" display-only field.

Highlights   Enter up to four highlights of your company. The four highlights are displayed, in that order, on the top of your company overview page.

When you are satisfied with your entries, click Detailed Description on the Content List. The Detailed Description worksheet appears, as shown in Figure 7-4.

The Detailed Description worksheet is used for entering a detailed description of your company.

Sample description

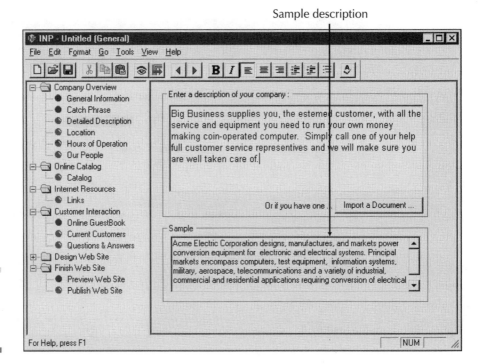

Detailed
Description
worksheet
Figure 7-4.

Enter a Description of Your Company   Customers that reach your page need to know what you do. This description will end up as the first thing on your company overview page. There is an example in the Sample box in the lower half of the worksheet.

If you already have a marketing document that tells your customers about your company and what it does, you can import it into PeachLink by clicking the "Import a Document" button and selecting a file from the standard Open File dialog (not shown). When you are satisfied with your selection, click OK. The text from the selected file will be imported into Detailed Description.

PeachLink will not be able to transfer indents and other complicated formatting onto your web page, but hard returns and other basic formatting will stay intact. A document must be in one of the following formats to import successfully:

◆   Microsoft Word 6.0 or 7.0 (.DOC)

◆   WordPerfect for Windows 6.0 (.WP)

◆   Plain ASCII text (.TXT)

◆   Rich Text Format (.RTF)

When you are satisfied with your entries, click Location on the Content List. The Location worksheet appears, as shown in Figure 7-5.

The Location worksheet is used for entering the location(s) of your company. Locations are displayed on your Company Overview web page. You can change a location you have already entered by selecting the location from the list in the "List of Current Locations" box, making the change, and then clicking Apply Modification.

T IP: It is not imperative that you include all the information requested for each of your locations, but having addresses for all locations is a good idea. The Web has made it fairly common for customers away from home to visit a branch of store they might otherwise not know about. Many Internet customers have begun looking up information about places they visit, and that includes shops and offices. Even if these customers do not feel comfortable ordering from your web site, they may feel better about a purchase if they can come to your store in person. At the very least, make sure that you provide the complete address and phone contact information for your main office. The more locations you enter on this worksheet, the more customers those stores will have.

7

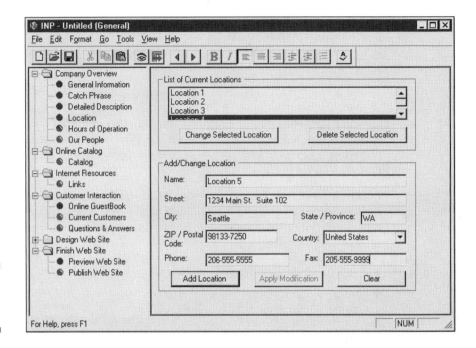

Location
worksheet
Figure 7-5.

List of Current Locations   This field lists the locations entered for the business's web page. Select a location in this list to modify or delete. To modify a location, click Change Selected Location. The location information appears in the fields in the lower portion of the worksheet. To delete a location, click Delete Selected Location.

CAUTION: PeachLink deletes the location as soon as you click Delete Selected Location. Make sure that you've selected the right location before deleting.

Name   Enter the name of this location.

TIP: If you are entering several locations, you may want to have an identifier in the name of the location, such as "Big Business—Seattle office" or "Big Business—Tucson office."

Street   Enter the street address for this location, including apartment or suite number.

City   Enter the city for this location.

State/Province   Enter the state or province for this location.

ZIP/Postal Code   Enter the ZIP code or postal code for this location.

Country   Enter the country for this location. You can also select a country name from the drop-down list.

Phone   Enter the telephone number for this location.

Fax   Enter the fax number for this location.

Add Location   Click this to add the location to the list (if you are adding a new location).

Apply Modification   Click this to save the changes in the fields when you modify the information for an existing location.

Clear   Click this to clear the information in the fields.

When you are satisfied with your entries and have added the location, click Hours of Operation on the Content List. The Hours of Operation worksheet appears, as shown in Figure 7-6.

The times you input on this worksheet are not configurable for each location, so it may be best to input the hours for your main office. You could list for your web customers the hours the switchboard at your main office is attended, or you could give them an idea of the best hours to catch your customer service representatives.

Opening Time   Enter the opening time for each day. You can adjust the time by selecting the hours, minutes, or A.M. or P.M. part of the time, and using the arrows to the right of the field to adjust the time up or down.

Closing Time   Enter the closing time for each day. You can adjust the time by selecting the hours, minutes, or AM or PM part of the time and using the arrows to the right of the field to adjust the time up or down.

Closed   Check this box if the office is closed on that day.

Special Comments   Enter information about which of your listed locations these hours apply to. This comment is especially important if you have more than one location, since the information from the Location worksheet will display next to that from the Hours of Operation worksheet on the Company Overview page.

7

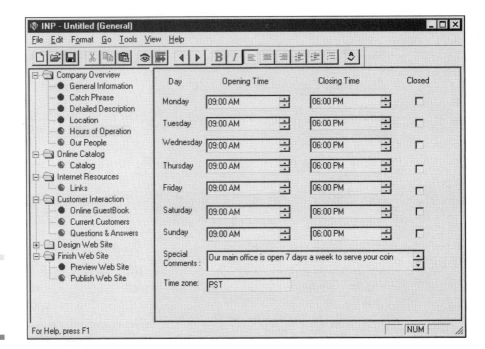

Hours of
Operation
worksheet
Figure 7-6.

CAUTION: If you have more than one location listed, make sure you note what location the hours are for.

Time Zone Enter the time zone.

When you are satisfied with your entries and have added the location, you can add another location. When you are done entering locations, click Our People on the Content List. The Our People worksheet (shown in Figure 7-7) appears.

You can enter a list of employees on this worksheet. The information on the Our People worksheet shows your web customers the people that make up your company and allows them to get to know them on their own time and at their own pace. It is common to list the company's CEO, President, and Vice-President-level employees, as well as HR and Customer Service managers.

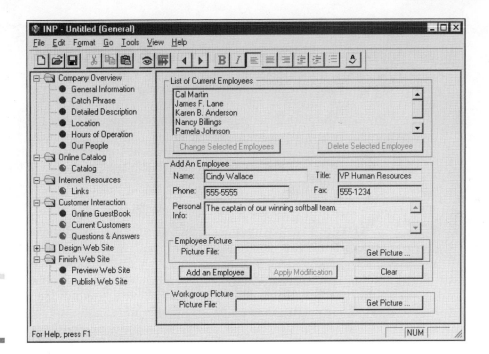

Our People
worksheet
Figure 7-7.

NOTE: Unless you are a very small company, you will probably not want to include all of your employees, although this is a decision that has as much to do with your marketing strategy as anything else.

List of Current Employees   This field lists the employees entered for the business's web page. Select an employee in this list to modify or delete. To modify an employee, click the Change Selected Employee button. The employee information appears in the fields in the lower portion of the worksheet. To delete an employee, click Delete Selected Employee.

7

CAUTION: PeachLink deletes the employee as soon as you click Delete Selected Employee. Make sure that you've selected the right employee before deleting.

Name   Enter the name of the employee.

Title   Enter the title of this employee.

Phone   Enter the telephone number for this employee.

Fax   Enter the fax number for this employee.

Personal Info   Enter any appropriate comments about the employee here.

Picture File   Enter the path and filename for the picture file for the employee. You can click Get Picture to the right of this field to browse your file directories.

NOTE: The picture must be in GIF or JPG format and should be no larger than 20K. If you're not familiar with how to create and manipulate graphics files, take a look at Chapter 9, "Using Advanced PeachLink Features," for information on using PaintShop Pro (which is on the CD accompanying this book). If you don't have a graphics file for the employee, you can leave this field blank and then enter it later.

It is not uncommon to see individual pictures for each of the people listed on a company's web site. However, including a picture with each entry may well make this page very large. Since this information is part of your Company Overview page, it is very important to make sure this section stays within reasonable size limits. Photographs are one of the largest kinds of image files, no matter which graphics format you use. You will want this to be a friendly part of your site, but do not include so many pictures that it causes your customers to lose interest.

Add an Employee   Click this button to add an employee to the list (if you are adding a new employee).

Apply Modification   Click this button to save the changes in the fields when you modify the information for an existing employee.

Clear   Click this to clear the information in the fields.

Picture File   Enter the path and filename for the picture file of the entire staff. Pictures of groups of employees have started to become popular, particularly because one group picture takes up much less space than the 20 or 30 it replaces. You can click Get Picture to the right of this field to browse your file directories.

NOTE: Harbinger offers scanning services for pictures. See your PeachLink manual for information. Many large copy centers also have scanning services. If you have a number of pictures to scan or you think you'll have an ongoing need to scan pictures, you may want to invest in a flatbed color scanner. Inexpensive scanners can be had for as little as $100.

When you are satisfied with your entries and have added the employee, you can add another employee. When you finish entering employees, you have completed entering the information for the Company Overview web page. You can preview your work at this point by clicking the Preview icon on the PeachLink toolbar. Netscape Navigator appears with the web page created from the information you've just entered, as shown in Figure 7-8.

You can use the Preview feature to look at the web page in progress at any time.

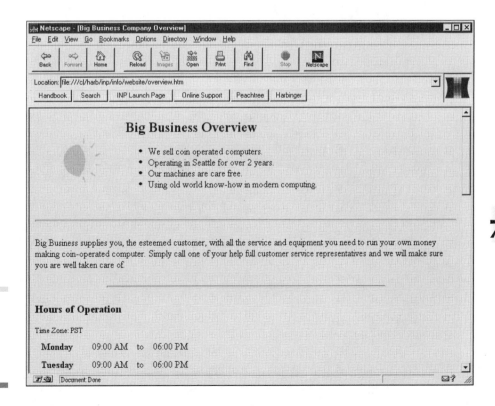

Preview of Company Overview web page **Figure 7-8.**

7

TIP: Previewing lets you experiment with your entries: if something doesn't look good on the web page, you can change the information in the appropriate worksheet and look at it again.

Creating an On-Line Catalog Web Page

To create the On-Line Catalog web page, click Catalog on the Content List. The Catalog worksheet (shown in Figure 7-9) appears.

The Catalog worksheet collects the information that will become your On-Line Catalog, where your customers will place their orders. The items you want your customers to be able to order on the Web will be listed here, as well as shipping and payment information. Inventory items and sales information make up the bulk of the Catalog page, which is linked to a final sales order form and a shipping worksheet.

Full Catalog Listing   This field lists the items currently in the catalog. Select an item in this list to modify or delete. To modify an item, click the Change Selected Item button. The item information appears in the fields in the lower portion of the worksheet. To delete an item, click Delete Selected Item.

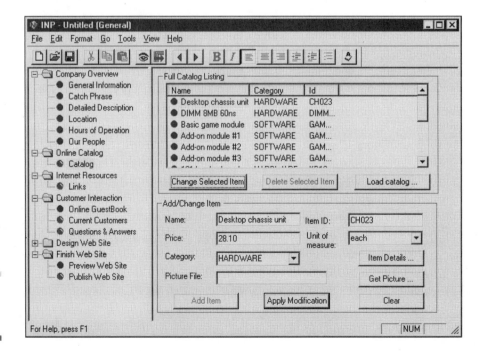

Catalog
worksheet
Figure 7-9.

CAUTION: PeachLink deletes the item as soon as you click Delete Selected Item. Make sure that you've selected the right item before deleting.

Load Catalog   Click to import an inventory list previously exported from Peachtree Accounting.

NOTE: Exporting data can be a complex process. If you are not already familiar with how to export data from your business, see the Peachtree Accounting manual or Chapter 13, "Management Tools and Procedures," of *Peachtree Complete Accounting for Windows Made Easy* for more information on the export process.

To export an inventory list for use in PeachLink, start Peachtree Accounting, open your company, and Select Import/Export from the File menu. Select Harbinger INP Product Catalog from the Inventory list, and click Export. Since you do not want to export every item you have listed in your database, you will need to filter the list using the Filter tab (not shown), where you select the information you wish to export.

Exporting data in the right format will depend on the type of inventory you carry and the design requirements for your web page. You may need to do several exports with different filtering options before you hit on the filtering options you need. As a general rule, start by filtering for just the stock items that are active.

The Layout tab (not shown) controls the format of the data you export. PeachLink will only accept the data if it has a specific layout, which is different than the default set by Peachtree Accounting. To set the correct layout, click Deselect All on the Layout tab. You then need to select the following fields for exporting in the order shown:

◆ Item Description
◆ Item ID
◆ Description of Sales
◆ Sales Price (can be any of the one to five prices listed, but only one of the five prices may be selected)
◆ Item Type
◆ Unit of Measure

Once you have the fields selected, you need to tell Peachtree Accounting where to put the exported file. The Option tab has the file path at the top of

7

its window. If you need to change the path, click the right arrow next to the field and enter the new path.

CAUTION: Do not click the Include Headers box on the Options tab. If headers are included in the exported file, PeachLink will create a new item with the heading information.

When you are satisfied with your entries, click OK. Peachtree Accounting starts the export process. After the export process is complete, close Peachtree Accounting, and return to the PeachLink On-Line Catalog worksheet.

Click Load Catalog on the On-Line Catalog worksheet. Select the file from the standard Windows box. (The default file and location is C:\WEBPAGE.CSV.) PeachLink imports the catalog and the items appear in the Full Catalog Listings area. You can then change or delete individual items.

If the exported file still needs major changes (above and beyond those made by selecting different parameters during the export process), you can edit the file by opening it in a text editor. Each inventory item will be separated by hard returns and all six fields will appear for every item, separated by a commas. It is vital that you do not add or remove commas or hard returns as you edit the document. Save the document as text only with the CSV extension and re-import it into PeachLink.

CAUTION: Be sure to delete all the entries from one import process before importing another file or else you'll have entries from both in the catalog.

Name Enter the name of this item.

Item ID Enter the item ID for this item.

CAUTION: The item ID should be the same item ID as appears in Peachtree Accounting; otherwise, your order processing won't be able to identify which item the customer is buying.

Price Enter the price for this item.

Unit of Measure   Enter the unit of measure for this item.

Category   Choose the appropriate category for the item from the drop-down list.

Item Details   Click this button to enter additional information about the item. The Item Details window appears:

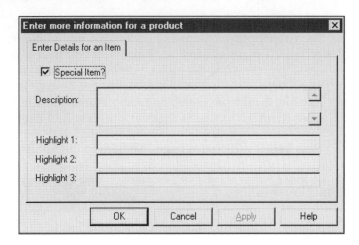

Special Item?   Check the box to identify this item as a "special" item. PeachLink adds a star on the web page next to the listing for each special item. This is useful for identifying sales or promotional merchandise.

Description   Enter an item description.

Highlights   Enter short highlights about the item. PeachLink displays the information you enter as bulleted items appearing after the item description.

NOTE: You cannot enter highlights if the Special Item box is not checked.

When you are satisfied with your entries, click OK to return to the On-Line Catalog worksheet.

Get Picture   Click this button to include a picture of the selected inventory item. Enter the path and filename for the picture file for the item or browse your file directories.

7

NOTE: The picture must be in GIF or JPG format and should be no larger than 20K. If you're not familiar with how to create and manipulate graphics files, take a look at Chapter 9, "Using Advanced PeachLink Features," for information on using PaintShop Pro (which is on the CD accompanying this book). If you don't have a graphics file for the item, you can leave this field blank and then enter it later.

As with employee pictures previously mentioned, be careful not to include too many pictures of your products. If you have a very short catalog or very small pictures (2 to 5K each), you may be able to include pictures of most items without going over acceptable size limits. However, if you have a large catalog, it may be best to include pictures for only the most important of your items, or for items that customers would need to see before ordering.

Add Item   Click this to add an item to the list (if you are adding a new item).

Apply Modification   Click here to save the changes in the fields when you modify the information for an existing item.

Clear   Click this to clear the information in the fields.

After you've finished entering these items, you will have completed your On-Line Catalog web page. You can preview your work at this point by clicking on the PeachLink toolbar. Netscape Navigator appears with the web page created from the information you've just entered, as shown in Figure 7-10.

NOTE: When a customer places an order through your web site, they see a web page that thanks them and shows the order number and contact information if they need to make changes. If Harbinger is your ISP, the customer will also receive e-mail confirming their order.

Internet Resources

The Web thrives on effective connections between web pages. The more links you can provide to and from your web site, the more customers are likely to visit your site and to recommend it to other people. The Predefined Links and Custom Links folders on the Internet Resources worksheet collect information about other web sites you would like to link your web site to. These links display on your Internet Resources web page.

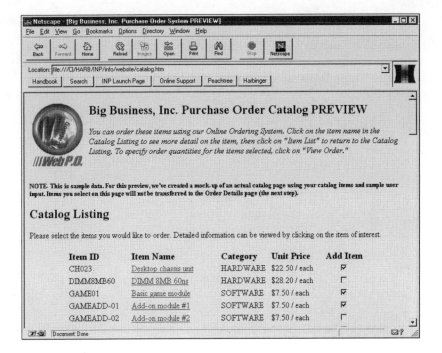

PeachLink
On-Line
Catalog page
Figure 7-10.

Click Internet Resources in the Content List. The Internet Resources worksheet (shown in Figure 7-11) appears with the Predefined Links folder already selected.

The Predefined Links folder lets you select from a list of predefined web sites that may be of interest to you. When you highlight some of the items in this list, a description appears below the list. Check the box to the left of the links you want to include on your web site.

When you are satisfied with your entries, click the Custom Links tab. The Custom Links folder (shown in Figure 7-12) appears.

The Custom Links folder lets you enter links to web sites that don't appear in the Predefined Links folder.

List of Current Custom Links This field lists the custom links currently entered. Select a link in this list to modify or delete. To modify a link, click Change Selected Link. The link information appears in the fields in the lower portion of the worksheet. To delete a link, click Delete Selected Link.

CAUTION: PeachLink deletes the link as soon as you click Delete Selected Link. Make sure that you've selected the right link before deleting.

7

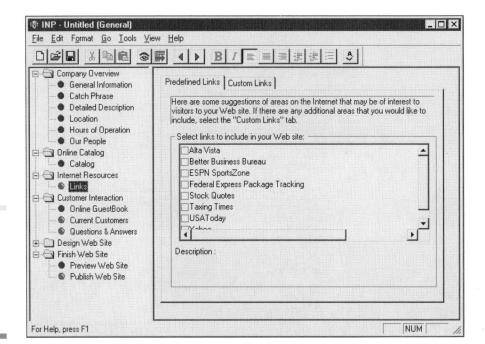

Internet
Resources
worksheet
showing the
Predefined
Links folder
Figure 7-11.

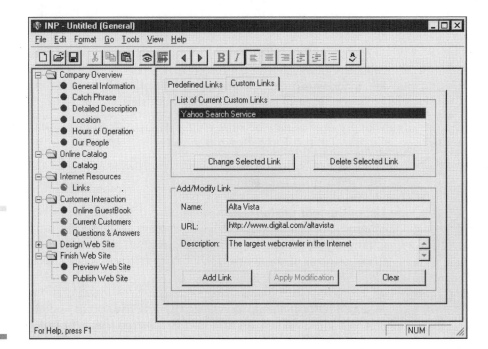

Internet
Resources
worksheet
showing
the Custom
Links folder
Figure 7-12.

Name   Enter the name of the link. PeachLink will display this information on the web page as the name of the link.

URL   Enter a URL (Uniform Resource Locator). All URLs for web sites start with http:// followed by the specific information for the web site. When you display a web page, the URL appears in the Location box on the Netscape Navigator browser.

Description   Enter a description of the link. This is optional but recommended.

Add Link   Click this to add a new link to the list.

Apply Modification   Click this to save the changes in the fields if you are modifying the information for an existing link.

Clear   Click this to clear the information in the fields.

 When you are finished entering links, you have completed entering the information for the Internet Resources web page. You can preview your work at this point by clicking the Preview icon on the PeachLink toolbar. Netscape Navigator appears with the web page created from the information you've just entered, as shown in Figure 7-13.

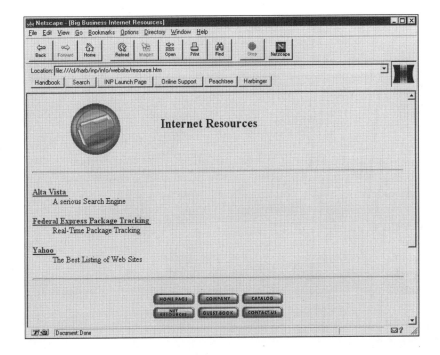

Internet
Resources
web page
Figure 7-13.

Customer Interaction

One of the strengths of the Web as a sales and marketing tool is that you can get information directly from your customers. PeachLink uses each of the Customer Interaction worksheets to create the following web pages of information for your customers: questions to ask your customers, a list of current and past customers (and their endorsements), and a Frequently Asked Questions (FAQ) list.

Online GuestBook

The Predefined Questions and Custom Questions folders on the Online GuestBook worksheet let you specify and enter questions that you want to ask your customers. Click Online GuestBook in the Content List. The Online GuestBook worksheet (shown in Figure 7-14) appears with the Predefined Questions folder already selected.

The Predefined Questions folder lets you select from a list of predefined questions that you may want to ask your customers. These questions appear when a customer goes to the Online GuestBook. Check the box for the questions you want to include on your web site. Table 7-1 shows you the information that PeachLink displays for each predefined question.

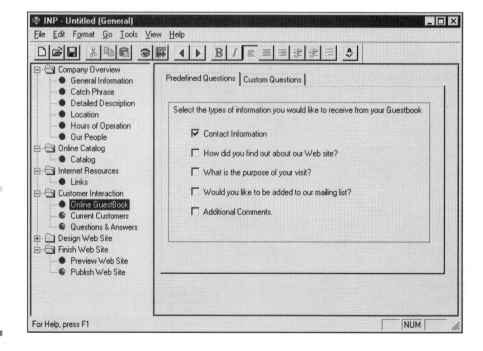

Online GuestBook worksheet showing the Predefined Questions folder

Figure 7-14.

Predefined Question	What PeachLink Displays
Contact Information	Form boxes for first and last name, title, company name, address (including city, state, ZIP code, and country), e-mail address, and phone and fax numbers.
How did you find out about our Web Site?	Checkboxes for: Listed in trade publication Searched Lycos, WebCrawler, Web Worm, Yahoo, etc. Noted in brochure or other publication from Short Name Followed link from other site A colleague told me about it Also includes a fill-in box for Other
What is the purpose of your visit?	Checkboxes for: Need Product Information Need to be included on Mailing List Need Representative to contact me
Would you like to be added to our mailing list?	Yes or No dialog box
Additional comments?	Large fill-in box

Predefined
Questions
Table 7-1.

When you are satisfied with your entries, click the Custom Questions tab. The Custom Questions folder (shown in Figure 7-15) appears. This folder lets you enter questions of your own that you want to ask your customers.

List of Custom Questions   This field shows a list of the custom questions currently entered. Select a question in this list to modify or delete. To modify a question, click Change Selected Question. The question as it is entered appears in the Question field in the lower portion of the worksheet. To delete a question, click Delete Selected Question.

7

CAUTION: PeachLink deletes the question as soon as you click Delete Selected Question. Make sure that you've selected the right question before deleting.

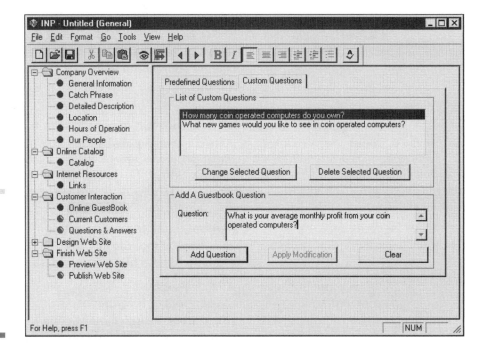

Online
GuestBook
worksheet
showing the
Custom
Questions
folder
Figure 7-15.

Question   Enter the question you want to ask the customer.

NOTE: All custom questions appear with a standard fill-in box on
the web site.

Add Question   Click this to add a new question to the list.

Apply Modification   Click this to save changes to the question when you
modify information for an existing question.

Clear   Click this to clear the information in the fields.

TIP: You can combine customer questions and predefined questions on
the same web site, but you should keep the total number of questions under
five. Internet customers are not known for their patience and will be
annoyed by a form that takes too long to fill out.

When you are finished entering questions, you have completed entering the information for the Online GuestBook. PeachLink displays a standard set of fields on the Online GuestBook web page (not shown) that requests name, address, and contact information from the customers, followed by the questions you've just entered on this worksheet. You can preview your work at this point by clicking the Preview icon on the PeachLink toolbar.

Current Customers

Click Current Customers in the Content List. The Current Customers worksheet (shown in Figure 7-16) appears.

The Current Customers worksheet collects endorsements from current customers for your company. You can also use it to create a list of your current customers on the Current Customers page on your web site.

NOTE: While you are proud of your customers, be sure to exercise appropriate professional discretion in advertising the names of your clients on your web site.

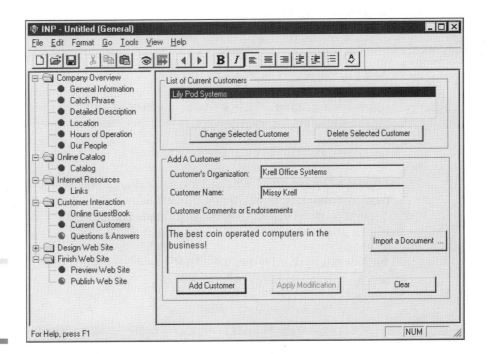

Current Customers worksheet
Figure 7-16.

List of Current Customers   This field lists the customers currently entered. Select a customer in this list to modify or delete. To modify a customer, click Change Selected Customer. The customer will appear in the Customer field in the lower portion of the worksheet. To delete a customer, click Delete Selected Customer.

CAUTION: PeachLink deletes the customer as soon as you click Delete Selected Customer. Make sure that you've selected the right customer before deleting.

Customer's Organization   Enter your customer's company name.

Customer Name   Enter the name of the primary contact for the customer.

Customer Comments or Endorsements   Enter any comments or endorsements made by this person or company that you want to display on your web page.

NOTE: Before quoting customers, you may want to get signed approval that this is all right with them and that the quote is complete and correct.

Add Customer   Click this to add a new customer to the list.

Apply Modification   Click this to save the changes in the fields after you've modified information for an existing customer.

Clear   Click this to clear the information in the fields.

Import a Document   Click to import a document. Select the document from the standard Open dialog (not shown) and click OK. If you have a document that details some of your satisfied customers, it can be imported if it is in any of these formats:

- ♦   Microsoft Word 6.0 or 7.0 (.DOC)
- ♦   WordPerfect for Windows 6.0 (.WP)
- ♦   Plain ASCII text (.TXT)
- ♦   Rich Text Format (.RTF)

When you are finished entering current customers, you have completed entering the information for the Current Customers web page. You can preview your work at this point by clicking on the PeachLink toolbar. Netscape Navigator appears with the web page created from the information you've just entered, as shown in Figure 7-17.

Questions & Answers

Click Questions & Answers on the Content List. The Questions & Answers worksheet (shown in Figure 7-18) appears.

The Question & Answers worksheet compiles a set of frequently asked questions (FAQ or FAQ list, in Internet parlance) for the Questions & Answers web page. The best questions and answers to feature on your web site are the ones that your customer service staff are asked most frequently. It is also a good idea to include answers to technical questions; for example, if you write software, you may include common installation problems and how to fix them.

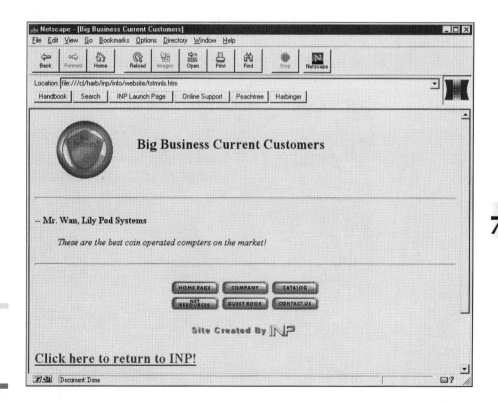

Current
Customers
web page
Figure 7-17.

7

The Questions & Answers page of your web site is one of the strongest draws to your customers. They may not even know your web site exists until they go looking for answers to a question they have about your products. Make sure this section is easy to understand and remember to update this page frequently.

List of Common Customer Questions   This field lists the frequently asked questions currently entered. Select a question in this list to modify or delete. To modify a question, click Change Selected Question. The question as it is entered appears in the Question field in the lower portion of the worksheet. To delete a question, click Delete Selected Question.

CAUTION: PeachLink deletes the question as soon as you click Delete Selected Question. Make sure that you've selected the right question before deleting.

Question   Enter a frequently asked question.

Answer   Enter the corresponding answer to the question entered above.

Add Question   Click to add a new question to the list.

Questions &
Answers
worksheet
Figure 7-18.

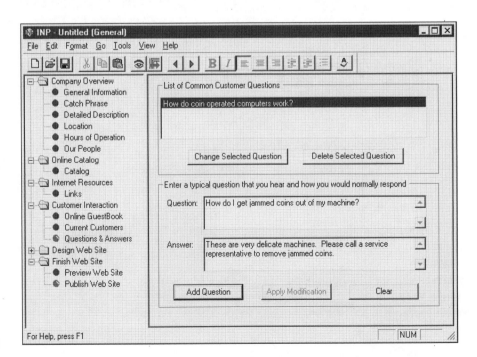

Apply Modification   Click this to save the changes in the fields when you modify the information for an existing question.

When you are finished entering questions, you have completed entering the information for the Questions & Answers web pages. You can preview your work at this point by clicking the Preview icon on the PeachLink toolbar. Netscape Navigator appears with the web page created from the information you've just entered, as shown in Figure 7-19.

Design Web Site

The Design Web Site section helps you make choices about the color and layout of your entire web site. The choices you make here will greatly affect the look and feel of your web site. You may wish to choose styles that correspond with your marketing strategy. You should also experiment extensively with layouts before publishing your web site on the Internet to make sure that you have selected the best layout and style for your web site.

Click Choose Layout in the Content List. The Choose Layout worksheet appears, as shown in Figure 7-20.

Your layout is the basic look of your web site. It affects how the text and clipart are arranged on your web site's home page. The layout will only minimally affect the other pages in your web site. The layout you choose should support your company's marketing strategy.

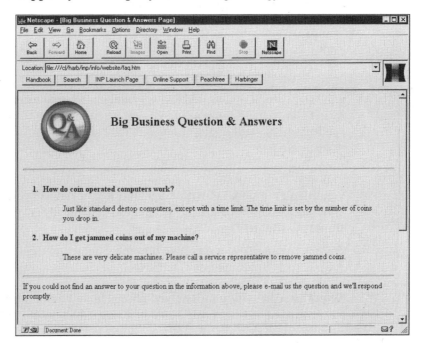

Questions
& Answers
web page
Figure 7-19.

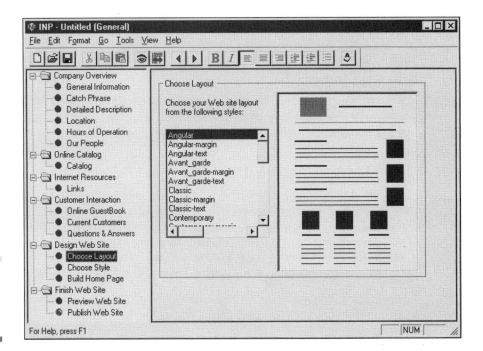

Choose
Layout
worksheet
Figure 7-20.

Select a layout from the list. When you highlight a layout, a thumbnail of the layout design appears to the right of the list. There are more than 30 layouts in PeachLink.

TIP: Layouts with text in the title will have fewer graphics on the home page, but they will have the same number of graphics on the other pages of your web site. If you would like a graphics-intensive site, layouts such as Avant Garde have more graphics on the home page. Since the graphics are used on individual pages, there is no file size savings by not having them on your home page.

When you are satisfied with they layout you have chosen, click on Choose Style on the Content List on the left. The Choose Style worksheet will appear similar to that in Figure 7-21.

The Choose Style worksheet will help you choose the background, text colors, and clipart for your entire web site.

Select an Icon Group to Be Used Throughout Your Web Site   Select one of the groups of icons. PeachLink comes with 13 sets of clipart for the

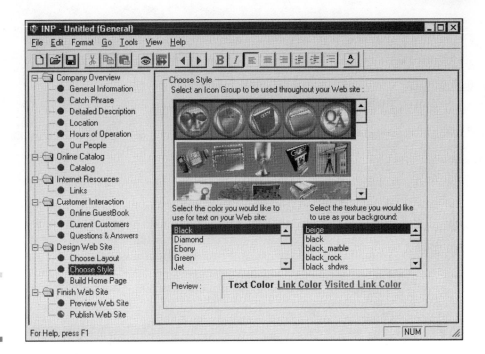

Choose Style
worksheet
Figure 7-21.

navigational buttons on your web site. PeachLink uses these icons throughout the entire web site, at various predefined locations.

The style of clipart should fit the type of business you do. It should also go well with the style of the text you included in the previous work sheets. Most notably, your clipart should not clash with the background and text on the page.

 NOTE: It is possible to include more sets of clipart or to use your own custom artwork in your web site. See the section "Adding Clipart" in Chapter 9, "Using Advanced PeachLink Features," for more information.

7

Select the Color You Would Like to Use for Your Text on Your Web Site
Select a color from the list. All text will appear in this color.

There is usually no reason to change the default text colors, as you may confuse your customers, who are used to the generic colors on web pages: black for text, blue for links, red for links you have visited. However, if the background you choose in the following field makes one or more of the default text colors invisible or hard to read, you may need to change text colors.

NOTE: In some cases, your choice of text colors can conflict with the text settings for some web browsers, which can cause errors in the way the browser displays the web page. Where possible, leave your text colors set to the default values.

Select the Texture You Would Like to Use as Your Background   Select a texture from the list. PeachLink comes with 80 backgrounds in various colors and patterns.

The graphical nature of the Web makes your color choices very important. The background color of your pages will be the first thing your customers notice since many will have to wait for the graphics and text to load. The color of your background is like the outside of your front door to your store or office. If it is confusing or gives the image of poor decorating decisions, your customers may jump to the wrong conclusion about you. Make sure your background color complements your company logo and the clipart you choose.

NOTE: It is possible to include more backgrounds to use with your web pages. See the section "Adding Backgrounds" in Chapter 9, "Using Advanced PeachLink Features," for more information.

When you are satisfied with the style choices you have made, click Build a Home Page from the Content List on the left. The home page is the first page your customers see when they visit your web site and it provides links to the other parts of your web site. Figure 7-22 shows the Build a Home page worksheet.

The text on this worksheet will appear on your home page as descriptions of the links to other parts of your web site. PeachLink provides default entries for the fields, but you should customize them to the look and feel of your company. The descriptions should be short and to the point, and should match the text style of the rest of your document. If you aren't using a feature, such as the On-Line Catalog, PeachLink ignores the description you enter.

CAUTION: Since the information here is on the first page your customers will see, the text must be free of spelling and grammatical errors. Use the spelling checker that comes with PeachLink and have the text proofread.

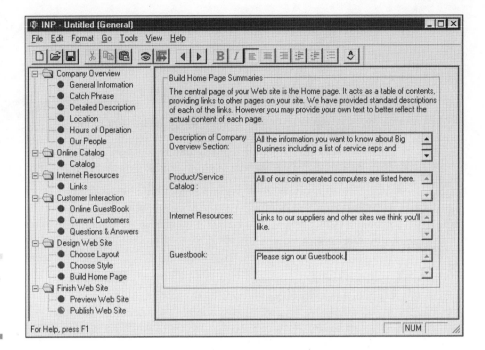

Build a
Home Page
worksheet
Figure 7-22.

Description of Company Overview Section Enter a description of the
Company Overview section.

Product/Service Catalog Enter a description of the Catalog section.
Mention any special features you want to draw attention to.

Internet Resources Enter a description of the Internet Resources section
and the types of links customers will find.

Guestbook Enter a description of the GuestBook and what the customers
can request from you.

When you are finished entering introductions, you have completed entering
the information for building your home page. You can preview your work at
this point by clicking the Preview icon on the PeachLink toolbar. Netscape
Navigator appears with the web page created from the information you've
just entered, as shown in Figure 7-23.

With the completion of this worksheet, you have entered all the information
necessary for your web site.

7

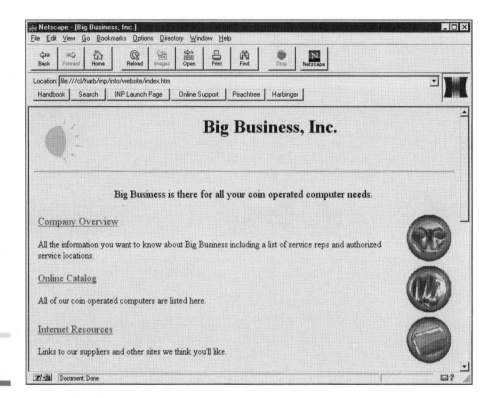

Home page
Figure 7-23.

Finishing Your Web Site

In the preceding sections, you have seen how to create your web pages by entering information on the various worksheets. In this section, you will complete the web site creation process by previewing your web site and then publishing it on the Web.

Previewing Your Web Site

The first step is previewing your web site. To preview your site, click Preview Web Site from the Content List on the left. The Preview Web Site worksheet appears, as shown in Figure 7-24.

The Preview worksheet allows you to see your web site before you upload it to your ISP. You can choose each page individually by clicking the associated button, or you can preview the entire site by clicking Preview Web Site to display the home page and then clicking on the links on the web pages to navigate through your web site just as your customers will.

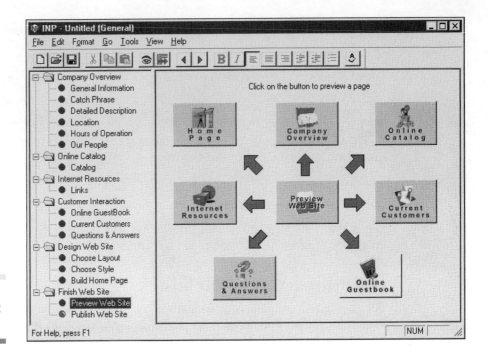

Preview Web
Site worksheet
Figure 7-24.

 TIP: It's important to take some time to review your web pages so you can identify and fix any errors. Furthermore, get other people in your office to review what you've done. Remember, your web site does not need every feature implemented when you first publish it, but everything you do have must be complete, correct, and free of spelling, grammar, and typographic errors.

Preview Web Site Click to preview the entire site and navigate through it as your customers will.

Home Page Click to preview just your home page.

The home page is the main point of entry for your web site. After you publish your site, you will be taken to this page. The URL for this page is the address you give to other sites when you are exchanging links. It is also the URL you give all Internet search engines (such as AltaVista, Yahoo, and Lycos) and have printed on your letterhead.

Internet Resources Click to preview your page of links to other web sites.

7

Current Customers   Click to preview your page of kudos from your customers.

Guest Book   Click to preview what your customers will see when they go to your GuestBook.

NOTE: Customers submit their contact information here. Your custom questions are at the bottom of the list.

Questions & Answers   Click to see your page of frequently asked questions.

When you have previewed all of the pages and are happy with the way your entire web site looks, you are ready to publish.

Publishing Your Web Site

Before you can publish your web site, you must register with Harbinger. If you have not yet registered with Harbinger, you must do so now. You also need to make sure that your ISP (whichever you decide upon) knows your web site will be uploaded to their system. In addition, if you want your customers to be able to pay for their orders with a credit card, you must make sure PeachLink is set up to accept credit cards. Do this by selecting the Option/Info option from the Tools menu, then verifying that the "Do you want to enable ordering capacity on your web site?" box is checked in the Web PO folder. You should also select Peachtree in the list for the order type and check the box that says "Do you want to accept credit card information on your order form?" Include any necessary shipping and tax information in the Payment Shipping Information box. When you are satisfied with your entries, click OK on the Options/Info window.

TIP: If you're accepting credit cards, it's a good idea to list the credit cards you will accept. Type the names of the credit cards after the "Credit cards accepted=" phrase in the Payment Shipping Information field and separate each with commas. Do not delete the equal sign or the words that precede it.

To publish your web site, click on Publish Web Site from the Content List on the left. The Publish Web Site worksheet appears as shown in Figure 7-25.

The Publish Web Site worksheet is the final worksheet in the web creation process.

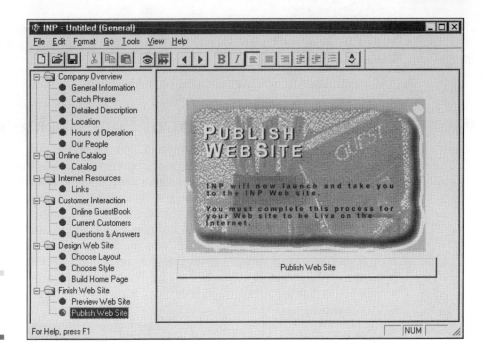

Publish Web
Site worksheet
Figure 7-25.

T IP: Before you publish your web site, make sure that all the of the pages are complete and correct. To fix errors after this point will require you to republish your web site.

Connect to Your ISP You must be connected to your ISP to publish your web site. After connection is established, click on the Publish Web Site button.

PeachLink will ask you which files you would like to publish. If this is the first time you are publishing your web site, select all of the files. (Later, you may want to update information on a few pages, in which case you would only select the pages you want to change.)

You will be asked for your password. Enter the password you selected during the Harbinger registration process. PeachLink will then upload the pages you have created. Uploading the files may take several minutes depending on the speed of your Internet connection and the size of the files.

After uploading has finished, you will be notified of a successful completion and asked if you would like to go to your new web site. Click Yes. (You will be making sure that the site published correctly and you will also need the

7

URL for your web page.) When Netscape opens your web page, write down the URL from the Location box. Then browse through your site and admire your handiwork.

Congratulations! You are now part of the World Wide Web!

Making the Web Part of Your Business

Now that you are part of the World Wide Web, you need to make allowances for it in your business practices. For example, your accounting flow will need to deal with orders from a source you have not used before. You will also need to network professionally for web links and other business concerns. You may even need to hire designers or web professionals (frequently just on a contract basis) to handle the new medium you have just become involved in. From this day forward, you need to think about the Web as a vital part of your business strategy; for example, you need to be constantly thinking of ways to get your URL in front of your customers. (Some ideas on how to do this are included in the "Marketing on the Web" section later in this chapter.)

Most importantly, you will need to make sure your web site is maintained. Maintenance of a web site is often more time consuming and expensive than creating one. Someone in your company will need to take the web site on as part of their daily job duties. Be sure to budget enough time for this: daily web site maintenance will average 30 minutes a day (or less), weekly maintenance about an hour, and monthly and yearly maintenance can easily take up an entire day. The specific requirements are detailed in the section, "Maintaining Your Web Site."

One of the largest changes to the way you do business will be the new orders from your web site. As you've seen, PeachLink integrates directly with your Peachtree software, which can help you get ahead of your competition on the Web. Orders from your PeachLink site will be seamlessly integrated with the computer side of your accounting, but the transition may not be as seamless for other parts of your accounting processes. If sales orders need to be printed on paper before they are processed by the Shipping department, you may have to create a new step in order processing to print web orders. If you keep paper files of each order, those will need to be printed as well. Some companies like to have the entire sales team informed of sales made that week, and web sales will need to be integrated into that process also. It is difficult to foretell how your new web site will directly affect your accounting processes, but it is very important to give some time and thought to accounting and your new web site. A little forethought on this subject can save you weeks of accounting headaches as you try to figure out where an order came from. It gets much harder to follow a paper trail when the order never started on paper.

Maintaining Your Web Site

As your business information changes, your web site will also need to change. Maintaining your site is not just important, it is vital. The Web is based on the premise that, for the first time in history, your customers are able to get up-to-the-minute information at all times. The bonus for your company having a web site is that it becomes a place were you can pass out the latest and greatest information about your products and services. What use would this be if it was out of date? If a web customer tries to order merchandise you do not currently carry, or tries to reach you and can't, they won't just be annoyed like a phone customer might be. A web customer may never order from you again because they've found out-of-date information on your web site, and they are likely to tell other potential customers of their bad experience. Outdated information on your web site can cost you dozens of lost customers every day. This section will take you through the steps for daily, weekly, monthly, and yearly maintenance of your web site, as well as help you identify what to look for if you decide to hire someone to maintain your site for you.

Daily Maintenance

To keep the information current on a daily basis, someone in your company must be in charge of maintaining your web site. It should be part of someone's regular tasks to make sure the site is current, and that the simple, yet expedient task of checking the web server is done every morning, to make sure it's still working and that customers can reach it without difficulty.

Most daily maintenance is very easy. Often, once the site has been built and uploaded, an employee with limited Internet experience can maintain the site day-to-day simply by logging into your web site and taking a few moments to look at all the pages. If your ISP changes their systems, it can affect how your site runs. You need to know about any malfunction or problems as soon as possible—with your web site open for business 24-hours a day, 7-days a week, you don't have time to waste. The first step to fixing a problem is finding a problem.

Your site maintainer should also check the ordering mechanism daily. The most common daily problems are with the programs that run the ordering mechanism. Changes made to the ISP's server that will affect your site will probably show up first in the ordering process.

7

TIP: Create a false account you can use to test the ordering system on your web site. You can easily delete orders from that account before entering them into Peachtree.

As you will see in the following sections, you will check each order before it is entered into Peachtree Accounting. This checking process will ensure that sending yourself a bogus order won't affect your accounting system. Even if you don't send yourself an order, at least make sure the system will let you into the order processing area and that it is possible to select items to order. All of the catalog pages require programs on the server that can be damaged from time to time, and if they are damaged, they may keep your customers from placing orders.

You should also make sure that e-mail is reaching you daily. This is easy to check because once you get used to e-mail as a business tool, you will likely check it first thing every morning anyway. As soon as you notice any e-mail problems, notify your in-house system administrator as well as the administrator on your ISP. Being without e-mail is like being without telephones, a problem that should be handled quickly. If your customers can't reach you, they can't give you their money, and once your web site is operating smoothly, some of your customers will be contacting you exclusively via e-mail. After you have made sure that these processes are working and that all of the pages on your web site can be accessed, your daily maintenance is complete.

Weekly Maintenance

It doesn't take long to get into the habit of checking your web site daily. Some companies simply make it a part of an executive assistant's daily tasks, much like opening the mail. Even if you decide to do the daily maintenance yourself, you can frequently complete it in less than ten minutes. All you need to do is to go to your site, look at the pages, and send yourself e-mail and an order or two. However, weekly maintenance can become much more involved.

Weekly maintenance will tend to focus on the noticeable—but not massive—changes to the web site that serve to keep the web site looking fresh and new. The person who does the weekly maintenance should already have some Internet experience and be able to do simple HTML coding. This person should also be able to republish the web site using PeachLink and check the web site to make sure that it is still functioning.

The value of making noticeable changes to your web site once a week is that most of your web customers are likely to visit your site once or twice a week as they become regular customers. The pace of business on the Web can be very fast and it is on the weekly level that most new web customers notice the difference. A web site that does not change frequently will lose the interest of the typical web customer who is comfortable with the rapid pace of the Internet.

The weekly changes don't need to be earth-shattering. As a matter of fact, the most common weekly change to business web sites is to change your highlighted items. These are usually stock items that may be new or different. It may even be stock that has had a price change in the last few days. One way to do this is to highlight the item using the catalog creation forms in PeachLink (in the detail window for each item, there is a checkbox that lets you highlight each item).

The items you highlight can be things other than products for your customers to order. For example, they can be important information for people in your business to know, such as news releases that affect how you do business. Highlighted items can also be important or exciting events at your company or in your city. You could even highlight the weather in your home town. As long as the information changes in some noticeable way every week, it is not vitally important how it changes. Your customers will observe the changes and feel reassured that your web site is up-to-date and accurate. Web sites that don't change often can give the appearance of not being maintained, which can make web customers nervous.

To make changes to your PeachLink pages, you will need to start PeachLink and select Open an Existing INP Web Site on the main window and click OK. Select your web site (it will probably be in the \Harb\inp\info\website folder). Go through the worksheets you would like to change and then publish your web site again.

TIP: When you publish weekly updated files, you don't need to republish everything—just the files that have changed. Make sure you know which files have changed and that all of them get republished. One of the more common publishing errors is to miss uploading an updated web page or graphics file, which may cause an error when someone views the web page.

7

By the way, source control—keeping copies of your files—is a vital part of the maintenance process. If your files are small, you may want to back them up to diskettes and save them whenever you make a change. If the files are large, you may want to store them somewhere on your network. In either case, though, you should always have at least one copy of the most recent version of the files for your web site stored offline in case you need to recreate the web site for any reason.

Once you have republished the pages you have changed and verified that the web site works, you have completed your weekly maintenance. You should be able to complete the weekly maintenance in about an hour or so, depending on the changes you make to your site. Remember to check for inaccuracies and misspellings before you republish. Keeping your customers up-to-date won't do you any good if your site is full of errors.

Monthly Maintenance

Where daily and weekly maintenance are relatively quick, monthly maintenance will take the better part of a day. On a monthly basis, you will be making major changes to your web site. You might compare monthly maintenance to doing improvements around the house. Deleting old information, re-exporting your product list from Peachtree, and even rewriting all the information on your home page are just some of the projects you may do each month. For monthly maintenance, you will need someone skilled in HTML and web design, possibly the same person that built your web site. This person should be familiar with both PeachLink and Peachtree and feel comfortable with the Internet and the Web. They should also have an understanding of your company's marketing strategy on the Web and should be able to write copy to fit. They may even need to work with the marketing group to verify that your web site still correctly reflects your company's image.

REMEMBER: Don't forget to make source control copies of your entire site before you start monthly maintenance. If there is a problem or system crash, your monthly backups may be the only way to recreate your web site.

To export a current list of products and services, you will need to go through the export process in Peachtree Accounting. As detailed previously in this chapter, you must open Select Import/Export from the File menu in Peachtree Accounting. (The "Creating an OnLine Catalog Web Page" section earlier in this chapter will help you through the steps for exporting.) Make sure you get all the information in the correct order with the correct fields. After you have successfully exported your updated list, you can import it into PeachLink on the Online Catalog worksheet.

Before you click the Import button on the Online Catalog worksheet in PeachLink, make sure to delete all the items currently in your catalog. If you forget to do this, you will have both item listings in the dialog box at the top of the work sheet. If you need to delete these items after importing a new list, you will need to delete them one at a time.

CAUTION: PeachLink will delete the selected item as soon as you click the DELETE key. Make sure you have selected the correct item before you click DELETE.

The newly imported catalog will need to have modifications made to it. You should highlight some of the items and make sure they all have complete descriptions. Don't forget to preview this page before you upload your monthly updates to the system. A current and correct catalog is as important to your web customers as it is to your other customers.

After you have imported a current catalog and created descriptions for the items, you should consider changes to other parts of your site as well. The Internet reinvents itself on a monthly basis and month-old information is useless on the Web. Your employee list can be updated at this point, including any changes in job descriptions or duties that have changed in the last month. Your customers will like to know who will be handling their order or who to call with a question. Keeping your employee list current will help this.

You may also consider changes to your company information page and home pages during your monthly update. You probably won't have updates to these pages every month, but you will need to change this information at least occasionally. To change the text on your company information pages or your home page, open PeachLink and go through the first few worksheets again. Make sure you also update the Home Page worksheet, highlighting changes that have been made to the pages that link to it.

Don't be afraid to make too many changes to the content of your web pages on a monthly basis. Web customers are used to reading pages that have changed every time they log into your site. However, you should not make frequent changes to the overall look and feel of your site. The monthly update is not for making changes to the color or layout of your web site; it is simply to make sure your site has the most current information possible. Your customers might get confused if the navigation and layout changed on your site every month.

Once you have made changes to your Online Catalog worksheet, your Company Information worksheets, and your Home Page worksheet, you are ready to republish your web site. At this point, it is a good idea to republish

7

the entire web site, even if some of the pages have not changed. It is important to make sure you don't miss any changes or new pages when you republish.

To republish, open your web site in PeachLink and go to the Publish worksheet. Click on Publish, and when PeachLink asks which files you would like to publish, make sure all the listed files are selected. Continue through the publication process, then view your site over the Internet to make sure all the changes were made. This completes the monthly maintenance on your web site.

Monthly maintenance is vital to your site. It is impossible to overstate the importance of keeping the content on your web site current and fresh. The few hours it takes to perform the monthly maintenance will be well worth the effort. Your customers will appreciate knowing they have the most current product list. Being conscientious about monthly updates will also make your subsequent weekly updates go more smoothly.

T IP: You should make big changes to the text on your web site on a monthly basis, but it is a good idea to leave the color and layout the same month to month.

Yearly Maintenance

A year on the Internet is like a decade in the normal business world. A year from now the Web will look completely different. "Yearly maintenance" may be a misnomer because on a yearly basis, your web site will need to reinvent itself. As each new browser comes out, or as new specifications are released for HTML, the entire look of your site will need to reflect the current trends. In addition, what looked new and exciting a year ago will have become rather dated and commonplace in the succeeding twelve months. Overhauling your web site to reflect all of these changes should be done at least once a year.

If your PeachLink web site has served you well for an entire year, you may consider visiting the Harbinger web site to see if there is a new version of their software. A new version of the creation software will probably require you to go through the creation process again. (Harbinger should be able to keep you updated with web services, including programs to run the newest generation of ordering software. Check the Peachtree web site at *http://www.peachtree.com* or the Harbinger web site at *http://www.harbinger.com* for information on new releases.)

If you feel you have outgrown your PeachLink site, you will need to examine your web requirements closely. It is likely that after your successful first year, you will feel a need for a larger and more dynamic site than can be produced directly with PeachLink. This type of site will handle fairly large traffic, probably more than 100 customers a month. You could include pages on individual products, or almost any other new kind of page you need.

This doesn't necessarily mean that you will have to give up your existing web site, as you may be able to still use your PeachLink pages on Harbinger's server and simply add a few custom pages. However, in order to do this you or your web site maintainer will need to learn some HTML. HTML is the language used to write web pages and is extremely easy to learn. (Chapter 9, "Using Advanced PeachLink Features," will walk you through the steps of creating your own custom web pages and linking them to your PeachLink web site.)

However, adding pages to your existing PeachLink web site will only allow you to access the most basic of HTML and you will still rely on Harbinger for your home page and basic support. If you feel your web site needs are even larger than can be handled with PeachLink, you will need to create your own site. You can use one of the commercially available web-designing tools or write the HTML yourself. This may sound daunting, but if you have a large volume of web customers, it may be worth the effort to create a site. If you don't have the time or inclination to create your own site, especially if you need a site with many pages, you should look into the costs of hiring an agency to create a new web site for you. The agency will be completely responsible for the creation and maintenance of a web site and will have its own HTML experts who create dozens or hundreds of web pages a week.

No matter the option you choose, you should seriously consider getting your own domain name. A domain name is the address of your site. For example, the domain name for Harbinger is harbinger.com, and the corresponding URL for their home page is *http://www.harbinger.com*. Having your own domain name will help establish name recognition and it will help your customers find you. Many web surfers, when looking for a new web page, simply enter *http://www.companyname.com* (where *companyname* is the name of the company they are looking for) first before they try any of the search services. If they can find your site that way, it will save them time and will get you more customers.

After a year on the web, having your own domain name is a logical next step. Sites without their own domain name are generally looked down on, and are often considered less professional. Talk to your ISP about the process to obtain a domain name, or visit *http://www.internic.net* to register a new name. Make sure that your service provider can handle your domain name, and that your web site is prepared to handle the address change.

7

CAUTION: To make the change to your own domain name you will probably need professional help to make sure your site can migrate to the new address.

The cost of any of these options depends a great deal on what you want your new site to do. As it applies to the Web, the statement that "you get what you pay for" is even more real. A more expensive site will generate more revenue; however, the cost of your web site needs to be carefully weighed against your other advertising costs. After your first full year on the web you should take time to rethink your company strategy on the Internet. Are you doing everything you could be? Is the new medium helping you make new sales? Is your web site generating revenue? Have all your customers found your site quickly and easily? Has your service been reliable?

Yearly maintenance can take anywhere from hours to months, depending on what you are trying to accomplish. Your web site should look entirely new at the end of the process. At the very least you should change the layout and colors, but you will probably want to do much more than that. As part of your first anniversary online, you may find you need an in-house professional to handle your web site. The "Hiring a Web Professional" section later in this chapter will help you learn what to look for.

Web Maintenance Checklists

This section contains checklists of the various tasks you need to perform on a daily, weekly, monthly, and yearly basis to keep your web site up-to-date and appealing to your customers. Feel free to photocopy these lists and use them to keep your web site current.

Daily Maintenance Checklist

- ☐ Log onto your ISP and read all system notices.
- ☐ Verify that you are receiving e-mail.
  This may require that you send yourself e-mail.
- ☐ Visit each page in your web site.
- ☐ Check the ordering system (if you are using one).

NOTE: You may need to create a fake customer account to send yourself an order. If you decide not to send yourself an order, make sure you check all of the catalog pages, including the final shipping information page.

Weekly Maintenance Checklist

☐ Finish daily maintenance.

☐ Make source maintenance copies of any pages you might change.

☐ Identify and change the currently highlighted items as necessary.
You can do this in the Online Catalog worksheet.

☐ Include any new office business that might interest your customers.
You can do this in either the Company Information worksheet or the Employee worksheet.

☐ Republish your web site.
This is done from the Publish Your Web Site worksheet. On a weekly basis, you only need to republish the pages that have changed.

Monthly Maintenance Checklist

☐ Finish daily maintenance.

☐ Finish weekly maintenance.

☐ Make source maintenance backups of your entire site.
This backup should be kept where other important digital media for your company is kept. In case of fire or theft, this may be your only record of the web site.

☐ Export a new catalog from Peachtree Accounting.
Select Import/Export from the File menu in Peachtree Accounting.

☐ Delete old catalog information from the Online Catalog worksheet in PeachLink.

☐ Import the new product listing into PeachLink.
Click the Import... button on the Online Catalog worksheet to do this.

☐ Include details for each item by selecting from the list and clicking Details.

☐ Use the Details dialog to select the currently highlighted items.

☐ Update your employee list on the Employee worksheet.

☐ Update the Company Information worksheet.

☐ Preview your updated web site. Remember to check spelling and punctuation.
You may need to have someone look at your site to be sure it is error-free.

☐ Republish your entire web site.

7

Yearly Maintenance Checklist

☐ Finish daily maintenance.

☐ Finish weekly maintenance.

☐ Finish monthly maintenance.

☐ Re-evaluate your web site.
Is the web site doing what it is supposed to? Is it reaching the customers it should reach? Can it be used more effectively to market or sell your company and its products? Is the web site cost-effective?

☐ Design and publish the updated web site.

☐ Start the process for acquiring your own domain name.

Hiring a Web Professional

As you do business on the Web, your web site will expand. After the rush of processing your first few web orders, you will settle into the day-to-day routine of doing business on the Internet. During the following year, your web site will generate an increasing amount of business. To accommodate this growth, you will eventually need a larger, more complex site. At some point, the care and feeding of your web site may become more than you can handle yourself and you may need to employ a web professional. This section will discuss how to find this person and will tell you what to expect from this new member of your business team.

The Internet is less than 20-years old. The youth of the medium tends to translate into a very unconventional group of professionals that specialize in it. Most web professionals have a young outlook that works well with the speed and youth of the medium. Web development agencies do their work at a price few other businesses can fathom. When the time comes for you to hire someone to create your second web site, remember that a web professional is unlike any of your standard employees. To specialize in the World Wide Web, your new web designer must love what they're doing. Web designers are generally not the type of person to leave their work at the office and are often found surfing the Web at home "just for fun." Web designers are a mix of artist and programmer that results in a unique kind of person. This section will help you better understand what you need from a web professional before you have one on your payroll.

 NOTE: It is worth mentioning that you may not need a web professional as a full-time employee; a contractor or design agency may be adequate. Think carefully about how much time you expect this person to spend creating your site, and how much time you expect them to spend maintaining it. A major advantage of contracting for a part-time web designer or a web design agency is that neither needs to work in your office; in fact, they need not even be in your part of the country. Much of the information in this section still applies to agencies or contractors, since they are often found in many of the same ways an in-house web professional is.

Advertising for a Web Professional

To find the right professional for your office, you will need to explore alternate avenues of obtaining applicants. Most people in this field don't read classified ads in the newspaper; instead, they tend to get their news off the Web. Most professionals are self-taught, so looking at college graduates may only slightly improve your chances. The best way to find a web professional is to advertise in the medium they know the best: the Web. There are many "help wanted" listing services on the web. Go to any search service and search for "jobs." This search should lead you to listing services.

Listing your position on your own web page may also be a good way to get results: you may wish to create a custom page on your web site for "Job Openings." From there, you could list all the openings in your company. (Advertising on a web page has become a common way to solicit for all kinds of applicants.) Wherever you list your position, make sure that you list your web address and request applicants to submit their résumé via e-mail.

Another excellent source for web designers is professional organizations, such as the Society for Technical Communication (*http://www.stc-va.org*) and the International Association of Business Communicators (*http://www.iabc.com*), both of which have local chapters throughout the US and Canada and can provide information on local web designers. Of particular interest is Webgrrls, an international professional organization for women in the Internet. Check out the Webgrrls home page at *http://www.webgrrls.com* (be sure to spell that correctly) for up-to-date references to web professionals in your area. Several of the URLs listed in Appendix B, "Online and Printed Resources," also advertise web design and consulting services.

7

It is also possible to find a web professional through an employment agency, though your success may be dictated greatly by your location. In areas where many computer professionals are employed, you are more likely to find web professionals listed through a service. The largest benefit of hiring a web professional from a service is that most of the first stage of screening has been done for you. You will also have an easier time negotiating salary.

Finding the Right Person

The Web is constantly changing. If you are hiring someone to maintain and run your web site, they need to be well-versed in the most current topics, programs, and design options. The best web professionals (and often the most expensive) are familiar with at least a couple of web development languages (such as Java, CGI, and Perl), have an intimate understanding of HTML, and have experience supporting someone else's web site already.

Having your applicants submit their résumés through e-mail ensures that they are comfortable with the Internet. (Being able to create and send a file over the Internet is a basic skill for the person you are looking for.) Once you have their résumé, open it and take a look at it on your computer screen. They should be able to create a document free of errors and with a pleasing layout. Creating for screen is a different, but related, skill to graphic design for paper. A good web designer will understand the difference and account for that when they send you their résumé. The layout may be non-traditional, but that is somewhat expected since a good web designer is often a non-traditional person.

NOTE: Any applicant worth their salt will also have a web site of their own. Be sure to review an applicant's web site to see if you like the applicant's design style.

Once you have selected résumés and are ready to proceed to the interview stage, you may consider doing the first stages of interviews over the telephone. If your company does not conduct telephone interviews as a general rule, you may want to find a book or other resource on the technique. In the computer industry, it has become common to do initial interviews over the telephone because many applicants may be in other parts of the country.

The location of your applicant need not be a concern if you're hiring an agency or contractor. As a general rule, if you are hiring someone part-time, your applicant will do most of the work in their own office. Because the Internet is global, it doesn't matter if your offices are in Hawaii and your web page was uploaded from Kansas. Because of this, web professionals tend to work non-traditional hours and in non-traditional ways. This doesn't mean they should be allowed to work less hard than any of your other employees; it simply means they are likely to work differently.

After you have spoken to enough applicants you feel necessary to make a first choice, you can treat your web professional as you would any other professional. Remember to ask them to bring in samples during their interview. The samples your applicants bring may be the only information you have about their skills before you hire them to run your web site. Don't hire anyone who hasn't got samples of their work.

The pay and benefits a web professional may expect vary greatly by region. Be sure to look at other listings for web professionals to get an idea of what a competitive salary is in your area. Similarly, you should solicit bids from several different agencies or contractors to get an idea of the range of prices you can expect to pay for your particular web site.

Marketing on the Web

You have a wonderful new web site. You are ready to take your customer's orders and are prepared to answer their questions. But what if you opened your web site and no one looked at it? How to get *hits* (people looking at your web site) can be a very real problem. Getting the customers to your site is what web pages are all about. The speed of the Web makes your Marketing department's job even harder, as you need to have a marketing strategy that will withstand the new speed of Internet business.

A successful web marketing plan takes into account the major differences between the Web and standard print advertising. What worked in print doesn't always work on the Web. You will need to do some research to understand the new market. Even if you hire a marketing firm to draw up your web marketing plan, you will need to see what you are up against. Take some time and tour the Web for yourself. An afternoon spent surfing the Web is worth thousands in marketing dollars and is probably more productive. You will gain more than an insight on the competition and you will also start to understand the expectations of your web customers.

T IP: Your web marketing plan should be about more than just the colors on your web pages and the icons you choose; it is about how to get the millions of potential customers to your site so they can give you their money.

The Web is like a neighborhood—everybody seems to know what everybody else is doing. It is a fact of Internet life that what "that other site" did will affect how your site is viewed by your customers. If your competition's site is giving away green plastic ducks, you will need to know about it as soon as possible. (Free toys, contests, and premiums are great way to attract attention on the Web, but be prepared for tens of thousands of people to enter their names on your web site. It can be worth the publicity if you can afford it.)

Your web customers will likely be very different from your phone or mail customers. They may be younger and they will probably be better educated. The best estimates say that more than 25 percent of Americans are logging in daily and that this will double by the turn of the century. In addition, the demographics of the Internet show that it is not just a cross-section of the

7

American population. Internet users tend to be highly educated and make more money than the average American, and those spending the most time surfing are generally the highest educated and make the most money. While this may change over the next few years, most of your web audience for now is very different than television, magazine, or most direct mailing audiences. All of this should be reflected in your marketing strategy. Be sure to spend some time thinking about what you are saying as well as to whom you are saying it.

Publicizing Your Web Site

Once you have decided how you want your web site to come across to the customer, you will need to publicize it. Although some customers will use search services to find your site (discussed in the "Search Services" section later in this chapter), most of your customers will find your site by seeing your URL listed in some other media. It may seem odd that most people will initially connect to your site because they saw it somewhere other than online first, but the statistics show this to be true. Magazines rate the best at getting your web page to the right people: more then 35 percent of the people responding to a survey say they find web pages when they are listed in magazines, either in ads or feature articles. Business cards and stationery are also popular. URLs on television rate the lowest, but there is speculation that the numbers of hits generated from television spots is rising.

How do you get your customers to see your URL? The best way is to make it part of everything you send out of your office so you can use your existing advertising to bring your URL to your customers' attention. Having your URL printed as part of your letterhead or business cards is an easy way to make sure it gets to your customer. Advertisements, press releases, flyers, and other promotional materials should always have your URL on them as well. Start thinking of your web site like you think of an 800 or 888 number: as a way for customers to communicate with you inexpensively and to make purchases. Over the last few years, some standards have developed for how and where to display your URL (shown in Table 7-2).

As you can see from Table 7-2, your URL has just become part of your normal business practices. Treat it like you would treat your address and phone number: the more customers you can tell about it, the greater your potential market will be. URLs are printed on the sides of buses, painted on delivery trucks, and even printed on food boxes. Any ad campaign or promotion should include your URL, and everything you send out of your office should announce that you have a web site.

Where to Place Your URL	Placement Standards
Letterhead	Your URL should go on your letterhead just like your street address or phone number. It should be on its own line in the same typeface as the rest of the printing. You should always include the entire URL, starting with *http://*, such as *http://www.yourcompany.com*.
Business Cards	With the limited space on a standard business card, you may wonder if it is worth putting your URL on each card. Surveys show that URLs on business cards are a highly effective marketing tool. In fact, new customers may only have your business card before they contact your web page. Place the URL as the last line on the card under the address and phone numbers. It is often printed in a bold or italic font the same size as the rest of the text on the card.
Press Releases	Your URL should be a central feature of all press releases. It should be right at the top next to the phone numbers of your company's press relations contact or agency. (Note: You may even want to consider a press release about your new web site. It can be an effective way to generate interest in you new web presence.)
Television	If you purchase television spots, you should consider printing your URL on the screen at the end of your spot. It is OK for a voiceover to bring attention to your URL, but having them pronounce it is not usually practical.
Magazines	Anytime your company is mentioned in a magazine article or buys ad space in a magazine, your URL should be printed near your company name. Potential customers will visit your web site to get more information on the products or services they're reading about.

Ways to
Publicize
Your Web Site
Table 7-2.

7

Where to Place Your URL	Placement Standards
Catalogs	If your company does any mail order business, all of your catalogs should have your URL wherever you might put a phone number. Many customers are more likely to visit your web site than call your 800 number. Even if you don't send out mail order catalogs, circulars, or product lists, any mail to your customers should promote your web site.
Phone messages	Many small businesses leave their URL on their answering machine. This way, when they are unable to help a customer after-hours, the customer has a way to get information or to place an order on their web site. (Be sure to pronounce the entire URL carefully, spell it out, then pronounce it again on the outgoing message.)

Ways to
Publicize
Your Web Site
(*continued*)
Table 7-2.

You should note that not all publicity is good publicity and that there are some ways to avoid publicizing your URL—where doing so may land you on the Blacklist of Internet Advertisers. (A current list of these advertisers is kept at *http://www.cco.caltech.edu/~cbrown/bl*.) The Blacklist is a list of advertisers that have engaged in massive, unsolicited e-mail campaigns to personal e-mail boxes, or who have engaged in excessive, inappropriate posts to newsgroups to advertise services or products that have nothing to do with the topic of the newsgroup. This kind of advertising is almost certainly directly against any Internet service contracts you have signed and will certainly cost you customer revenue. If you engage in this type of advertising, your ISP is likely to cancel your account, costing you your web access and your web site's address. This will, in turn, take away your marketing momentum for people who are used to finding your web page at the same place. However, the penalties can be more severe than bad PR and lost business: those who launch massive e-mail campaigns have been successfully taken to court for the lost revenue they caused. Remember that your customers are paying for their Internet services, just like you pay for yours. Do not send unsolicited e-mail messages, no matter how easy or promising it seems. It is a breach of good manners that can land you in court.

High-Priced Marketing Options
If you have a great deal of money to spend on your new web site, you have many options for how to spend it. Increasing the amount you spend on your

web site often gets you many more customers on the Web. There seems to be a direct relation to how much you spend in your first year and how many people visit your site. If you feel like you really need to make your site known in the first year and you have a healthy marketing budget, the following list will give you some ideas of ways you can spend it to get instant publicity for your site:

♦ The Yahoo! search service will showcase new sites on its "Web launch" service. This has been proven to provide massive exposure to your site, probably more than a million people will visit your site in the first month. Go to *www.yahoo.com* for more information.

♦ Consider buying a *banner*—a small advertisement at the top of the screen—on a popular search service or a site for a large, related business. For example, if you are selling auto parts, you may be able to advertise through a car dealer's web site.

♦ Television spots, both local and national, can generate millions of hits over the course of a few months. Simply adding your URL to television spots you are already running may help generate lots of hits without paying for an entirely new television spot.

♦ Large direct-mail campaigns that announce your web site can have a massive effect on the traffic on your sites. Mailing out toys and chocolates are both favorites of web surfers and are almost guaranteed to get you a visit from most people who receive your advertisements.

♦ A billboard, either locally or in a market that you think would be useful, will help get your site out into the public mind-set. Don't forget to make your URL readable. Similarly, a banner with your URL pulled behind an airplane will generate a great deal of attention for your web site. It will reach more people than most billboards, but may only be practical if you have your own short domain name.

Web Marketing on a Budget

7

Not every web marketing idea requires that you have television ads or that you send thousands of small plastic toys all around the country. A major benefit of business on the Internet is that it is relatively inexpensive, and that advertising can be even cheaper.

After you have plastered your URL on every piece of paper in your office, the next step is to make sure that those who will look for you on the Web can find you easily. This means registering with several of the search services and then starting to work your existing professional connections to generate links to and from your site.

Search Services

The people who don't find your web page by seeing the URL printed in a magazine or on the business card of one of your company representatives will most likely find you through a search service. A search service is a listing agency, much like a phone directory. Search services help web surfers find what they are looking for by running a search for all the sites about a particular topic. Most web surfers will turn to search services to find your company if they try *http://www.companyname.com* and it doesn't work. Harbinger will register you with some of the largest search services, but not all of them. You should take the time to make sure your web site is in all the search services it needs to be.

There are two basic types of search services: listing services and crawling services. *Listing services* work like a web site encyclopedia: they will only list the sites that have been listed with them. *Crawling services* will search the entire web and return a list of all existing web pages about a particular topic. There is no way to make sure a crawling service will send customers to your page, but there are techniques they use to find pages that you can take advantage of.

Listing services require that you register with them. One of the largest listing services is Yahoo! (*http://www.yahoo.com*). Yahoo! is also the oldest listing service on the Web, and many web surfers rely on it to get to the sites they want. If you have chosen to host your site with Harbinger they will register you with Yahoo! and a few other sites.

If you have your own independent ISP, you will need to register yourself with Yahoo! and the other large listing services. You can either do this by going to each individual site you'd like to register with or you can use the !Register-It! registration service (*http://www.register-it.com*). !Register-It! takes your web site's important information and submits it to all the major listing services. Submit-it! (*http://www.submit-it.com*) is another excellent registration service. Both services provide you with a list of the services they register you with on their respective web sites.

It's worth noting that these registration services have not yet figured out how to solve the hardest problem about registering with listing services: what to use as keywords for your site. Since listing services work like encyclopedias, your web site needs to be listed in the right categories so your web customers can find it when they go looking. If you are listed under the wrong keywords, when your customers run a search looking for your type of business, the listing services will not lead those customers to your site. It might be a good idea to do your own searches on a few listing services before you register your site so you understand the lexicon of web site listing.

Crawling services are more complex and can also be more accurate. In order for your customers to find your site when they run a search on a crawling service you have to make sure your site has the right words on it. Crawling services search the Web every day. They look for new or different sites and create a current database of what is listed on the pages. Then when a customer runs a search, the crawler returns thousands of sites that have those topics on their pages. The best-known crawling service is AltaVista (http://altavista.digital.com), but there are many other excellent crawling services available.

Since crawlers look at the content of your site, they can lead customers directly to you. However, the manner in which a crawler catalogs a site varies greatly from day to day and from site to site, and your web site may never come up in a crawler search. The best you can do is make sure your pages include the most common keywords a customer might use to search for your site. One of the most effective ways to do this is to list on your site the slang and technical terms that a customer might know about your type of business. The crawling services will find these terms and add them to their catalogs.

Links

If your customers don't find your web site with a search service or see your URL printed somewhere, there is still another way to find you: they can follow a link to your web site. These customers may not be looking for your specific company, but they will be looking for someone like you. This type of customer is just spending time following links from one page to another looking for new and interesting sites. Although this way will likely get you the fewest new web customers, compared to the other ways of advertising your web site, using web links to attract new customers still has the potential for massive revenues and should be given serious consideration.

To get the web surfers to your site, you need to have links to your web site on lots of other pages. *Link exchanges* (where you link to someone else's page and they link to your page) have made the Web interactive and interlinked. The ability to move from one related site to another can bring you customers, but only if your links are on other pages. The link exchanges you used to create the list of links on your Links worksheet in PeachLink are just the start of it. You need to make sure that you have links to your pages from all possible sources.

The first step to creating a strong network of links is to work your existing business connections to create new web links. If you know a CEO or board member of a related company, drop them an e-mail and let them know you

7

would like to exchange links on your respective web pages. Or you could call any of your business connections and propose a link exchange. (Most business contacts will be interested in swapping links—it's a win for everyone.) A sample e-mail to create a link exchange with a business contact might look like this:

```
To: John Doe

From: Sally Jones, Big Business Marketing Director


Subject: Let's exchange links

Hi John!

I just looked at your company's new web site. It looks great! I love the way
you put the ducks on the first page; it's really an attention grabber.

Have you seen our site? It's at http://www.ourcompanyname.com. Take a look some-
time. We're really proud of the way the company logo works with the text and
background.

Now that we're both on the Web, I was wondering if you wanted to exchange links
on our web pages. Send me mail and let me know what you think.

Congrats again on your new site. I'll talk to you at the conference next week.

Sally
```

Once you have exchanged links with all your business connections, there are still more ways to create links to your site. One of the most popular is the *web ring*. A web ring is where you and a group of related businesses create links to each other's pages so that you navigate from page to page in a large circle or ring. Your job would be to link to the sites before you and after you in the list. Once everyone has linked to their web ring neighbors, the head hooks to the tail and you have a circle of links. This will enable your customers to find your site even if they only find one of the related sites; they can follow the ring around until they reach your site. Adding sites to the web ring is simply a matter of changing links on two sites (which will be coordinated by the appointed web ring administrator). Web rings are becoming more popular, paralleling the growing use of search services as a method for customers to find sites (since they ensure more hits for more people).

Another way to create links to your site is to search the web for any good press about your products or company. Many magazines have gone online and more have plans for extensive web sites, including reviews of millions of products. If you can find a link to a review for a product you sell or make, you should contact the system administrator (or webmaster) for that web site via e-mail (the webmaster's e-mail address is usually listed at the bottom of the pages). Let them know that you have a web site for those products and suggest that they link the review to your pages, in exchange for which you'll be glad to link to them from your web site. What better way to gain new customers than from a positive review of what you sell?

Marketing Benefits from the Web

The Web is not just something for you to advertise with, it is also a wonderful way to test new strategies and to ask your customers marketing questions. Your PeachLink site has a Guestbook with customizable questions. Those questions are perfect for you to gauge customer response to new products, new marketing ideas, and even about the marketing of existing products.

Research on the Web is almost painless for the amount of information it generates. You can ask web customers almost any question and they are likely to answer. The love of filling out surveys on the Web can greatly benefit all of your marketing plans, not just those focusing on the Web. Surveys on the Web can be even more effective than phone surveys: one recent survey generated 150 times more responses in two days on the Web than they would have generated in the same time by phone.

What questions should you ask your web customers? That depends a great deal on the information you are trying to generate. If you want to know what customers will think of a new product, you might create a custom page that details the product and then ask questions about it. Web customers are notoriously opinionated and they will be happy to tell you what they think. You can even try first introducing a new product on the Web as a cheap, easy way to see how a new item will be accepted. A new product promotion like, "You can only get it on our web page" can be a big draw to your site as well as helping you gauge response. You can also ask your customers what they would change or improve about your products.

7

If nothing else, web surveys provide an inexpensive and effective way to get to know your web customers. Those who fill out the surveys on your page are either already your customers or are probably considering becoming customers. What better survey base can you ask for?

TIP: Make sure you have clear, well-worded questions that accurately present the points you want to make. Consider having a few people outside of your office take a look at your survey questions before you post them on the Web.

Other Resources

There are numerous books available on every aspect of the Internet. The following are some books that you may want to purchase for further information on creating an effective web site and marketing your company over the Web:

♦ *The Non-Designer's Web Book* by Robin Williams and John Tollett (Peachpit Press, 1998). This book tells you everything you need to know about web basics, the elements of web page design, technical information such as using graphics, fonts, and colors, and how to maintain and promote your web page. This book is particularly attractive in that it is printed in color, so you can clearly see the differences in choosing one combination over another.

♦ *Creating Commercial Web Pages* by Laura Lemay and Brian Murphy (SamsNet, 1996). This book provides information for the intermediate and advanced user on how to add technical features to your web pages. The book comes with a CD-ROM containing a variety of utilities, sample applications, and programs.

♦ *Web Marketing Cookbook* by Janice King, Paul Knight, and James H. Mason (Wiley and Sons, 1997). This book will help you adapt your sales and marketing material to the Web, generate publicity, and market your company's services online. The book comes with a CD-ROM with a variety of templates, resources, and tools.

♦ *Webmaster Answers: Certified Tech Support* by Chris Ditto (Osborne/ McGraw-Hill, 1997). This handy troubleshooting guide is packed with answers to frequently asked questions about Web page creation and management, as well as solutions to common problems.

♦ *NetMarketing* by Bruce Judson (Wolff New Media, 1996). This book introduces you to the concepts of commercial web design by showing you commercial web sites for dozens of large corporations.

♦ *Getting Hits* by Don Sellers (Peachpit Press, 1997). This book focuses specifically on how to get more people to visit your web site by registering with search engines, using Internet newsgroups, and inspiring repeat business and recommendations from your customers.

There are new books appearing all the time. Check the bookstores and publishing web sites for new listings frequently.

 **Summary**

In this chapter, you saw how to design and create a web site with PeachLink, and how to use Netscape Navigator to view the web pages you've created. You also saw how to publish your web site and become a part of the World Wide Web. In the next chapter, you'll see how to take the orders your web site generates and import them into Peachtree Accounting. You'll also see how to handle credit card orders and e-mail confirmations.

8

Using PeachLink
Order Processor

In the last chapter, you saw how to design and create a
web site with PeachLink and how to use Netscape
Navigator to view the web pages you created. You also
saw how to publish your web site and become a part
of the World Wide Web. In this chapter, you'll see
how to take the orders your web site generates and
transfer them to Peachtree Accounting. You'll also

learn how to handle credit card orders, process sales orders, and enter new web customers in Peachtree Accounting.

What Is PeachLink Order Processor?

PeachLink Order Processor allows you to seamlessly add orders from your web site to your business in Peachtree Accounting. PeachLink Order Processor logs onto your account through an open Internet connection, retrieves the order from your web site, and displays them in the PeachLink Order Processor window. You select the orders to pass on to Peachtree Accounting and PeachLink Order Processor formats the order to conform to Peachtree Accounting's standard order procedure.

Using PeachLink Order Processor and your web site makes taking orders easier than any other method of order collection. PeachLink Order Processor can make your web site become profitable, helping your customers make their purchasing decisions.

PeachLink Order Processor installs as part of the PeachLink installation process, so there is nothing additional you have to do to install it. You're able to start processing orders from your web site immediately.

Getting to Know PeachLink Order Processor

To start PeachLink Order Processor, select PeachLink Order Processor from the Peachtree Accounting program folder on the Start menu. The PeachLink Order Processor password dialog box appears:

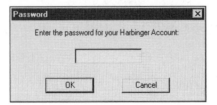

NOTE: PeachLink Order Processor will only ask for your password if you have selected to allow orders with credit cards on your web site. You can turn this option off in the Options menu.

Enter your Harbinger password and click OK. The main PeachLink Order Processor window appears, as shown in Figure 8-1.

Take a moment to get to know PeachLink Order Processor. As you can see in Figure 8-1, the PeachLink Order Processor window has the following three parts: the upper left portion of the window is the Order InBox, which shows orders to be processed; the lower left portion of the window is the Processed Orders List, which shows the orders that have been sent to Peachtree Accounting; and the large portion of the window on the right is the Details screen, which shows the details of each order as it is highlighted.

The PeachLink Order Processor window is somewhat different from the Peachtree Accounting windows you may already be familiar with. Table 8-1 shows the menu items and what they do.

You'll see how to use the menu and its options later in this chapter.

PeachLink Order Processor has a toolbar for selecting some of the most commonly used menu options. The buttons and their descriptions are listed in Table 8-2.

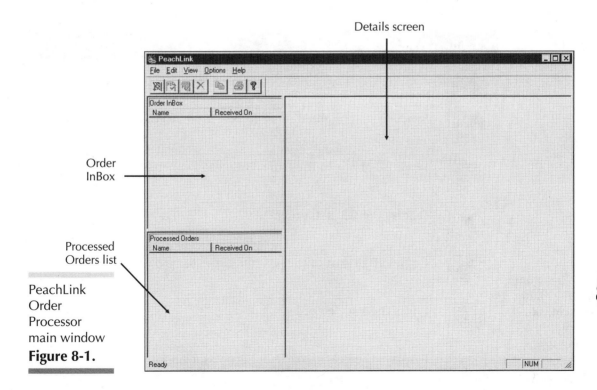

Details screen

Order InBox

Processed Orders list

PeachLink Order Processor main window

Figure 8-1.

Menu
Items on the
PeachLink
Order
Processor
Window
Table 8-1.

Menu	What It Does
File	Retrieves, processes, deletes, or prints orders; exits PeachLink Order Processor
Edit	Cuts, copies, and pastes information within orders
View	Turns the toolbar and status bar on or off; alters the split screen
Options	Turns "accept credit cards" on or off; alters security
Help	Accesses help files

Using PeachLink Order Processor

PeachLink Order Processor allows you to handle orders taken from your web site. The following procedures will show you how to process the orders, detailing the steps from retrieving orders from the Internet, to adding them to Peachtree Accounting.

Toolbar Icons
on the Main
PeachLink
Order
Processor
Window
Table 8-2.

Icon	What It Does
	Logs in and gets new orders
	Sends the highlighted order to Peachtree Accounting
	Sends all orders in the Order InBox to Peachtree Accounting
	Deletes the selected order
	Copies all or part of the selected order to be pasted as text
	Prints the selected order
	Displays the PeachLink Order Processor About window

Retrieving Orders

You begin by logging on to your ISP. PeachLink Order Processor must have a live Internet connection to retrieve the orders from your Internet site. Next, start PeachLink Order Processor, enter your password, and click OK. The main PeachLink Order Processor appears (refer to Figure 8-1).

To start retrieving orders, select the Retrieve Orders option from the File menu. The Get Orders dialog box will appear, showing your order downloading progress. PeachLink Order Processor connects to your ISP and downloads orders. After all the orders have been downloaded, they appear in the Order InBox. If there are no new orders from your web site, a "No New Orders Waiting" message will appear in the Get Orders dialog box.

Once you have downloaded the orders, you need to verify them.

Verifying Orders

The free information exchange that characterizes the Internet helps your web site do a lot of business. Your web site can make you money without any direct attention from you. In fact, your web site may generate orders simply because your customers don't have to deal with sales people. However, the technology is still fairly new and many people aren't used to it; they may not get the order correct, they may leave information out, or they may even lose their connection such that the information can become corrupted. Moreover, the fact that the Internet is unmonitored creates the potential for intentionally bogus sales orders generated by people surfing the Web at random (sort of the Internet equivalent of prank phone calls).

In order to determine if an order is valid, you will need to look at the details of each order. Click on an order in the Order InBox to highlight it and the details will be displayed in the Details screen to the right.

Valid orders will have most of the contact fields completed and will have one or more ways to easily reach the customers who entered them. Current customers will be easy to recognize. New customers will often request information from you before they place an order or sometimes will include requests for information within their new order. Invalid orders are frequently obvious: requests for an excessive number of items; an easily recognized, phony mailing address (1600 Pennsylvania Avenue, for example). Invalid orders rarely have contact information or other fields completed. Bogus orders entered by pranksters can cause expensive mistakes. Check all unusual orders to make sure they are real.

8

In general, it is a good idea to phone or fax new customers to confirm their orders. It is also a good idea to confirm orders with your existing customers for the first few months after you start taking orders online, to make sure that they are comfortable with the process.

PeachLink Order Processor allows you to delete any order. Simply highlight the order you want to delete and select Delete from the File menu. You can also click the delete button on the tool bar.

Transferring Orders to Peachtree Accounting

Once you have verified your orders, you are ready to transfer them to Peachtree Accounting. Start your Peachtree Accounting software and open your company so PeachLink Order Processor can transfer the orders to the company files.

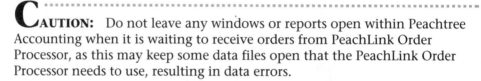 **C**AUTION: Do not leave any windows or reports open within Peachtree Accounting when it is waiting to receive orders from PeachLink Order Processor, as this may keep some data files open that the PeachLink Order Processor needs to use, resulting in data errors.

PeachLink Order Processor directly interfaces with Peachtree Accounting. You can transfer orders to Peachtree Accounting individually or as one large batch.

Transferring a Single Order

Highlight the order you want to transfer to Peachtree Accounting. Select the Process Selected option from the File menu. (You can also click the Process Order button on the PeachLink Order Processor toolbar.) The Process Orders dialog box will appear, showing you the progress of the orders being sent to Peachtree Accounting.

When the order has been transferred, Peachtree Accounting will open a new sales order containing the information from the web order. You can now process the sales order as described in "Processing Orders in Peachtree Accounting" later in this chapter. (If your web order contained credit card information, see "Transferring Credit Card Information" later in this section.)

Transferring All Orders

Select Process All from the File menu. (You can also click the Process All Orders button on the PeachLink Order Processor toolbar.) Again, the Process Orders dialog box will appear, informing you that all the orders are being processed.

When the orders have been transferred, Peachtree Accounting will open a new sales order containing the information from the first web order in the batch. You can now process the sales order as described in the "Processing Orders in Peachtree Accounting" section, later in this chapter. (If any of your web orders contained credit card information, see "Transferring Credit Card Information" next.)

Transferring Credit Card Information

Credit card numbers are not automatically transferred to Peachtree Accounting. To transfer credit card information to Peachtree Accounting, you must copy it from PeachLink Order Processor and post it into Peachtree Accounting. The easiest way is to cut the credit card information from PeachLink Order Processor and paste it into the appropriate field in Peachtree Accounting. You can store this information at the customer level, in custom fields, or in the Peachtree Accounting invoice note.

You will also need to independently verify the credit availability of the credit card number given on the web order. This verification step may be a good first line of defense when trying to establish whether an order is genuine. If a credit card verification fails, you can contact the customer via the contact information from the web order form.

Processing Orders in Peachtree Accounting

When you transfer an order to Peachtree Accounting, it will use the information to create a new sales order in the Peachtree Accounting Sales Order window, as shown in Figure 8-2.

The Sales Order window is similar to the standard Peachtree Accounting Sales Order window; however, PeachLink Order Processor alters many of the fields that you usually are responsible for. PeachLink Order Processor inserts information in some customer fields, some line item fields, and takes advantage of fields Peachtree Accounting normally leaves blank. The following shows you the changes PeachLink Order Processor makes to the Peachtree Accounting sales order form.

 NOTE: Fields that are the same as in the Peachtree Accounting Sales Order window are not listed here.

8

Customer ID   Enter the customer ID. Your web customer may have entered this on the web page. If your customer did not enter this field on their web order, and you know they are not a new customer, you can select the customer ID from the drop-down list. (If the customer ID field is entered by the customer, this information will appear automatically.) If it is a new

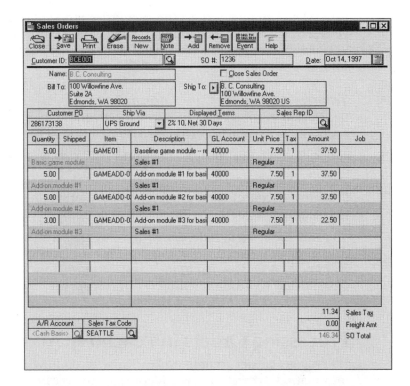

Sales Order
window, with
information
from several
sample orders
Figure 8-2.

customer, you will need to add them as a customer. (See "Adding Web
Customers" later in this chapter.)

When you select the customer ID, Peachtree Accounting enters the customer
name, Bill To, and Ship To addresses in the appropriate fields. If your
customer has entered different information on the web order, you may
need to update your customer information within Peachtree Accounting.
Peachtree Accounting will also enter customer defaults such as the Ship Via
information, Displayed Terms, Sales Rep ID, GL Account, A/R Account, and
the Sales Tax Code in the appropriate fields.

SO #   Peachtree Accounting automatically increments the sales order
number, or invoice number, for your web order. You are also supplied with a
purchase order number by PeachLink Order Processor, which is inserted into
the Customer PO field.

Date   Enter the date for the invoice if you want to change it from the
default inserted by PeachLink Order Processor. Click the Calendar icon or
right-click in this field to display the date-selection calendar.

Ship To   Peachtree Accounting displays the default shipping address from the customer record in this field. You can select an alternate Ship To address by clicking the button and selecting from the Ship To Address window (not shown). The customer record you entered earlier can have up to nine Ship To addresses to select from. Click the "Drop Ship" box in the Ship To Address window if you want this to be a *drop shipment*; that is, if you want your vendor to ship the order directly to your customer. When you enter or modify information for one of the Ship To addresses, Peachtree Accounting updates the customer record appropriately.

REMEMBER: Verify in PeachLink Order Processor that the customer has not entered a drop-ship address in the special instructions field or in the standard address fields. The only way to do this is to crosscheck the information in PeachLink Order Processor with the information as it appears in Peachtree Accounting.

Customer PO   Peachtree Accounting displays the default PO number assigned by PeachLink Order Processor in the customer record. You should not change this default PO since it will help you identify web orders from this customer. The information displayed here will be printed on the customer invoice.

Ship Via   Peachtree Accounting displays the default shipping method for the customer (if you set one up in the customer record). You can select an alternate shipping method by clicking the button to the right of the field and selecting a shipping method from the drop-down list. Keep in mind the shipping methods displayed on your web site. If a customer has a standing arrangement for a shipping method other than the one entered on the web order, you may want to contact that customer and verify how they would like their order shipped.

Sales Rep ID   Peachtree Accounting displays the default sales rep ID you entered for the customer (if you set one up). You may want to enter a dummy sales rep that stands for your web orders. This would allow you to find all of your web orders with greater ease and you can tally the total sales for your web site on your sales information screens. Creating a dummy sales rep to stand for your web site orders may help you figure the revenue and profits your web site brings in.

8

Line Items   PeachLink Order Processor adds all the line items from the order to your invoice. If you need to add or remove line items for any reason, you can do so with the Add or Remove toolbar button at the top of the Sales Order window. You can add up to 140 line items per invoice.

TIP: The invoice information you enter depends on the items and prices set up in the Inventory section and are related to the item prices on your web site. If the prices you see in the line items seem incorrect, check against the prices currently displayed on your web site.

Quantity   PeachLink Order Processor will enter the quantity of the item purchased as downloaded from the web order.

Item   PeachLink Order Processor will enter the item ID in this field. If you need to change the item ID or other item information, you can do so by clicking on the field you want to change.

Description   The default description (from Inventory) is the description for the item. You can enter up to 160 alphanumeric characters in this field.

GL Account   The default General Ledger account number is the General Ledger account number for the item. If you want, you can enter a different General Ledger account number for this item. This will be one of your Income accounts or, in the case of physical goods, a Cost of Goods Sold account.

Unit Price   The default unit price is the unit price for the item as displayed on your web site. If you have set up multiple price levels for an item in Inventory (in Peachtree Accounting), you can click the button or right-click in the field for a drop-down list of unit prices. If the customer is eligible for a lower price than the one displayed on your web site, you may want to confirm the new pricing with them the first time they place an order.

Tax   The default sales tax type is the sales tax type for the item. You can right-click in the field for a drop-down list of tax types.

Amount   Peachtree Accounting computes the extended amount from the unit price and the quantity. You can accept the computed amount or enter a different amount.

Job   The Job column appears only if you have set up a job through the Maintain Jobs window as described in the Peachtree Accounting manual (and in my earlier book, *Peachtree Complete Accounting for Windows Made Easy*

[Osborne/McGraw-Hill, 1997]). Enter the job ID that this invoice should be applied to.

A/R Account   Enter the General Ledger account to apply the invoice to. The default entry for this field is the last account entered in the field. This will be an Asset or Accounts Receivable account type. Group these accounts as you would your departments or units, or just summarize the whole company into one account. You will be able to get aging and payment reports from Accounts Receivable to use as an analysis tool.

Sales Tax Code   The default entry for this field is the default sales tax code for the customer.

Sales Tax   Peachtree Accounting computes the sales tax based on the tax rate specified by the sales tax code and the total amount of the invoice. You can accept the computed amount or enter a different amount.

Freight Amount   Enter the freight charges (if any) for this sales transaction.

SO Total   Peachtree Accounting computes the invoice total as the sum of the sales tax, the freight amount, and the invoice amount. This field is display-only.

When you are satisfied with your entries, you can save and post the invoice by clicking Save on the toolbar. You can also post the invoice and print it by clicking Print on the toolbar. You will need to go to the Reports menu if you want to print a batch of invoices.

NOTE: Peachtree Accounting will automatically print the invoice if you save or post an invoice without an invoice number in the SO# field.

Adding Web Customers

If your web order is from a new customer, you will need to set them up as a customer in your Peachtree Accounting database. There are four types of information you enter to set up customer records: general customer information, customer invoice defaults, custom fields, and customer history. You may also need to enter a beginning balance for the customer. PeachLink Order Processor enters most of this information for you when it processes an order. However, in case you need to fill some of it in manually, this section shows you how to enter all of this information.

8

Entering General Customer Information

From the Setup Checklist, click the "Enter customer records" item. (You can also display this window by selecting the Customers/Prospects option from the Maintain menu.) The Maintain Customers/Prospects window appears with the General folder already selected (as shown in Figure 8-3).

Enter information for a customer as follows:

Customer ID   Enter the customer ID. Customer IDs can be up to 20 characters long, and they can contain any characters except the asterisk (*), question mark (?),or plus sign (+). Although you have up to 20 characters to deal with, you should keep your customer IDs simple, perhaps 6 or 8 characters long. A common way to create a customer ID is to begin the ID with the first few letters of the customer's name, and follow that by a number. For example, if the customer's name is "Oberon Computers," the customer ID should be something like OBE001. If there is another company with the same first three letters, such as "Oberto & Calamari," their customer ID could be OBE002. Using the first few letters of the customer's name gives you a reasonably intuitive way of looking up the customer in the file, without requiring a lot of typing.

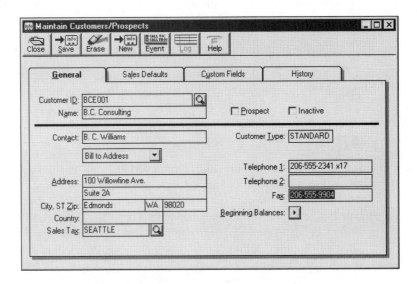

Maintain
Customers/
Prospects
window
showing the
General folder

Figure 8-3.

REMEMBER: As with General Ledger account IDs, customer IDs are case-sensitive, so Peachtree Accounting treats the customer IDs OBE001 and obe001 differently. You may want to set a policy that all letters in customer IDs be entered as capital letters.

Whatever you choose as a customer ID system, be sure that it can expand with the business. All the Accounts Receivable transactions that you enter for a customer are keyed to the customer ID. Once you set up a customer, you cannot change the customer ID without deleting the old ID and setting up a new one. Also remember that Accounts Receivable sorts customers on reports in order of the customer ID. If you are using just a six-digit number for each customer ID, you may have to look through many pages to find a particular customer.

Name   Enter the customer's name from the web order. You can enter up to 30 characters in this field. Accounts Receivable will list the customer name on customer invoices and statements, and on both the Aged Receivables report and the Invoice Register.

Prospect   Check this box to identify this customer as a prospect rather than an actual customer. Prospects are not included on the customer reports. Clearing the checkbox or creating an invoice will cause Peachtree Accounting to treat this record as a customer.

Inactive   Check this box to set the customer to "inactive" status. Although you can update the name and address information, Peachtree Accounting will warn you if you try to post a sale to an inactive customer. Peachtree Accounting will also display "<Inactive Customer>" in the drop-down lists of customers.

NOTE: Setting a customer to "inactive" may be easier than deleting the customer. If the customer should ever become active again after you deleted them, you would have to re-enter the customer information.

8

Contact   Enter the contact name for the customer. This field may be up to 20 characters. Accounts Receivable includes the customer contact name on the Customer List. If your web customer did not enter a contact name, you could put their e-mail address here.

Customer Type   This is a custom field in which you can enter up to eight characters to identify the type of customer or prospect. You can decide on a standard that assigns a customer type that starts with a "W" to all your new customers gained through your web site. This field allows you to group customers by their type, perhaps for printing statements or reports, and is especially helpful when you are trying to identify all the customers that have contacted you over the Web. For example, you might set up a customer-type system to group your web customers by geographic region, sales territory, type of business, type of purchase, or by the amount of money the customer is likely to spend in the future. For instance, for web customers that ordered in the third quarter of 1998 from Dallas, you can assign a customer type of "WDALL398." This field is case-sensitive.

Bill to/Ship to Addresses   Select one of the Bill To or Ship To options from the drop-down list. You can enter one Bill To and up to nine Ship To addresses for each customer. Your new web customers are likely to provide only one Ship To address with their first order, but it is possible that they will provide more as they place more orders.

Address   Enter the street address. If you have only one line of address information, enter it on the first line and leave the second line blank. This information will be stored under the appropriate Bill To or Ship To address option selected in the previous field.

City, ST Zip   Enter the city, state, and ZIP code for this address. This information will also be stored appropriately.

Country   Enter the country for this address. This information will also be stored.

Sales Tax   Enter the sales tax code for this customer. (Sales tax codes are set up as part of the Accounts Receivable setup process.) The default sales tax code you set up for a customer is automatically applied to customer sales.

Telephone 1   Enter the primary telephone number for the customer.

Telephone 2   Enter any other important telephone number for the customer. You could also enter the customer's e-mail address in this field.

Fax   Enter the fax number for the customer.

Entering Customer Sales Defaults

After you have entered the general customer information, click the Sales Defaults tab. The Sales Defaults folder appears, as shown in Figure 8-4. (You'll see how to enter a beginning balance for customers later.)

You set sales defaults for such things as the customer's sales rep (usually WEB for web customers, if you have set up WEB as a sales rep), shipping options, pricing level, and terms of sale.

As you can see, the information in the top part of the Sales Defaults folder is carried forward from the information you entered in the General folder. You can work with this customer or select another one by clicking on the magnifying glass or right-clicking in the Customer ID field. You can also change the name, prospect, and inactive information for the customer from this folder.

Enter the sales defaults as follows:

Sales Rep   Enter the ID of the sales rep for this customer, if any. The name of the sales rep must already be entered in your business's list of employees. You can set up a web sales rep in the Payroll portion of Peachtree Accounting.

GL Sales Acct   Enter the default General Ledger sales account for the customer's sales activity. (You will normally want to use an Income account.)

Maintain
Customers/
Prospects
window
showing the
Sales Defaults
folder

Figure 8-4.

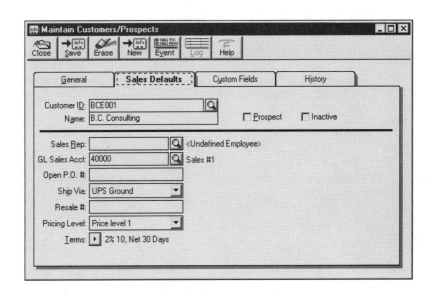

8

Open P.O. #   Enter the PO number for the customer as generated in PeachLink Order Processor. This is the open PO number for this customer. This default purchase order number will be set by each web order processed for this customer. You can override it during invoicing or leave it blank if there is no purchase order for this customer.

Ship Via   Enter the default shipper for this customer. This information is the default used for this customer's invoices (set up in Inventory). Shipping methods are entered as part of the default information for Inventory and are also displayed on your web site. If you need to change the shipping method, you may want to contact the customer to verify the change.

Resale #   Enter the customer's resale or seller's permit number. Resale or seller's permit numbers are required in many states for a customer to legally buy wholesale and to avoid paying sales tax on items purchased for resale. This field is display-only and does not affect the sales tax calculation. Set up and use an exempt tax authority and sales tax table for these customers. If you suspect your new web customer may be a retailer and they did not include their resale number, you will need to contact them to get it.

Pricing Level   Select the pricing level from one of five pricing levels.

NOTE: Pricing levels are usually based on customer purchasing patterns or group discounts, with price breaks for quantity or payment record. You have set a default pricing level on your web site. If this customer is eligible for a different pricing level, you will need to change it here and on each order they submit from your web site. If this is the case, you should send your web customers e-mail letting them know they can expect different pricing for each item every time they order from your web site.

Terms   The default value for payment terms appears to the right of the Terms button. (These terms are based on the customer defaults you entered when you set up the basic customer information in Peachtree Accounting.) Click the button to select the terms. The Customer Terms window appears:

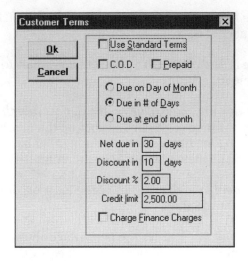

You use the Customer Terms window to select the terms you want to use for this customer. The default options and fields are the same as those you set in Peachtree Accounting in the Payment Terms folder of the Customer Defaults window.

Enter customer terms as follows:

Use Standard Terms   Check this box to use the standard terms for this customer (as determined in Peachtree Accounting in the Payment Terms folder of the Customer Defaults window).

NOTE: The default for any customer is to use the standard terms. When the Customer Terms window first appears, the Use Standard Terms checkbox is checked and all other options are grayed out. You must clear the Use Standard Terms checkbox to select another option in the window.

Due on Day of Month   Select this option to make payments due on a specific day.

Due in # of Days   Select this option to make payments due in a specific number of days.

Due at End of Month   Select this option to make payments due at the end of the month.

Net due in ... days/Due on the ... next month   Enter the number of days after the date of the invoice before the invoice comes due. Typically, you will enter 0 (due immediately) or a number between 10 to 30 days. If you have selected "Due on Day of Month," enter the day the invoice is due.

Discount in ... days   Enter the limit on discounts. This would typically be from 0 to 15 days.

Discount %   Enter the percentage allowed for the discount. Peachtree Complete Accounting will calculate the default discount amount for you based on this percentage.

Credit Limit   Enter the default credit limit for your customers. For example, you may want everyone to have a nominal $500.00 credit limit.

T **IP:** If you don't use or don't want to assign a credit limit, enter a large default, such as $10,000.00. This is a useful technique because whenever a customer exceeds their credit limit, Peachtree Complete Accounting gives you a warning. If you entered a credit limit of $0.00, Peachtree Complete Accounting would warn you every time you entered any activity for the customer.

Charge Finance Charges   Check this box if you want to charge finance charges for this customer.

When you are satisfied with your entries, click OK to accept the changes you've made, or Cancel to exit without changing the payment options.

There are no differences or special considerations for entering the information in the Custom Fields or History folders. Enter the information as you would for a typical customer, as described in the Peachtree Accounting manual.

When you are satisfied with your entries in all the folders in the Maintain Customers window, click Save to save the customer record in Peachtree Accounting.

Troubleshooting PeachLink Order Processor

Most problems with PeachLink Order Processor occur when it is interfacing with either your web site or Peachtree Accounting. The following are the four most common problems and their likely solutions:

♦ **Unable to retrieve orders.** Make sure you have a live Internet connection. Some services will disconnect you if your connection is not active for a few minutes. It is also possible that there are no new orders. Verify your connection and then try again. If the Get Orders dialog box says "No New Orders To Retrieve," no orders will appear in your Order InBox.

♦ **Credit card numbers do not appear in Peachtree Accounting.** Credit card numbers never automatically appear in Peachtree Accounting. You will have to manually copy and paste the numbers into Peachtree Accounting.

♦ **The prices for each line item in Peachtree Accounting are incorrect for this customer.** PeachLink Order Processor imports the prices as they appear on the web site. It is possible that some of your customers may not use the prices you have set in your web catalog. Simply change the prices in Peachtree Accounting when you process the order. It is also a good idea to confirm the new prices with the customer the first time they place an electronic order.

♦ **The customer address or Ship To address in Peachtree Accounting is incorrect.** The address you see in Peachtree Accounting is the one your customer entered when placing the order from your web site. In case of a conflict, you will need to return to PeachLink Order Processor and decide what address the customer entered. It is possible that the address is a Ship To address, or it may be a new address for the customer.

Summary

In this chapter, you've seen how to take the orders your web site generates and transfer them to Peachtree Accounting. You've also seen how to handle credit card orders, process sales orders, and enter new web customers in Peachtree Accounting. In the next chapter, you will see how to use HTML to expand your web site's capabilities, add your own clipart (for icons, backgrounds, and other files), and manipulate graphics files.

8

REMEMBER: For additional information on processing customer orders, see the Peachtree Accounting manual. For detailed information on using Peachtree Complete Accounting for Windows, look at *Peachtree Complete Accounting for Windows Made Easy* (Osborne/McGraw-Hill, 1997). For detailed information on using Peachtree Accounting for Windows, see *Peachtree Accounting for Windows Made Easy* (Osborne/McGraw-Hill, 1995).

Using Advanced PeachLink Features

In the preceding chapter, you saw how to use PeachLink Order Processor to add web site orders into your Peachtree database. You also saw how to add a new customer in Peachtree Complete Accounting for Windows and how to screen your web orders for accuracy in PeachLink Order Processor. In this chapter, you will see how to add clipart and backgrounds to the web site you created with PeachLink, and how to change the look of your web site by using HTML. You will also learn the basic concepts behind web page creation and HTML, and how to integrate your customer's web pages into your PeachLink web site.

Creating Clipart Sets

When you created your web site with PeachLink, you chose a set of clipart from the Choose Style content worksheet in the Design Web Site section of the Content List (recall Chapter 7, "Using PeachLink"). But what do you do if you want to use your own images as buttons on your web pages? How do you carry over the look of your in-house marketing documents onto your web page? How do you use images you have created in-house? In order to begin answering these questions, you will need to create a clipart set of your own that PeachLink can read and understand.

The first step in the process is creating copies of your images in GIF format (.GIF) using a graphics utility such as Paint Shop Pro.

NOTE: Paint Shop Pro is an award-winning graphics utility. A shareware version comes on the CD that accompanies this book. The examples and figures in this chapter show you how to manipulate graphic images using Paint Shop Pro.

Creating the Images

To create a complete clipart set you will need to have six separate, fairly small images. These images will become the clipart for each of the following six sections of your web site:

♦   Overview

♦   On-Line Catalog

♦   Current Customers

♦   Internet Resources

♦   Q & A

♦   Guestbook

Look at your images and decide which of the six categories each best represents.

Next, you'll need a folder on your system into which you can save the images after you have finished getting them in the correct format. PeachLink looks for graphic files in the C:\Harb\inp\info\icons directory (if C: is the drive you installed PeachLink to). Whenever you create a set of clipart, you need to save it to its own group. Since PeachLink currently ships with 13 groups of icons and clipart, you can put your first set of custom clipart into C:\Harb\inp\info\icons\group14. You will save the final versions of your images to this folder.

If your images are small and already in GIF format, you'll only have to rename them in order to use them in PeachLink. However, if you need to create smaller versions of your images, save the images in GIF format, or to make any other changes, you must do so in a graphics utility such as Paint Shop Pro.

If you do not already have Paint Shop Pro or some other graphics utility installed on your system, you will need one before working with graphic images. Information on installing Paint Shop Pro from the CD accompanying this book can be found in Chapter 11, "Peachtree Accounting Add-ons and Other Software."

To open Paint Shop Pro, select Paint Shop Pro 4 from the Paint Shop Pro program group in your Start menu. The Paint Shop Pro Registration screen will appear:

Click Start Paint Shop Pro. The Paint Shop Pro main window appears, as shown in Figure 9-1.

9

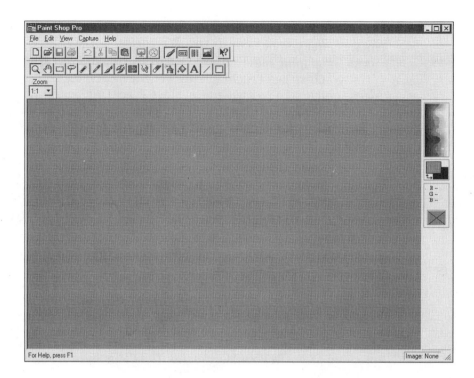

Paint Shop Pro
main window
Figure 9-1.

TIP: Paint Shop Pro is a powerful program with many features. The following instructions will show you how to do simple graphic manipulation, but you may want to spend some additional time exploring the things you can do with the program.

To work on a graphic image, you first need to open it in Paint Shop Pro. First, select File | Open, then select the image filename in the Open dialog box and click Open. Your image will open in the Paint Shop Pro window. To save the image in GIF format, select Save As from the File menu and choose "GIF - CompuServe" from the Save as Type drop-down list.

After your images are in GIF format, you will need to rename them to correspond to their appropriate sections and save them to the directory you created earlier (C:\Harb\inp\info\icons\group14). PeachLink looks for specific file names for each of the graphic images. Table 9-1 lists the six sections of the PeachLink web pages and the names your images must have to correspond with them.

Section	Filename
On-Line Catalog	catalog.gif
Overview	oview.gif
Current Customers	metal.gif
Internet Resources	resource.gif
Questions and Answers	faq.gif
Guestbook	gbook.gif

File Names for
Clipart Images
Table 9-1.

Although each image needs to be small (less than two inches on a side) to be used on the web pages, you can use Paint Shop Pro to alter the size of larger images. Select Resize from the Image menu. The Paint Shop Pro Resize window will appear:

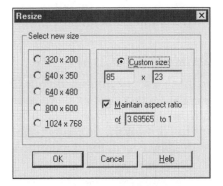

Enter the new dimensions for your image. Make sure the "Maintain aspect ratio" box is checked. After you have resized your image you can save it as you did before. Shrinking very large images will result in a loss of detail when the image is displayed on the user's monitor screen. Be sure to test your clipart for legibility before you publish it on your web site.

Creating the Group Image

After you have the final, correctly named versions of each image saved to the C:\Harb\inp\info\icons\group14 directory, you will be ready to create a composite image that combines your clipart images together. The group image will allow you to select your new clipart group in the PeachLink Choose Style worksheet. The image will not be displayed as part of the web page and can be saved in bitmap (.BMP) format.

9

To assemble this image with Paint Shop Pro, select File | Open, select oview.gif from the C:\Harb\inp\info\icons\group14 directory, and click Open. Repeat this procedure with resource.gif, metal.gif, gbook.gif, and faq.gif, until you have five images open in Paint Shop Pro. (There are only five images in a group image so you don't need to open the catalog.gif file.)

Now select New from the File menu. Paste a copy of each of the .GIF documents you have open into the new document. Line up each of the images so your group image looks like the sample shown here (from PeachLink's group1 directory):

When you are satisfied with your group image, select Save As from the File menu. Select "BMP - OS/2 or Windows Bitmap" from the Save as Type drop-down list and name the file group14.bmp. Click Save.

Finishing the Clipart Set

You now have a set of images in your C:\Harb\inp\info\icons\group14 directory that includes all six of your original images (in GIF format) and the composite image you created (group14.bmp). The last step in the creation process is to copy all the generic image files for buttons and other web page graphics used by PeachLink. Open the C:\Harb\inp\info\icons\group01 directory and copy all the files to your group14 directory except for the GIF files with the same names as the graphic files already in the group14 directory.

CAUTION: Do not copy over the files with the same names as your new graphic files. This will erase your images and you will need to start again.

You now have a new clipart set you can add to your web site from PeachLink.

Creating Custom Backgrounds

In addition to creating custom clipart sets, you can further customize your web site by including custom backgrounds. To use a custom background with your PeachLink web site, you must have an image that can be repeated, or tiled, seamlessly and one that will be appropriate as a backdrop for the text and clipart on your pages. Good background images are usually lightly textured and almost monochromatic. They should be small and have few features that will detract from the text and pictures that will go on top of them.

Backgrounds, like clipart images, must be in GIF format. (If you need to convert your image to GIF format, please see the preceding section, "Creating Clipart Sets," for information on using Paint Shop Pro to change image format.) Once you have a GIF version of your background, you will need to copy it to the directory where PeachLink can find it during the creation process. Copy your background image to C:\Harb\inp\info\ textures. This will allow you to choose the new background from the Choose Style worksheet in PeachLink's Design Web Site folder.

After you have created a custom background for your web site, be sure to experiment with the backgrounds before publishing. A background that looks good by itself may clash with the text or the clipart. Be conservative in your choices until you have a good idea of what works well in web page design.

If you would like a site customized beyond the level of changing clipart and backgrounds, you can create your own web pages with HTML.

What Is HTML?

HTML is an acronym for HyperText Markup Language. It is the basis for all web page creation. (Hypertext is a way of presenting text, pictures, and sounds in a document that lets you move through the document non-sequentially. Windows help files and web pages are examples of hyptertext documents.) HTML was originally developed as SGML (Standard General Markup Language) for government and university purposes. Years later, SGML was greatly simplified to create a new standard, HTML. HTML was adopted as the standard for the Web in the early 1980s. Today, HTML is used for almost all hypertext documents you see, including many of the help files in your favorite software packages.

HTML is a simple system for tagging information that creates web pages. Web browsers, such as Netscape, look at the tags in a text document and use them to format the page on your screen. Browsers have been programmed to find the HTML tags and display the text on your screen formatted as the HTML directs.

HTML is not difficult to write. Most HTML is simply a way to tell your browser things like "Center this line" or "Insert a hard return here." If you are

9

familiar with formatting text in any modern word processor, you should have no trouble writing text with HTML formatting tags.

What Is an HTML Tag?

An HTML tag holds HTML formatting instructions. A tag tells the browser what each piece of text should be, where it should go on the screen, and how it functions within the document. Tags tell the browser the difference between normal text, lists, links, titles, and even pictures.

Tags generally work with an on-off mentality. For example, to create bold text, you need to turn the bold notification on at the start of the text you would like to be bold, and then you need to turn the bold notification off at the end of that text. Each tag tells the browser something different, so it is important that you use the tags for their intended purpose. Do not try to put one kind of tag inside another tag unless it is specifically designed for it. Using a tag the wrong way can make someone's browser crash. The last thing you want your customer's computer to do at your site is crash. You can't make a sale if they can't see your site.

If you do not see a tag in this section that does what you would like, refer to the list of HTML references at the end of this chapter to find what you're looking for.

The Format of HTML Tags

To display web pages on browsers, the Internet community had to agree on a standard for HTML tags. The standard format for HTML tags is to enclose the name of the tag inside angle brackets. For instance, the tags for turning on and off italics are

```
<I> and </I>
```

Every tag in HTML follows this same format. Every tag is enclosed in angle brackets. The "on" tag is simply the tag symbol enclosed in the brackets. The "off" tag is the same symbol, which may be a word, preceded by a slash. For example, the feature that centers text it looks like

```
<CENTER>This text would be centered on the page</CENTER>
```

and would be displayed by a browser like the following:

This text would be centered on the page

Each individual tag must be spelled correctly and have the correct formatting for the browser to display it on your customer's screen. Tags are not case-sensitive—however, they will appear exclusively uppercase in this book for simplicity.

Creating HTML Documents

An HTML document is a simple text document. When you write the HTML documents that will become custom web pages, you will probably find it easiest to create them in your favorite word processor and then save them as "text only" with an .HTM extension.

Remember that none of the formatting created in your word processor will appear on the web page, so any page layout or other text formatting in the HTML document must have the appropriate HTML tags.

REMEMBER: Most computers that you publish your web pages to are case-sensitive. That means you will always access your HTML files by typing the name exactly as you typed it when you saved it. For this reason it is probably a good idea to save HTML documents and files always with all lowercase or all uppercase names.

Basic HTML Tags

The definition of an HTML document is that it contains HTML tags. These HTML tags tell your browser that the document can be displayed on your screen with the formatting and links that you have become familiar with on the Web. Since there are literally hundreds of possible tags in HTML (and thousands of ways to display text and pictures), the standards committee decided to define a basic HTML document as one containing the HTML elements shown in the following example:

```
<HTML>
<HEAD>
<TITLE>Basic HTML document</TITLE>
</HEAD>
<BODY>
<H1>This would be the header.</H1>
<P>And here is the start of the normal text.
From here you could create documents of any size.</P>
<P>With paragraph breaks whenever you want them.</P>
</BODY>
</HTML>
```

Figure 9-2 shows this document as displayed by a browser.

9

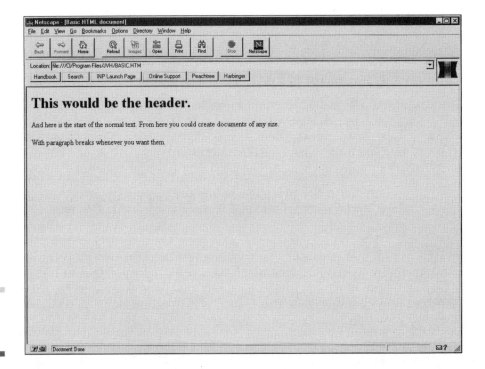

The tags in the basic HTML document tell the browser where the text should be displayed. Each of the tags, like <TITLE> and <H1>, tells the browser where the text should appear and in what format the text should be. The following several sections will show you in detail how each of the tags from this sample document works.

<HTML> Tag

The HTML tag is the first and last tag in your document. It tells your browser that this is an HTML document and not a graphic file or a program. Consequently, it must be the first tag in your document, and its corresponding </HTML> tag must be the last tag in your document.

Look again at the previous example, find the first and last lines, and note the placement of the <HTML> tag. The <HTML> tag is extremely important and must not be forgotten. Many web pages have crashed because their designer forgot this simple first step. In fact, if you are creating your web pages within a word processor, you may want to set up a document template for all of your HTML documents: one that has some of the basic tags, like <HTML>, and the other tags described in this section. This way you won't forget "the basics" when you are creating new HTML documents.

<HEAD> Tag

The <HEAD> tag tells the browser to expect the title of the document and heading commands that deal with the format or nature of the document, as well as the web page titles and other formatting elements. In fact, the web page title and formatting elements belong within the <HEAD> tag. All HTML documents must have a <HEAD> tag.

<TITLE> Tag

The title tag contains the title of the document and is intended to give some basic information to your customers. The text between <TITLE> and </TITLE> will be displayed on the title bar of the browser window. In Figure 9-2, the title bar of the window reads "Netscape - [Basic HTML document]," corresponding to the text placed between the <TITLE> and </TITLE> tags. The <TITLE> tags must be within the <HEAD> and </HEAD> tags.

It is a good idea to include a useful title with your document. If your customers bookmark your page, or even if they simply want to find out what it is about, they will be looking at the title. The information in the <TITLE> tag is also sometimes used by search services and could affect who finds your page. It is also considered good Net etiquette to give meaningful titles to your documents. A classic example given in many HTML-basics books is of the new web-page designer that created a web site with "Page One," "Back Page," and "Front Page" page titles. This type of titling can only confuse your customers since they won't necessarily understand what "Back Page" means nor how to use it. Creating useful titles for your documents makes your customer's visit to your site more understandable.

<BODY> Tag

The <BODY> tag tells the browser to look for the body text, the text and links that make up your web page and represent the bulk of the document. The <BODY> tag comes right after the </HEAD> tag, informing the browser that the formatting and title information is finished and that the bulk of the information that is to be displayed to the screen has begun.

Inside the <BODY> tags of your document, you will place all of the text and graphics, as well as the links and lists that will be displayed to your customer's screen. The <BODY> tag is one of the few HTML tags meant to enclose many other tags. The </BODY> tag will end the body of your document, and only the </HTML> tag follows it.

Header Tags

Header tags create text in larger and bolder fonts within your HTML document. There are six header tags in the format <H1>, <H2>, <H3>, and so on up to <H6>. Unlike the <HEAD> tag, these tags tell the browser how to

9

display text in the document. Header text is larger and bolder than standard text. Headers go inside the <BODY> tag, and tend to precede the bulk of the text on your page.

<H1> defines the largest, boldest text on your page. <H1> is analogous to a title in a standard word processing document. In general, it displays on the top of the page and is usually the first part of the <BODY>.

Generally speaking, it's a bad idea to use all six levels of header on one web page as the page will look too "busy" and be difficult to read. It is more likely that you will only need one or two header levels to create an adequate introduction on your page. You should also carefully plan what will go in each header: it is a good idea to start with <H1>, but not necessary. You can also skip header numbers. For instance, you can have <H1> and then <H4> with no intervening headers (of course, you must close <H1> with </H1> before you go on to <H4>). You may want to experiment with each header level and how they look on your own browser before you use them in your web pages.

Paragraphs and Hard Returns

Just like in your word processor, paragraph marks and hard returns define when a new paragraph starts or a line ends. Since HTML is not dependent on the formatting you see on your screen as you write it, you must insert these line breaks with HTML tags instead of simply pressing ENTER on your keyboard. Also, the line wrap you see on your word processor has no effect on how the text is displayed by the browser. The following examples appear differently in a word processor, but will display the same on a browser screen:

Example One

```
This is line one.
This is line two.
```

Example Two

```
This is line one. This is line two.
```

In fact, both of the examples will appear on your browser screen like Example Two. The new line and hard returns expected in Example One are not interpreted by the browser without the <P> and </P> tags.

<P> is called the paragraph mark. You place <P> at the start of your new line, and </P> at the end of one. For instance, to make Example One display in a browser on two lines, the HTML would have to look like this:

```
<P>This is line one.</P>
<P>This is line two.</P>
```

<P> tells your browser that you are starting a new paragraph and </P> tells the browser you have just ended one. When you are creating text for your web page, you will want to use <P> in situations where you would normally hit the ENTER key in a word processor. The browser will line-wrap the text between the <P> and </P>, thus making the length of a line dependent on the width of the screen displayed by your customer's browser. It will create some extra space before a <P> mark and after a </P> mark to help distinguish a paragraph from surrounding text, images, or links.

If you do not want the extra space created by the <P> mark, or if you simply would like to control when a line ends, you can use the <BR> mark.
 is referred to as a "break." Break tells your browser that the line ends at that point and it is one of the few tags that has no corresponding off tag. </BR> means nothing to your browser. It is HTML convention to make only limited use of the <BR> feature, since some of your customers may be making use of the line wrap feature to get as many words on their screen as possible. The most common use of <BR> is when you need several lines of space before or after text. For example:

```
<P>This is the start of my text. It will have several lines of
blank space to force you to scroll down your window.<BR>
<BR>
<BR>
<BR>
Now you are at the bottom.</P>
```

Since <BR> does not create the extra space, you can also use it inside <P> to control line breaks within your paragraph. This is not a common usage, but you could do this for a dramatic effect like

```
<P>It was a dark and stormy night.<BR>
At least that's what he said.<BR>
But I didn't believe him.</P>
```

Either way <BR> will give you a hard return without the extra white space before the tag like <P> will.

REMEMBER: Only <P> and <BR> will allow you to control the end of a line. All lines without these tags will be formatted by line wrap, regardless of how they look on your word processor screen.

Now you are ready to learn more about HTML. The best way to begin understanding how HTML works (after you've learned the basics) is to look at HTML other people have written for their own pages. To see the HTML text of a web page, select View Source from the View menu on your browser's menu bar. This will open a window showing the underlying HTML document of a web page. Although some pages may have extremely complicated HTML, it is not required to create a nice looking page. Look for the basic structure of HTML that you are familiar with when you look at other pages. Look for the <HTML> and <HEAD> tags, as well as all the other tags introduced in this section. Examples from the Web will give you ideas on how to improve the HTML you write.

More HTML

Now that you can create a web page with HTML, including text with controlled line breaks, how do you include links and pictures on your pages like you see on other web pages? How do you make lists and other page-layout decisions? There are HTML commands to help answer these and many other questions you might have.

After plain text, the most common items on web pages are *links*. The following are four broad categories of links you can create with HTML:

♦ **Page links** When you click a page link, you jump to another page or an entirely different web site.

♦ **Graphic links** Graphic links insert a picture, such as a scanned photo, a design, or a graphic file, into your web page.

♦ **File links** When you click a file link, you start downloading a file.

♦ **E-mail links** When you click an e-mail link, you can send e-mail to a predefined address.

To create any of these four links, you use HTML tags to tell the browser how to format and display the link.

Creating a Page Link

Page links let you connect to other web pages within your site or in another site entirely. Links usually appear as blue underlined text. (You have already seen page links in the pages you created in Chapter 7, "Using PeachLink.") The Internet Resources page you created, shown in Figure 9-3, is an example of how links are often integrated into a web site.

NOTE: When you link to another web site, you will probably want to link to their home page unless you have a prior agreement with their site manager.

To insert a page link you need to learn a new kind of HTML tag, the <A HREF=> tag. Links to other pages use the URL for the page as a name in the tag, so instead of the standard tag like <BODY>, page links have tags like <A HREF= "basic.html">, where basic.html is the name of the page you are linking to. It is turned off with a </A>.

Suppose you want to create a link inside a block of text. In the following example, the bold phrase will take you to a web page when you click it:

I found a really great page on monitor problems and fixes. **The monitor page** has lots of information that other pages lack. You should really check it out.

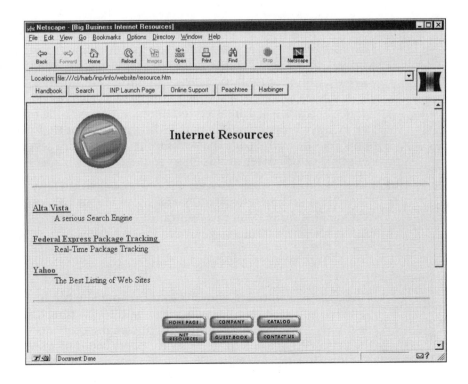

Internet
Resources
page
Figure 9-3.

The corresponding HTML would look like

```
<P>I found a really great page on monitor problems and fixes.
<A HREF="http://www.monitorwurld.com/monitor.html">The monitor page</A> has
lots of information that other pages lack. You should really check it out.</P>
```

As you can see from the example, a link to a page has three parts: the URL, the text, and the </A>.

The URL

The URL tells the browser which page to link to and is placed directly after the equal sign and enclosed in quotes. You need to include the entire URL for pages that are not part of your own web site. In the preceding example, the URL is *http://www.monitorwurld.com/monitor.html.*

CAUTION: Don't forget the final closing bracket or to enclose your URLs in quotes. Both are very common mistakes and forgetting them will turn your page into a mess.

There are two kinds of URLs discussed in this chapter: absolute URLs and relative URLs. The URL *http://www.monitorwurld.com/monitor.html* is an absolute URL because it includes everything your browser needs to find it anywhere on the Web. A simple example of a relative URL is "monitor world." Relative URLs are used to reference a page or file on your own web site. When a browser sees a relative URL, it looks for that page or file in the same web site as the page that calls for it. You will see several examples of each type of URL later in this chapter.

To link to another page in your web site (for example, if you are trying to make a link on a page created by PeachLink), your URL only needs to be relative. This means you can omit most of the absolute URL. The basic relative reference to this page would look like this:

```
<A HREF="monitor.html">The monitor page</A>
```

If the page you would like to link to is on your site but in a different directory, you will need to include the path to the directory. For instance, the monitor page could be in the \hardware directory and the referring page (the page with the link to the monitor page) could be in the \software directory. In such a case, the link looks like the following:

```
<A HREF="hardware\monitor.html">The monitor page</A>
```

TIP: It is important to always know what directory you are in as well as the directory of the page you are trying to link to. Keeping directory structure in mind while you are creating a page will prevent many headaches later on.

Relative references give your site mobility. If you change ISPs or alter your web site's directory structure, you do not need to rewrite all of the URLs you place in the pages you create. Even under a massive reworking of your web site, you would probably only need to add a couple of directory references to URLs already in pages, instead of having to rewrite all the URLs.

The Text

The text part of the <A HREF=> tag is the text your customers see as a link. It is inserted in the link reference between the <A HREF=> and </A> tags like this:

```
<A HREF="http://www.monitorwurld.com/monitor.html">The monitor page</A>
```

The text "The monitor page" will show up on the page highlighted as a link. As with other links, this link will usually appear blue to the customer before they click it, and red or purple after they click it. In the example at the start of this section on page links, the text part was indicated by the bold text.

The text you insert between the <A HREF=> and the </A> is the text your customers will see for that link—in this example, the text is "The monitor page." You need to choose the text carefully: it should be informative, as this may be the only insight the customer will receive about this link. It has become standard practice to attempt to work links into text seamlessly to avoid phrases like:

```
Click here to go to the monitor page: The monitor page.
```

Instead, the link should look like it is part of the sentence or paragraph, only distinguishable as a link because of its difference in color from the surrounding text, as in the following:

```
Click here to go to the monitor page.
```

The text for a link always comes after the closing bracket (>) of the URL reference and before the opening bracket of the link closing tag </A>.

</A>

</A> is the link closing signal. It tells the browser it can resume displaying text as normal black text. If you forget the closing link, the browser will display all text after the link as if it were the link; in fact, all the text will be part of the link. This means it will all be underlined, blue text that you can click.

By convention, there is no space between the last character of your link text and the opening angle bracket of your link closing tag. However, there is a space after the closing angle bracket of the signal and the next character of text. These conventions will make your text look normal on the page.

Graphic Links

Graphic links insert a picture, such as a scanned photo, a design, or a graphic file, into your web page. Linking to a graphic file is much like linking to another web page except that instead of taking the customer to a new page, the browser will display the file in the page. To enclose a graphic you will use the <IMG SRC=> tag exactly as you used the <A HREF=> tag in the previous section.

NOTE: To include a graphic file as a link you must have it saved in either GIF (.GIF) or JPEG (.JPG or .JPEG) format. If you are not already familiar with creating and manipulating graphic files, see the "Creating Clipart Sets" section earlier in this chapter.

Suppose you want to include an image of a duck, which you have given the name duck.gif. Insert a line of HTML text like this:

```
<IMG SRC="duck.gif">
```

When the customer loads this page, the browser looks at this HTML tag and displays the file duck.gif.

REMEMBER: You must upload the graphic files along with the HTML files that make up your web pages, otherwise, the browser will not know what to display on the customer's screen (because it can't find it).

As you can see, there is no closing tag for an image reference since it is simply a placeholder that tells the browser where to display the image.

<IMG SRC=> operates like <A HREF=> as far as the URL portion is concerned. You can have either relative or absolute URLs between the quotes, but for most images you will want to place the image within the directory of the page that calls it.

If you want to include an image that PeachLink is already using, you will need to know its filename and directory. It may be a useful exercise to learn this for your company logo graphic since PeachLink already uploads and uses the logo for the pages it creates. To learn about PeachLink's HTML and file structure, see the "Integrating with PeachLink" section later in this chapter.

Aligning Graphics

You can control the way your image displays on your customer's browsers. There are commands for alignment, dimensions, and borders that you can add to the basic image tag.

Whenever you have text and image together you will want to give some thought to how the text looks with the image. You use the ALIGN= tag to control that. For text to accompany an image there must be a paragraph mark or hard line break between the image tag and the text. You insert the ALIGN= tag inside the image tag like this:

```
<IMG SRC="URL", ALIGN=TOP>
```

The alignment can be TOP (to align the text with the top of the graphic), MIDDLE (to center the text vertically, with respect to the graphic), or BOTTOM (to align the text with the bottom of the graphic). The default alignment is BOTTOM, which uses the lower horizontal line of the image as the bottom of the text to accompany the image. This formatting holds only until the text wraps around the screen. For example, suppose you want to insert your duck image with some text. The HTML to align the text looks like the following and goes in the body of your document:

```
<P><IMG SRC="duck.gif" ALIGN=bottom>
And this is the image of a duck with bottom alignment.</P>
<P><IMG SRC="duck.gif" ALIGN=middle>
And this is the image of a duck with middle alignment. </P>
<P><IMG SRC="duck.gif" ALIGN=top>
And this is the image of a duck with top alignment. </P>
```

 NOTE: As you saw earlier, you can put line breaks in the HTML commands anywhere to improve the readability of the HTML without affecting the finished web page.

This HTML would create a web page that looks like the one shown in Figure 9-4.

Dimensions

Dimension control works very much like alignment control insofar as you add a dimension tag to the end of your image tag. Unlike the alignment tag, however, the dimension tag has two parts: WIDTH and HEIGHT. To alter the size of an image, insert the following HTML into the body of your document:

```
<IMG SRC="duck.gif" WIDTH="X" HEIGHT="Y">
```

"X" and "Y" represent the dimension of the image in numbers of pixels. Dimensions are always in terms of number of pixels.

The image can be reduced or enlarged, depending on the default pixel size of the graphic and the assigned width and height. The following HTML is an example of changing an image's size using the WIDTH and HEIGHT commands.

```
<P><IMG SRC="duck.gif" WIDTH="40" HEIGHT="40">This is a 40/40 image</P>
<P><IMG SRC="duck.gif" WIDTH="180" HEIGHT="180">This is a 180/180 image</P>
<P><IMG SRC="duck.gif" >And this is the unaltered image</P>
```

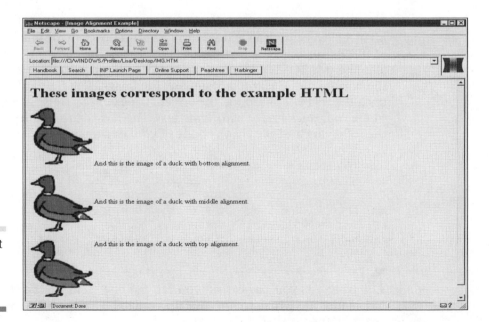

Image and text alignment example

Figure 9-4.

The web page as it will look in a browser is shown in Figure 9-5.

TIP: Enlarging and reducing can greatly alter the look of an image and, consequently, the web page.

An examination of the enlarged duck image (labeled 180/180) shows a loss of image clarity. This is because the dimension tags simply do what your office copier would do: they stretch the image to fit the dimensions you specify. Just like repeated enlarging or reducing with your copier will do to your paper documents, repeated redimensioning will hurt the integrity of your image.

CAUTION: It is not a good idea to use the dimension tag to enlarge the image more than a few percent. If you would like a substantially larger or smaller image, use a graphics program such as Paint Shop Pro to change the default dimensions of the graphic file.

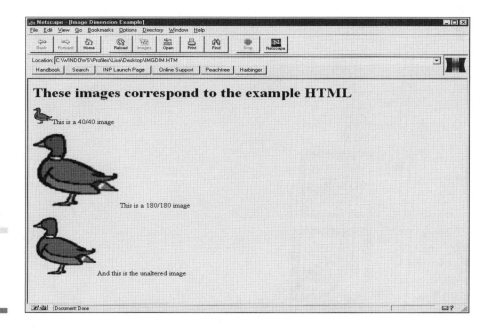

Image
dimension
example
Figure 9-5.

Adding Borders

You can frame an image with a border using the BORDER command. Similar to the dimension and alignment commands, the BORDER command is an additional tag that must be added to the IMAGE tag. The HTML syntax looks like this:

```
<IMG SRC="duck.gif" BORDER=#>
```

Replace the # with a number (in pixels) that will be the width of the border. The following HTML placed in the body of your document illustrates the BORDER command for borders of three different sizes.

```
<P><IMG SRC="duck.gif" BORDER=2>This is a 2 pixel border.</P>
<P><IMG SRC="duck.gif" BORDER=10>This is a 10 pixel border.</P>
<P><IMG SRC="duck.gif" BORDER=20>This is a 20 pixel border.</P>
```

This web page is shown in Figure 9-6.

Borders will always be square or rectangular because your browser sees the image as square or rectangular. Borders are very useful for making an image stand out on a web page.

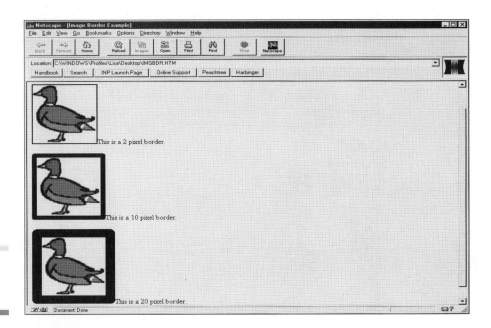

Image border
example
Figure 9-6.

File Links

Using HTML, you can add a link to your page linking a file that your customers can download when they click it. With file links, your web page can link to virtually any available file on the Internet.

File links are formatted just like page links. They even use the same <A HREF=> tag. To connect to a file, you will need to insert the following tag into the body of the document:

```
<A HREF="URL">text</A>
```

The URL in the previous HTML refers to the relative or absolute URL of the file, and the text is what you want the highlighted link to read on the page. The same rules for page links apply to file links: you need to remember the quotes and you need to close the link with the </A> tag.

The main difference between file and page links will be noticed mostly by your customers. After clicking a file link, your customers will see a download dialog instead of another web page. A good strategy for your file links is to keep the file as small as possible in order to minimize time spent by your customer downloading. By using a compression utility to shrink your file's size, you can potentially save your customers an enormous amount of time. Included on the CD accompanying this book is WinZip, a standard among file compression utilities. You can use WinZip to compress files into sizes manageable for your customers.

Don't forget the issue of absolute versus relative file references and remember to include full paths and directories if you need them. It is also imperative to be sure that the files you offer for downloading are bug-free and virus-free. If a customer downloads a virus from your site, you will have one fewer customer. There are many virus scanning programs available both on the Internet and commercially. Get one and use it regularly. You should also check for updates to the virus program's data files to keep up with the latest viruses.

REMEMBER: Scan and compress all files right before you upload them to your system. Only then can you ensure they are as small as possible and virus-free.

E-mail Links

The last type of HTML link is an e-mail link. You can put an e-mail link on your web page. When someone clicks it, their browser starts their mail program and addresses the e-mail using the address in the link. This is most typically used for things like e-mailing information to a specific person or group.

As with links in the preceding sections, you use the <A HREF=> tag to create an e-mail link. For example, the following HTML example will create a line of text that sends e-mail to sales@yourcompany.com when the user clicks on the word "Sales" (which will be highlighted on their browser screen):

```
For more info, e-mail our <A HREF=mailto:sales@yourcompany.com>Sales</A> team.
```

TIP: It's a good idea to embed e-mail links in several places throughout your web site so your customers can reach you easily.

Lists

List tags create numbered or bulleted lists on your web page. Creating lists on your web page can have outstanding page layout effects when used correctly. As far as browsers are concerned, there are only two types of lists: bulleted lists and numbered lists. Bulleted lists, or unnumbered lists, are displayed with the standard bullet. The bullets are slightly different for each browser, but most look like the bullets found in your word processor. Numbered lists can start with any number or letter and will be incremented by one for each item.

Bulleted List

To create a bulleted list in the body of your HTML document, you will need to use the following set of tags: <UL> defines an unnumbered, or bulleted, list; <LI> indicates a line item; and </UL> turns off the list tag.

You combine the tags in the body of the HTML document like this:

```
<P>My Grocery List for this week is:</P>
<UL>
<LI>Eggs
<LI>Milk
<LI>Bread
<LI>Orange Juice
</UL>
```

which will create a list that looks like the following on your web page:

My Grocery List for this week is:

- ◆ Eggs
- ◆ Milk
- ◆ Bread
- ◆ Orange Juice

Bulleted lists can be any length and are commonly used to list points or arguments about a subject. You can include bulleted lists anywhere on your web page as if you were desktop publishing the document. Remember, however, that the bulleted list will always appear flush with the left margin.

Numbered Lists

To create a numbered list in the body of your HTML document, you will need to use the following set of tags: <OL> defines this as an ordered, or numbered, list; <LI> indicates a line item; and </OL> turns off the listing tag.

You combine the tags in the body of the HTML document like this:

```
<P>Here are our top three support questions.
The answers are on the Questions and Answers page.</P>
<OL>
<LI>How do I create a list?
<LI>What can lists do for me?
<LI>Where does the list go in the HTML document?
</OL>
```

The previous example will create a list that looks like this:

Here are our top three support questions. The answers are on the Questions and Answers page.

1. How do I create a list?
2. What can lists do for me?
3. Where does the list go in the HTML document?

Like bulleted lists, numbered lists can be any length, and are commonly used for listing items you would see in tables of contents or other informational listings. You can include numbered lists anywhere on your web page as if you were desktop publishing the document.

9

Nesting Lists

All lists may be nested; that is, you can have one list inside another list. (The HTML list commands are among the few HTML commands that you can place inside another command.) You can nest a numbered list in a bulleted list, a bulleted list in a numbered list, a numbered list in a numbered list, or a bulleted list in a bulleted list. The nested list will be slightly indented, to indicate it is a nested list. The following is a simple example of how to format a nested list in HTML:

```
<P>My Grocery List for this week is:</P>
<UL>
<LI>Eggs
<LI>Milk
<LI>Bread
<OL>
<LI>Rye
<LI>Wheat
<LI>Oat Bran
</OL>
<LI>Orange Juice
</UL>
```

This will appear on the browser screen something like the following:

My Grocery List for this week is:

- Eggs
- Milk
- Bread
  1. Rye
  2. Wheat
  3. Oat Bran
- Orange Juice

It is very important to remember to turn off the nested list (done in the preceding example with a </OL>); otherwise, the remainder of your list will become nested.

For more information about the many features of lists, refer to the list of resources provided in the section "HTML References," at the end of this chapter.

Formatting Text in HTML Documents

Normally, the text you input when you create an HTML document will display on your customer's screen in whichever font they have set as the default for their browser. Links will be highlighted and listed text will be indented, but other than those two changes, all of the text in the body of your document (excluding headings) will look like basic characters. There are ways to change this. The tags you will be introduced to in this section will give you many ways to change the way text is displayed to your customer's screen.

Using Preformatted Text

The <PRE> (for "preformat") tag reformats text. Preformatting forces the browser to display the text that follows the <PRE> tag exactly as it is formatted in the HTML document.

The <PRE> tag was used heavily in the early days of the Web. Before the advanced formatting features of today's browsers, using <PRE> was the only way to create tables and lists that would display correctly. Today, the <PRE> tag is often used to display lines of code or other text that would be harmed by line wrap or a font change. The off tag for <PRE> is </PRE>. For instance, to create preformatted text, use HTML similar to the following in the body of your document:

```
<P>To create a new directory, type:</P>
<PRE>
C:\ md new
</PRE>
<P>where new is the name of the new directory.</P>
```

The resulting display of the preceding HTML will look like:

To create a new directory, type:

    C:\ md new

where new is the name of the new directory.

Notice that all preformatted text is displayed in a monospaced (or non-proportional) font. This means each character takes up the same amount of space regardless of the space it needs. For instance "O" and "l" take up the same space in a line even though they have very different character widths. This makes preformatted text ideal for listing code or other information

9

that might be hurt by a proportional font. Unfortunately, it does not look as nice as the standard browser font. For this reason, you should restrict your use of preformatted text to information that truly needs the appearance of non-proportional fonts.

Changing the Text Format

Beyond preformatted text, there are several ways you can change the look of the text your customers see. You can control the formatting of any text on your web page. It can be centered, right- or left-justified, in bold or italics, and even underlined. Most of these formatting tags work the same, so the following examples should give you an idea of how to use any text formatting tags.

Suppose you wanted your company name on your web page. You could use your company name to create a line in the body of your document like this:

```
<P>Big Business, Inc</P>
```

Since left-justified text is the default for all browsers, this line alone would simply be left-justified on your customer's screen in a standard proportional font.

But suppose you wanted to center your company name on the page to give it more impact. To tell the browser to center this line you need to include the <CENTER> tag and its corresponding </CENTER> tag. The preceding example would look like this with the center tag:

```
<P><CENTER>Big Business, Inc</CENTER></P>
```

Now suppose you would like to have your company's name in bold as well as centered. You need to include the bold tag as well. The bold tag uses <B> to turn on and </B> to turn off, as in the following example:

```
<P><CENTER><B>Big Business, Inc</B></CENTER></P>
```

It has become an HTML standard to place paragraph marks and hard returns on the outside of a line, the <CENTER>tag next, and the text formatting tags closest to the text. These standards help you understand what the text will look like on your web page and it will help browsers display text correctly. Creating HTML that follows standards is also easier to test and debug.

All other text formatting tags work the same as the bold tag. For example, suppose you want your company name in italics instead of bold. The preceding HTML would look like

```
<P><CENTER><I>Big Business, Inc</I></CENTER></P>
```

where <I> is the tag for italics (and </I> turns off italics).

To underline your company name instead italicizing it, use the <U> tag and its corresponding </U> tag, as in the following:

```
<P><CENTER><U>Big Business, Inc</U></CENTER></P>
```

CAUTION: Links are normally already underlined, so it is not a good idea to use underlined text very often.

Right-Justifying Text

The one type of text formatting that does not work like the preceding examples is right justification. However, right justification does work like one of the tags you have seen before: the <IMG SRC="", ALIGN=> tag.

If you want to right-justify your company name on your web page, use the <P ALIGN=> tag. It works much like the tag you used when you aligned your images. The TOP, BOTTOM, and MIDDLE of the <IMG SRC="", ALIGN=> has been replaced with LEFT, RIGHT, and CENTER for the <P ALIGN=> tag. Since left-justification is the default and the <CENTER> tag is used for centering text, the <P ALIGN=RIGHT> is really the only option used on web pages. To right-justify your company name, you would use something like this:

```
<P ALIGN=RIGHT>Big Business</P>
```

You should note that the tag is actually a <P> tag into which the ALIGN= command has been integrated. As expected, the <P ALIGN=> tag is turned off with the standard off paragraph mark, </P>.

You can use any of the text formatting tags, except <CENTER>, with the <P ALIGN=> tag. For instance, to display your company name right-justified and bold, you would do this:

```
<P ALIGN=RIGHT><B>Big Business</B></P>
```

9

Special Characters

HTML reserves several special characters, such as the open angle bracket (<), for its own use. Therefore, if you need to display them in your web page, you must use coded versions of these characters. For example, to display an open angle bracket, you will need to use "&lt" instead. All special characters start with the ampersand sign (&) and are followed by a brief code to identify the special character. Table 9-2 lists the most common special characters.

Including a special character is not as difficult as it may seem. The following example has several special characters.

```
<P>To center a line of your web page you will need
to use the &ltCENTER&gt tag. The &ltCENTER&gt tag, &amp its companion,
the &lt/CENTER&gt tag, will fulfill all your line centering needs.</P>
```

The preceding HTML would appear on your page like this:

```
To center a line of your web page you will need to use the <CENTER> tag. The <CENTER> tag,
                  & its companion, the </CENTER> tag, will fulfill
                             all your line centering needs.
```

The "HTML References" section at the end of this chapter provides resources that list all the special characters, including the accented characters used in most European languages and many foreign currency symbols.

Creating Tables in Web Pages

The <TABLE> tag allows you complete control over the layout of your web pages. Before tables, the only way to make sure your text aligned correctly was to use the <PRE> tag, carefully counting spaces and then previewing your pages. With tables, you can format your text in columns, which lets you create web pages with the layout you want. Tables are probably the most common element used to control formatting in web pages today. Even some

Special Characters in HTML
Table 9-2.

Character As Displayed	Code That Must Be Inserted in Text
<	&lt
>	&gt
&	&amp

of the pages you created with PeachLink contained tables, such as the catalog pages. This section will familiarize you with tables and give you some examples of how to use them to display information for your customers.

CAUTION: Tables are the most advanced HTML concept addressed in this book, and should only be included in your custom web pages after you are comfortable with the HTML techniques previously discussed in this chapter.

Defining the Table

The on-off formatting of HTML works with the <TABLE> tag. All tables must start with <TABLE> as their first tag and end with </TABLE> as their last tag. However, the <TABLE> tag does not define any part of your table, it simply tells the browser to prepare to display a table. (It is important to remember the </TABLE> tag since if you forget it your customer's browser may crash as it tries to turn the rest of the web page into a table.) Table formatting happens with the row and cell tags <TR> and <TD>, described in the following section. HTML tables are also not automatically displayed with grid lines (called borders in HTML). The "<BORDER>" section will explain how to create tables with grid lines.

<TR> and <TD>

In your word processor, a table is defined by the number of rows and columns it has. HTML works on a similar principle, but the freedom of HTML means that you can connect cells within the table giving the impression of a different number of columns for some rows. This means that your web pages can look like they have a different number of columns in different parts of the table giving you many options for formatting your tables. This formatting option is available because HTML tables are not defined as a whole piece, as they are in a word processor, but instead they are defined row by row.

Row definition means that you must include the <TR> tag (also known as the *table row* tag) for each row you want in your table. As with most other HTML tags, you must also have a </TR> tag at the end of each row. Within each row, you will define a cell with the <TD> tag (also known as the *table data* tag). Since there is no way to explicitly define columns in a table, you use the <TD> tag to define your columns: your table will have the same number of cells for each row, and this determines the number of columns in your table.

Whichever row has the most cells determines the number of columns in your table. For example, if row 1 needed three cells, row 2 needed two cells and row 3 needed four cells, then your table would have three rows and four columns. The extra cells that are not needed for a given row are simply left blank. (There are ways to deal with blank cells, known as spanning, which will be discussed later in this chapter.)

 REMEMBER: The largest number of cells within any row in the table defines the total number of columns in a table. Make sure you have decided the maximum number of columns you will need so you can handle them throughout the table.

The default width of your columns is defined by the total amount of text within the column. The column will shrink to fit the widest line within it. Rows behave the same way, shrinking to fit the text within them. This means the default appearance of a table is dependent only on the size of the information within it. Although this is very convenient for general information that is all roughly the same size on the screen, you may have a great deal of text or a picture in one cell that may affect the layout of your table by wrapping to the next line. You'll see how to override the default formatting shortly.

To create a basic table you will need to use at least three different sets of tags:

♦ <TABLE></TABLE> to start and stop the table

♦ <TR></TR> to start and stop each row in the table

♦ <TD></TD> to start and stop each cell in the row

The HTML for a simple table example would look like this:

```
<TABLE>
<TR>
<TD>Cell 1 row 1</TD>
<TD>Cell 2 row 1</TD>
<TD>Cell 3 row 1</TD>
</TR>
<TR>
<TD>Cell 1 row 2</TD>
<TD>Cell 2 row 2</TD>
<TD>Cell 3 row 2</TD>
</TR>
<TR>
<TD>Cell 1 row 3</TD>
```

```
<TD>Cell 2 row 3</TD>
<TD>Cell 3 row 3</TD>
</TR>
</TABLE>
```

The preceding HTML would look like the table shown in Figure 9-7.

You can configure the basic table extensively by the use of row or column spanning, alignments, borders, and images as you will see in the next section.

Formatting and Text Layout in Tables

As you've seen, creating a basic table is fairly simple, but the default formatting may not be adequate for your needs. As with many other HTML commands, you can include alignment and other information in row tags to change the appearance of individual rows in the table. You control the look of the columns, rows, and of the entire table with formatting tags. Column and row spanning allow you to make your table look like it has fewer cells. Alignment changes the way text is displayed in each row, and borders add grid-lines to your tables.

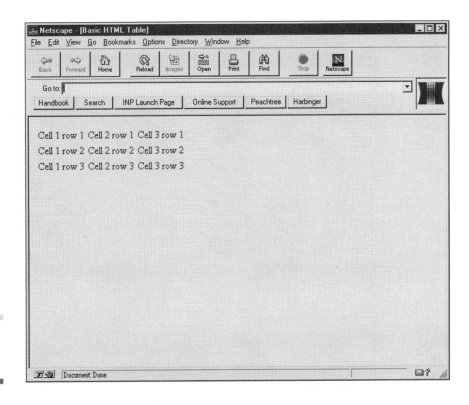

Simple table example
Figure 9-7.

9

To start with, you can use the formatting tags you've already seen in this chapter. You can create bold text inside a table cell by using the <B> tag. You can center text inside a cell with the <CENTER> tag. Almost all the tags that worked to format text outside of tables will function just fine within them. The following example shows you one way in which you might use some standard formatting tags to enhance the appearance of individual cells in a table.

```
<TABLE>
<TR>
<TD><U>Name</U></TD>
<TD><CENTER><B>Fred Jones</B></CENTER></TD>
</TR>
<TR>
<TD><U>Corporation</U></TD>
<TD><CENTER><B>Big Business, Inc.</B></CENTER></TD>
</TR>
</TABLE>
```

Figure 9-8 shows you how this looks when displayed in a browser.

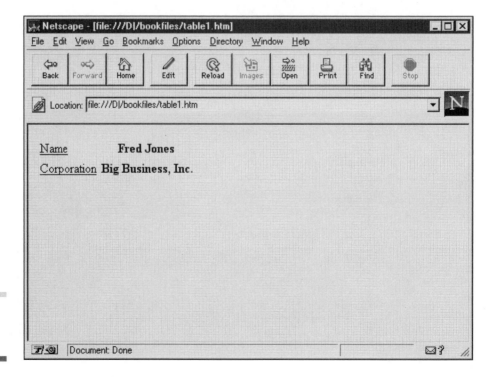

Formatting
in tables
Figure 9-8.

As with many other HTML features, you should experiment with the various options to see what looks best on your web page.

Column and Row Spanning

The flexibility of the HTML commands allows you much greater control over the appearance of your tables than is normally available to you in a typical word processor. In addition to the standard formatting commands available to you, there are some specific HTML commands used for formatting tables: the COLSPAN and ROWSPAN tags. These tags go inside the individual <TD> tags to tell the browser that a particular cell includes more than one column or row. The ability to span columns or rows lets you alter the appearance of your table so that it does not look like it has a fixed number of columns or rows.

For example, if you wanted to make a table that included a very long sentence spanning several cells, you could use something like the following HTML example:

```
<TABLE>
<TR>
<TD>Name</TD>
<TD>Fred Jones</TD>
</TR>
<TR>
<TD>Corporation</TD>
<TD>Big Business, Inc.</TD>
</TR>
<TR>
<TD COLSPAN=2>Fred Jones works for Big Business, Inc., and is an
honored customer of this company.</TD>
</TR>
</TABLE>
```

This table is shown in Figure 9-9 as it would appear to your customers. The number of columns included, or spanned, in one cell is defined by the number after the equal sign in <TD COLSPAN=>. The spanned cell will appear with the total width of cells it includes. For example, if you have spanned three cells with COLSPAN, the resulting cell will be three columns wide. As you can see in Figure 9-9, the last cell in the column spans the entire width of the table because it takes up all the cells in its row.

You can also span rows to increase the vertical space available for a specific item. One of the most common uses of row spanning is when the information in one cell needs to apply to information in two other cells, such as when you display a set of complicated definitions in a table. To have a cell span rows, you will need to use the ROWSPAN tag. ROWSPAN works

9

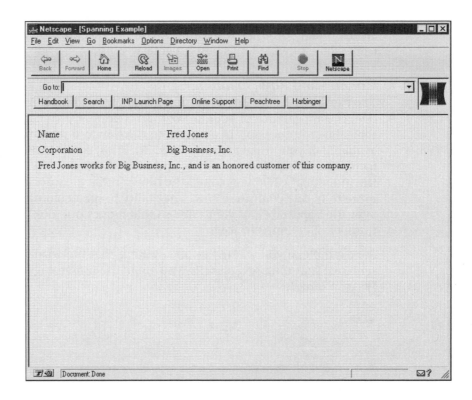

COLSPAN
example
Figure 9-9.

the same way COLSPAN does. For example, to have a cell span three rows, the tag would look like: <TD ROWSPAN=3>.

You can also combine the ability to span rows and columns to create very large cells. For example, to create a cell spanning two columns and two rows you would use: <TD COLSPAN=2 ROWSPAN=2>.

NOTE: When you are spanning columns and rows, don't forget to make adjustments for any cells that are not part of the spanned area but are in the affected column or row.

<WIDTH>

So far, you have seen how to format individual cells or rows. You'll now see how to control the width of your table and individual columns using the <WIDTH=> tag.

<WIDTH=> overrides the "smallest fit" that is the default for all tables, and creates a table or column as wide as you specify. It is important to always test your tables when you have set the width, since you are able to set the width of a table or column too wide or too narrow, so that the information within it can become badly formatted. The automatic line-wrap feature will make sure no line in truncated (unless you suppress it with the NOWRAP tag), but the table may not display the information the best possible way. You can use the <WIDTH> tag in either the <TABLE> tag or the <TD> tag.

The number after the equal sign in the <WIDTH> tag can refer to either a number of pixels or a percentage of the browser window. For instance, if you wanted your table to fill 75% of your customer's window you would use <TABLE WIDTH=75%>. If the percent sign is not included, the browser will assume the number refers to a fixed width in pixels. If you wanted a table 75 pixels wide you would use the same tag without the percent sign: <TABLE WIDTH=75>.

It's important to note that the number of pixels on your customer's screen is extremely dependent on screen size and resolution and should not be assumed to be something specific as you create your table. However, a rule of thumb has developed that 640 pixels is usually considered to be the largest default window the majority of web viewers can see on their screen without scrolling to the left or right. If you leave 40 pixels for the up-down scroll bar and other browser features, you can assume a 600-pixel table is the widest your customers can see easily. The disadvantage with using pixels rather than percentages is that a 600-pixel table will appear exactly the same no matter the size of your customers' monitors: unlike defining your table or column width by percentages, a pixel-defined table will not increase with size as the browser window increases. As a result, you should view all pixel-defined tables on several different monitors before you include them with your web site. A badly drawn table can make your site look messy, which could lose you customers.

You can also use the <WIDTH=> tag with the <TD> tag to define the width of a column. For example, to create a column that is one-third of the width of the table, you would use <TD WIDTH=33%>. Although the width of an entire column is defined by the width of the widest cell within it, it is a good idea to include the <WIDTH=> for all the cells in a column, as some browsers can have trouble formatting a table correctly without the redundant tags.

CAUTION: Some browsers may have trouble when you define the width of a column without also defining the width of the table. Remember to set the width in the <TABLE> tag, even if you simply set it at 100% or 600 pixels.

9

You can combine the use of the <WIDTH=> tag with the COLSPAN tag. For example, if you have defined a column as being 25% of the width of the entire table, you could still span cells to accommodate a single cell that is wider than the other cells in the column.

VALIGN=

Earlier in this chapter, you saw how to use the ALIGN= tag to set the horizontal alignment left, right, or center. You can also set the vertical alignment using the VALIGN= tag.

The default vertical alignment is centered in the cell. The VALIGN= tag specifies the vertical alignment of the text within the cells by placing either TOP, BOTTOM, or MIDDLE after the equal sign. For instance, if you wanted to align all the text within a row to the bottom of each cell, you would use <TR VALIGN=BOTTOM>.

As with many other formatting tags, you can use VALIGN= with either the row tag, <TR>, or the table cell data tag, <TD>. If VALIGN= is used with the <TD> tag, all of the text in that row will be aligned as specified by VALIGN=; if it is used with the <TD> tag, only one cell will be aligned by the VALIGN= tag.

You can also use the VALIGN= tag to set a baseline for a row that will align all the text in that row to an average baseline by entering VALIGN=BASELINE. However, the BASELINE option is only valid when used with the row tag, <TR>.

Finally, you can combine the use of the ALIGN= and VALIGN= tags to set the horizontal and vertical agreements. The following example shows the ALIGN and VALIGN tags used in a simple table definition.

```
<TABLE>
<TR ALIGN=LEFT VALIGN=TOP>
<TD>Cell 1 row 1</TD>
<TD ALIGN RIGHT VALIGN BOTTOM>Cell 2 row 1</TD>
<TD>Cell 3 row 1</TD>
</TR>
<TR>
<TD>Cell 1 row 2</TD>
<TD>Cell 2 row 2</TD>
<TD ALIGN=RIGHT VALIGN=TOP>Cell 3 row 2</TD>
</TR>
</TABLE>
```

In this example, the first row will be horizontally aligned to the left of the cells and vertically aligned to the top of the cells except for the second cell, which is aligned to the right and the bottom of the cell. The second row uses the default alignment settings except for the third cell, which is aligned to the right and the top of the cell.

Whenever you use the ALIGN= and VALIGN= tags, the alignment settings are reset to the defaults with the cell or row end tag (</TD> or </TR>).

Borders

HTML does not automatically include grid-lines for your table. To create these grid-lines you will need to use the <BORDER> tag. <BORDER> is always included in the <TABLE> tag and will draw a one-pixel grid-line around every cell in your table.

NOTE: A table border affects the entire table. There is no way to turn borders on and off for each individual cell.

If you want to change the width of the border from the default, you can enter the tag as <BORDER=> followed by the width of the border in pixels. You can define any pixel width you want. For example, if you wanted to define a border of five pixels you would use <TABLE BORDER=5>. Remember that a custom border is part of the table's width. If you define a custom border width, you will need to compensate for that in the total 600-pixel width used as the standard for full-page tables.

The following example uses many of the tags described in this section to create a custom table.

```
<TABLE WIDTH=200 BORDER=2>
<TR VALIGN=BOTTOM>
<TD WIDTH=100><CENTER><B>Country<BR>
Full Name</B></CENTER></TD>
<TD WIDTH=50><CENTER><B>City</B></CENTER></TD>
<TD WIDTH=50><CENTER><B>State</B></CENTER></TD>
</TR>
<TR VALIGN=MIDDLE>
<TD WIDTH=100>The United States of America</TD>
<TD WIDTH=50>Seattle</TD>
<TD WIDTH=50>WA</TD>
</TR>
<TR VALIGH=MIDDLE>
<TD WIDTH=100>Italy</TD>
<TD COLSPAN=2 WIDTH=100>Rome</TD>
</TR>
</TABLE>
```

9

As you can see in Figure 9-10, the preceding HTML displays the text in the first row in bold and centered. Since most text formatting tags work inside the table tags, you can create almost any text layout and design you can imagine. It is very important when you have so many nested tags that you be sure to remember the closing tags every time. If you forget to close a tag, it will likely cause your customers' browsers to crash.

Almost the entire range of HTML tags and options are available to you for use within tables. For example, you can put links of all kinds into your tables, including displaying images in individual cells (as shown in the following section). However, it is always a good idea to test your HTML on a few computers with different configurations and (if possible) several different browsers and versions of browsers before you place it on your web site.

Images Within Tables

It is possible to display images within tables. To include an image inside a table, you will need to include the link to it inside a table cell. Since most images will be larger than the standard text size, you will want to make sure you include an alignment tag for all the other text in the row. In addition, it

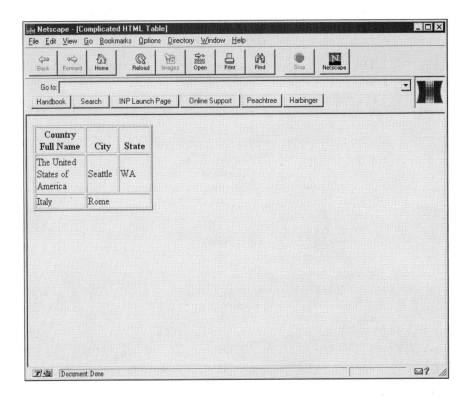

Complex table
example
Figure 9-10.

may be a good idea to use standard text formatting tags to deal with other text in the cell. The following HTML will include the DUCK.GIF image file in several table cells:

```
<TABLE BORDER>
<TR VALIGN=MIDDLE>
<TD><IMG SRC="duck.gif"></TD>
<TD>This is the image of a duck in a table</TD>
</TR>
<TR VALIGN=MIDDLE>
<TD><IMG SRC="duck.gif" WIDTH=40 HEIGHT=40></TD>
<TD>And this is a smaller image of a duck in a table</TD>
</TR>
</TABLE>
```

As you can see in Figure 9-11, the images display in the tables just as you would expect them to from your experience with images earlier in this chapter.

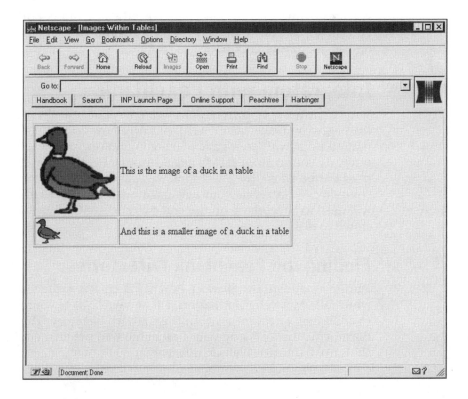

Images with
in tables
Figure 9-11.

9

Table Titles

The last new tag for tables you will learn about is the <CAPTION> tag. This tag provides a caption, or title, for your tables. The <CAPTION> tag is placed after the <TABLE> tag, but before any of the <TR> tags. By default, captions are displayed above the first row of your table, spanning all columns. Any text can be between the <CAPTION> tag and the </CAPTION> tag, and the text can be modified by any standard text formatting tags.

You can also display the table title at the bottom of the table by using the <ALIGN=> tag with the <CAPTION> tag. The <ALIGN=> tag can have either top or bottom after the equal sign. For instance, if you wanted your table to have a title at the bottom you would use:

```
<CAPTION ALIGN=BOTTOM>This would be a caption at the bottom</CAPTION>
```

<CAPTION> does not affect the layout of your table in any way, but it may become useful if you have several tables on a page and need to clearly identify them.

You've now seen how to create many kinds of web pages using several dozen different tags and formatting options. It is time to start linking your custom pages into the pages you created with PeachLink. The next section will help you create links to your new pages with the PeachLink Links page. It will also show you how to upload your images and custom pages when you upload your PeachLink pages.

Integrating with PeachLink

You've created your own custom web page, but how do you make it link to the pages you made with PeachLink? And how do you publish any graphics that go along with your page when you publish your PeachLink pages? To integrate your custom HTML pages into the PeachLink web site, you will need to find where the PeachLink web pages are stored on your own computer. To integrate your new pages with the PeachLink pages, you will need to be working on the computer where the PeachLink pages were stored to disk.

Finding the PeachLink Directories

During a standard installation, PeachLink creates a directory (C:\Harb) to which all of its web information will be saved. All of your web files are kept in additional directories within the C:\Harb directory. The HTML documents that make up your PeachLink web site are kept in the C:\Harb\INP\Info\Website directory.

You will see many HTML documents in this directory, distinguishable by their .HTM file extension. To verify that these are HTML documents, double-click one of them, Netscape will open, and you will see a page as it looked when you previewed your site with PeachLink. You will also see several files with the .HTT file extension and some files with various other extensions. These are PeachLink files that you can ignore when integrating your custom web pages. (This directory also contains another directory, Images, that you will be using later in this section.)

T IP: Examine the HTML files here and note the filename of each PeachLink page. You may need them later during the integration process or you may wish to include links to them on your custom web pages. If you have more than one custom web page you can include links to all of them on the Custom Links Tab, or you may want to include only one link to a page that would then have links to other custom pages.

You will need to copy the custom HTML documents to the C:\Harb\INP\ Info\Website directory so they will be uploaded to the Harbinger web site when you republish. Once you have copied all of your custom pages to this directory, you will need to copy all of the images that go with those pages to the Images directory. (All of your images must be in GIF or JPG format when they are copied to this directory.)

Making Links in PeachLink

After you have copied your custom files to the C:\Harb\INP\Info\Website and your images to the C:\Harb\INP\Info\Website\Images directories, you are ready to link your new pages to PeachLink. Because of the structure of the PeachLink web site, you must create links to your custom pages on your Internet Resources page. To do so you must launch PeachLink by selecting TrustedLink INP from the Harbinger program group in your Start menu. Select the "Open an Existing INP Website" radio button and click OK. Select the web site you built earlier (it will have an .IVW extension) and click Open.

After you have opened PeachLink, click Links in the Internet Resources folder. Click the Custom Links tab on the Links worksheet. The Custom Links folder on the Links worksheet will appear, as shown in Figure 9-12.

The custom links you have already added will be shown in the List of Current Custom Links box. To add your custom pages as a link, you will need to fill in the empty fields in the Add/Modify Link area of this window.

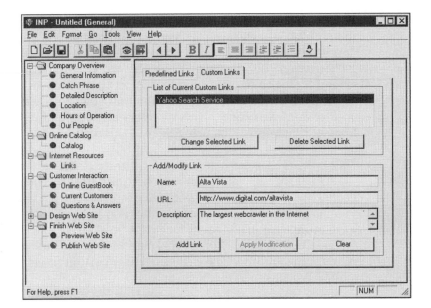

Links
worksheet
showing the
Custom Links
folder

Figure 9-12.

NOTE: If you have more than one custom web page you can include
links to all of them on the Custom Links Tab, or you may want to include
only one link to a page that would then have links to other custom pages.

Name   Enter the name of your custom web page as you would like it to
appear on the Links page.

URL   In the URL field, insert the URL for your custom web page. (See
Chapter 7, "Using PeachLink," for more information on this worksheet.)

If you are unsure what the URL will be for your custom page, remember that
all URLs on the Harbinger site are in the following format: *http://www.harb.net/
yourbusinessname/nameofwebpage*. This ensures that the first part of all URLs
for your web site is the same. Therefore, your custom web pages will have
a URL like *http://www.harb.net/yourbusinessname/customwebpagename.htm*,
where *yourbusinessname* is some form of the Short Company Name you
provided on the General Information page, and *customwebpagename* is the
filename of your custom web page. For example, if you wanted to include a
custom HTML document, basic.htm, on the Big Business web site example
from Chapter 7, "Using PeachLink," the URL would look like the this: *http://
www.harb.net/bigbusiness/basic.htm*

TIP: Look at the URL for your home page to help you figure out the standard URL for your web site.

Description   Enter a short description (256 characters or less) of your custom web page.

When you are satisfied with your entries, click Add Link. PeachLink adds the link to the list.

After you have created the link to your custom pages you may want to alter the text for the Internet Resources description that will appear on your home page. To change the text on your home page, from the Content List (right side of the window), select Build Home Page in the Design Web Site folder. The Build Home Page Summaries worksheet will appear, shown in Figure 9-13.

Change the text in the Internet Resources box to indicate that this page will also include links to your custom pages. For example, you may want to include text like, "A selection of links to our suppliers and business partners, as well as links to our own pages on government policy and how Internet commerce is affecting the computer industry."

After you have finished creating your links and altering the text for your Internet Resources page, you are ready to republish your web site with the new information and your custom web pages.

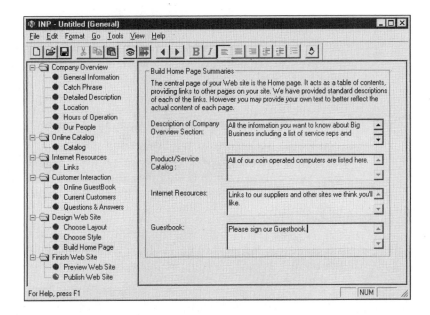

Build
Home Page
Summaries
worksheet
Figure 9-13.

9

Republishing Your Web Site

Once you have added links to the Internet Resources page and have copied your custom web page to the correct directory, you are ready to republish your updated web site. Republishing your web site is almost identical to the publishing procedure outlined in the "Publish Your Web Site" section of Chapter 7, "Using PeachLink." The only difference is some files will not be selected in the Publication Wizard Window. You will need to go through the entire publication process to place your custom web pages on your web site.

NOTE: If you have any images on your custom web pages, they will not be automatically included in the publication process. You will need to use FTP to upload your images to the images directory on your Harbinger web site. For more information about FTP, see the "Using an Independent ISP" section later in this chapter.

When the Publication Wizard informs you that it has completed your update, it will ask if you would like to go to your web site. Click Yes.

Your Home Page will appear with links to all the other pages you created using PeachLink. If the new text for the Internet Resources Page does not appear next to its link, click the Refresh Button on the Netscape tool bar. This forces Netscape to load the most current version of this page.

Click the Internet Resources Link. When the Internet Resources Page has loaded, if you do not see links to your custom web pages, click the Refresh button on the Netscape tool bar.

Now click the link to your custom web page and admire your handiwork. You have just created your very own web page, and it is now on the Web for everyone to see.

Using an Independent ISP

If you would like to use an ISP other than Harbinger, you will need to FTP your files to their computers. FTP stands for File Transfer Protocol, and is the most common way to copy files from personal computers to large computers on the Internet. To use FTP you need to have an FTP program on your machine.

Most ISPs will gladly help you through the process of putting your web site on their server, but not all parts of the web site you created in PeachLink will work on another ISP. It is particularly important to note that the On-Line Catalog portion of your PeachLink web site requires files on the Harbinger web site, so if you would like to use the PeachLink On-Line Catalog feature you must use Harbinger as your ISP.

The following is a very brief overview on how to use FTP to place your web pages on your independent ISP's web server. If you have never used FTP or other UNIX utilities before, please refer to the documentation for your FTP program or a complete FTP primer (there are some listed in Appendix B).

Using FTP

If you are using Windows 95 or NT, you already have a basic FTP program on your computer. If you do not have Windows 95 or NT, you may install WS_FTP from the CD accompanying this book.

To use the Windows 95 FTP program to copy your files to your ISP, you must have a live connection to your ISP when you start FTP. To open an FTP window in Windows 95 or NT, select Run from your start menu. Type **FTP** in the command line field and click OK. An FTP window will open like the one in Figure 9-14.

At the FTP> prompt type **open isp.net** where isp.net is the name of your independent ISP. A login prompt will appear. Enter your username and password at the prompts to log in to the computer. Use the change directory command (cd) to move to the directory of your account on your ISP's web server. Use the put command (put) to place your web pages up on your ISP's Web server. After you have finished, close the connection by typing **quit** at the FTP> prompt.

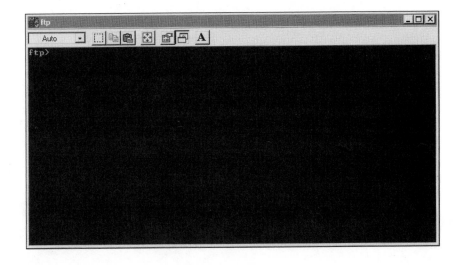

FTP window
Figure 9-14.

9

You may prefer to use WS_FTP for file transfers because it has a Windows interface that lets you see the files you are transferring. See Chapter 11, "Peachtree Accounting Add-ons and Other Software," for more information on WS_FTP.

HTML Resources

There are many different online and printed resources for learning more about HTML. These are listed in Appendix B, "Online and Printed Resources."

Summary

In this chapter, you saw how to add clipart and backgrounds to the basic creation process of PeachLink and how to change the look of your web site by using HTML. You also learned the basic concepts behind web page creation and HTML and how to integrate your custom web pages into your PeachLink web site. In the next chapter, you will see how to use Electronic Bill Payment to automate your check writing process.

10

Using Electronic Bill Payment

The preceding chapters in this section have told you how to use PeachLink to create and maintain your company's web site. This chapter will show you how to use Electronic Bill Payment to automate your check writing process.

What Is Electronic Bill Payment?

Electronic Bill Payment, a service of ADP-Electronic Banking Services, gives your small business the convenience of making payments through the Accounts Payable module of Peachtree Accounting, paying bills in minutes without having to write checks. Use the Electronic Bill Payment Feature to transmit payments to the ADP processing center and you can avoid buying and printing checks, stuffing envelopes, and adding postage. ADP will do all this for you at a fraction of what it would cost you to do it yourself.

NOTE: If you have an earlier version of Peachtree Accounting, you may know this product as *e*-Check.

Electronic Bill Payment enables you to do the following:

♦ Select one or all invoices from the same vendor for payment

♦ Make payments from up to 11 bank accounts to any bank in the U.S.

♦ Take advantage of Peachtree Accounting features for payment information to supply to vendors, including discounts and adjustments taken

Security through Electronic Bill Payment includes encryption of transmitted data and several levels of security codes and passwords, ensuring that only authorized personnel have access to your data.

Setting Up Electronic Bill Payment

Although Electronic Bill Payment is a standard feature of Peachtree Accounting, you must set it up before you can use it. To set up Electronic Bill Payment, you will need to fill out an enrollment form, sign up with ADP, link disbursement accounts with your General Ledger cash accounts, and so on.

Filling Out the Enrollment Form

Fill out an enrollment form from ADP. Enrollment forms are included in the Peachtree Accounting product box. If you do not have the form or you need to ask questions, call (800)327-3997. You will need to supply the following information on the enrollment form:

♦ A voided check from your company's primary bank account and a voided check from each of the secondary bank accounts you plan to use for disbursements

◆ A four-digit personal security code (which you create)

◆ Your federal tax ID, which will be used as the Master Account ID

You are permitted to specify one primary bank account for electronic disbursements and up to ten secondary bank accounts (each one requiring its own Electronic Bill Payment Secondary Account form).

Fax the completed enrollment form to (770) 650-6201. It will be processed within 72 hours and ADP will mail you a Startup Kit, which contains a brochure with information on Electronic Bill Payment, a Quick Start Guide to help get started, and a statement of the Terms and Conditions of the service.

NOTE: Users of some earlier versions of Peachtree Accounting may also receive a free software upgrade that lets them use the bill payment service.

Activating Electronic Bill Payment

Once you receive your Startup Kit, you are ready to activate Electronic Bill Payment. From the Maintain menu of Peachtree, select Company Information. The Maintain Company Information window appears (as shown in Figure 10-1).

NOTE: The fields will default to what is already entered for the company in Peachtree Accounting.

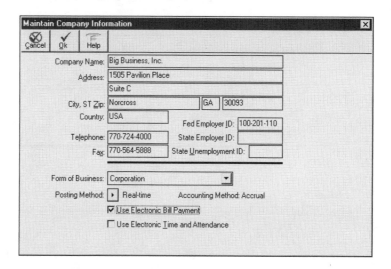

Maintain
Company
Information
window
Figure 10-1.

Company Name   Enter the company name (up to 30 characters) that will be printed on electronic bill payment to the vendor.

Address   Enter the valid company mailing address. The first line is required, the second is optional. Electronic Bill Payment will recognize only the first 28 characters on either line.

City, ST Zip   Enter the city, state, and ZIP code. The city name can be up to 28 characters. The ST information must be one of the two-letter Postal Service abbreviations for a state (or DC for the District of Columbia, PR for Puerto Rico, and VI for the U. S. Virgin Islands). The ZIP code must be a valid five- or nine-digit number.

Telephone   Enter a ten-digit number, area code first.

Check Use Electronic Bill Payment and click OK. Peachtree Accounting displays a message window (not shown) that tells you that you will need to select Electronic Bill Payment from the Maintain/Default Information window; click OK. You now have access to all the areas of Peachtree Accounting that have to do with Electronic Bill Payment, and you are ready to set up your modem and configure Electronic Bill Payment.

Setting Up Your Modem

The next step in setting up Electronic Bill Payment is to set up your modem. From the Maintain menu, select Default Information and then Electronic Bill Payment. The Modem Setup window appears:

Port   Select a port from the drop-down menu. Most modems are on COM1 or COM2.

Speed   Select a modem speed from the drop-down menu. ADP can accommodate between 2,400 and 28,800 bps. See your modem documentation for the correct speed. ADP recommends using a modem speed of 9,600 bps for the most consistent results.

Dial Type   Choose either Tone or Pulse. Virtually all phone lines are now tone.

Initialization String   This is usually set to ATZ. You can customize this if you wish. See your modem documentation for a listing of valid modem commands.

Dialing Prefix   Enter the characters or digits the modem should dial first. Usually this is a number needed to get an outside line, typically a 9. Sometimes it is a code used to disable call waiting—typically *70 or 70#. A comma following this number or numbers causes the modem to pause for two seconds. If your phone system takes longer to connect to an outside line, you may wish to enter more than one comma (for example, 9,, or *70,, or *709,,). If the computer on which you are setting up Electronic Bill Payment is not going to be used to transmit data to ADP, check No Modem at the bottom of the window.

When you are satisfied with your entries, click OK. The Electronic Bill Payment Initial Setup window appears:

Electronic Bill Payment Initial Setup	✕
Master Business ID:	25-001630
Security Code:	****
Re-enter Security Code:	****
Transmission Phone #:	515-6000
Transmit **Cancel** **Help** **Test**	

You use this window to enter the basic information for your company's Electronic Bill Payment account.

Master Business ID   Enter the Master Business ID. This is the federal tax ID that was on the enrollment form you received from ADP. If you enter more than one company in Peachtree Accounting, you will need to contact ADP for another Master Business ID.

Security Code   Enter the security code. This is the four-digit personal security code you entered on the Enrollment Form.

CAUTION: Put this security code in a safe place! If you lose it, you cannot change it, and you will need to call ADP to find out what your code is.

Re-enter Security Code   Enter your four-digit personal security code again to verify it.

Transmission Phone Number   Enter the telephone number your modem dials to transmit information to ADP. (This number is provided in your Quick Start Guide.)

You're now ready to test your modem setup. Click Test at the bottom of the window. Peachtree Accounting will test the modem setup by dialing the number. If you get no connection or get an error message, first check your modem setup, then the information you just entered in the Electronic Bill Payment Initial Setup window, and finally the Session Log, if needed. (See "Displaying the Session Log" later in this chapter for more information on how to examine the Session Log.)

Select Transmit to accept the setup as entered. Peachtree Accounting will initialize the modem, call ADP's bill payment processing center, and log you on to the Electronic Bill Payment Network. ADP will then verify the data entered in the Electronic Bill Payment Initial Setup window, verify your bill payment account, and download your bank account information. The Transferring Data window (not shown) displays status information (that the transfer was successful) and that a new Electronic Bill Payment bank account has been added and needs to be assigned to a GL Cash Account. Click OK to continue. You will then see the message, "In order to use Electronic Bill Payment, Electronic Bill Payment accounts must be assigned to General Ledger cash accounts. Proceed to Maintain Chart of Accounts now?" Click OK to continue. You are now ready to link disbursement accounts and General Ledger cash accounts.

Linking Disbursement Accounts and GL Cash Accounts

Before you can use an Electronic Bill Payment primary or secondary disbursement account to make electronic bill payments, you must link the disbursement account to a General Ledger cash account. First, select Chart of Accounts from the Maintain menu, then click the Electronic Bill Payment tab. Figure 10-2 shows the Maintain Chart of Accounts window with the Electronic Bill Payment folder displayed.

NOTE: Only one Electronic Bill Payment account at a time can be linked to a General Ledger cash.

Account ID   Select a General Ledger account ID from the drop-down menu.

Electronic Bill Payment Account   Select an Electronic Bill Payment account from the drop-down list to link to the account ID you chose in the preceding field.

Once the link is established, Peachtree Accounting displays the Bank Name, Routing Number, and Account Number. Click Save to save the information.

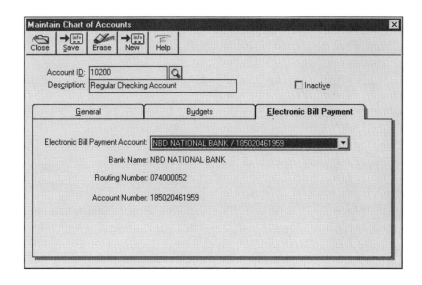

Maintain Chart of Accounts window with the Electronic Bill Payment folder displayed
Figure 10-2.

NOTE: From now on, in any Peachtree Accounting window that has an Account ID lookup list, "Cash/E-Pmt" will be displayed in the Account Type column for this General Ledger cash account.

You may link other General Ledger cash accounts to Electronic Bill Payment disbursement accounts. When you are through, click Close.

Setting Up Vendors for Electronic Bill Payment

After you have linked General Ledger cash accounts to Electronic Bill Payment disbursements accounts, confirmed and saved vendor data, and closed the Maintain Chart of Accounts window, the Maintain Vendors window appears, with the General tab selected (as shown in Figure 10-3).

Vendor ID   Select a vendor ID from the drop-down menu, or enter a new one.

NOTE: Electronic bill payments cannot be made to government agencies. This requires more information than can be entered for vendors, and sometimes requires personal signatures. Electronic bill payments must also be larger than zero and no larger than $9,999,999.99.

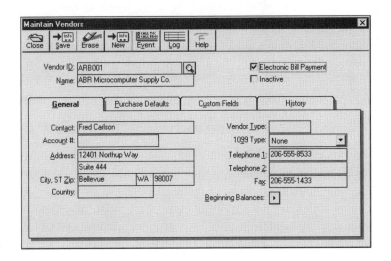

Maintain
Vendors
window
Figure 10-3.

Electronic Bill Payment Box   Check this box to enable the vendor for electronic bill payment. If the Electronic Bill Payment box does not appear in the window, electronic bill payment is not activated.

Name   Enter the name of the vendor to receive the electronic payment. This field is required.

Contact   Enter the name of the contact person at the vendor.

Account #   Enter the number assigned to your company by the vendor. This field is required.

Address   Enter the vendor address to which ADP is to send payments. ADP will accept only the first 28 characters on each line. The first line is required, and the second line is optional.

City, ST Zip   Enter the city, state, and ZIP code. This information is required and has the same limitations described previously in the "Activating Electronic Bill Payment" section.

Telephone 1   Enter a ten-digit number, area code first. This field is required.

Telephone 2   Enter a second vendor telephone number.

Fax   Enter a fax number for the vendor (optional).

When you are satisfied with your entries, click Save to save the vendor record. Peachtree Accounting automatically assigns a payee number for the vendor to the right of the Electronic Bill Payment box. You can continue setting up more vendors the same way. When you are finished, click Close.

Transmitting New Payee Data to ADP

Before you can transmit an electronic bill payment to a vendor, you must transmit the vendor information to ADP. Select Electronic Bill Payment from the Tasks menu, then select Transfer Data. Figure 10-4 shows the Transfer Electronic Payment Data window after clicking the Vendor Maintenance tab.

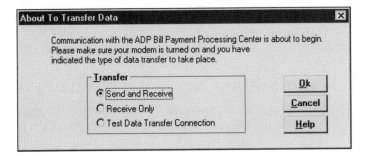

Transfer
Electronic
Payment Data
window with
the Vendor
Maintenance
folder
displayed
Figure 10-4.

The Vendor Maintenance folder lists the vendors you just enabled for
Electronic Bill Payment. When you are satisfied with your entries, click the
Connect button on the toolbar to start data transfer to ADP. The About to
Transfer Data window appears:

The About to Transfer Data window notifies you that communication with
ADP is about to begin. Click the "Send and Receive" radio button and then
click OK to start the transfer. A progress window shows the status of the

connection. Once the connection is made, Peachtree Accounting displays transfer results as follows:

◆ **The Transfer Was Successful** The vendor information was transmitted to ADP successfully.

◆ **The Transfer Failed** The vendor information was not transmitted to ADP. See "Handling a Failed Data Transfer" later in this section for more information.

A message appears in both windows showing that a Session Log has been created, recording all activity during the transmission.

When you have examined the transfer results to your satisfaction, click OK. A warning window appears, offering you the opportunity to back up your data. Click Backup to create a backup, or Continue to end this process without creating a backup.

CAUTION: Back up your data after each transmission! See the Peachtree Accounting manual or *Peachtree Complete Accounting for Windows Made Easy* (Osborne/McGraw-Hill, 1997) for information on how to back up your data.

Once ADP has received the new vendor information, Electronic Bill Payment vendors are set up for transmission of payments. To confirm this setup, print the Electronic Bill Payment Vendor Maintenance report (described later in this chapter). The status of the vendor you just added will be one of the following:

◆ **Confirmed** ADP received the new vendor information as transmitted.

◆ **Pending** ADP did not receive the new vendor information. Try transmitting it again. (Information will only be pending if you've never transmitted it.)

◆ **Returned** The transmission failed to ADP. Refer to the Session Log for more information. (See "Displaying the Session Log" later in this chapter.)

When you have transmitted vendor data, the setup and configuration of Electronic Bill Payment for your company is complete. You're now ready to enter vendor payments.

Entering Vendor Payments

Entering vendor payments with Electronic Bill Payment is very much like entering them for payment by check: you check available funds and select invoices for payment. There are two ways to select invoices for payment with Electronic Bill Payment. The first (and easier) method is to use the Select for Payments window, which lets you select invoices for payment based on selection criteria you enter. The second is to use the Payments window, which lets you select individual invoices for payment.

Transaction Detail	Difference
Check Number	Peachtree Accounting provides a payment reference number in place of the usual check number. This number will be used as the check number when your payments are processed.
Date	This is the date on which the Electronic Bill Payment transaction is posted to the General Ledger. It is not necessarily the same date as when the payment is transmitted to ADP, or when ADP writes the vendor a check.
Electronic Bill Payment as Prepayment	To make any kind of electronic invoice payment, you must have an invoice number. You cannot use Electronic Bill Payment for applying the prepayment to the purchase and nothing else.
Vendor Payee Address Changes	Changes to the information in the Maintain Vendors window must also be transmitted to ADP as a maintenance update. (You may want to do this before transmitting electronic payments for the vendor, to make sure the changes have been accepted. However, you can send vendor changes at the same time as payments to the vendor, if you prefer.)
Pay to the Order of	While Peachtree Accounting lets you use the "Pay to the Order of" button to change the address information for regular (non-electronic) payments, ADP's address for that vendor reverts to the default vendor address in the Maintain Vendors window.
Total	The Total Electronic Bill Payment parameters must be greater than zero and less than $10,000,000.00. If you must remit a total of $10,000,000.00, make several electronic bill payments that total the desired amount.

Differences Between Direct Payments and Electronic Bill Payments
Table 10-1.

Considerations

Before you enter electronic bill payments, there are some limitations you need to be aware of. First, you cannot set up payments in Electronic Bill Payment for processing in advance, nor can you set up or edit recurring payments with Electronic Bill Payment. Moreover, once you have transmitted a pending electronic payment to ADP, you cannot edit it. ADP processes transmitted transactions immediately, and mails out payment on the next business day. If the transaction date you assigned is different from the next business day, it is overridden.

There are several differences between payments made with Electronic Bill Payment and those made directly through Peachtree Accounting. One of the most significant differences is that electronic bill payments have two posting dates, the *transaction date* and the *process date*. The transaction date is when the transaction is posted to the Peachtree Accounting General Ledger via the Payments, Select for Payments, Cash Manager, or Payment Manager window. The process date is when the transaction was transmitted to ADP. Table 10-1 shows some of the other differences.

Making Individual Payments with Electronic Bill Payment

The following are two types of electronic bill payment that can be made singly:

◆ Direct expenses or other disbursements that do not involve invoices

◆ Payments applied to invoices already entered as purchases

To make individual payments, select Payments from the Tasks menu. The standard Payments window appears, as shown in Figure 10-5. Select a vendor from the drop-down list. The Electronic Bill Payment box should be checked automatically if the vendor is set up as an Electronic Bill Payment payee. Peachtree Accounting also automatically supplies the vendor account number in the Memo field, the Electronic Bill Payment account information at lower right, and the Process icon (in place of the Print icon).

Enter the payment information on the Apply to Invoices or the Apply to Expenses folder as usual. When you are satisfied with your entries, click Process. Peachtree Accounting then saves or posts the payment, in accordance with the posting method you've selected in the Maintain Company Information window, and then puts the transaction into the Pending category for transmission to ADP.

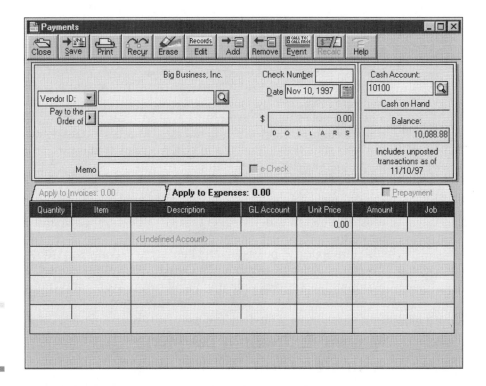

Payments
window
Figure 10-5.

Applying Payments to Purchase Invoices

You can apply payments to purchase invoices with Electronic Bill Payment. On the Apply to Invoices folder on the Payments window, enter a vendor ID to display open purchase invoices. As with regular payments, you may apply payments to all or part of any invoice.

NOTE: Entering electronic bill payment information is the same as applying regular payments to vendor invoices, except that instead of posting or saving the data, you click Process to process the information. ADP gets a transmission including invoice number, discount amount, and amount paid.

Applying Payments to Expenses

Direct vendor expenses are usually payments for which there is no invoice. To apply payments to expenses, select the Apply to Expenses tab on the Payments window. Enter the line item amount (required), and any of the following (all optional): Quantity, Item ID, Description, Unit Price, Job ID; then click Process to process the information.

10

Entering Prepayments

To enter prepayments, select the Apply to Expenses tab of the Payment window, then check Prepayment. Enter the prepayment data, including a positive prepayment amount, then click Process to process the information.

Applying Prepayments

A prepayment is considered a negative invoice in Peachtree Accounting. To make any kind of electronic invoice payment, you must have the invoice number. Once the prepayment is transmitted, the payment reference number serves as an invoice number if payment is to be applied to an outstanding invoice. Otherwise, the number of the check used in prepayment serves as the invoice number.

Click the Apply to Invoices tab from the Payments window. Select the invoice number for the prepayment already entered, then enter the amount of payment to be applied. For example, for a $750 invoice, a prepayment of $100 would be entered as -100.00 in the Amount Paid column. You would then find the outstanding invoice(s) to be paid, and enter the amount of payment. To pay for the remainder of the $750 invoice, the check amount would be $650 ($750 less the $100 prepayment). Click Process to process the information.

Failure to apply the prepayment could create a problem if no payment is made to the purchase invoice for a long time. Aged Payables would not reflect the correct invoice balance owed as long as the prepayment was still available but not applied.

Keep in mind that you cannot use Electronic Bill Payment for applying just the prepayment to the purchase and nothing else. The total check amount would then be zero after applying the prepayment. To correct the situation when a prepayment is the only payment anticipated, clear Electronic Bill Payment in the Payments window. Enter 100.00 in the Pay column. The total payment amount is zero, which does not change the amount in the General Ledger cash account.

Making Multiple Payments with Electronic Bill Payment

Making multiple payments with Electronic Bill Payment is similar to what you're already used to doing in Peachtree Accounting: you select the invoices to pay from the Select for Payment window. The basic differences for Electronic Bill Payment are as follows:

♦ The Process icon replaces the Print icon on the Select for Payment window.

♦ A new column appears to the right of the Chk column—E-Pmt. You can check invoices for payment via Electronic Bill Payment here.

♦ The bank name and account number used as the Electronic Bill Payment disbursement account appears at the bottom left of the Select for Payment window.

♦ The Check Date is the date the payment is posted to the General Ledger.

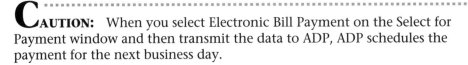

CAUTION: When you select Electronic Bill Payment on the Select for Payment window and then transmit the data to ADP, ADP schedules the payment for the next business day.

For more information on making multiple payments using the Select for Payment window, see your Peachtree Accounting manual or *Peachtree Complete Accounting for Windows Made Easy* (Osborne/McGraw-Hill, 1997).

Processing Payments

Once you have entered payments, the next step is to process them. Processing is preparing the payments for transmission to ADP. Click Process to begin processing payments. Peachtree Accounting starts the About to Create Electronic Bill Payment Transactions sequence for payments to be made via Electronic Bill Payment. If you are making payments by check, the payment process occurs the same way as it does if Electronic Bill Payment is not activated: Peachtree Accounting starts the standard Print Forms sequence.

The cash account box is at the top of the Select for Payment window and is selected when the checks are being selected. Peachtree Accounting moves the payments to Pending status and sends them to ADP during your next transmission. You may view the list of pending transactions (see Figure 10-6) by selecting Electronic Bill Payment from the Tasks menu and then selecting Transfer Data.

You may cancel payment by Electronic Bill Payment by selecting Cancel in the About to Create Electronic Bill Payment Transactions window or in the Writing Electronic Bill Payment window.

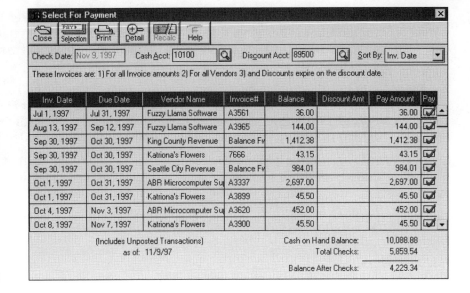

Select for
Payment
window
displaying
selected
invoices
Figure 10-6.

10

Managing Electronic Bill Payments

Managing Electronic Bill Payments is much like managing direct payments
from Peachtree Accounting, but there are a few differences. These are
described in this section.

Viewing and Editing Electronic Bill Payments

You can view any Electronic Bill Payment transaction, regardless of status,
in any of these three ways:

♦ Select Payments from the Tasks menu, then select Edit Records in the
Payments window.

♦ Select Electronic Bill Payment from the Tasks menu, then select Transfer
Data. Choose a payment and double-click it to display detail.

♦ Select a report from the list of Electronic Bill Payment Accounts Payable
reports on the Reports menu. Choose a payment and double-click it to
display detail.

You can edit electronic payments only if they are Pending, Confirmed, or
Returned. You can't edit payments that have a Sent status.

You can edit payments from the Payments window of the Tasks menu, as
follows: select the Edit Records icon. The Electronic Bill Payment reference
numbers appear in the Reference column. If the transaction has not yet been

transmitted, the notation e-<Pending> also appears in the Reference column. (If information has already been transmitted, the payment reference number appears above the Date field.) Select the electronic payment you wish to edit, and click OK.

You can also double-click Electronic Bill Payment from the Transfer Data window just before transmitting transactions to ADP. Select Electronic Bill Payment from the Tasks menu, then select Transfer Data. All pending electronic payments appear. Select a transaction and click Detail.

Finally, you can edit electronic bill payments from reports that permit double-clicking a line item to display detail. These reports are listed here:

♦ Cash Disbursements Journal

♦ Vendor Ledgers

♦ Check Register

♦ Pending Electronic Bill Payments

♦ Pending Electronic Bill Payment Transfer Data

♦ Electronic Bill Payment History

♦ Electronic Bill Payment Register

♦ Electronic Bill Payment Status

Printing Electronic Bill Payment Records

You can print a record of a payment that has been transmitted to ADP. To print a copy of an Electronic Bill Payment, select Payments from the Tasks menu, then select Edit Records from the Payments window to display the Select Payment window. Select and double-click the Electronic Bill Payment for which you want to print a duplicate copy. The Payments window appears with the transaction data.

Select Print from the File menu. The Print Forms: Disbursement Checks window appears. Select the check form and click OK, then select Real in the Print Forms window. The form is printed with "Void" in the signature area and "Duplicate" close to the check number field.

Stopping Electronic Bill Payments

Once an Electronic Bill Payment has been transmitted and received by ADP, it cannot be stopped. You must call the bank where the disbursement account is located to issue a stop payment.

Voiding Electronic Bill Payments

Void electronic bill payments as you would check payments once they have been confirmed by ADP. Payments with Sent status cannot be voided.

Contact the vendor directly to handle payments made in error. ADP does not debit your disbursement account except for the monthly ADP service charge.

When you void an electronic bill payment, Peachtree Accounting generates a reversal of the payment via the General Ledger. At account reconciliation, the original transaction and the voided transaction are automatically cleared. View the voided payment in the Deposits and Debits section of the Account Reconciliation window.

Reconciling Electronic Bill Payments

Select Account Reconciliation from the Tasks menu. When the Account Reconciliation window appears, enter or select the account to reconcile.

The Reference column will display either the account's transaction numbers or the notation <Pending E-Pmt>. The transaction number should match the ADP draft number.

TIP: Select the General Ledger account linked to the Electronic Bill Payment account when reconciling payments.

Transmitting Electronic Bill Payment Data

Once electronic bill payments have been processed, the transactions are put into the Pending category until they are sent to ADP with your next transmission, which can also include these other kinds of data:

♦ Vendor changes or deletions

♦ Electronic Bill Payment account deletions

♦ Company data changes

♦ E-mail messages

In addition, during data transfer from ADP, you may also receive any of the following:

♦ New Electronic Bill Payment disbursement account data

♦ Electronic payment confirmations and rejections

♦ Responses to e-mail from ADP

♦ Vendor or account maintenance confirmations and rejections

Reviewing Data to Be Transmitted

Data transfers to ADP can be among the following: sets of instructions for sending electronic bill payments; additions or changes to vendor, account, or company information; or e-mail covering special circumstances. Once you perform maintenance or enter payments, this data is held as "pending" until the next transmission to ADP.

Before you transmit data to ADP, you should review it for accuracy. To review data, select Electronic Bill Payment and then Transfer Data from the Tasks menu. The Transfer Electronic Payment Data window appears (as shown in Figure 10-7).

The payments ready for transmission appear on the Payment Transactions folder.

NOTE: Payments cannot be transmitted until the vendor has been enabled for Electronic Bill Payment and the data has been transmitted. The send option for payments will be disabled until the vendor information has been transmitted successfully to ADP.

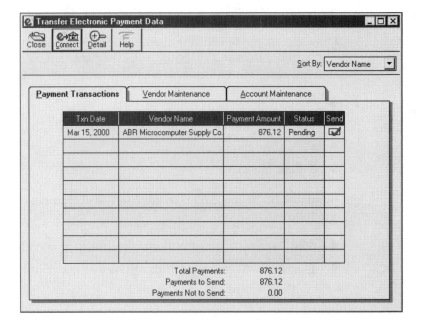

Transfer
Electronic
Payment Data
window with
the Payment
Transactions
folder
displayed
Figure 10-7.

Review the payments to make sure that the information about to be transmitted is complete and correct. You can select a sorting option—Vendor Name, Txn (transaction) date, or Status—in the Sort By field in the upper-right corner of the window to change the order in which data is displayed. Note that the Status field displays data for both pending and returned transactions.

You can edit a returned transaction by selecting the item and then clicking Detail. Edit the payment and click Close to return to the Transfer Electronic Payment Data window. The edited item will appear on the Payment Transactions folder with a status of Pending. You can select or deselect specific payments for transmission by checking the Send box for the payment.

When you are satisfied with your entries, click the Vendor Maintenance tab. The Vendor Maintenance folder appears (as shown in Figure 10-8).

Review the information on this folder for accuracy. As with the Payment Transactions folder, you can sort the information by selecting an option from the drop-down list in the Sort By field (in the upper right corner of the window), and you can edit vendor maintenance information by selecting the item and then clicking Detail.

When you are satisfied with your entries, click the Account Maintenance tab. The Account Maintenance folder appears (as shown in Figure 10-9).

As you can see, the Account Maintenance folder is divided into two parts. The Electronic Bill Payment Account Deletions section shows all

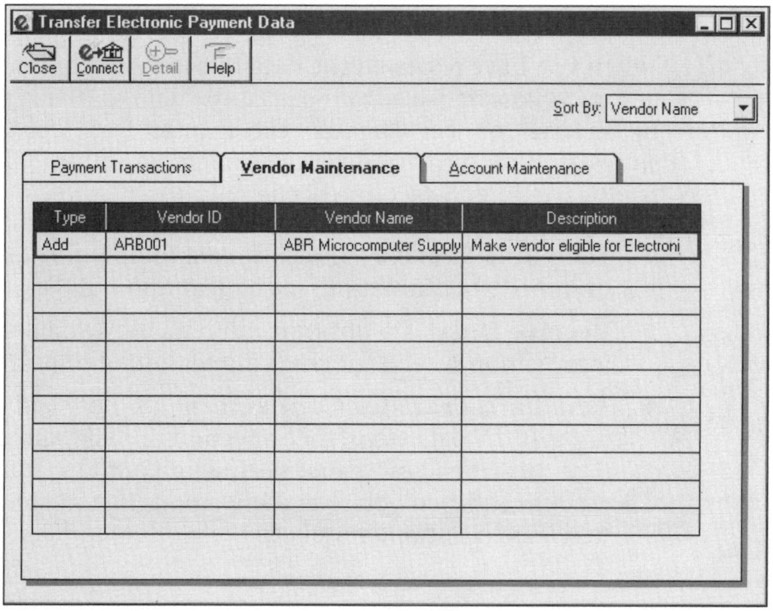

Transfer
Electronic
Payment Data
window with
the Vendor
Maintenance
folder
displayed
Figure 10-8.

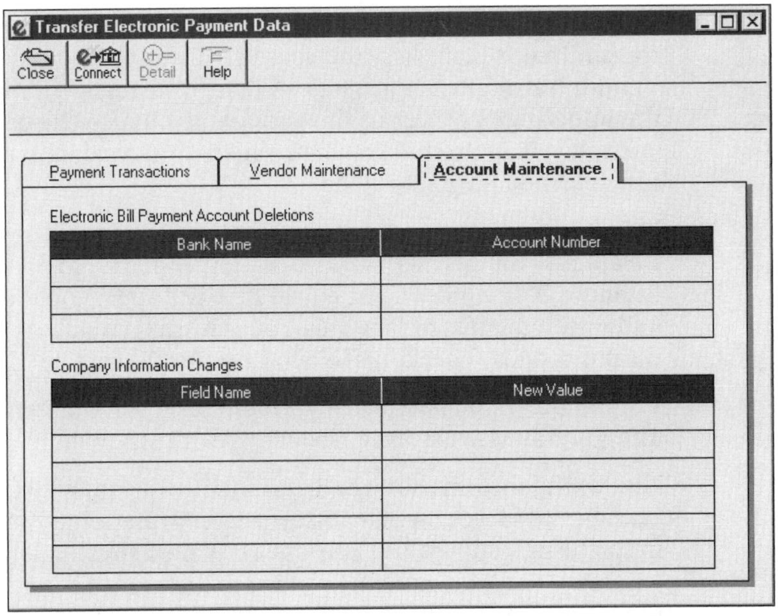

Transfer
Electronic
Payment Data
window with
the Account
Maintenance
folder
displayed
Figure 10-9.

disbursement accounts you deleted in from Maintain | Default Information |
Electronic Bill Payment Information. The Company Information Changes
section displays changes you made in the Maintain Company Information
fields, such as changed security codes.

Starting the Transmission

When you have reviewed the data in the folders and are satisfied with its
accuracy, you are ready to transmit the data to ADP. Start the transmission
by clicking Connect. The About to Transfer Data window appears (not
shown) with information about connecting your modem and offering
transfer options. Select one of the following:

♦ **Send and Receive** Transmit data to ADP and receive information
from ADP (confirmations, e-mail, and so on)

♦ **Receive Only** Do not transmit data to ADP, but receive any
information (useful for checking for e-mail responses and the like)

♦ **Test Data Transfer Connection** Do not send or receive anything;
just test the data transfer connection to make sure it's working correctly.
(Use this when you're first setting up your Electronic Bill Payment
account or when you're making changes to the security code or
transmission phone number.)

Select one of these transfer options and click OK. Peachtree Accounting will transmit the data to ADP, after which one of two windows will appear: Transfer Successful or Transfer Failed, depending on the results of the transmission. In either case, a Session Log is created to show all transmission activity. See "Displaying the Session Log" later in this chapter for information on how to view the Session Log.

Click OK after you have read the message window. The Backup After Transmitting Data window appears:

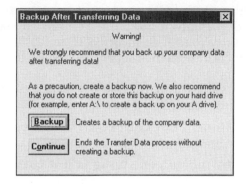

Select Backup to back up data or Continue to end data transfer without backup.

CAUTION: *Always* back up your data after each transmission to ADP. Unless you do so, you are unlikely to keep your data in sync with ADP if you need to restore data from a previous backup.

Handling a Successful Data Transfer

When you transmit data successfully, you will receive one of the following messages in the Transfer Successful window:

♦ **A new Electronic Bill Payment bank account has been added. This needs to be assigned to a GL cash account** You must link the new account to a General Ledger cash account. See "Linking Disbursement Accounts and GL Cash Accounts" at the beginning of this chapter.

♦ **Billing Information has been received, please see your E-Pmt Billing Report** ADP has deducted its monthly service charge from your primary Electronic Bill Payment disbursement account.

♦ **E-mail from the ADP Bill Payment Processing Center has been received** To view messages from ADP, select Electronic Bill Payment from the Tasks menu, then select Mail.

♦ **One or more transactions could not be transmitted** All transactions have been returned due to a synchronization error, such as duplicate payment reference number. The Session Log has detailed information about this error.

Handling a Failed Data Transfer

Although the data transfer process is fairly simple, there can be problems with the transmission. If the connection fails, it may be due to an invalid security code or an incorrect transmission phone number. Other problems can occur with the modem, including the following:

♦ **Modem not turned on** Check the connection to the outlet and try turning the modem off, and then on again.

♦ **Modem not connected to the correct port** Make sure the communications port is not being used by another accessory.

♦ **Initialization string is not correct as entered** Check your modem documentation and enter the correct command.

♦ **No dial tone** Check the dialing prefix.

♦ **Modem speed too high** If the baud rate for your modem doesn't match the baud rate in the Modem Setup window, you will not get a connection.

Displaying the Session Log

You should always check the Session Log after each transmission to ADP. To display the Session Log, select Electronic Bill Payment from the Tasks menu, then select View Session Log. The Session Log contains the following information:

♦ **Batch Number** Session sequence number for the transmission

♦ **Transfer Date/Time** Beginning transmission date and time taken from your system clock

♦ **Summary Information** Transactions sent, not sent, or received, organized according to transaction type

♦ **Detail Information** Individual transaction data, including whether transmission was successful and a reason code if it was not

All transmission information shown in the Session Log is for the latest transmission. For earlier transmission data, see the E-Pmt Service History report.

T IP: It's good practice to print each Session Log as part of your audit trail, as error messages do not appear on the History report. You can select Print from the File menu to print the Session Log.

Processing Service Charge Information

To review billing for ADP services (which is deducted from the primary Electronic Bill Payment disbursement account), select E-Pmt Billing Information from the Report menu.

Enter the service charge information—date, payment reference number, and amount—by selecting Payments from the Tasks menu. The Payments window appears. Next, enter the ADP vendor ID or type their name in the "Pay to the Order Of" field. (You should already have set up a vendor named ADP in the Maintain Vendors window—but not as an Electronic Bill Payment payee.) Enter the billing date, type of charge, and amount from the Electronic Bill Payment Billing Information report. You may also enter a reference number (such as the receiving batch number). Record this transaction by selecting Save or Post. For more information, see "Reconciling Electronic Bill Payments" earlier in this chapter.

Confirming Electronic Bill Payments

During transmission, ADP accepts all pending electronic payments that appear in the Transfer Data window and sends back a temporary confirmation number for each received payment. After ADP has processed payments and sent out checks on the first business day after the transmission, a final confirmation number is sent to you in the next transmission. The confirmation number in both cases is the same for all items transmitted in the same session. To see if you have received final confirmation of Electronic Bill Payments, check the Electronic Bill Payment Status report or the Session Log for items with a Confirmed status.

Confirming Vendor and Account Maintenance

After transmission of maintenance data, and in the same transmission session, ADP sends a confirmation of receipt. You can then transmit Electronic Bill Payments to the vendors whose new data you just transmitted. As with verifying electronic bill payments, you should verify the information you've transmitted by checking the appropriate Electronic Bill Payment

Maintenance report or by checking the Session Log for items with a Confirmed status.

Handling Returned Electronic Bill Payments

Electronic bill payments that are rejected by ADP will be returned. Check the Session Log for detailed information about the rejected transaction, including the reason the payment was rejected. The error message will also give you ideas on how to resolve the error condition. If you need more information on resolving a particular problem, contact ADP.

Handling Returned Checks from Vendors

If your Electronic Bill Payment to a vendor bounces due to insufficient funds, you must deal with the vendor directly. ADP does not debit your primary disbursement account except for monthly service fees.

Maintaining Electronic Bill Payment Data

Once you've set up your company to handle electronic bill payments, entered vendors as Electronic Bill Payment payees, and set up Electronic Bill Payment accounts, you can begin maintenance of the data by entering new data or deleting old data from the windows. You must also maintain Electronic Bill Payment data via backups.

Maintaining Company Information

Should you need to edit the company name, address, or phone number, enter the changes in the Maintain Company Information window. If you delete required information, you will be warned to replace it before you can save the changes. Once saved, the changes will be automatically queued for transmission to ADP. These changes can be reviewed before transmission, as shown earlier in this chapter.

A word of caution: if you turn off the Electronic Bill Payment option, you will lose *all* Electronic Bill Payment setup information, including the following:

♦ Master Business ID

♦ Security code

♦ Transmission telephone number

♦ General Ledger account links to Electronic Bill Payment accounts

♦ Vendor payee numbers

♦ Current e-mail message

If you do turn off Electronic Bill Payment and turn it back on again, you will need to re-enter all the setup information and call ADP, to tell them about deactivating and reactivating Electronic Bill Payment. It will take 24 hours to re-activate your account.

Modifying Default Electronic Bill Payment Setup Information

You cannot modify the Master Business ID once you have set up Electronic Bill Payment, but you can update your security code and the transmission telephone number. You can also delete secondary disbursement accounts. To modify the default Electronic Bill Payment information, select Default Information from the Maintain menu, then select Electronic Bill Payment. The Maintain Electronic Bill Payment Information window appears (as shown in Figure 10-10).

From this window, you can do any of the following:

♦   Change your security code

♦   Change the transmission phone number

♦   Add or change Electronic Bill Payment accounts

♦   Delete secondary disbursement accounts

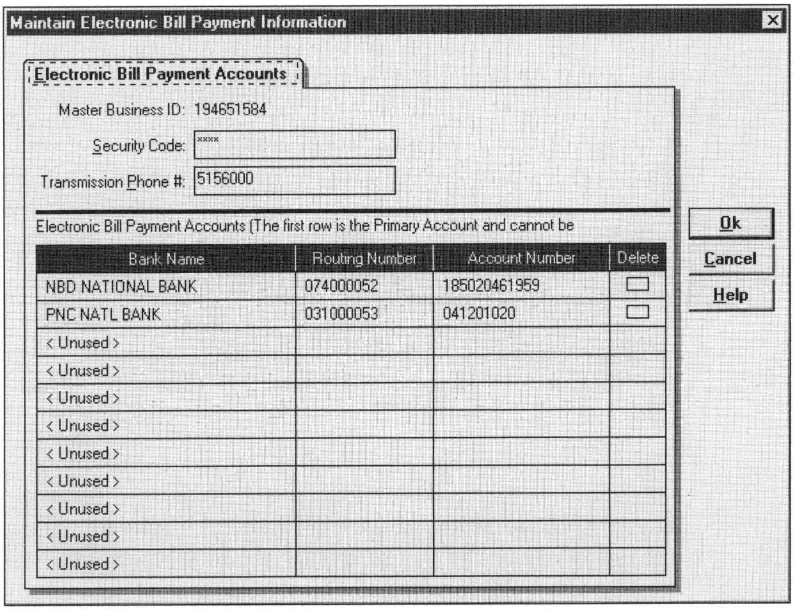

Maintain
Electronic Bill
Payment
Information
window
Figure 10-10.

Maintain Electronic Bill Payment Information

Electronic Bill Payment Accounts

Master Business ID: 194651584

Security Code: ****

Transmission Phone #: 5156000

Electronic Bill Payment Accounts (The first row is the Primary Account and cannot be

Bank Name	Routing Number	Account Number	Delete
NBD NATIONAL BANK	074000052	185020461959	☐
PNC NATL BANK	031000053	041201020	☐
< Unused >			
< Unused >			
< Unused >			
< Unused >			
< Unused >			
< Unused >			
< Unused >			
< Unused >			
< Unused >			

Ok

Cancel

Help

Changing Your Security Code

It is good practice to change your security code occasionally to prevent someone from discovering it and making unauthorized Electronic Bill Payment transmissions. To change your security code, you must first obtain an Electronic Bill Payment Security Code Change form from ADP. You must supply a four-digit number for the new security code, then return the form by mail or fax to ADP.

Once you have received confirmation of the security code change from ADP, you can enter the new security code in the Security Code field and click OK. A message appears asking if you have confirmed the new security code with ADP. Click Yes if this is true or No to exit from the Maintain Electronic Bill Payment Information window.

The Verify Security Code window appears (not shown). Enter the previous security code in the Old Security Code field and enter the changed security code in the New Security Code field. Peachtree will compare the new code to the one entered in the Maintain Electronic Bill Payment Information window. Click OK to accept the new security code. The Maintain Electronic Bill Payment Information window reappears. Click OK again. The change will be effective after your next data transmission to ADP.

CAUTION: Once ADP has made the Security Code change, no payments can be sent until the Peachtree security code is updated in Peachtree. You cannot transfer new payment information until after the new security code has been transmitted to ADP.

Don't forget the new security code—you'll have to call ADP to find out what it is if you do. Write it down and put it in a safe place.

Changing the Transmission Phone Number

You may want to change the transmission phone number for several reasons. Maybe you need to transmit data from a site away from your office, and don't wish to incur long-distance charges. Or perhaps you have obtained a new modem and need to switch to a transmission number that works with the new baud rate.

For a new transmission phone number in your area, call the Local Access Number Information Line at (800)263-7628. An automated service for Electronic Bill Payment clients will help you to obtain the number.

After you have the new number, enter the new phone number of up to 16 characters in the Transmission Phone # field on the Maintain Electronic Bill Payment Information window. (Any extra digits for accessing an outside line or canceling call waiting need to be entered through Modem Setup on the Options menu.) Click OK to save the change and update the telephone number.

Adding or Changing Electronic Bill Payment Accounts

You can add or change Electronic Bill Payment account information at any time. Contact ADP to obtain a Bank Account Change Form or Secondary Account Form.

NOTE: You can phone, fax, or e-mail ADP for the form(s). Peachtree recommends using e-mail for your requests. E-mail questions to ADP-Electronic Banking Services at *billpayhelp@Iadp-ebanking.com*. Include your fax number in the e-mail, so they can fax you the necessary forms.

You must supply a voided check from your company's new primary bank account and a voided check from each of the new secondary bank accounts that you're changing. After you have faxed the completed form(s) and the voided check(s) to ADP, ADP will verify and establish the new account data under your Master Business ID. This will take one to two business days.

After confirmation of the new account data is transmitted to you from ADP, select Electronic Bill Payment from the Tasks menu. Select Transfer Data. The Transfer Electronic Payment Data window appears. Click the Connect button. When the About to Transfer Data window appears, select Send and Receive if you wish to transmit data to ADP, or select Receive Only if you don't have anything to transmit, then click OK.

The Transfer Successful window appears, displaying data on your transmission. If you updated the primary disbursement account, you will receive no message in this window. However, the Session Log will note that you received the update. If you added secondary disbursement accounts, the message, "A new Electronic Bill Payment bank account has been added. This needs to be assigned to a GL cash account" appears. Select OK to close this window.

Click Backup to back up your company data. (Remember, you should do this after every transmission.)

Return to the Maintain menu. Select Default Information and then Electronic Bill Payment to see the updated list of disbursement accounts (shown in the Maintain Electronic Bill Payment Information window). If you do not see the updates in the window, contact ADP.

To link new accounts to Peachtree General Ledger cash accounts, see "Linking Disbursement Accounts and GL Cash Accounts" earlier in this chapter.

Deleting Secondary Disbursement Accounts

The primary disbursement account cannot be deleted if you wish to continue to use Electronic Bill Payment. However, any secondary disbursement account can be deleted at any time. On the Maintain Electronic Bill Payment Information window, check the Delete box next to the secondary disbursement account to be removed, then click OK. The pending transaction you just created will appear on the Account Maintenance folder. The account you just marked for deletion will be deleted by ADP the next time you transmit data and you will receive confirmation of the deletion from ADP.

To reverse (clear or "undelete") a secondary disbursement account deletion before it is transmitted to ADP, uncheck the Delete box for the account you wish to reinstate, then click OK. The deletion will not be transmitted to ADP.

Maintaining Vendor Information

To enter new vendor information (such as name, address, phone number), select Vendors from the Maintain menu. When the Maintain Vendors window appears, select the General tab, then enter a Vendor ID. Enter the new or changed vendor information and click Save to save the new data. This transaction will be sent to ADP in the next transmission.

CAUTION: You must wait to send electronic payments to recently updated vendors until after ADP confirms the updates. You may check confirmation by looking at the Electronic Bill Payment Vendor Maintenance report or the Session Log after the data has been transmitted.

Adding and Deleting Employee Passwords

To safeguard Electronic Bill Payment transactions, you should set up employee passwords that restrict access. Passwords are not required but they're a good idea for security.

From the Maintain menu, select Passwords. The Maintain Passwords window appears:

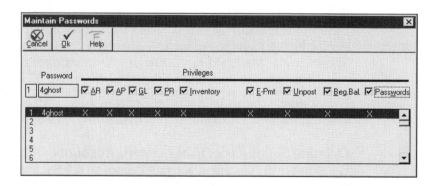

To set up a new employee password, choose the next available number from the list at the bottom of the window. Enter the new password, and then check the boxes for each part of Peachtree Accounting to which you want the employee to have access. When you have entered all the new passwords and have assigned access to each, click OK. To delete a password, select it, press the BACKSPACE key to clear it from the password field, and then click OK. Any additions or deletions you make to passwords will appear the next time you open the company in Peachtree Accounting.

Backing Up Electronic Bill Payment Data

Backing up your company data is absolutely critical for keeping your data synchronized with ADP. If you need to restore data after a power fluctuation or other problem, use the most recent backup of company data. You should have made this backup immediately after your last transmission to ADP.

CAUTION: If your data is not synchronized with ADP, or if you must use a backup that was made *before* your last transmission, the only way to correct it is to call ADP immediately. ADP will walk you through the steps needed to avoid duplicate transmission errors.

For information on backing up your data, see the Peachtree Accounting manual or Chapter 13, "Management Tools and Procedures," of *Peachtree Complete Accounting for Windows Made Easy* (Osborne/McGraw-Hill, 1997).

Printing Electronic Bill Payment Reports

There are two groups of reports that keep you informed of Electronic Bill Payment activity in Peachtree Accounting: Accounts Payable reports that incorporate Electronic Bill Payment data, and new Electronic Bill Payment reports designed to track Electronic Bill Payment transactions, both pending and transmitted.

The new and expanded reports are displayed, customized, and printed in the same way as other Peachtree Accounting reports. First, select Accounts Payable or Electronic Bill Payment from the Reports menu, then select the report you want to print.

NOTE: The standard reports do not include Electronic Bill Payment fields. You must select the new Electronic Bill Payment fields in the Layout folder.

Accounts Payable Reports

Some Accounts Payable reports incorporate Electronic Bill Payment data if Electronic Bill Payment is activated in the Maintain Company Information window. These reports are listed here:

♦ Vendor List

♦ Vendor Master File List

♦ Vendor Ledgers

♦ Check Register

♦ Cash Disbursements Journal

Vendor List and Vendor Master File List

The Vendor List and the Vendor Master File List have two new fields of Electronic Bill Payment information that you can display. Go to the Layout folder for the report and check the Show box next to the following field names: Eligible for E-Pmt and E-Pmt Payee Number. The former will report whether the vendor is set up as an Electronic Bill Payment payee and the latter shows the ADP's Vendor ID number.

Figure 10-11 shows a sample Vendor Master File List with the Electronic Bill Payment information displayed.

Vendor Ledger, Check Register, and Cash Disbursements Journal

The Vendor Ledger, Check Register, and Cash Disbursements Journal have a new field, Payment Type, which shows whether a payment was made by check, cash, or Electronic Bill Payment. Go to the Layout folder for the

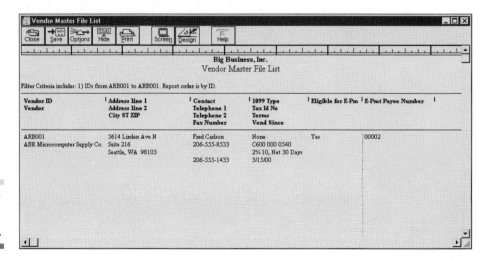

Vendor Master
File List
Figure 10-11.

report and check the Show box next to Payment Type to display the information in these reports.

In addition, the Check Register and Cash Disbursements Journal display an ADP check reference instead of a check number. The Vendor Ledgers report shows a transaction number instead of a check number. Figure 10-12 shows a sample Vendor Ledgers report with the Payment Type field. Figure 10-13 shows a sample Cash Disbursements Journal with an ADP check reference number.

Electronic Bill Payment Reports

When you set up Electronic Bill Payment, you have a whole new category of reports available to you in Peachtree Accounting: Electronic Bill Payment reports. The new reports are as follows:

◆ Electronic Payment Register

◆ Pending Transfer Data

◆ Electronic Payment Status

◆ Vendor Maintenance

◆ ADP E-Pmt Billing Information

◆ E-Pmt Account Maintenance

◆ E-Pmt History

◆ Pending Electronic Payments

◆ Pending Vendor Maintenance

◆ Pending Account Maintenance

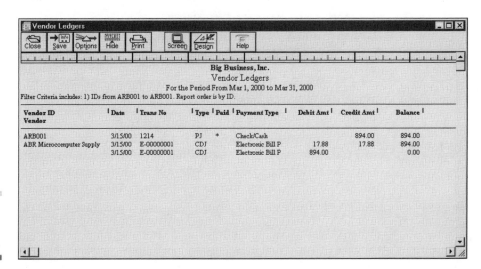

Vendor
Ledgers
Figure 10-12.

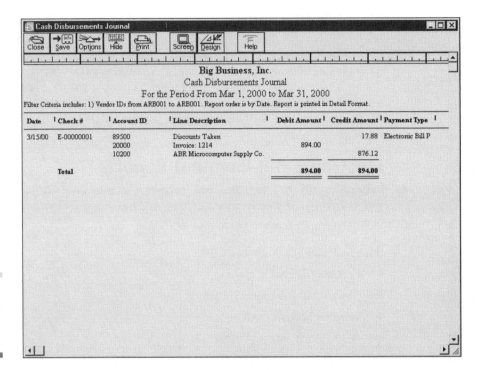

Cash
Disbursements
Journal
Figure 10-13.

NOTE: If your company uses passwords but you do not have password privileges, you will not have access to these Electronic Bill Payment reports.

Electronic Bill Payment Register

The Electronic Bill Payment Register report (shown in Figure 10-14) looks very much like the Peachtree Check Register report, except that it lists payments by reference number instead of check numbers. The default setting for print includes all Pending, Sent, Returned, or Confirmed Electronic Bill Payments for the current accounting period.

The Payment Reference Number is the number assigned to the payment by ADP after transmission to them. If there is no number, the payment has not been transmitted. The Check Date is the date the transaction was posted to the General Ledger. The Cash Account is the General Ledger cash account linked to the Electronic Bill Payment disbursement account. The Amount is the payment total.

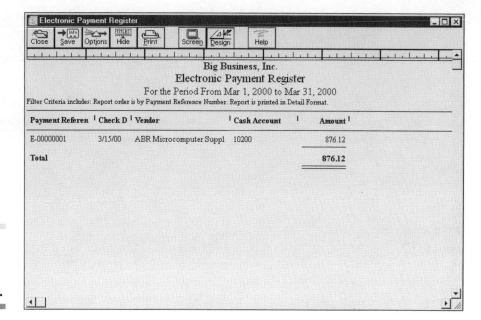

Electronic Bill
Payment
Register
Figure 10-14.

Pending Transfer Data

The Pending Transfer Data report, shown in Figure 10-15, presents information that hasn't been transmitted. This report lists all electronic bill payments, plus vendor, account, and company information maintenance. The Pending Transfer Data report lists the same information as is displayed in the Transfer Data folders. You can use this report for reviewing your data to be transmitted.

On this report, the Status column shows the maintenance transaction status, either pending or returned, as of the ending date of the report. The Transaction Type identifies whether this is for an Account, Company, Payment, or Vendor. The Maintenance Type is add, change, or delete. Vendor ID shows the associated Vendor ID. The remaining information is the bank name or bank account number of the Electronic Bill Payment disbursement account.

Electronic Payment Status

The Electronic Payment Status report presents detailed transaction data, specifying the status of each payment: Confirmed, Pending, Returned, or Sent (as shown in Figure 10-16).

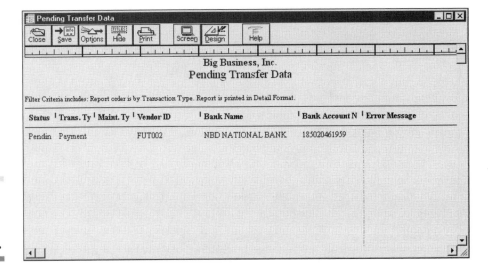

Pending
Transfer
Data report
Figure 10-15.

On this report, the Date Sent column is the date the payment was
transmitted to ADP. The Payment Reference Number is the number assigned
by ADP to the payment. (If there is no reference number, the payment has
not been sent to the Processing Center.) The Amount is the total electronic
bill payment. The Status is the payment status as of the report ending date
(Pending, Sent, Confirmed, or Returned). The Error Message is the message
returned from the Processing Center concerning the payment, if the
payment is rejected.

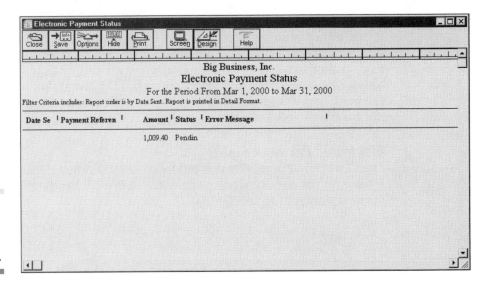

Electronic
Payment
Status report
Figure 10-16.

Vendor Maintenance

The Vendor Maintenance report presents detailed information for Electronic Bill Payment vendor maintenance—additions, changes, and deletions to vendor records. You will usually use this report (shown in Figure 10-17) to determine why a vendor maintenance transaction was rejected.

On this report, the Date Sent column shows the date the maintenance transaction was transmitted to ADP. The Vendor ID is the associated vendor ID. The Maintenance Type is add, change, or delete. The Status is the maintenance transaction status as of the ending date of the report (Pending, Sent, Confirmed, or Returned). The Error Message is the message returned from the Processing Center concerning the payment, if it was rejected.

Account Maintenance

The Account Maintenance report presents detailed information about Electronic Bill Payment account maintenance—updates to all account data (additions, changes, deletions), plus changes to Peachtree Accounting company data. Use this report (shown in Figure 10-18) to determine the reason for rejection of account or company maintenance, and to see if the security code was changed.

On this report, the Date Sent column shows the date the maintenance transaction was transmitted to ADP. The Maintenance Type is add, change, or delete. The Transaction Type shows whether this was a company or account maintenance. The E-Pmt Account Group is the bank name or bank account number of this Electronic Bill Payment disbursement account. (This field is not displayed if the Transaction Type is Company.) The Status is the maintenance transaction status as of the ending date of the report (Pending,

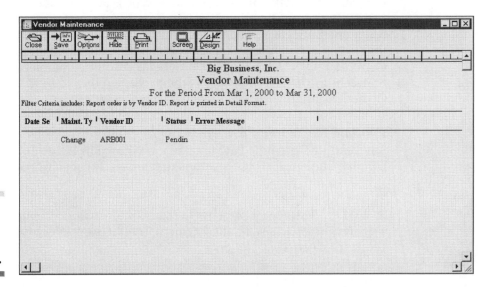

Vendor Maintenance report
Figure 10-17.

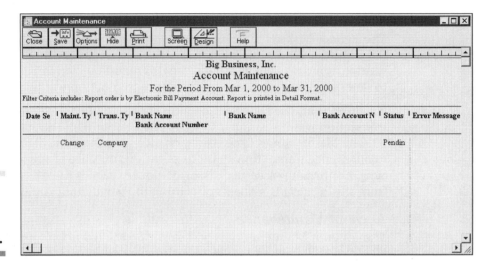

Account
Maintenance
report
Figure 10-18.

Sent, Confirmed, or Returned). The Error Message is the message returned
from the Processing Center concerning the transaction, if it was rejected.

E-Pmt Service History

The E-Pmt Service History report (shown in Figure 10-19) lists all Electronic
Bill Payment history that has not been purged, including all Electronic Bill
Payments and all maintenance transactions—vendor, account, and company
data—during the current accounting period, plus the processing
confirmation number of each transaction.

On this report, the Date Sent column shows the date the transaction was
transmitted to ADP. The Maintenance Type is add, change, or delete. The
Transaction Type shows whether this is payment, vendor, account, or
company transaction. The Status is the maintenance transaction status as of
the ending date of the report (Pending, Sent, Confirmed, or Returned). The
Confirmation Number is ADP's number confirming completion of the
transaction. The Error Message is the message returned from the Processing
Center concerning the transaction, if it was rejected.

Pending Electronic Payments

The Pending Electronic Payments report (shown in Figure 10-20) shows all
pending and returned transactions that are ready for transmission to ADP.

NOTE: This report presents the same information as appears in the
Transfer Data window on the Payment Transactions folder for the current
accounting period.

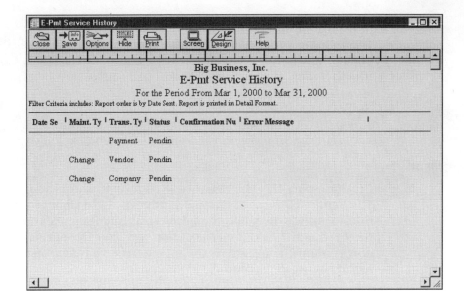

E-Pmt Service
History report
Figure 10-19.

On this report, the Check Date column shows the date the transaction was posted to the General Ledger. The Vendor ID and Vendor Name are the associated vendor ID and vendor name. The Status is the payment status as of the ending date of the report.

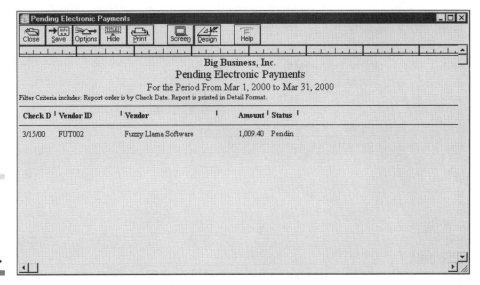

Pending
Electronic
Payments
report
Figure 10-20.

Pending Vendor Maintenance

The Pending Vendor Maintenance report (shown in Figure 10-21) lists all updates to all vendor data for vendors set up for electronic bill payment, plus the status of each transaction.

NOTE: This report displays the same information as is displayed on the Transfer Data window on the Vendor Maintenance folder.

On this report, the Maintenance Type column shows add, change, or delete. The Vendor ID is the associated vendor ID. Field Changed is the name of the field for which the value changed in this maintenance transaction. Old Data shows what the field used to contain and New Data shows what the field now contains. The Status is the maintenance transaction status as of the report ending date (Pending or Returned).

Pending Account Maintenance

The Pending Account Maintenance report (shown in Figure 10-22) lists all pending and returned updates to Electronic Bill Payment account data and Peachtree Accounting company data. This report displays the same information as appears in the Transfer Data window on the Account Maintenance folder.

On this report, the Maintenance Type column shows add, change, or delete. The Transaction Type is either Account or Company. The E-PmtAccount Group is the bank name and account number of the Electronic Bill Payment disbursement account. (If this is a Company maintenance item, this field

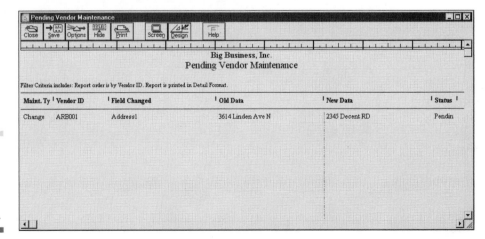

Pending
Vendor
Maintenance
report
Figure 10-21.

10

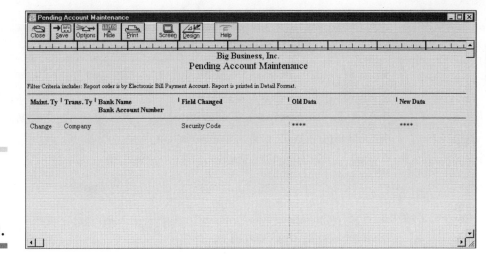

Pending
Account
Maintenance
report
Figure 10-22.

will be blank.) Field Changed is the name of the field the value for which changed in this maintenance transaction. Old Data shows what the field used to contain and New Data shows what the field now contains. The Status is the maintenance transaction status as of the report ending date (Pending or Returned).

Contacting ADP

You may have questions that require answers from ADP. This section describes how to determine whom to call and how to contact ADP, and includes detailed information on how to use the built-in Mail feature.

Determining Whom to Call

Call Peachtree Client Support if you need help with the following:

♦ Installing Peachtree Accounting

♦ Reconciling accounts

♦ Performing General Ledger transactions

♦ Entering payments in Peachtree Accounting

♦ Viewing and customizing reports

If it has been less than 30 days since you registered your copy of Peachtree software, call (770)279-2099. If has been more than 30 days, call (900)555-5005. You will be billed for calls to the 900 number.

Call ADP Client Services if you require help with the following:

♦ Setting up and activating Electronic Bill Payment service

♦ Solving transmission and modem initialization problems

♦ Making electronic bill payments

♦ Producing Electronic Bill Payment reports

♦ Obtaining ADP billing information

♦ Synchronizing Electronic Bill Payment data

Choose one of the following methods to reach ADP :

♦ Use the built-in Electronic Bill Payment Mail feature (the fastest way to reach ADP Processing Center).

♦ Call or fax the Client Services department. You can call the Client Services Helpline at (770)650-6200 ADP from 8:30 AM to 8 PM (EST), Monday through Friday, or fax Client Services at (770)650-6201. The Local Access Number Information Line, (800)263-7628, is open 24-hours a day to provide transmission phone numbers.

♦ Write to ADP at:

ADP Electronic Banking Services
Client Service, 3rd Floor
5800 Windward Pkwy
Alpharetta, GA 30005

Using the Mail Feature

You can e-mail ADP via the Internet at *billpayhelp@adp-ebanking.com,* or send e-mail using the Mail feature of Electronic Bill Payment. The chief difference is timing: Internet e-mail is sent immediately; mail with Electronic Bill Payment is sent during your next transmission to ADP.

ADP Client Services staff reads mail received with other transactions, and then sends responses, where necessary, when you transmit data to ADP again.

All e-mail correspondence under Electronic Bill Payment appears in the Electronic Bill Payment Mail window. This same window is used to create an e-mail message. The Mail feature can be used only to correspond with ADP.

Opening Mail

First select Electronic Bill Payment from the Tasks menu, and then select the Mail option. The Electronic Bill Payment Mail window appears (as shown in Figure 10-23).

The Electronic Bill Payment window displays all e-mail messages, those you've sent or received, one line per message, sorted by date and time. Each message line displays the following information:

♦ Author of the message

♦ Date the message was created

♦ Subject of the message, assigned by the author

♦ Status of the message—whether it is pending or sent, received or read

Reading a Message

To read a message displayed in the Electronic Bill Payment Mail window, either double-click the message or select the message and then select Detail. The Electronic Bill Payment Mail Document window appears (as shown in Figure 10-24).

You can view any message. However, you can edit only pending messages—those that have not yet been transmitted to ADP. (See "Editing a Message" in this section.) Select Print to print the message. Select Close to close the message and return to the Electronic Bill Payment Mail window.

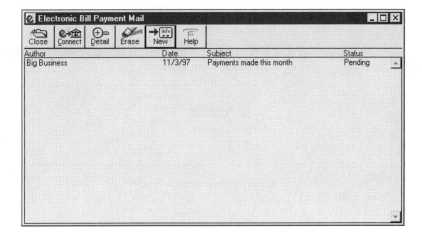

Electronic Bill
Payment Mail
window
Figure 10-23.

Writing a Message

Click New on toolbar of the Electronic Bill Payment Mail window and the Electronic Bill Payment Mail Document window appears (refer to Figure 10-24). The To field will always display "Electronic Bill Payment Center," and the Date field will always display the current system date on your computer. Enter the name of the person sending the message (your name or someone else's) in the From field, and a subject of up to 30 characters in the Subject field.

Enter the message text in the Message box. Your message can be up to 560 characters and spaces. Press ENTER to start a new paragraph. When you are finished, select Save. The Electronic Bill Payment Mail window appears, displaying the line for the message you just wrote, with a status of pending.

Editing a Message

You can edit only pending messages (pending in the Status column). Select the message you wish to edit and then select Detail, or double-click the message. The Electronic Bill Payment Mail window appears. Make your changes in the necessary fields (From or Subject) and the message text. When you are satisfied with your changes, click Save to save or Close to leave the message unchanged.

Erasing a Message

You can delete any message displayed in the Electronic Bill Payment Mail window. Select the message you want to delete, and then click the Erase

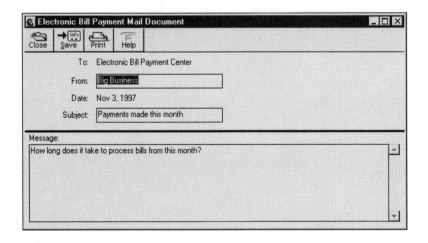

Electronic Bill
Payment Mail
Document
window

Figure 10-24.

toolbar button. A warning message appears. Click Yes to confirm that you want to delete the message, or No to cancel the deletion.

Transmitting Messages

Pending messages can be sent to ADP in one of two ways. The first is by selecting Connect from the Electronic Bill Payment Mail window. Using this method, only your messages are sent to and received from ADP; no Electronic Bill Payment information is transmitted. When the About to Transfer Data window appears, select Send and Receive and click OK. The Transfer Successful window appears. Click OK. A warning appears, suggesting backing up your company data. Click Backup.

CAUTION: Remember to back up your company data after each Electronic Bill Payment transmission!

Pending messages can also be sent by clicking Connect from the Transfer Electronic Payment Data window. However, when using this method, all messages, plus all payment data, and vendor and account maintenance data are sent to ADP.

Using Import/Export with Electronic Bill Payment

To use the import/export feature of Peachtree Accounting, both the company you're exporting data to and the company you are importing data from must be set up to use Electronic Bill Payment and have Electronic Bill Payment activated. Once companies are activated in Electronic Bill Payment, more fields are available for import and export in Peachtree Accounting. Peachtree Accounting uses the new fields in the following three areas:

◆ Vendor List
◆ Chart of Accounts List
◆ Payments Journal

CAUTION: None of the new fields are selected on the Fields folder of the Import and Export windows. To include Electronic Bill Payment information, select the fields.

Vendor List

Once Electronic Bill Payment is activated, the Electronic Bill Payment ID field shows a value for each Peachtree Accounting Vendor. This value can be one of the following:

♦   Zero (0) if the vendor is not set up as an Electronic Bill Payment payee

♦   The payee number if a vendor is set up as an Electronic Bill Payment payee

For a complete list of conditions for importing payees, see "Conditions for Importing Electronic Bill Payment Payees" in Appendix A of the Electronic Bill Payment user's guide.

Chart of Accounts

Once Electronic Bill Payment is activated, each General Ledger account listed in the Chart of Accounts will have the three following new fields for Electronic Bill Payment Account information linked to it:

Field	Contents
E-Pmt Bank	Bank name
E-Pmt Acct	Bank account number
E-Pmt RTN	Routing transmit number

A General Ledger cash account must be linked either to an Electronic Bill Payment account when Electronic Bill Payment is used or to no account whatsoever.

NOTE: You cannot import or export Electronic Bill Payment Accounts. These accounts must be set up in Electronic Bill Payment before they are linked to imported General Ledger accounts.

Exporting General Ledger Cash Accounts
Linked to Electronic Bill Payment Accounts

When you export a General Ledger cash account linked to an Electronic Bill Payment account, three fields that contain account information are added:

10

Field	Contents
Bank Name	Up to 30 characters and spaces (blank if not linked to an Electronic Bill Payment Account)
Bank Account Number	Up to 19 digits and spaces (blank if not linked to an Electronic Bill Payment Account)
Routing Transit Number	A positive number (zero if not linked to an Electronic Bill Payment Account)

Importing General Ledger
Cash Accounts Linked to Electronic Bill Payment Accounts

Before Peachtree Accounting accepts imported General Ledger cash account information linked to an Electronic Bill Payment account, Peachtree Accounting confirms that the following two conditions are true:

♦ The importing company has Electronic Bill Payment activated in the Maintain Company Information window.

♦ The Electronic Bill Payment account linked to the imported General Ledger account is defined in the Maintain Electronic Bill Payment Information window.

Both of these conditions must be met, or Peachtree Accounting will halt the import and display an error message. Error conditions will result for General Ledger accounts already linked to Electronic Bill Payment accounts and Electronic Bill Payment accounts already linked to General Ledger accounts.

Electronic Bill Payments

Once Electronic Bill Payment is activated, payment records display more fields containing payment data. The following new fields will appear:

Field	Contents
E-Pmt Flag	Whether or not payment is an electronic bill payment
E-Pmt Status	The current payment status
E-Pmt Send Batch	The transmission batch number used when the payment was sent to ADP

Field	Contents
E-Pmt Send Date	The transmission date
E-Pmt Send Time	The transmission time
E-Pmt Receive Batch	The transmission batch number used by the Processing Center to confirm or reject payment
E-Pmt Receive Date	The date that transmission was received
E-Pmt Receive Time	The time that receipt of payment as confirmed or rejected was received
E-Pmt Error	The error code received from the Processing Center about the payment
E-Pmt Bank	The name of the bank for the Electronic Bill Payment account used for this payment
E-Pmt Acct	The bank account number for the Electronic Bill Payment account used for this payment
E-Pmt TRN	The transit routing number for the Electronic Bill Payment account used for this payment

Exporting Electronic Bill Payments

If the exporting company has Electronic Bill Payment activated, the following fields are added to the payment record:

Field	Contents
E-Pmt Flag	1 for electronic bill payment, 0 for non-electronic bill payment
E-Pmt Status	0 for non-electronic bill payments; for electronic bill payments, 0 = pending, 1 = sent, 2 = confirmed, 3 = rejected, 4 = canceled
E-Pmt Send Batch Number	A positive integer for electronic bill payment; 0 otherwise
E-Pmt Send Batch Date	A date for electronic bill payment; none otherwise
E-Pmt Send Batch Time	A time for electronic bill payment; none otherwise

Field	Contents
E-Pmt Receive Batch Number	A positive integer for electronic bill payment; null otherwise
E-Pmt Receive Batch Date	A date for electronic bill payment; none otherwise
E-Pmt Receive Batch Time	A time for electronic bill payment; none otherwise
E-Pmt Error	A positive or negative number for electronic bill payment; 0 otherwise
E-Pmt Bank	A string up to 30 characters long for electronic bill payment; null otherwise
E-Pmt	A string up to 10 characters long for electronic bill payment; null otherwise
E-Pmt RTN	A positive number for electronic bill payment; 0 otherwise

Importing Electronic Bill Payments

Before you import payment records that include electronic bill payments, you must do the following:

♦ Define the Electronic Bill Payment account in the Maintain Electronic Bill Payment Information window

♦ Activate Electronic Bill Payment in the Maintain Company Information window for the importing company

If these two actions are taken, the payment record import will occur. If the record is pending, the Transfer Electronic Payment Data window will appear, and the transaction will be queued for transmission to ADP. Otherwise, Peachtree Accounting will display an error message and halt the import.

Rebuilding or Transferring an Existing Company's Data

There are several reasons why you may wish to rebuild data for a company that's already set up in Peachtree Accounting. You may want to change your accounting method from accrual to cash, or cash to accrual. You may want to change the annual number of accounting periods or the fiscal year setup.

Or you may want to transfer data from one company you have set up in Peachtree Accounting to another, new company.

You may transfer list items, such as data for customers, vendors, and the Chart of Accounts, from a company set up on an accrual basis to a cash basis, or from a cash basis to an accrual basis. However, you cannot transfer journal entries from one type of setup to another.

Rebuilding or transferring an existing company's data requires special steps when using Electronic Bill Payment, as described in the rest of this chapter.

CAUTION: While you may "recycle" a Master Business ID by using it for a new company, you may not use the same Master Business ID for both an existing and a new company. If you try to transmit data from the old company after having set up the new company with ADP with the existing Master Business ID, serious out-of-sequence transaction errors will result.

Telling ADP About the Rebuild

Before you do anything else to rebuild your company in Peachtree Accounting, contact ADP and first tell them that you are rebuilding a company already set up in Peachtree. Next, ask for a current list of all Electronic Bill Payment accounts used during the initial setup transmission. This will take 24 hours to produce. Finally, ask for an Electronic Bill Payment payee list (to use in verifying your records).

ADP will notify you when it is time to receive the list of accounts.

Disabling the Multimedia Version of New Company Setup

The multimedia version of New Company Setup does not copy all the default information you will need from the old company to the new company. However, the previous version of New Company Setup, which does copy all the necessary data, is also part of Peachtree Accounting.

To disable the multimedia version of New Company Setup, close Peachtree Accounting. From Windows 95, select Start and then Run on your desktop. (If you are using Windows 3.1, select the Program Manager's File menu and then select Run.)

When the command line appears, type **PAW50.INI** (or the name of the configuration file for your version of Peachtree Accounting) and click OK. When Notepad opens displaying the PAW50.INI file, look in the [Options] section for the following line:

```
DisableNewCompanySetup=No
```

Change "No" to "Yes." (Be sure not to change the uppercase and lowercase in the line.) Finally, select Save from the File menu, then select Exit.

After rebuilding your old company, you may wish to use the New Company Setup feature. In that case, return to PAW50.INI and either change the value after the equal sign in the line you just typed to read "No," or delete the entire line.

Creating a New Company

Creating a new company is the first step in rebuilding your old company. First, enter company information by selecting New Company from the File menu and click OK. After the New Company Setup window appears, select Continue. Enter your new company's information in the appropriate fields. The Form of Business (corporation, S corporation, partnership, or sole proprietorship) should be the same as the old company, if you are doing a rebuild. Click OK. When windows for posting and accounting methods appear, select the appropriate methods and then click OK. Click Continue.

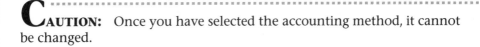

CAUTION: Once you have selected the accounting method, it cannot be changed.

The second step is to copy company defaults. After the Copy Company Defaults window appears, select the old company and then Options. When the default areas appear, check all of them except accounting periods. (If you use the payroll and sales reps features of Peachtree, you must select Employee Defaults, otherwise, errors will occur when you import data.) Click OK to return to the Copy Company Defaults window. The company whose data you want to copy should be highlighted in the box. Click OK again. A window appears that describes the copy process.

The third step happens after the copy process is complete. The standard Set Up Accounting Periods window appears (as shown in Figure 10-25).

Number of Accounting Periods in the Fiscal Year   Enter the number of accounting periods (usually 13).

First period in Which You Will Be Entering Data   Enter the first period in which you are entering data. Note that if you are setting this company up during a period, such as period 8, and you don't want to enter the prior period detail, Peachtree Accounting will default to period 8 when you complete the new company setup.

Calendar Year   Enter this payroll year.

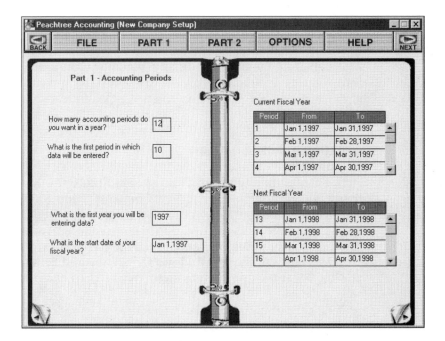

Set Up
Accounting
Periods
window
Figure 10-25.

Current Fiscal Year Accounting Periods Table   Fill the From and To date
columns for Period 1. Peachtree Accounting will automatically enter the
dates for the rest of the year. Scroll down to verify the year's dates.

Next Fiscal Year Accounting Periods   Scroll down to verify the year's dates,
and click OK.

When a warning message appears about verifying the dates, click Continue
to save the data entered on this screen. The New Company Setup window
reappears. Click Close.

Activating Electronic Bill Payment for the New Company
You must activate Electronic Bill Payment before you can build your new
company data. Once Electronic Bill Payment is activated, the fields to be
used for payments can be imported.

NOTE: If Electronic Bill Payment was used in your existing Peachtree
company, but is not necessary for the new company, you are still required to
activate Electronic Bill Payment so Peachtree Accounting knows from where
to import all the data. Once the company data is rebuilt, you need not use
Electronic Bill Payment; you can deactivate it if you wish.

Select Company Information from the Maintain menu. The Maintain Company Information window appears. Check Use Electronic Bill Payment, and click OK. After the message appears telling you that Electronic Bill Payment has been activated, click OK.

Rebuilding a Company

The next part of the rebuild process involves transferring data from the existing company to the new company. You must follow this process in the order in which it is shown below. But before proceeding with a company rebuild, be sure to back up the new company data.

1. **Copy Report and Tax Data.**   Close the new company file and exit Peachtree Accounting, then copy the following files from the old company subdirectory to the new subdirectory:

   ♦ taxcode.dat (for sales tax)

   ♦ taxauth.dat (for sales tax bodies)

   ♦ taxtable.dat (for payroll taxes)

   ♦ report.dat (for financial reporting)—copy only if you customized at least one financial report. If in doubt, copy.

   ♦ rptdata.dat (for reports other than financial)—copy only if you customized at least one financial report. If in doubt, copy.

2. **Export Maintenance Data.**   Open Peachtree Accounting and the file for the original company. Choose Select Import/Export from the File menu, and export these items in the following order:

   ♦ Chart of Accounts List from General Ledger

   ♦ Employee List from Payroll

   ♦ Vendor List from Accounts Payable. Select the Layout tab before exporting, and select the field Electronic Bill Payment ID

   ♦ Customer List from Accounts Receivable

   ♦ Inventory Item List from Inventory

   ♦ Job List from Jobs

3. **Import Maintenance Data.**   Close the old company and open the new company, then import these items in the following order:

   ♦ Chart of Accounts List from General Ledger

   ♦ Employee List from Payroll

   ♦ Vendor List from Accounts Payable. Select the Layout tab before importing, and select the field Electronic Bill Payment ID

♦ Customer List from Accounts Receivable

♦ Inventory Item List from Inventory

♦ Job List from Jobs

4. **Enter Inventory Item Beginning Balances and Job Beginning Balances, if there are balances.**

NOTE: If you are switching accounting methods from cash to accrual basis, or vice versa, this is the end of the import process. Transaction files in companies with different accounting methods cannot be imported.

5. **Set up Electronic Bill Payment for the new company.** Before you can set up Electronic Bill Payment and establish payment accounts for the new company, you must be instructed by ADP to re-transmit the initial setup information and Electronic Bill Payment account data. After this is done, follow the same procedure you used to set up Electronic Bill Payment for the old company, as described at the beginning of this chapter. However, when you are prompted during the setup process to go to the Maintain Vendors window, click Cancel, and then verify that your Electronic Bill Payment account data has been received. Verify by selecting Default Information from the Maintain menu, then Electronic Bill Payment. The same Master Business ID should appear for both the old company and the new company, and the Electronic Bill Payment account list should also be the same for both companies. Finally, back up the new company data immediately!

6. **Export and import journal entries.** Now close the new company. Open the original company. On the Filter tab, change the date range to ALL. Set the beginning date several years past (to assure that all the necessary data is exported). Export the journals shown below in the following order:

♦ General Journal from General Ledger

♦ Purchases Journal from Accounts Payable

♦ Payments Journal from Accounts Payable

NOTE: Select the Layout tab before you proceed and also check these: E-Pmt flag, E-Pmt Status, E-Pmt Send Batch, E-Pmt Send Date, E-Pmt Send Time, E-Pmt Receive Batch, E-Pmt Receive Date, E-Pmt Receive Time, E-Pmt Error, E-Pmt Bank, E-Pmt Acct, and E-Pmt RTN.

10

- ♦ Assemblies Journal from Inventory
- ♦ Adjustments Journal from Inventory
- ♦ Sales Journal from Accounts Receivable
- ♦ Cash Receipts Journal from Accounts Receivable
- ♦ Payroll Journal from Payroll

Now close the original company and open the new company. Import the same journals that you just exported, in the same order.

7. **Compare the two companies.** Post and print all of the necessary reports, and make any adjusting entries that are required. Because the new company will be using the same Master Business ID as the old company, you must not use the older company data. If you are going to use Electronic Bill Payment for the new company, the data should be correct and complete.

Summary

This chapter has shown you how to use Peachtree's Electronic Bill Payment Feature to automate your check writing process. The next (and final) chapter describes the programs on the CD-ROM accompanying this book and additional programs of interest to Peachtree Accounting users.

PART 3

Using Peachtree Accounting with Other Products

The third and final section of this book focuses on products that you can use with Peachtree Accounting and Windows to make them even more powerful and effective. These programs include add-ons specifically designed for Peachtree Accounting, and popular programs such as Time & Chaos32, Visio, WinZip, Paint Shop Pro, Eudora, Free Agent, and CompuShow for Windows. Many of the programs featured in this section appear on the CD accompanying this book, giving you a chance to try the programs out immediately.

11

Peachtree Accounting Add-ons and Other Software

The previous chapter showed you how to use Electronic Bill Payment. This final chapter shows you how to further enhance the effectiveness of Peachtree Accounting with an assortment of add-ons and other useful programs. Some of the products described here offer specific enhancements and extensions to the Peachtree Accounting software; others are more general but have gained laudable reputations as indispensable tools for the small business or home office user. Below each product description, you'll find contact information and company web site or e-mail addresses for your convenience. In addition, many of the programs described here appear on the CD that accompanies this book.

The Peachtree Accounting add-ons featured in this chapter (all of which appear on the CD) extend Peachtree Accounting's features in a variety of ways.

♦ PAW/et (Peachtree Accounting for Windows Extension Tool) from Multiware, Inc. lets you import and export data between Peachtree Accounting and other programs.

♦ The Peachtree Backup Utility from Datasoft Corporation lets you automatically back up tax files and form files along with your data files for one or many companies in a single operation.

♦ Wizard's Utility Pack for Peachtree contains five programs that let you perform a diverse selection of tasks, including delete General Journal entries, calculate the weight of a shipment and the number of items shipped, print receipts for large numbers of invoices, track information on the inventory items actually shipped, and print reports of chart of accounts ending balances and budget forecasts for a specified period.

♦ Three demo programs from Wizard Business Solutions, Inc. let you issue certified payroll reports (a requirement of many federal construction projects and most state and local projects that utilize federal funds) from Peachtree Accounting information, print checks on blank check-stock paper rather than on expensive preprinted forms, and create Federal W-2 reports on magnetic media.

In addition to these add-ons for Peachtree Accounting, this chapter also describes a number of useful programs and tools that can help you to conduct business—both on the Web and in general, as follows:

Programs	Type of Software
Time & Chaos32	A personal information manager for managing your time, tasks, and contacts
Expert Software	A series of CDs with tutorials about Windows 95 and the Internet, adding fonts to your system, providing libraries of clipart for web sites, and many other programs and libraries

Programs	Type of Software
WinZip	A tool for compressing large files and groups of files
Arachnophilia	An HTML editor for creating and maintaining web pages
Dunce	A handy utility that adds options to the standard Windows 95 Dial-Up Networking feature
Eudora Lite and Eudora Pro	Two programs for sending and receiving e-mail
Free Agent 1.11	A reader for Internet newsgroups
WinCode	A handy utility that decodes Internet files that aren't otherwise decoded
Visio Standard Test Drive	A tool for creating effective business charts
Paint Shop Pro 4.14	A paint program that lets you create and modify graphics files for business and for your web site
CompuShow for Windows	A graphic viewing program, particularly effective at looking at groups of graphic files
F-PROT, McAfee Virus Scan, NAV, Anyware	A variety of programs for detecting and cleaning viruses from your system

11

Many of the companies whose products are described in this chapter have shareware or demo versions on the CD-ROM accompanying this book. Other products, while not included on the CD-ROM, are available through the companies' web sites. You'll find company web site and contact information after each product description.

NOTE: Although the versions of the software featured on the CD are the latest available as of press time, many of these programs change frequently. You are strongly encouraged to check the manufacturer's web sites for later versions of these products and additional program information that may have appeared after this book and CD were produced.

In general, the software in this chapter requires a Windows 95-compatible computer. If you are already running Windows 95, you should have enough capacity on your system to use the software. For Peachtree Accounting add-ons, you will also need a copy of Peachtree Accounting installed on your system. Any requirements that differ from these basic requirements are listed with the program's contact information.

What Is Shareware?

Shareware is software that is distributed on a "try before you buy" basis. You can load the software on your system, try it out, and if you like it, you register with the author for a small fee. Shareware is usually cheaper (and frequently better) than many of its commercial counterparts. You can share the software with anyone, hence the name. Somewhat similar to shareware is "freeware," products that are distributed free of charge, with no registration fee. Like the commercial software you purchase in a store, shareware (and freeware) products are copyrighted and their authors retain all rights to that software. In other words, you can use it yourself, but you should not distribute the software without permission from the author. The terms for each program are laid out in the program's license agreement.

 NOTE: Your financial contributions help the shareware authors recoup some of their development and distribution costs, and enable them to finance further developments to their products. Wherever possible, pricing and contact information have been included for your convenience, but the availability of products, pricing, and contact information is subject to change.

Most shareware programs are offered on a limited-time basis. After the time period expires, you should register the program with the author or delete it from your system. Registering your shareware offers you the chance to receive advance notice of upgrades and new releases. There may also be additional benefits to you, such as technical support, and many shareware users are offered the chance to become beta testers for new releases of products.

Peachtree Accounting Add-ons

In addition to the standard features you'll find in Peachtree Accounting, there are also several programs on the market that have been specifically designed to extend the features and capabilities of Peachtree Accounting. Three companies, Multiware, DataSoft, and Wizard, have been at the

11

forefront of developing Peachtree Accounting add-ons. Their programs are featured in the next few sections of this chapter.

A word of caution before you begin: Peachtree Accounting and the functions it performs are complex. *Always* be sure you have current backups before using any add-on product with Peachtree Accounting. Always verify the accuracy of the information whenever you write a record from an add-on application to the Peachtree Accounting files. And if you try a new application that is intended to extend Peachtree Accounting, you'll want to test the way the two applications work together. Because the information may be posted across different parts of the application, be sure to check the related Peachtree Accounting files to ensure that the information is being updated correctly. For example, try varying or omitting information in some fields to understand how it might affect your results.

PAW/et

PAW/et (an acronym for "Peachtree Accounting for Windows Extension Tool") from Multiware, Inc. extends the capability of the basic Peachtree package by enabling you to export data from your Peachtree Accounting database to other programs, and to import data from other programs into Peachtree Accounting. With this capability, you'll be able to extend the effectiveness and efficiency of your Peachtree Accounting software. PAW/et is especially valuable because Multiware has done the background research into importing and exporting data from the Peachtree Accounting database. (A demo of this product has been included on the CD.) You can download free reference documentation from the company's web site which covers installation, using the product, and important precautions about using this type of application with Peachtree Accounting. The PAW/et main window appears in Figure 11-1.

PAW/et comes in two versions: PAW/et2 is the original application and PAW/et95 is a variation that is compatible with MS Access 95, but is much slower. You'll want to use PAW/et2 if speed is important to you.

CAUTION: Be careful during installation of this product. Even though PAW/et95 is compatible with Microsoft Access 97, it was developed in Microsoft Access 95. If you install PAW/et95 and you are using Access 97, the product will ask if you want to convert PAWET951.MDB to an Access 97 database. Choose Yes. However, be careful not to convert PAWDATA.MDB. According to Multiware, this file must remain in Access 95 format so that PAWENG.EXE can access it properly.

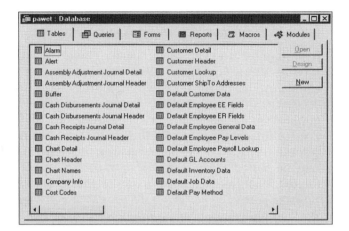

PAW/et main
window
Figure 11-1.

Besides working with Peachtree Accounting for Windows and Peachtree
Complete Accounting for Windows, PAW/et also works with Peachtree First
Accounting. However, there are a few limitations of which you should be
aware. There are some tables that were not in First Accounting. You will not
be able to attach the Alarm Table, the Alert Table, nor the Tax Table, since
they are not included in First Accounting.

CAUTION: Be careful whenever you write data back to Peachtree
Accounting files. Because you are modifying data without giving Peachtree a
chance to validate it, you may accidentally corrupt files if the data you write
back is not correct or complete.

PAW/et

Minimum System Requirements:

♦ Standard minimum requirements

♦ Microsoft Access Version 2.0 (for PAW/et2) or Microsoft Windows 95 or
NT, and Microsoft Access 95 or 97 (for PAW/et95)

Price: $179 for full product and one year of support and updates

Multiware, Inc.
216 F Street, Suite 161
Davis, CA 95616
Phone: (916) 756-3291
Fax: (916) 756-3292
http://www.dcn.davis.ca.us/~walraven/pawet.htm

Peachtree Backup Utility

11

Peachtree Accounting just comes with basic backup facilities. Although you've seen in the Peachtree Accounting manual and in *Peachtree Complete Accounting for Windows Made Easy* how to use the Windows backup program to back up your files, this is not as effective as having a single backup utility that lets you back up everything for all your companies in one simple step. DataSoft Corporation has produced the Peachtree Backup Utility, a handy little program that lets you back up data files, tax files, and custom form files either for a single company or for multiple companies as a single backup operation.

You can download a demo version of the Peachtree Backup Utility from DataSoft's web site at *http://www.dscorp.com*.

Peachtree Backup Utility

Minimum System Requirements:

◆   Standard minimum requirements

Price: $49.99 plus shipping and handling

DataSoft Corporation - MPLS
12 South Sixth Street
Suite 323
Minneapolis, MN 55402
Phone: (612) 399-0115
Fax: (612) 399-0121
Fax-on-demand: (612) 399-0118 (24 hours)
datasoftmpls@compuserve.com
http://www.dscorp.com

Wizard's Utility Pack for Peachtree

Wizard's Utility Pack for Peachtree is a feature of the CD accompanying this book. It contains the following programs:

Program	Description
Delete General Journal Entries	Deletes out-of-date general journal entries.
Invoice Screen Display Weight and Units Shipped	Calculates the total weight of a shipment and the number of items shipped on this invoice.
Payment Reports	Lets you print receipts that contain more than ten invoices.
Units Invoice	Creates invoices outside of Peachtree Accounting that let you specify each item's unit of measure and then computes the appropriate invoice amounts.
Variance Report	Exports the ending balances for your chart of accounts so you can specify the financial period and the accounts you want to compare to create a variance report.

Each of these programs is discussed briefly in this section. (Complete documentation for each program appears on the CD in the directory for the program.)

Delete General Journal Entries

The Delete General Journal Entries program lets you delete out-of-date general journal entries. This may be helpful if you are running short of disk space or if processing is taking too long when doing general journal reports.

Invoice Screen Display Weight and Units Shipped

The Invoice Screen Display Weight and Units Shipped lets you calculate the total weight of the items in a given shipment and the number of items shipped. The information displayed by Invoice Screen Display Weight and Units Shipped doesn't appear on the invoice; it is only for use by you and your company's Shipping department.

Payment Reports

The Payment Reports let you print receipts that have more than ten invoices. These reports aren't programs, but are rather report files that you copy to your Peachtree Accounting program directory (or, if you running Peachtree Accounting on a network, you need to copy the files to the

Peachtree Accounting data path). The reports will then appear on the Reports menu in Peachtree Accounting under Accounts Payable.

Units Invoice

The Units Invoice program lets you track information on the inventory items you have shipped. You can use this program to track the unit of measure for the line items that appear on the invoice: the Units Invoice program calculates the price for each item based upon the quantity and the unit of measure. The program furthermore lets you create invoices independent of Peachtree Accounting, which lets you specify the unit of measure for the line items and calculates the invoice amounts from that information.

11

Variance Report

The Variance Report worksheet lets you export the ending balances for your chart of accounts so you can specify the financial period and the accounts you want to compare to create a variance report. You can use this report to compare General Ledger ending balances with the forecasted budget amounts.

To run the Variance Report, you will need to start Peachtree Accounting and then open the varrept.xls file in Microsoft Excel. Click the following three tabs to gather the information and generate the report:

♦ The Account-Filter tab creates a worksheet from the General Ledger chart of accounts for your company.

♦ The Period-Filter tab creates a worksheet of accounting period information for your company.

♦ The Report tab creates a worksheet containing the variance report information. This worksheet is based on the accounts and periods you have selected.

Wizard Demo Programs

In addition to the programs in Wizard's Utility Pack for Peachtree, there are three additional programs in demo versions on the CD accompanying this book, as listed in the following table:

Demo Program	Description
CertPay Wizard	Lets you issue certified payroll reports (a requirement of many federal construction projects and most state and local projects that utilize federal funds) from Peachtree Accounting information.
CheckWizard	Lets you print Peachtree Accounting checks on blank check-stock paper rather than on expensive preprinted forms.
WizMag W-2	Lets you use employee information in your Peachtree Accounting files to prepare magnetic media 1997 Federal W-2 reports that are compliant with the Social Security Administration publication TIB-4. WizMag W-2 also lets you print reports of the employee information written to magnetic media.

CertPay Wizard

Do you need to issue certified payroll reports? The United States Department of Labor imposes many requirements on federal construction projects and most state and local projects that utilize federal funds. One of these requirements is that contractors and subcontractors on these projects report weekly certified payroll data (the Davis-Bacon Act). The information must be reported on form WH-347, issued by the Department of Labor. Although this can be a significant task, CertPay Wizard from Wizard Business Solutions can reduce the time you need to spend on the task.

You can use CertPay if you are using Peachtree Complete Accounting Plus Time and Billing for Windows. CertPay extracts the payroll data and formats it for the WH-347 form. After you print it out, the only thing left to do is sign it and send it in. CertPay Wizard can be used with one company or multiple companies, and includes fields for entering race/gender information for use in specific reports to the government.

NOTE: If you want to install CertPay Wizard, be sure to fill in your registration information. CertPay uses this as the source for your company information, so it's important not to skip this step.

CertPay uses Peachtree's time tickets, which you use to enter Employee Hours for payroll and invoicing functions.

Using Time Tickets

For each employee, you'll create a time ticket in Peachtree Accounting, as you would normally for Payroll. Next, you export the time tickets for the employees from the current pay period from Peachtree Accounting to the CertPay Wizard. To do this, open the company in Peachtree Accounting, then Select Import/Export from the File menu. In the Select Import/Export Window, choose Time/Expense, and Time Ticket Register. Choose the information you want to export, then click Export. The Time Ticket Register appears (not shown). On the Options tab, make sure that Include Headings is selected, then choose the destination for the information and click OK. (For more information on how to change the accounting period, see your Peachtree Accounting documentation or see Chapter 13, "Management Tools and Procedures" in *Peachtree Complete Accounting for Windows Made Easy* [Osborne/McGraw-Hill, 1997].)

Using CertPay Wizard

Using CertPay Wizard is fairly straightforward. You'll be guided through the 7-step procedure, with cues from the title on the top of the main windows, such as Step 2 of 7. The following steps give you a quick overview of the process. (Complete documentation can be found on the CD in the CERTPAYD.DOC file in the \Wizard\CertPay folder.)

Step 1. Fill out the Welcome Screen.

Enter the information for the employee's payroll fields, payroll levels, race and gender information (optional; for state and federal anti-discrimination requirements), the location of export files, and information on when to refresh the information for the accounting period.

Step 2. Open or start a contract.

You choose either a new or existing contract to fill out for reporting purposes.

Step 3. Enter the contract information.

Enter, review, and edit information about a specific contract.

Step 4. Select Employees.

You'll need to enter at least one employee for this screen, which lists the employees assigned to the contract you selected.

Step 5. Specify the payroll number.

Here you'll group together the paychecks for a particular period for this contract.

Step 6. Enter the payroll number information.

Enter, review, and edit information about the payroll for a specific period.

Step 7. Print the CertPay reports.

Print the Payroll Report, Other Fields Report, and the Statement of Compliance Report to your printer.

NOTE: During printing, the program disables the Exit and Finish buttons to ensure that the information is not corrupted by an interruption. Once the information is sent to the printer, you'll be able to use the Exit and Finish buttons again.

CertPay Wizard

Minimum System Requirements:

♦ Standard minimum requirements

♦ Peachtree Complete Accounting for Windows Plus Time & Billing or Peachtree Accounting for Windows (Batch 4.0 and later versions)

Wizard Business Solutions, Inc.
3630 Capital Blvd.
Raleigh, NC 27604
Phone: (919) 981-0505 or (800) 322-4650
Fax: (919) 981-0099
http://www.wizard-net.com

CheckWizard

The CheckWizard utility is simple but remarkably effective: it lets you print Peachtree Accounting checks on blank check-stock paper rather than on

11

expensive preprinted forms. For companies that print large numbers of payroll checks, this can result in substantial savings.

Installing the CheckWizard program is very simple: you simply copy the files to a directory and use the Fonts option on the Control Panel to install the three MICR (magnetic-ink character recognition) fonts for printing the numbers on the checks. After you configure the program with the information for your checks—bank name, account number, company name and address, and so on—you import payroll checks from Peachtree Accounting. You can set up CheckWizard to use multiple banks and accounts for checks. You can add, modify, or delete the information for checks as necessary.

WizMag W-2 '97 Federal Edition

Are you filing your W-2 reports on magnetic media? If so, you'll want to use WizMag W-2 from Wizard Business Solutions. WizMag W-2 extracts payroll data from Peachtree Accounting and then formats the information as required by the Social Security Administration and the Internal Revenue Service. WizMag W-2 then copies the payroll data onto a 3.5" or 5.25" diskette. Wizard Business Solutions also offers programs for filing State W-2 reports on magnetic media.

NOTE: To set up WizMag W-2, you must first copy the files in the \Wizard\W2 Demo directory to the \Windows\Temp directory on your hard disk, and then run setup.exe. You cannot install WizMag W-2 directly from the CD that accompanies this book.

Before you use WizMag W-2, Wizard Business Solutions recommends you follow these steps:

1. Open Peachtree Accounting.
2. Ensure that the company whose payroll information is being reported is operating in the accounting period ending December 31, 1997.
3. Be sure that the calendar year is set to 1996 or 1997, even if you have already entered data for 1998 and have been operating in a 1998 accounting period.

NOTE: To change accounting periods, select System from the Tasks menu, then select Change Accounting Period. For more information on how to change the accounting period, see your Peachtree Accounting documentation or see Chapter 13, "Management Tools and Procedures" in *Peachtree Complete Accounting for Windows Made Easy* (Osborne/McGraw-Hill, 1997).

4. Be sure that *all* payroll data for 1997 has been entered. If you make any changes after WizMag W-2 writes the W-2 reports, the reports will be invalid.

5. Make sure that your company address information is complete and correct by selecting Company Information from the Maintain menu. WizMag uses this information to report to Social Security.

6. Check the directory structures. All companies must be one directory below the DATAPATH directory specified in PAW*xx*.INI, where *xx* is 35 or 36 (in Peachtree Accounting for Windows 3.5), 40 or 41 (in Peachtree Complete Accounting for Windows 4.0), or 45 (in Peachtree Complete Accounting Plus Time & Billing).

7. Close the company, but don't exit Peachtree Accounting. Peachtree Accounting must be running without an open company or WizMag will not work properly.

CAUTION: Never attempt to enter or change company data while WizMag is running.

Running WizMag W-2 for the First Time

The first time you run WizMag W-2, you will need to select a company name from the list that WizMag W-2 extracts from Peachtree Accounting. Occasionally during this process, you might see an error message that reads "System Error 11." Wizard Business Solutions recommends that you ignore the message and instead keep trying until you are able to select the company name for which you want to run the W-2 report.

Generating W-2 Reports for Magnetic Disk

The first screen you see after you select the company name is the WizMag W-2 main window, shown in Figure 11-2.

From the Setup menu, you can choose between Standard Payroll Fields and Custom Payroll Fields. Standard Payroll fields contain common information such as Gross Wages, Federal Withholding, Social Security Withheld, and

WizMag W-2
main window
Figure 11-2.

11

Medicare Withheld. Your company may use Custom Field Names, such as Gross instead of Gross Wages, or Ssecur, instead of Social Security. On the Custom Field Names screen, you input the field names used by your company for these specific categories. If you have other field names that are more distinctive or different, you can use the Custom Field Names window to enter these names.

There is no cancel button in the Custom Field Names window. To cancel any changes you've made to a row, press ESC. To delete an entire row, click the mouse once on the left of a field name and then press DELETE on your keyboard.

NOTE: When naming field names, you cannot use spaces, hyphens, slashes, or any punctuation or special characters (except for underscores) in the name. For example, you can use "FringeBenefits," and "Fringe_Benefits," but not "Fringe Benefits," "Fringe-Benefits," or "Fringe/Benefits."

You'll also need to fill out the information on the Other Information window. This information includes the prior reported employer ID and information about the transmitter, the person or organization that is preparing the data and sending it to the federal government. This window also requests the following information:

♦ **Prior Reported Employer ID** This is your company's employer identification number, if it changed during the tax year.

♦ **Establishment Number** You probably won't have this unless you're a State agency. If you don't have one, just leave it blank.

♦ **Names Stored By** This reports whether your employees are stored in Peachtree Accounting by their first names or by their last names.

♦ **Employment Type** This categorizes the kind of business in which your company is engaged. Most respondents will select Regular.

Once you've supplied the information requested, you can click Accept.

Writing the Information to Disk

The next step in the process is to write the information to a magnetic disk. You do this by clicking Write on the WizMag W-2 main window. Select the drive you want to use, and then insert a disk into the requested drive. WizMag W-2 extracts the information from Peachtree Accounting, reformats it, and saves it to your disk.

Printing Reports and Totals

After you write the information to disk, you can generate reports to check the accuracy of your data. There are two reports, the Employee Report and the Totals From Disk report, that you should generate.

To print the Employee Report, go to the WizMag W-2 main window and choose Print from the File menu. This reads the data directly from the disk you just created. You can print the report either according to your employee's social security numbers, or in the order that the information was retrieved from Peachtree Accounting.

To print the Totals From Disk report, choose Print Totals From Disk from the File menu in the main window. This reads the data directly from the disk you just created. The report includes the Intermediate Totals, the Employer Totals, and the File Totals figures and places them in a report. The "totals" in this report refer to the following:

◆ **Intermediate Totals** This total records increments of 41 employees as they are reported to disk. In smaller companies (fewer than 41 employees), this total will be zero.

◆ **Employer Totals** These are the totals for the selected company in Peachtree Accounting.

◆ **File Totals** These are the totals of all employees reported on the W-2 report.

 NOTE: Before printing, you can preview the Intermediate Totals, the Employer Totals, and the File Totals, which are compiled into the Totals Report.

Ensuring Accuracy

Ensuring the accuracy of your W-2 information is very important. You can compare the Employer Totals and the File Totals to the data you've created in the Yearly Earnings Report in Peachtree Accounting.

Checklist for Mailing W-2 Magnetic Media

Once you've prepared your diskettes, you need to label each diskette with the tax year, the Federal Employer Identification Number, the name, city, and state of the company transmitting the information, an inventory control number, the operating system the diskette was created with, and the volume number (if the data is on more than one diskette).

CAUTION: Always keep backup copies of any diskette you file with the government for audit purposes (and in case the diskette is lost or damaged). You must also make backups of the company data used to create the W-2s and keep them on file for four years.

11

Fill in a copy of form 6559 in TIB-4 for each diskette you're sending. (The instructions come with the form.) Store copies of the completed form 6559 with the other backups. Pack your diskettes in a diskette mailer or other secure package together with the form 6559 and mail to the Social Security Administration. (Current addresses are in the WizMag W-2 '97 Federal Edition documentation.) Don't use rubber bands, staples, or paper clips on diskettes, as they can bend and damage the diskettes.

NOTE: If you are submitting diskettes for more than one company, you must package and ship the diskettes for each company separately.

WizMag W-2

Minimum System Requirements:

- Standard minimum requirements
- 10 MB free hard disk space
- Peachtree Accounting for Windows 3.5, Peachtree Complete Accounting for Windows 4.0, or Peachtree Complete Accounting for Windows Plus Time & Billing

Wizard Business Solutions, Inc.
3630 Capital Blvd.
Raleigh, NC 27604
Phone: (800) 322-4650 or (919) 981-0505
Fax: (919) 981-0099
http://www.wizard-net.com

Other Peachtree Add-ons
from Wizard Business Solutions

Wizard Business Solutions also offers many other fine programs that extend the functionality of Peachtree Accounting software. For more information on the programs or for pricing information on any of the programs in this section, contact Wizard Business Solutions, Inc.

Sales to Purchases Wizard

In many businesses, sales are custom orders and materials and parts are purchased from vendors after the sales orders are taken. If this describes your company, you may find the Sales to Purchases Wizard useful. This program can be further customized to whatever business specifications may be needed, such as the following:

◆ Quotes to Purchase Orders

◆ Quotes to Purchases

◆ Invoice to Purchase Orders

◆ Invoice to Purchases

One or more purchase orders are generated for each line item in the sales invoice, which can be printed through Peachtree Accounting. Multiple line items for the same vendor are included in the purchase order for that vendor. You can use Sales to Purchases Wizard whether you use Inventory or not.

Delete All Wizard

Ever had the urge to just delete everything and start over? Now you can. This automatic deletion program deletes all Journal Entries, Payments, Receipts, and Invoices. Any entry that can be deleted with the Erase toolbar button can be deleted with this program.

WizMag CA DE-6

California companies are not required to file State W-2 forms. However, if you file Federal W-2s on magnetic media, then you must file Form DE-6 on magnetic media quarterly. This program is designed specifically for those companies in California to whom these rules apply.

WizMag 1099

If you work with vendors who are designated as 1099, you'll need to file a special 1099 form with the IRS. You can use WizMag 1099 to quickly extract Accounts Payable data, convert it into the IRS format, and then copy the data onto a 3.5" floppy disk. WizMag 1099 is intended for use with Peachtree Accounting for Windows Release 3.5 and Peachtree Complete Accounting for Windows Release 4.0.

Consolidation Wizard

Sometimes, financial reports need to be created from financial data of multiple companies or subsidiary companies. Consolidation Wizard from Wizard Business Solutions can extract data from each company and then consolidate the data into one company, which you select. This company can then issue the required reports using this consolidated data.

11

Recurring Entries Wizard

Unfortunately, Peachtree Accounting does not provide users with a way to set up recurring entries past the last open period. With the Recurring Entries Wizard, you'll be able to set up recurring journal entries, invoices, or payments beyond the last open period. It also expands the choice of periods. For example, with Recurring Entries Wizard, you can set up your recurring entries for every second month, on a week-to-week basis (or for just about any schedule you can think of, for any period of time).

Conversion Wizards

Have you been wrestling with converting your DOS versions of Peachtree Accounting to a Windows version? Many Peachtree DOS users have made the upgrade, only to face the dilemma of being unable to export their historical data from either the General Ledger or from the open A/P or A/R invoices to the Windows version of Peachtree Accounting. If you find yourself in the same situation, you'll want to check out the Conversion Wizard from Wizard Business Solutions. With the three following Wizards, you can export the data from your Peachtree Accounting for DOS version to Peachtree Accounting for Windows or Peachtree Complete Accounting for Windows:

◆   G/L Conversion Wizard

◆   A/P Conversion Wizard

◆   A/R Conversion Wizard

You can purchase the conversion programs separately or bundled at a discount. You'll get the best results if you run the conversions while you are working in the second year. Ordinarily when you are working with the Accounts Payable and Accounts Receivable, only the beginning balances carry over for vendors and customers. The A/P Conversion Wizard and the A/R Conversion Wizard open the invoices for those balances so that aged payables and receivables print properly, and so that you can apply payments or receipts properly.

Managing Time with Time & Chaos

Personal information managers, or "PIMs," can offer you increased efficiency in your contact management and in managing your daily tasks. One of the best PIMs is a shareware product called Time & Chaos32, by iSBiSTER International, Inc.

Time & Chaos32 is a personal information manager for Windows 95/NT. With Time & Chaos32, you get a calendar, a "To Do" list, an address and telephone book, and an autodialer feature. You can use Time & Chaos to keep track of all your business and personal contacts. You can also use it to dial the phone, send faxes and e-mail, link to web sites, and merge letters, mailing labels, and envelopes.

You can track your daily appointments, their start and end times, and notes describing what you need to do. The "To Do" list is particularly useful; you can assign priorities to various tasks and mark them after they're completed. The current version of Time & Chaos also features an improved Print Preview option and has upgraded the printing performance. Figure 11-3 shows a typical Time & Chaos32 window.

Time & Chaos32 is a first-rate, inexpensive PIM for Windows. It has an impressive array of features, comparable to the best commercial PIMs, and

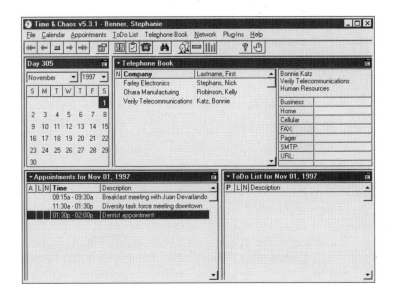

Time & Chaos32 window

Figure 11-3.

good documentation. Take a look and see for yourself!

Time & Chaos32

Minimum System Requirements:

◆ Standard minimum requirements

◆ Windows 95 or NT

Price: 21 days free, then $45

iSBiSTER International
1111 Belt Line Road
Suite 204
Garland, TX 75040
Phone: (972) 495-6724
Fax: (972) 530-6566
sales@isbister.com

11

Tutorials

If you are new to using either Windows 95 or the Internet, you'll want to take a look at these tutorials from Expert Software. These tutorials were chosen because they go beyond the realm of "read this, do that." Incorporating animation, sound, and video, these tutorials make learning about these new technologies entertaining and effective.

Windows 95 Personal Tutor

If you or your staff are just coming up to speed on Windows 95, you'll want to check out Windows 95 Personal Tutor from Expert Systems. Hosted by computer expert Daniel Will Harris, this is an entertaining and informative introduction to using Windows 95. The topics covered include basic elements of file management and more advanced topics such as dragging and dropping. Harris, as the host, offers knowledgeable and occasionally amusing advice. The lessons are well-paced, although difficult information is repeated to ensure that the concept is absorbed. Throughout the lessons, eager viewers can choose the Interact feature, with enables you to temporarily exit the program to try out your new knowledge.

Although there is no online help or documentation included with the product, the interface is simple enough that documentation is not really necessary. Even the glossary is excellent, with well-written definitions. As an added bonus, after reading the definition for a term, you can play a video clip or "movie" that illustrates how to use the feature. A typical window from the Windows 95 tutorial appears in Figure 11-4.

Sample
Windows 95
tutorial
window
Figure 11-4.

T **IP:** There are many sound clips with this program. If you don't already have a sound card for your computer, you should seriously consider getting one or you'll miss much of the impact of this multimedia tutorial.

Windows 95 Personal Tutor

Minimum System Requirements:

♦ Standard minimum requirements

♦ 8-bit or higher sound card

Expert Software
800 Douglas Road
Coral Gables, FL 33134
Phone: (305) 567-9990
Fax: (305) 443-0786
support@expertsoftware.com
http://www.expertsoftware.com

Internet Tutorial

Expert Systems also offers Internet Tutorial. First time users of the tutorial will probably find it helpful to browse through the help file that accompanies the tutorial as the interface can be challenging to novices. The Internet Tutorial covers a lot of information for the novice user, so the feature that enables you to take online notes is helpful. Accessing the Internet, the Web, URLs, domain names, e-mail, and newsgroups are all covered. Along with this basic information, the tutorial also includes more in-depth discussions of FTP and other advanced topics. Aspects of doing business on the Internet are touched on, but not in great depth. Throughout the tutorial, key words are hyperlinked to either glossary definitions or to other areas of the tutorial. Figure 11-5 shows a sample window from the Internet Tutorial.

11

The information is presented in windows, accompanied by text and animations. There are some audio clips, but they are accompanied by a text window (which appears in Figure 11-5) that transcribes the audio script, so you don't need to have audio capabilities.

Internet Tutorial

Minimum System Requirements:

♦   Standard minimum requirements

Expert Software
800 Douglas Road
Coral Gables, FL 33134

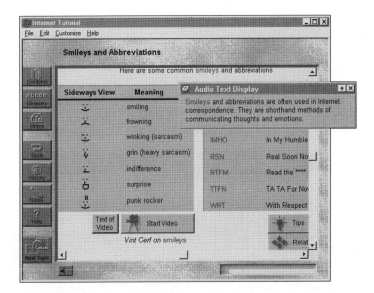

Sample
Internet
Tutorial
window
Figure 11-5.

Phone: (305) 567-9990
Fax: (305) 443-0786
support@expertsoftware.com
http://www.expertsoftware.com

Other Products from Expert Systems

Expert Systems has a wide range of inexpensive and useful products that can make business and home computing easier and more enjoyable. Some of their CD titles are:

- ◆ **Forms** Create, edit, and print forms
- ◆ **Labels** Create labels, envelopes, and bar codes for standard or custom-sized labels.
- ◆ **Stationery Shop** Design your own letterheads, business cards, and fax cover sheets

Expert Systems also has a wide range of CDs that provide fonts, clipart, photos, and other products for the business user. They also offer entertainment, educational, and other titles. For a complete list of products, be sure to check out the Expert Systems catalog on their web page at *http://www.expertsoftware.com/catalog.htm*.

Compressing Files with WinZip

By compressing data, such as a text file, before you send it over the Internet, you can significantly decrease the time it takes to transfer your information. The most common method of compressing data is known as *zipping*, named after the popular PKZIP compression utility. Many companies who post large documentation files on the Internet are using zipping to compress files and reduce the time it takes for customers to download the information. You want to consider compressing files in the following situations:

- ◆ Storing archival files that involve multiple files of related information
- ◆ Archiving files that you need to save, but that you don't anticipate accessing often
- ◆ Sending multiple files to another person

WinZip, from Nico Mak Computing, is one of the world's most popular programs for handling file compression and decompression. In 1996, WinZip brought home numerous awards, including PC Magazine's "Best Utility" Shareware Award. WinZip is popular because it's easy to use and powerful. It handles an enormous variety of file formats, including zip,

UUencode, MIME, TAR, gzip, UNIX compress, and BinHex. It's particularly popular with people who are managing large archives of files. You can view lists of files in your archive, add or delete files from individual archives, view individual files, and even test files in archives. Figure 11-6 shows the WinZip main window with a sample zip file displayed.

Are you sending zipped files to users who may not be very familiar with compression technology? If so, you can create files that unzip by themselves with WinZip's Self-Extractor Personal Edition, which comes with WinZip. (Keep in mind that there is a more robust version of WinZip Self-Extractor, which is available for $49. This version is intended for users who distribute software in large quantities to novice users.)

T IP: If you are a novice, you may want to try working with the WinZip Wizard. The Wizard provides a slightly scaled-back interface and more user assistance until you get your feet wet.

WinZip also features automatic disk spanning capabilities. This means that you can compress directories, and even groups of directories, into a single large file and store them on more than one diskette. (Many compression programs don't allow for disk spanning, limiting you to files that fit on a single diskette.) To make a zip file that spans multiple disks, simply create a zip file on a diskette or other removable disk, then add files to the zip as you normally would. If the disk fills during the Add operation, WinZip will

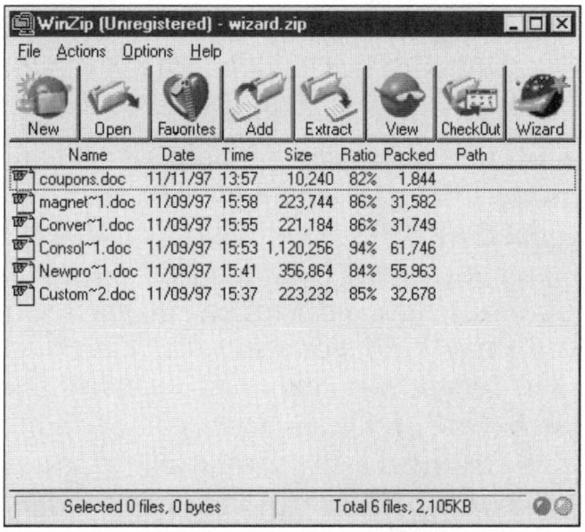

WinZip main window
Figure 11-6.

prompt you for another disk. Simply insert the next disk and click OK. (WinZip won't format disks on the fly, though, so be sure that the disks are already formatted.)

WinZip

Minimum System Requirements:

♦   Standard minimum requirements

List Price: $29

Nico Mak Computing
P.O. Box 919
Bristol, CT 06011
Phone: (800) 242-4775
Fax: (713) 524-6398
http://www.winzip.com

Internet Tools

One of the fastest growing classes of software is tools for using the Internet more effectively. This section shows you a selection of tools you can't afford to be without.

Arachnophilia HTML Editor

The chapters in this book covering PeachLink show you how easy it can be to establish a web site for your company. Perhaps you want to go further with your web site, but have been put off by the notion of learning HTML and other programming languages. Investing the time and money to learn these tools or to hire resources isn't necessarily a good idea until you decide whether a web presence will even be helpful for your business. In addition, many companies overlook a very important aspect of having a web presence: the cost and time commitment involved in updating a web site.

Arachnophilia is a comprehensive web editor designed to be used by beginners. It includes a very extensive online help system and an excellent tutorial that walks you through creating an HTML document and then uploading it to the Internet. You can use Arachnophilia in two ways. First, if you already have a document in Microsoft Word format (DOC) or in rich text format (RTF), you can use the product to convert the document to HTML. Second, you can try your hand at creating an HTML document from scratch. One of the challenges HTML editors must overcome is the handling of pre-existing, highly formatted information, such as a table. Arachnophilia handles this particularly well, easily converting the information to a format that will reproduce well on your web site. The main Arachnophilia window appears in Figure 11-7.

11

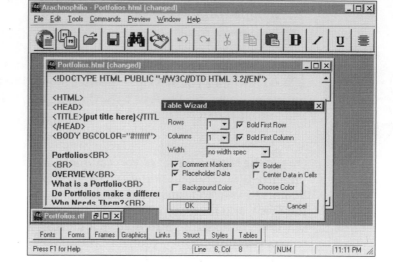

Arachnophilia
main window
Figure 11-7.

Creating the actual content of a web page is only half the battle. Many novice webmasters forget to preview their creations on different web browsers. Arachnophilia comes to the rescue again, giving webmasters the opportunity to preview on six different common web browsers.

If you are more experienced with using HTML, you'll appreciate the convenience of the customizable HTML tags and Arachnophilia's ability to work with JavaScript and CGI, two programming languages used for augmenting HTML. Arachnophilia is a good tool, not only for smaller web sites, but also for larger, multi-page web sites. It includes a global search-and-replace feature. For example, if the name of a product changes, updating the name change across all the web pages will be much easier using this feature of Arachnophilia.

Some users have encountered error messages while trying to preview their pages in Arachnophilia, especially with Microsoft's Internet Explorer. If you see an error message during preview, it means that there's a problem with the browser pointing to the right page. Here's how to fix the problem:

1. Save your file.

2. Click Preview at the right end of the Arachnophilia toolbar.

3. Click OK on the error message.

4. Switch to whichever Internet browser you are using.

5. In the address line, erase the part of the URL that reads " ~temp.005" (the number will vary, depending on your project).

6. Enter the file name of the actual file you are using, for example, **jobopenings.htm**.

7. Press ENTER.

NOTE: Once you have the browser pointed to the right page, any further previews can be done by saving the file, switching to your browser, and selecting Refresh from the menu.

One of the biggest mistakes you can make when you decide to create a web presence is misunderstanding the short attention span of most viewers. Visitors to your web site will definitely expect to see fresh information when they visit, and most companies are adhering to monthly, or even weekly, schedules of updating information and adding fresh material. All this means to you is that someone—probably you or a member of your staff—needs to spend time doing this. However, there are a number of products on the market that can make creating and maintaining a web site fast, easy, and even fun. You'll find Arachnophilia to be useful as you begin developing a web site. It can be used by both beginners and by more advanced users to create professional-looking web pages.

Paul Lutus of Ashland, Oregon developed Arachnophilia, and with it also developed the concept of distributing the software as CareWare. Essentially, as payment for using the program, Mr. Lutus will accept the performance of a good deed or an act of kindness toward another person. If you'd like to read more about this concept for software distribution, check out his web page at *http://www.arachnoid.com* and download a copy of Arachnophilia today.

Arachnophilia, v3.2

Minimum System Requirements:

♦   Standard minimum requirements
♦   Windows 95 or NT

List price: Free (CareWare)

Author: Paul Lutus
http://www.arachnoid.com

Dunce

One of the advantages of Windows 95 is the simplicity with which you can connect to the Internet, but it's still not as convenient as it could be. If you get a busy signal or have a problem connecting to your ISP, you may need to click Connect on your Dial-up Networking profile for quite a while. With the increase in the number of times you need to log on to the Web through your ISP, it's in your best interests to simplify the process as much as you can.

Dunce (an acronym for "Dial-Up Networking Connection Enhancement") from Vector Development lets you automate most of your connection process. Dunce will bypass the standard "Connect To" dialog box, redial until it connects, then minimize the dialog box. Dunce will also let you start as many as four programs automatically when you connect to your ISP. Dunce will even automatically reconnect you to your ISP if you get disconnected and will schedule connections at pre-set times (so you can download your e-mail or files late at night during off-hours, for example). Figure 11-8 shows you the main Dunce window.

For more advanced users, there is Dunce Gold. Dunce Gold supports more than one Dial-Up Networking profile (Dunce only supports one) and has more advanced scheduling features available.

Dunce 2.52 and Dunce Gold

Minimum System Requirements:

♦ Standard minimum requirements

♦ Microsoft Windows 95 only

Price: Dunce 2.52 is freeware; Dunce Gold is $20 (with online delivery), $25

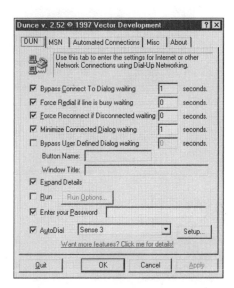

Dunce main
window
Figure 11-8.

for a diskette mailed to a North American address, or $30 for a diskette mailed to an address outside of North America.

Vector Development
P.O. Box 831
Manhattan, KS 66505-0831
Phone: (913)539-6106
http://www.vecdev.com

Eudora Lite

As e-mail becomes more prevalent as a communications tool, the volume of e-mail you and your staff handle will increase. If you and your company are just beginning to explore e-mail, you'll want to try out Eudora Lite by Qualcomm Corporation. Eudora Lite is a full-featured e-mail program that helps you manage e-mail efficiently. A sample message window from Eudora Lite appears in Figure 11-9.

You can attach files to your e-mail (including spreadsheets, video clips, and sound files) by simply dragging and dropping the required file onto your e-mail message. (Eudora Pro has an added feature: if someone sends you a message with a URL, you can click on the URL within the message and Eudora Pro will start your web browser and load the URL automatically.)

Another powerful capability of Eudora Lite is *e-mail filtering*. E-mail filters let you automatically channel incoming messages. You can automatically

Sample
message
window in
Eudora Lite
Figure 11-9.

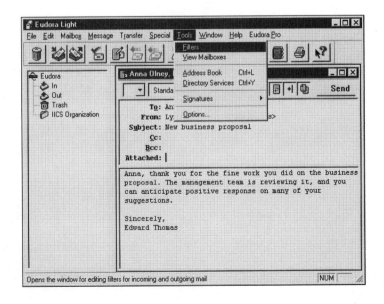

funnel e-mail from specific sources into preset folders and even automatically delete e-mail from certain sources. (This is very helpful for dealing with the unpleasant increase in junk e-mail, commonly known as "spam.") You can also set up filters to alert you with a sound when you receive a message, or you can create folders and have e-mail messages automatically go to the folders without appearing in your inbox. You can also redirect e-mail to another recipient with filters.

If you use Eudora Lite, you'll want to go ahead and register as a user with the company. Registering gets you a subscription to the excellent newsletter. Filled with tips, new features, and step-by-step how-to's for using the product, the newsletter will be e-mailed to you on a quarterly basis. You should also check out the company's web site at *http://www.eudora.com* for product information, FAQs, and extensive documentation.

11

Eudora Lite is a light version of Eudora Pro, one of the world's most popular Internet e-mail products. In addition to the plethora of features available with Eudora Lite, Eudora Pro includes the following features that are not included in Eudora Lite: customizing the toolbar; accessing multiple e-mail accounts; and spell-checking. Also, Eudora Pro 3.0 extends the powerful filtering capabilities of Eudora Lite, enabling you to set up your mail to include auto-reply and forwarding. You can also color-code and include URLs in your messages. Eudora Pro extends the filters by enabling you to automatically reply to requests for information, or to label certain messages from important contacts as high priority.

Eudora Lite

Minimum System Requirements:

♦ Standard minimum requirements

♦ Winsock 1.1 API-compliant networking package (if you're using Windows 3.1; Windows 95 has Dial-Up Networking built-in)

♦ An e-mail account with an ISP or Internet-style network

♦ Access to your e-mail account via a modem or an Internet-style connection

Qualcomm Incorporated
6455 Lusk Boulevard
San Diego, CA 92121-2779
Phone: (619) 587-1121
Fax: (619) 658-2100
http://www.eudora.com

Free Agent

One of the most valuable resources on the Internet are the thousands of Usenet newsgroups that exist. Many of them may be valuable to your business. Are you considering marketing a new gardening tool? Check into the newsgroups on gardening and find out more about your target audience. Trying to figure out which desktop publishing program will suit your needs? Find out if the programs you are considering have a newsgroup (which can often be unofficial), and ask the participants about various strengths and weaknesses of the programs. There are newsgroups on virtually any subject; there are more than 30,000 newsgroups currently in existence.

All newsreaders enable you to read the messages; the best ones provide sophisticated sorting and filtering techniques to keep you from drowning in useless information. One of the very best newsreaders for Windows 95 is Free Agent from Forté. Free Agent is extensively customizable and has an easy-to-use interface. Figure 11-10 shows the Free Agent main window.

There is a lot of information to be found online and Free Agent can help you manage how you store and maintain various newsgroup articles. Free Agent can build and maintain a database of your favorite headers and articles, and you can set the length of time you want to keep the articles. You can use Free Agent to navigate the complex threads of articles. This feature in itself makes the product valuable; combing through the threads, which are often out of order, can be very time consuming. If you discover a particularly annoying or interesting thread, you can set Free Agent to either ignore it or watch for it.

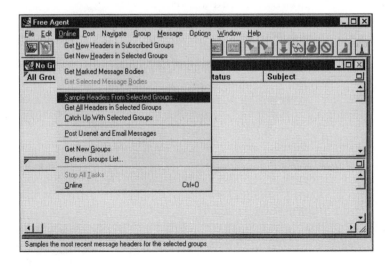

Free Agent
main window
Figure 11-10.

You can reply to an article directly on the newsgroup or privately via e-mail; the current version of Free Agent has a built-in e-mail program, if you wish to use the same program for newsgroups and e-mail. There is even a spell-checker to ensure that the articles and e-mail you send via Free Agent don't have spelling errors. Programs, templates, spreadsheets, and other files are often distributed on newsgroups. Free Agent is capable of retrieving them and automatically decoding many of these files for you.

Free Agent is particularly useful if you need to limit the time you connect to the Internet. You can configure Free Agent for either online mode (if you have a direct connection to the Internet and connect time is not an issue) or offline mode. In offline mode, Free Agent retrieves only the headers of articles for you to examine offline. You can then flag only the articles you want and have Free Agent retrieve them, minimizing your connect time.

11

As with most freeware, Free Agent does not come with technical support. However, Forté does collect e-mailed inquiries and periodically e-mails registered Free Agent users with lists of tips and answers to frequently asked questions. The Free Agent web site (*http://www.forteinc.com*) has FAQs, tips, and information for Free Agent users.

Free Agent is free, but you can buy a more powerful version called Agent. As with Eudora Pro and Eudora Lite, Agent has all the features of Free Agent and many more. One of the handiest things the current version of Agent will do is create a Watch List to watch for specified information in the newsgroups. You can select certain authors or particular topics and Agent will automatically download them for your convenience. This is a very useful addition for selectively gleaning the latest information from newsgroups. You can also create Kill Lists, which screen postings from selected people or containing certain topics. This is particularly useful after you've gotten to know the various participants on certain newsgroups through their e-mails.

If you are into serious information gathering, you know that it's pretty common for people to post the same information to different newsgroups. Agent is able to recognize when you've read a message in one newsgroup, and marks it as already read when it finds it in another newsgroup. This reduces the amount of time you spend re-reading the same message.

For working with articles, Agent gives you the ability to store articles in different folders, increasing your ability to organize and access the information you need. Purchasing Agent entitles you to 90 days of free technical support (via e-mail) and upgrades, which can be very useful if you're unfamiliar with using e-mail or newsreaders.

One general tip about newsgroups: some newsgroups have little patience for "newbies" or newcomers. Before trying to participate or posting a question, find out if the group has archives or a list of frequently asked questions (FAQs). Before posting marketing or advertising information on any newsgroup, be sure you understand whether it's considered OK. In many newsgroups, this is frowned upon and can result in your being deluged with angry e-mail messages.

Free Agent

Minimum System Requirements:

♦ Standard minimum requirements

♦ Winsock 1.1 API-compliant networking package (if you're using Windows 3.1; Windows 95 has Dial-Up Networking built-in)

♦ Access to an Internet news server (contact your ISP for more information)

Price: Free Agent is free; Agent 1.5 is $29

Forté, Inc.
2141 Palomar Airport Road, Suite 200
Carlsbad, CA 92009
Phone: (760) 431-6400
Fax: (760) 431-6465
http://www.forteinc.com

WinCode

When files are transmitted over the Internet, they're often encoded into one of several encoding formats. The program on the other end handles the decoding. Unfortunately, there's always going to be a format that your program isn't able to handle. That's where a good encoding and decoding program, like WinCode (shown in Figure 11-11), comes in.

There are several kinds of encoding/decoding you can perform. Two of the most prevalent are MIME and UUencoding. WinCode can handle both of these types of encoding/decoding, as well as less common types like BinHex and BOO. In UUencoding, for instance, ASCII (text) files are converted to binary files and vice versa. Using WinCode is fairly easy; you can set it up to do the encoding/decoding functions automatically, so you won't have to tag files and try to determine which formats you have or don't have (which is one reason it's become so popular). If you need to convert more than one file, be aware that WinCode offers a feature that will enable you to group the files and convert them, saving yourself some effort.

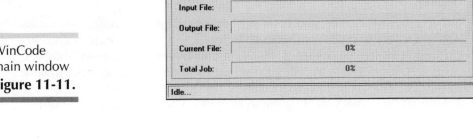

WinCode
main window
Figure 11-11.

NOTE: Encoding files is not the same as compressing them, but WinCode uses PKZIP and PKUNZIP to automatically zip or unzip files while encoding or decoding. WinCode can be set up to automatically zip or unzip files for encoding or decoding, as well as automatically decoding or encoding your e-mail messages.

WinCode also offers the ability to hook into other applications so you can save some time by converting files from within the applications you are working. This is a very handy feature if you are working with many different applications.

WinCode

Standard minimum system requirements

Price: Freeware

Contact: George Silva
http://www.winsite.com/info/pc/win3/util/wincode.zip

Creating and Modifying Graphics

In the day-to-day flurry of running a small business, you'll often need to whip up simple diagrams and flowcharts, or to create and edit simple graphics. Need to create an organization chart for a new business proposal? Want to quickly add cool graphics to your company newsletter? If so, check out Visio and Paint Shop Pro. You'll be able to use Visio to generate organization charts and to diagram your work process flows. Use Paint Shop

Pro to create and edit graphics to add to your marketing materials or enhance your web site.

Visio

Do you ever need to diagram complex manufacturing or ordering processes? Are you trying to train your team to follow accepted corporate decision-making processes? Sometimes, the most effective way to convey complex process information is by using flowcharts and process diagrams. However, as you've probably discovered, creating these graphics can be as complex as the actual processes you're trying to simplify. That's where Visio Standard comes in.

Like Paint Shop Pro, Visio Standard is another award-winning graphics product. You'll find a demo of the product included on the CD in this book. Visio products, from the Visio Corporation, have made creating professional-looking business diagrams and flowcharts remarkably simple. The baseline product in the series is Visio Standard, which can be extended with Visio Technical and Visio Professional editions. You can use the products to create a wide range of projects, including organization charts, office layouts, business process flowcharts, and maps. However, it's the process and decision flowcharting that is the true strength of Visio. Figure 11-12 shows a typical org chart created with Visio.

Visio products enhance the creation of graphics by using pre-existing shapes

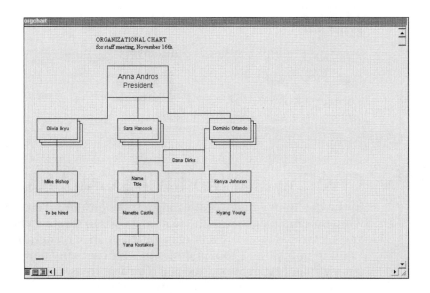

Sample Visio organization chart

Figure 11-12.

that you select and then drag onto your drawing. It's as simple as that. There are over a thousand shapes, grouped together into logical "stencils." There are shapes available to diagram the processes for everyday business use, manufacturing, chemical engineering, software product development, and many others. The shapes use SmartShapes® technology, which means that the shapes can be resized without distortion and can be customized. Adding text to your diagrams is as simple as selecting the shape and typing in your text.

In addition, the shapes can be connected with a wide variety of lines, segments, and arrows, which resize automatically as the shapes are moved and resized. The connectors also change angles, stretch, or shorten as you move the SmartShapes® symbols. For complex drawings, you may want to layer your shapes. By doing this, you can move all the shapes on one layer without affecting the others. You can edit, print, or hide various layers according to your needs.

The product itself is fairly intuitive and includes a well-written help system. However, to simplify your tasks even more, Visio includes a number of Wizards for the more common tasks. Wizards help to walk you through complex tasks, such as creating an organization chart, for example. Instead of moving through the menus, adding shapes and text, and making various selections, the Wizard requests specific information from you and then completes the task for you.

Visio Standard includes the basics you'll need to develop organization charts, flowcharts, maps, and block diagrams. However, don't let the ease of use fool you. There is even more power behind the product. You can layer information within the graphics to be referred to later as needed. For example, in your organization chart, you can include last-promotion date information, or you can layer the names of individual team members into development flowcharts. Information from your diagrams can be linked to databases to ensure regular updating. More advanced users will want to customize their control handles, and customize the shapes to your specific needs.

If you decide that you need even more power, try one of the other products in the series, Visio Professional or Visio Technical. Visio Professional contains more advanced shapes for designing and illustrating information and business systems. Use this edition if you need to illustrate network designs, business processes, or software designs. You'll also want this version if you post your diagrams on your intranet or on the Web. Try Visio Technical if you want to diagram more technical processes, such as chemical or electrical engineering.

If these editions don't satisfy your thirst for shapes and cool tools, you may want to investigate the Visio Solutions Library, located on the Visio Corporation web site. This library includes additional shapes and more complex Wizards. Regular users of Visio will also want to check out their user's forum on the Internet. Visio fans use the forum to share tips, hear the latest news, and get technical support from Visio employees. As Visio notes on their homepage, this forum is not intended to replace their paid support programs or warranty programs.

Visio Standard Test Drive

Minimum System Requirements:

♦ IBM-PC compatible 486/66 processor (minimum—Pentium processor or higher is recommended)

♦ Microsoft Windows 95 or Windows NT 4.0

♦ 16 MB of RAM (Windows 95); 24 MB of RAM (Windows NT)

♦ 15 MB of free hard disk space for a minimum installation; up to 90 MB of free hard-disk space for a full installation

Visio Corporation
P.O. Box 1500
Fairport, NY 14450-9825
Phone: (800) 24VISIO (that's 248-4746) or (716) 586-0030
Fax: (716) 586-0820
http://www.visio.com

Paint Shop Pro

Paint Shop Pro is one of the most popular graphics programs around. It has won numerous awards from industry reviewers and acclaim from its many users. In 1997, PC Magazine announced it as the "Program of the Year" in the Ziff-Davis Shareware Awards. There are a number of good reasons for all the hoopla.

Paint Shop Pro offers all the tools to create and edit all kinds of images—from web pages and photographs, to screen shots and line drawings. If you have graphics in one format that need to be converted to another, you can use Paint Shop to handle the conversions and to edit the images, including cropping and resizing. Figure 11-13 shows the Paint Shop Pro main window.

If your company needs graphics and screen shots to illustrate training materials or user documentation, you'll want to take advantage of the Paint Shop Pro feature called Screen Capture. In order to use the Screen Capture

Paint Shop Pro
main window
Figure 11-13.

11

feature, follow the steps in the excellent help file, which is accessed by choosing Help from the main toolbar.

NOTE: As Paint Shop Pro begins the capture process, it may appear that nothing is happening. Be patient; it takes a few seconds for the capture to occur.

To summarize, Paint Shop Pro is an exceptional program with more features than you're ever likely to use (but it's nice to know that they're there if you need them). The Windows 95 version is included on the CD. There are also Windows 3.1 versions available on the JASC web site.

Paint Shop Pro v4.14

Minimum System Requirements:

♦ Standard minimum requirements

♦ Windows 95 or Windows NT 4.0

Jasc, Inc.
PO Box 44997
Eden Prairie, MN 55344
Phone: (612) 930-9171
Fax: (612) 930-9172
http://www.jasc.com

CompuShow for Windows

CompuShow for Windows from Canyon State Systems started as a DOS shareware program (known as CSHOW) in 1987 for viewing graphics files. It was extremely popular and is probably the only program in this chapter to have been used on the Space Shuttle. The Windows version, first released in 1996, is no less amazing.

CompuShow for Windows will display files in an enormous variety of graphic file formats (including GIF, JPG, BMP, TIF, ICO, and WMF and many others). In addition, you can use this program to play movies and sounds, print pictures, and even convert pictures from one format to another. One of the best features of CompuShow for Windows is that you can view groups of files (all the JPG files in a directory, for example) or build a list of files to view in a "slide show" format, where the pictures are displayed one after another. Figure 11-14 shows the main window of CompuShow for Windows.

There is also a Gallery feature, which gives you a database of all the pictures on your system. You can create *thumbnails*—small versions of picture files that let you quickly identify and sort the picture files—that you can use to search for pictures and display, print, or convert them, regardless of their location on your system. The CompuShow Gallery can also be set for automatic update so that you always get the most recent thumbnails for the picture files in a directory or a drive.

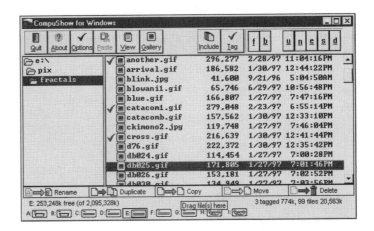

CompuShow
for Windows
main window

Figure 11-14.

CompuShow for Windows is an exceptional program for web designers, as it lets you view groups of files in a directory quickly and easily to find just the right one. The shareware version appears on the CD accompanying this book. Registering the program will give you additional benefits, including notification of upgrades to a new version and tech support.

CompuShow for Windows v3.00a

Price: $35.00 for registration and shipping; add $3.00 for shipping outside the U.S.

Canyon State Systems
P.O. Box 86
Sedona, AZ 86339-0086
Voice: (520) 282-5070
76555.167@compuserve.com
bobberry@aol.com
http://ourworld.compuserve.com/homepages/BobBerry
http://members.aol.com/BobBerry

Anti-Virus Protection

If you've never thought about using an anti-virus product, think again. There are currently over 5,000 known computer viruses, about 20 of which are considered common. Your systems may be in danger of infection if you or your employees ever transfer information from one computer to another using floppy disks, download information from the Internet, share files, use e-mail, or simply reuse disks from unknown sources. Some viruses have even appeared on the disks for commercial programs from major software manufacturers! Some viruses are intended as harmless pranks, designed to play a song or display a message, but others are much more damaging—erasing information, reformatting hard drives—resulting in a costly loss of information.

Whether a virus scanner is really effective is determined, in part, by how it searches for potential viruses. Virus scanners comb systems for search strings of code called signatures. Each virus has an identifiable signature, and that's how the scanners are able to identify which virus you're dealing with when you're infected. Some programs go a bit further, searching for signatures that "appear" to be virus-like. While this can lead to some inaccuracies (referred to as "false-positives"), many users share the belief that it's better to err on the side of caution.

As anti-virus software becomes more sophisticated, virus authors are becoming more cunning about hiding their handiwork. Most viruses can be identified or "fingerprinted" by lines of their code. The anti-virus programs can scan for the well-known fingerprints or for indications of file alterations. Recently, more sophisticated virus authors have begun developing viruses that mutate, destroying and altering the virus "fingerprints" that could be used to detect and remove them. Creating multiple, operational copies of themselves reduces the likelihood that a virus scan will detect all the variations of the virus. These mutating viruses, called *polymorphic viruses*, are very difficult to detect. Other viruses, called *stealth viruses*, are able to hide the evidence of the tampering and damage that they are doing to files and allocation tables. Like polymorphic viruses, these stealth viruses are difficult to find and remove.

Fortunately, there are a number of good anti-virus software programs on the market. What are some of the factors you should look for in a good anti-viral software product?

♦ **Ease of use and understanding** Your employees (and you) will be more inclined to use the product on a more frequent basis if the interface is familiar and the process for scanning and removing viruses is simple.

♦ **Flexibility** A good anti-virus product needs to be able to scan whole systems and drives, boot disks, floppies, files being downloaded from the Internet, zipped files, and e-mail. A good product offers detection, virus removal, and immunization. It should be capable of on-demand inspection or automatically scanning at a set time.

♦ **Customizability** To save time, you may only want to scan particular files or particular sections of your drive. The product you choose should allow this. Many software companies offer both desktop (stand-alone) versions of their products and versions that can be deployed over a company's network. Which one you'll need depends on your company's needs.

♦ **Company Support** The company offering the software needs to be current with new virus developments and aggressive about releasing solutions to new viruses.

While no product can protect your system completely from the many new forms of viruses, the products described in this section are easy to use and will prove invaluable in protecting your vital business information.

NOTE: Virus checkers are updated constantly to deal with new viruses as they appear. An old version of a virus scanner is worse than no scanner at all, because it lets the user believe that they're protected from infections, while the fact is that they are not. Therefore, rather than include any of the following virus scanning programs on the CD that accompanies this book, you should contact the manufacturers through their web sites and download the latest versions of the products.

F-PROT

Installing the shareware version of F-PROT requires a bit of experience with MS-DOS. The documentation, in the form of text files, clearly spells out the procedure, so if you're good at following manuals, you shouldn't have too many difficulties. You can actually customize F-PROT to check for certain types of viruses during the install, although it's in your best interest to do a full install if you are at high risk for infection.

F-PROT has a reputation for being more thorough and effective than many other products on the market. Fridrik Skulason, the program's author, updates the product frequently (six to eight times a year), maintaining its effectiveness against current viruses. Figure 11-15 shows the main F-PROT window.

There is also an extended version, available at a higher cost from Command Software Systems, that enables you to schedule the program to scan for viruses. This way, you can set the program to automatically check for viruses when you know you'll be away from your desk.

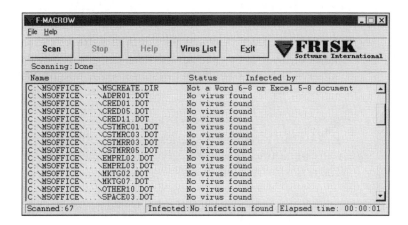

F-PROT main
window
Figure 11-15.

11

F-PROT 2.28

Price: Free for individual users. (For a $15 US fee, Fridrik Skulason will mail you a registered copy.)

http://www.datafellows.com/f-prot

F-PROT Professional for Windows 95, version 3.0

Minimum System Requirements:

- Standard minimum requirements
- Microsoft Windows 95

Price: $169.90

Command Software Systems
Jupiter, FL 33458
Phone: (800) 423-9147 or (407) 575-3200
Fax: (407) 575-3026
http://www.commandcom.com

McAfee VirusScan for Windows 95

McAfee virus scanning products are some of the most popular in the world. McAfee VirusScan for Windows 95 scans and detects viruses on Internet files, CD-ROMS, boot areas, compressed folders and files, e-mail, floppy disks, networks, and macros. VirusScan is able to detect over 11,000 of the known viruses, including many polymorphic and stealth viruses. You can also use McAfee to create an emergency recovery disk. In the event of a serious infection, you'll be able to use this disk to recover. The McAfee VirusScan main window appears in Figure 11-16.

If you are not very familiar with the issues of software viruses, you'll want to check out McAfee's extensive documentation. Not only does the documentation cover detecting, removing, and immunizing your systems, it also includes general information on viruses.

NOTE: VirusScan searches very aggressively for permutations of known virus signatures, which has given it a reputation for more "false-positive" diagnoses than other products.

The company actively solicits samples of viruses from customers in order to analyze and develop vaccines and detection mechanisms. With millions of users worldwide, that's a lot of input and is one of the reasons McAfee has been able to keep pace with the virus authors. McAfee virus scanning

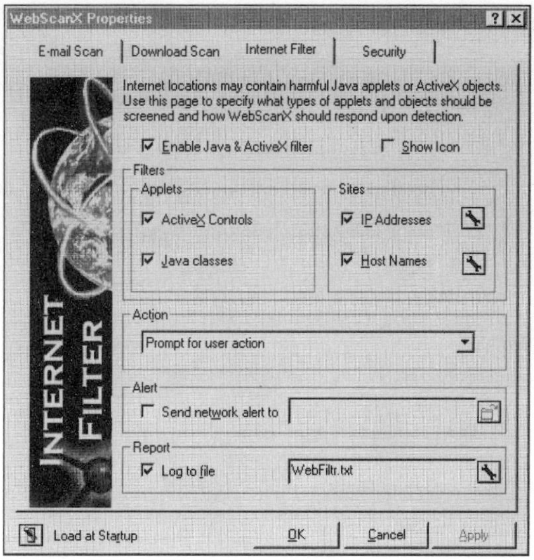

McAfee
VirusScan
main window
Figure 11-16.

products are also backed by a global team of virus specialists. Posted in Tokyo, Silicon Valley, and Amsterdam, their mission is to identify and develop antidotes for new viruses.

Along with other viruses, savvy virus authors are now using ActiveX controls and Java applets as carriers of their destructive work. As these proliferate, you'll want to consider adding McAfee's WebScan X version 3.1.1a to your arsenal. Along with the "traditional" scans it runs of e-mail attachments and files, WebScanX goes one step further. It actually will serve as a barrier to certain ActiveX controls, Internet addresses, or certain types of Java applets currently "in vogue" with virus designers.

McAfee VirusScan for Windows 95

Minimum System Requirements:

♦ Standard minimum requirements
♦ 4.9 MB of free hard disk space
♦ Microsoft Windows 95

Shareware: 30-day Trial Version

http://www.mcafee.com

McAfee's WebScan X

Minimum System Requirements:

- ♦ Standard minimum requirements
- ♦ 5.3 MB of free hard disk space
- ♦ Microsoft Windows 95 or Windows NT

Shareware: 30-day Trial Version

http://www.mcafee.com

Norton AntiVirus

If you're looking for anti-virus protection software that's easy to use and understand, you'll want to try this popular program. Norton AntiVirus, from Symantec Corporation, has been winning awards for years and for very good reasons. Norton AntiVirus (shown in Figure 11-17) has an interface similar to Windows 95, making it easy to understand for Windows 95 users.

Norton AntiVirus scans and detects viruses in files, floppy disks, CD-ROMs, and boot sectors. While Norton AntiVirus does detect viruses in the top level of zipped files, it does not detect infections in zipped files nested within other zipped files. There is some question of how effective AntiVirus is against detecting viruses in e-mail attachments.

Norton AntiVirus 2.0 is very effective at detecting and cleaning traditional viruses, but is less effective in catching and immunizing against the polymorphic viruses. Norton AntiVirus can scan for some unknown viruses and the company offers a support feature called LiveUpdate that automatically downloads updates from the company's web site.

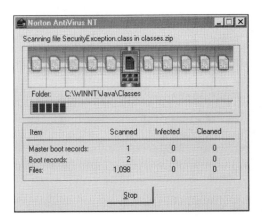

Norton
AntiVirus
main window
Figure 11-17.

Once a virus is detected, you have several options: you can ignore the infected file, stop the system and deny access to incoming infected files, or attempt to clean or delete the file. When an infected file is found, the Repair Wizard guides you through the procedures for cleaning the file of the virus. You can schedule automatic scans hourly, daily, weekly, monthly, or yearly.

NOTE: Norton AntiVirus lacks the specificity of some other products. For example, although you can set the program to autoprotect mode, you cannot choose which directory or files it immunizes.

11

Norton AntiVirus 2.0 for Windows 95

Minimum System Requirements:

♦   Standard minimum requirements

♦   Windows 95 or Windows NT

Symantec Corp.
10201 Torre Ave.
Cupertino, CA 95014
Telephone: (800) 441-7234
http://www.symantec.com

Anyware Antivirus for Windows 95

Anyware Antivirus 3.0 offers many of the same features as the other anti-virus products listed here. However, the authors of this program claim it to be three times faster than either Norton or McAfee. Since anti-viral detection and cleaning can be time-consuming if done on a regular basis, it's worth checking into this product. Anyware Antivirus offers two options for the time-crunched user: Smart-Scan and Fast-Scan options. Smart-Scan provides the longer, more thorough search-and-destroy ability. Figure 11-18 shows the Anyware Antivirus main window.

Anyware Antivirus checks local drives, directories, and files (regular and compressed), hard disks, floppy disks, and LAN drives, boot sectors, and partition tables. It also is effective at detecting infections on e-mail, shared files, and network drives.

Like the other products included here, Anyware does a superb job of detecting existing viruses and protecting against new, unknown mutations. Upgrades and new virus information are available through the company's web site. This product can be effective on either standalone computers or on

Anyware
Antivirus main
window
Figure 11-18.

LANs. If you choose to purchase the network version of Anyware, you can have all your connected PCs automatically updated from the server.

Anyware also inspects zipped and compressed files, an asset if you frequently download these types of files from the Internet or if you are frequently working with compressed files.

One of the handiest features is that you can customize Anyware Antivirus to scan specific parts of your system, saving you additional time. For example, if you know you are installing numerous files to a particular drive, you can save time by directing the product to analyze only that drive. If you're certain you've been infected and you want to figure out exactly where the virus is residing in your system, you can use this feature to analyze disks, drives, files, memory, DOS system files, or even specific compressed files.

Anyware Antivirus

Minimum System Requirements:

♦ Standard minimum requirements

♦ Windows 95

Anyware Software, Inc.
http://www.helpvirus.com

Other Programs

There are hundreds of programs, utilities, and files that you can add to your system to tailor it more closely to your needs. Be sure to check out the lists of URLs and newsgroups in Appendix B, "Online and Printed Resources," as a source of programs and information that may be helpful to you. Other resources you might check out are CDs of shareware (such as those from Walnut Creek CD-ROM) and many of the online computer news services.

11

Summary

This chapter showed you how to further enhance the effectiveness of Peachtree Accounting software with an assortment of add-ons for Peachtree Accounting as well as other useful programs. You are also encouraged to explore shareware sites on the Internet for the latest releases of the freeware and shareware programs described in this chapter as well as other programs that you may find useful or interesting.

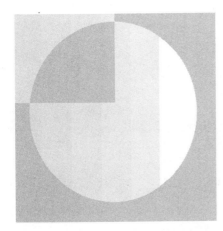

PART 4

Appendixes

A

Commands and Keywords in Peachtree Report Writer

This appendix describes the commands and keywords used in Peachtree Report Writer. A *command* is an instruction that tells Peachtree Report Writer to perform a specific action, such as "add two columns" or "format information for printing." Commands start with a command keyword, have user-specified information and other keywords, and end with a period. *Keywords* are words that have a special meaning and are reserved for specific use by Peachtree Report Writer. Peachtree Report Writer looks for these words as it processes a procedure.

The Peachtree Report Writer manual has the basic command syntaxes—the specific structure of each of the commands. This appendix will provide you with additional information about the various commands and their options, together with examples of what typical commands look like.

Conventions Used in This Appendix

The commands in this appendix are described using the following conventions:

♦ Words that appear in all CAPITAL letters are keywords.

♦ Words that appear in *italics* are information that you supply, such as a column name, a value, or text.

♦ Text that appears in a command is usually enclosed by single quotes.

A complete list of keywords appears at the end of this appendix in Table A-8.

ADD

The ADD command adds two numeric columns, or a column and a temporary column or a value, to produce a temporary column as the result. You can add numeric, date, date-time, and interval columns and temporary columns. If you add a temporary column to a date column, Peachtree Report Writer treats the temporary column as days. If you add a temporary column to a time, date-time, or interval column, Peachtree Report Writer treats the temporary column as a quantity of seconds.

Examples

```
ADD ADJUSTED-CHECK PLUS BONUS-AMOUNT GIVING BONUS-CHECK-AMOUNT.

ADD 1 TO COLUMN-COUNTER.

ADD START-DATE PLUS 90 GIVING INSURANCE-ELIGIBILITY-DATE.

ADD LOGGED-HOURS TO CURRENT-HOURS GIVING TOTAL-HOURS.
```

Comments

♦ You can use the ADD command inside an IF command.

♦ You can add the system columns CURRENT-DATE, CURRENT-TIME, and CURRENT-DATETIME with the ADD command.

♦ The ROUNDED and TRUNCATED options in the command let you round or truncate the result.

AUTHOR

The AUTHOR command centers an author name of up to 50 characters on the second line of a page of columnar or matrix reports. You can only use the AUTHOR command with the COLUMNAR, GRAPH, CHART, and MATRIX commands.

Example

```
AUTHOR "Dr. Melvin Morsmere".
```

Comments

◆ *Author-name* can contain up to 50 characters, including alphanumeric and other characters and spaces.

CHART

The CHART command defines a report in chart format. You can create any one of the following six different charts using this command:

◆ Bar
◆ Stacked Bar
◆ Area

◆ Pie
◆ Line
◆ Scatter

You can also use the various report options to set the colors in the charts, add titles and legends, use patterns, grids, borders, and add special effects such as 3D shading.

A

Examples

```
CHART STACKED_BAR X_AXIS PERIOD X_TITLE 'PERIOD' Y_AXIS TOTAL
NET-CHECK-AMOUNT Y_TITLE 'NET-CHECK-AMOUNT' BORDER HORIZ_GRID
FOREGROUND 7000000 BACKGROUND bffffff.

CHART PIE X_AXIS INVOICE-NUMBER VALUES '1' TO '999' LEGEND 'x
axis legend' COLOR 1ff0000 PATTERN 2 X_TITLE 'INVOICE-NUMBER'
GROUP BILL-TO-ID VALUES '0' TO '999999' , '3433434' TO '9999999'
LEGEND 'Y-axis legend' , 'second y-axis' Y_AXIS TOTAL CUSTOMER-
BALANCE Y_TITLE 'vertical axis legend' 3D BORDER HORIZ_GRID
FOREGROUND 8404040 BACKGROUND 30000ff.

CHART BAR X_AXIS CUSTOMER-CONTACT X_TITLE 'Who to call' Y_AXIS
TOTAL CUSTOMER-BALANCE Y_TITLE 'Amount owed' FOREGROUND 7000000
BACKGROUND bffffff.
```

```
CHART PIE X_AXIS EMP-NAME Y_AXIS TOTAL FED-DED 3D BORDER
FOREGROUND 9808080 BACKGROUND 30000ff.
```

Comments

♦ The CHART command replaces the COLUMNAR command in a report procedure.

♦ CHART *chart-type* identifies the type of chart. *Chart-type* can be BAR, STACKED_BAR, AREA, PIE, LINE, or SCATTER.

♦ COLOR *color-code* lets you specify a color (in hexadecimal notation) to use for the chart. The color code has the format *nnRRGGBB*, where RR, GG, and BB are the hexadecimal values for the red, green, and blue components of the colors, respectively. Values for each of these can be from 00 to FF. The smaller the value for the color component, the more color appears. For example, 01FF0000 would be a strong red and 010000FF would be a strong blue, whereas 01550000 would be a light red and 01000055 would be a light blue. Table A-1 shows the codes for the colors in the drop-down list on the chart windows.

You can specify custom colors by editing the color codes in the Edit Procedures window. The CONTROL.INI file in your Windows directory has the hexadecimal codes for the colors used in Windows.

Color Codes
Used with
the CHART
Command
Table A-1.

Desired Color	Color Code
Red	01FF0000
Green	0200FF00
Blue	030000FF
Cyan	0400FFFF
Magenta	05FF00FF
Yellow	06FFFF00
Black	07000000
Dark Gray	08404040
Gray	09808080
Light Gray	0AC0C0C0
White	0B000000

NOTE: When you are using colors other than the colors in Table A-1, the first two characters should be set to 00.

♦ X_TITLE *x-axis-title* identifies the title for the X-axis, which will appear in the lower right corner of the chart.

♦ PATTERN *pattern-type* lets you enter a specification for the pattern for the bars or solid areas of a chart. Table A-2 shows the possible entries for *pattern-type*. The default for *pattern-type* is solid (1).

♦ *Report-type* can be TOTAL, AVERAGE, MINIMUM, or MAXIMUM.

♦ Y_TITLE *y-axis-title* identifies the title for the Y-axis, which will appear in the upper left corner of the chart. (The Y_TITLE does not appear for pie charts.)

♦ SUPPRESS tells Peachtree Report Writer to omit labels for individual data items.

♦ MONO suppresses color in the chart, including any color specifications used with the COLOR, FOREGROUND, and BACKGROUND keywords. Peachtree Report Writer uses black and white patterns for the areas of the chart instead of colors.

♦ 3D tells Peachtree Report Writer to use three-dimensional effects on the chart. (The 3D option does not apply to area or line charts.)

♦ BORDER tells Peachtree Report Writer to put a border around the chart.

♦ HORIZ_GRID tells Peachtree Report Writer to display horizontal grid lines on the chart. (The HORIZ_GRID option does not apply to pie charts.)

A

Desired Pattern	Pattern Type
Solid	1
Horizontal stripes	2
Vertical stripes	3
Forward diagonal stripes	4
Backward diagonal stripes	5
Cross-hatch	6
Diagonal cross-hatch	7

Pattern Types Used with the CHART Command **Table A-2.**

- VERT_GRID tells Peachtree Report Writer to display vertical grid lines on the chart. (The VERT_GRID option does not apply to bar, stacked bar, and pie charts.)

- FOREGROUND *color-code* lets you specify a color (in hexadecimal notation) to use for the foreground color of the chart. (The color code has the same characteristics as the color code for the COLOR option.)

- BACKGROUND *color-code* lets you specify a color (in hexadecimal notation) to use for the background color of the chart. (The color code has the same characteristics as the color code for the COLOR option.)

COLUMNAR

The COLUMNAR command defines a columnar report. The COLUMNAR command is used for creating the output for most procedures. You can use the COLUMNAR command to create simple reports with one or two columns or you can create reports with detailed sorting, subtotaling, and information breaks. You can summarize column information to provide a count, a total, an average, a minimum, or a maximum value in the column. You can also create running summaries or summarize for specific report breaks.

Examples

```
COLUMNAR EMP-ID.

COLUMNAR EMP-NAME ADJUSTED-CHECK BONUS_CHECK_AMOUNT ON EMP-NAME
CHANGE SUBTOTAL ADJUSTED-CHECK BONUS_CHECK_AMOUNT.

COLUMNAR EMP-NAME SSN.

COLUMNAR BY EMP-NAME TOTAL QTD-3-AMT-EE-1-30#1.
```

Comments

- The [ON *summary-column-name* CHANGE SUBTOTAL {*numeric-column-name*[, *numeric-column-name*...]}] option tells Peachtree Report Writer to subtotal the specified numeric column(s) each time the value in *summary-column-name* changes. (The *summary-column-name* should be a column you are sorting on.) Peachtree Report Writer will also calculate a grand total of the specified numeric columns at the bottom of the report.

- The BY {*column-name*[, *column-name*...]} option tells Peachtree Report Writer to sort and summarize the report by the values in the column(s) specified. These columns don't need to be numeric. If this clause does not appear in the COLUMNAR command, Peachtree Report Writer does not subtotal the information in the selected rows.

♦ The [TITLE *"report-title"*] option tells Peachtree Report Writer to add a report title. Using the TITLE command elsewhere in the procedure will override this option.

CONCATENATE

The CONCATENATE command joins two columns or text strings to create a temporary column. You can trim additional spaces or insert a space between columns being concatenated.

Examples

```
CONCATENATE CITY AND STATE TO CITY-STATE.

CONCATENATE 'SEATTLE ' AND EMP-ID TO SEATTLE-EMP-ID.

CONCATENATE EMP-ID AND EMP-NAME TO SORT-EMP-ID NO TRIM NO-SPACE.

CONCATENATE CONTRACT-DATE-STARTED AND CONTRACT-HOUR-STARTED TO
CONTRACT-TIME-STARTED.
```

Comments

♦ You can use the CONCATENATE command inside an IF command.

♦ The NO-TRIM option tells Peachtree Report Writer not to trim trailing blanks from the information in the first column. (The default is for Peachtree Report Writer to trim trailing blanks.)

♦ The NO-SPACE option tells Peachtree Report Writer not to insert a space between the information from the two columns in the resulting temporary column. (The default is for Peachtree Report Writer to insert a blank.)

A

CONVERT

The CONVERT command can convert information in one of the three following ways:

♦ From an interval column to a numeric column

♦ From a numeric column to an interval column

♦ From a numeric column using one type of time or date measurement to a numeric column using a different type of time or date measurement

Examples

```
CONVERT CONTRACT DAYS DAYS TO HOURS GIVING CONTRACT-HOURS ROUNDED.

CONVERT CONTRACT-LENGTH TO DAYS GIVING CONTRACT-DAYS SCALE 5.0.

CONVERT CONTRACT-DAYS DAYS TO INTERVAL GIVING CONTRACT-DURATION
TRUNCATED.
```

Comments

♦ You can use the CONVERT command inside an IF command.
♦ The ROUNDED and TRUNCATED options in the command let you round or truncate the result.

DEVICE

The DEVICE command overrides the default device Peachtree Report Writer uses for the output of a procedure. You can use the DEVICE command to create a procedure that outputs information to a disk file when you run it.

Examples

```
DEVICE = PRINTER.

DEVICE = DISPLAY.

DEVICE = FILE emp-list.rpt.
```

Comment

♦ The FILE *filename* option creates an ASCII file that has no control codes for page breaks or line length.

DIAG

The DIAG (short for "diagnose") command tells Peachtree Report Writer to display the number of rows processed and selected as it generates the report.

Examples

DIAG.

Comments

This command has no options.

DIVIDE

The DIVIDE command divides one numeric column, interval, or value by another numeric column, interval, or value to create a temporary column.

Examples

```
DIVIDE CONTRACT-HOURS BY 8 GIVING WORK-DAYS.

DIVIDE QTD-2-AMT-EE-1-30#1 BY CONTRACT-HOURS GIVING AVG-CONTRACT-
HOURLY-RATE.
```

Comments

♦ You can use the DIVIDE command inside an IF command.

♦ You can divide using the system columns CURRENT-DATE, CURRENT-TIME, and CURRENT-DATETIME with the DIVIDE command.

♦ The INTERVAL option tells Peachtree Report Writer to force the result to be an interval. Use this when you are dividing or dividing by an interval column.

♦ The ROUNDED and TRUNCATED options in the command let you round or truncate the result.

FORMAT

The FORMAT command lets you override the default output format and create output in any of the formats shown in Table A-3.

Examples

```
FORMAT = FILE WORD_WIN COLUMNAR TITLES.

FORMAT = FILE EXCEL.
```

A

File Type	Description
ASCII_CSV	Comma-delimited ASCII. (Almost all spreadsheets, databases, and word processors will be able to read comma-delimited ASCII files.)
ASCII_FIXED	ASCII file with fixed-length columns
DBASE_2	dBASE II format
DBASE_3	dBASE III format
DIF	Data Interchange Format, used mostly by older DOS-based programs
DISK	Straight ASCII file. (This file includes titles and page numbers, where the fixed and comma-delimited ASCII files do not.)
EXCEL	Microsoft Excel version 3.0
LOTUS_123_1A	Lotus 1-2-3 version 1A
LOTUS_123_R2	Lotus 1-2-3 version 2
LOTUS_123_R3	Lotus 1-2-3 version 3
MULTIPLAN	Microsoft Multiplan symbolic file format.
WORDMARC	WordMARC (can be either document or mail-merge format)
WORDPERFECT_42	WordPerfect version 4.2 for DOS (can be either document or mail-merge format)
WORDPERFECT_51	WordPerfect version 5.1 for DOS (can be either document or mail-merge format)
WORD_WIN	Word for Windows version 2.0 (can be either document or mail-merge format)

Output File
Formats
Table A-3.

Comments

♦   TITLES tells Peachtree Report Writer to include the column titles in the output. You can use this for spreadsheet and word-processing files, but not for mail-merge files.

♦   MAILMERGE tells Peachtree Report Writer to output information in a mail-merge format. COLUMNAR tells Peachtree Report Writer to output information in a document format. Both the MAILMERGE and COLUMNAR options are available only when outputting to a word-processing format.

♦ The DISPLAY format tells Peachtree Report Writer to use a 23-line page length with an infinite line width.

♦ The PRINTER format uses the default entries for page length and line width as determined in the IQCONFIG.DAT file. If the default output device in the IQCONFIG.DAT file is not a printer, Peachtree Report Writer uses the page length and line width configuration as set for the default printer.

♦ The FILE DISK format has an infinite page length (no embedded page breaks) and line width. This option suppresses all control codes in the output.

♦ The Excel and Lotus formats can be used for columnar or for matrix reports. All other formats listed in Table A-3 can only be used for columnar reports.

IF

The IF command evaluates the condition(s) in the first part of the command, then, if the condition(s) are true, performs the commands included in the THEN clause. If the IF command also has an ELSE clause, Peachtree Report Writer will perform the commands in the ELSE clause if the conditions evaluate as false.

Examples

A

```
IF ADJUSTED-CHECK > 5000.00 THEN
        ADD ADJUSTED-CHECK PLUS BONUS-AMOUNT GIVING BONUS-CHECK-AMOUNT.

IF ADJUSTED-CHECK > 5000.00 THEN
     MOVE 600.00 TO QUOTA-BONUS
     MOVE .005 TO BONUS-COMMISSION
     MOVE 'Sales Superstar!' TO COMMENT-COLUMN.

IF ADJUSTED-CHECK > 5000.00 THEN
     ADD ADJUSTED-CHECK PLUS BONUS-AMOUNT GIVING BONUS-CHECK-AMOUNT
ELSE
     ADD ADJUSTED-CHECK PLUS STANDARD-BONUS-AMOUNT GIVING BONUS-CHECK-
     AMOUNT.
```

```
IF  ADJUSTED-CHECK  >  5000.00  AND  EMP-TYPE  =  'SALES2'  THEN
    MOVE  .075  TO  COMMISSION-PERCENT
ELSE
        MOVE  .06  to  COMMISSION-PERCENT.
```

Comments

- ◆ IF commands can contain any of the following commands as part of the command blocks in the THEN and ELSE clauses:

ADD	MOVE
CONCATENATE	MULTIPLY
CONVERT	SUBTRACT
DIVIDE	SUBSTRING

- ◆ You can use wildcards in comparison strings. The asterisk (*) represents zero or more characters of any type. The question mark (?) represents one character of any type. You can use the asterisk wildcard in equals or not-equals comparisons only.

- ◆ You can combine AND and OR options within a condition, but you must use parentheses to establish which set of conditions is evaluated first. Peachtree Report Writer will evaluate the conditions in the innermost parentheses first, then work outwards through the conditions until all the conditions have been evaluated.

- ◆ All the commands to be performed in the IF command must be complete and correct, but they do not have a period after them. The only period in the IF command occurs after the final command to be performed in the THEN or ELSE clause.

- ◆ You can use mathematical symbols instead of the abbreviations shown in the condition syntax, as shown in Table A-4.

- ◆ The CASE option tells Peachtree Report Writer to do a case-sensitive comparison (for example, "abcde" would not be the same as "ABCDE"). The default is for Peachtree Report Writer to ignore case when doing comparisons.

INITIALIZE

The INITIALIZE command tells Peachtree Report Writer to create a temporary column and set it to a specified value.

Mathematical Symbol	Abbreviation	Meaning
=	EQ	Is A equal to B?
<>	NE	Is A not equal to B?
>	GT	Is A greater than B?
>=	GE	Is A greater than or equal to B?
<	LT	Is A less than B?
<=	LE	Is A less than or equal to B?

Mathematical Symbols Used with the IF Command
Table A-4.

Examples

```
INITIALIZE BONUS-CHECK-AMT TO 1000.00 NUMERIC 5.2.

INITIALIZE BIRTH-DATE TO '3/21/98' DATE.

INITIALIZE START-DATETIME TO 3/21/98 '08:00:00 am' DATETIME.
```

Comments

♦ You can use the column-type option to specify the type of column being initialized and the column format or the column size.

♦ Peachtree Report Writer performs each INITIALIZE command only once, when it begins the procedure.

LABEL

The LABEL command is used to create labels or other multi-column output in either character or graphical mode. It is closely related to the REPORT command (discussed later in this chapter).

Examples

Character mode:

A

```
LABEL OFFSET 1 REPEAT 3 WIDTH 60 LENGTH 10
DETAIL NEXT LINE NEXT LINE 6 EMP-ID TRIM BOLD 35 EMP-NAME TRIM
BOLD 10 HIRE-DATE
NEXT LINE 1 ADDRESS
NEXT LINE 1 CITY TRIM 19 ',' 21 STATE 24 ZIP
NEXT LINE.
```

Graphical mode:

```
LABEL GRAPHICAL WINDOWS ENGLISH MARGIN '0.000' '0.000' '0.000'
'0.000' VPITCH '1.00' HPITCH '4.19' HEIGHT '1.00' WIDTH '4.00'
LBLACROSS 3 LBLDOWN 11 FONT 'Arial' SIZE 10.00 BOLD 400 COLOR
00000000 DETAIL
NEXT LINE 0.00 EMP-ID ALIGN 0
NEXT LINE 0.00 EMP-NAME ALIGN 0
NEXT LINE 0.00 EMP-ADDRESS-1 TRIM ALIGN 0
NEXT LINE 0.00 EMP-ADDRESS-2 TRIM ALIGN 0
NEXT LINE 0.00 CITY-STATE-ZIP ALIGN 0
NEXT LINE.
```

Comments

Comments on general label options:

♦ The *position* option for an object tells Peachtree Report Writer where to print the object. This value is in characters if it is a character label, or in the unit of measure (metric or English) as specified in the LABEL command.

♦ The *repeat_count 'text'* option for an object tells Peachtree Report Writer to print the specified text string *repeat_count* times.

♦ The SIZE option for an object tells Peachtree Report Writer to use a specified column width for a character column rather than the column's default width. This value is in characters if it is a character label, or in the unit of measure (metric or English) as specified in the LABEL command.

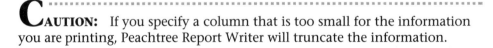

CAUTION: If you specify a column that is too small for the information you are printing, Peachtree Report Writer will truncate the information.

Comments on labels in character mode:

♦ The OFFSET option tells Peachtree Report Writer which column to print the first character of each line for the first column of labels.

- The REPEAT option tells Peachtree Report Writer how many labels to print across the page.
- The WIDTH option tells Peachtree Report Writer how wide each print column is. This includes spaces between the label's columns.
- The LENGTH option tells Peachtree Report Writer how high (in lines) each label is. This includes the blank lines between labels.
- The DETAIL option tells Peachtree Report Writer what to print.
- The *character-typestyle* can be bold, italic, and/or underlined.

Comments on labels in graphical mode:

- The METRIC option tells Peachtree Report Writer to interpret the measurements as metric values, while the ENGLISH option tells Peachtree Report Writer to interpret the measurements as English values.
- The MARGINS option tells Peachtree Report Writer where to set the label margins.
- The VPITCH option tells Peachtree Report Writer what the vertical pitch of the label is to be set to.
- The HPITCH option tells Peachtree Report Writer what the horizontal pitch of the label is to be set to.
- The HEIGHT option tells Peachtree Report Writer what the height of the label is to be set to.
- The WIDTH option tells Peachtree Report Writer what the width of the label is to be set to.
- The LBLACROSS option tells Peachtree Report Writer how many labels to print across the page.
- The LBLDOWN option tells Peachtree Report Writer how many labels to print down the page.

A

NOTE: You must enter an extra NEXT LINE clause at the end of the LABEL command to tell Peachtree Report Writer to align each label.

LIMIT

The LIMIT command tells Peachtree Report Writer to limit the number of records processed.

Examples

```
LIMIT TO 100 RECORDS SELECTED.

LIMIT TO 50 OUTPUT.
```

Comments

♦ The PROCESSED, SELECTED, and OUTPUT options are the same if you are not searching or sorting the information in the procedure with a SEARCH or SORT command.

♦ Peachtree Report Writer will only perform a single LIMIT command in a procedure. If you have multiple LIMIT commands, Peachtree Report Writer will only perform the last one.

♦ The PROCESSED option (the default) tells Peachtree Report Writer to read only the number of records specified.

♦ The SELECTED option tells Peachtree Report Writer to keep processing records until finding the number of records specified that match the criteria in a separate SEARCH command in the procedure.

♦ The OUTPUT option tells Peachtree Report Writer to process all data but to only output the number of rows specified. (This should be used with a SORT command.)

MATRIX

The MATRIX command creates a matrix report. Matrix reports let you print multiple levels of information.

Examples

```
MATRIX COLUMNS EMP-TYPE ROWS EMP-NAME TOTAL NET-CHECK-AMOUNT MISSING-
DATA BLANKS.

MATRIX COLUMNS EMP-TYPE ROWS EMP-NAME MAXIMUM PAY-RATE-1-10#1.
```

Comments

♦ The FORMAT option tells Peachtree Report Writer how to output the information. (See the FORMAT command for more information on the options and features of this clause.)

♦ The IN *count* option only applies for numeric rows or columns.

♦ The MISSING-DATA option tells Peachtree Report Writer what to enter in cells in the matrix when there are no rows that contain both the row and the column value for that cell. (This overrides the default information in the IQCONFIG.DAT file.)

♦ The SUPPRESS LABELS option tells Peachtree Report Writer to suppress the column labels on the matrix.

♦ You can only use the LEGEND option with the VALUES option. You must have a legend for each value.

♦ The TITLE option tells Peachtree Report Writer what title to use for the matrix. (The TITLE command will override this specification.)

MOVE

The MOVE command tells Peachtree Report Writer to move the value of a column or temporary column, a text string of up to 60 characters, a number, or a date, time, or interval to a temporary column. If the temporary column does not already exist, Peachtree Report Writer will create it as part of the MOVE command. You will use the MOVE command most frequently as part of an IF command to set an output value or adjust a temporary column used in a calculation.

Examples

```
MOVE '**INVALID ENTRY**' TO SENIORITY.

MOVE 0.6 TO COMMISSION-PERCENTAGE.
```

A

Comments

♦ If the MOVE command is creating a new temporary column, Peachtree Report Writer will format the temporary column based on the information you are moving. If you move a text string in quotes (such as '5') to a temporary column, Peachtree Report Writer treats the temporary column as an alpha column. If you move a string without quotes (such as 5), Peachtree Report Writer treats the temporary column as a numeric column. If you move a date, Peachtree Report Writer treats the temporary column as a date column.

♦ The ROUNDED and TRUNCATED options in the command let you round or truncate the result.

MULTIPLY

The MULTIPLY command creates a temporary column as the result of multiplying one column, temporary column, or value by another.

Examples

```
MULTIPLY NET-CHECK-AMOUNT TIMES -1.000 GIVING ADJUSTED-CHECK SCALE 5.2.

MULTIPLY CONTRACT-HOURS TIMES TOTAL-STAFF GIVING TOTAL-CONTRACT-HOURS.
```

Comments

◆ The MULTIPLY command can be used in an IF command.

◆ You can multiply using the system columns CURRENT-DATE, CURRENT-TIME, and CURRENT-DATETIME with the MULTIPLY command.

◆ The ROUNDED and TRUNCATED options in the command let you round or truncate the result.

PROMPT

The PROMPT command lets you prompt for information as part of a procedure and moves this information to a temporary column. You can use the information as part of your procedure processing.

Examples

```
PROMPT 'Enter the bonus amount.' TO PROMPT_BONUS_AMOUNT NUMERIC 5.2 .

PROMPT 'Enter starting date:' TO EMP-START-DATE DATE.
```

Comments

◆ The *prompt-message* is the string that Peachtree Report Writer will display to the user when the procedure is performed.

◆ The PICK-PROCEDURE option tells Peachtree Report Writer to perform a procedure if the user selects Values on the User Prompt dialog box when the procedure is performed. This will create a picklist of values to select from.

♦ The PICK-COLUMN option specifies a column that Peachtree Report Writer will query if the user selects Values on the User Prompt dialog box when the procedure is performed. Peachtree Report Writer uses the values in the column to create a picklist.

REPORT

The REPORT command defines a custom report. It is closely related to the LABEL command (discussed earlier in this chapter).

Examples

Character mode:

```
REPORT WIDTH 80 LENGTH 60 FOOTER 3
HEADING 15 ' ' 43 'TOTAL' NEXT LINE 12 'EMP-NAME' 36 'QTD-3-AMT-EE-
1-30#1'
DETAIL SUBTOTAL BREAK ON EMP-NAME 1 EMP-NAME 39
SUBTOTAL QTD-3-AMT-EE-1-30#1 FORMAT '9999999999.99-' ZERO TOTAL 39
TOTAL QTD-3-AMT-EE-1-30#1 FORMAT '9999999999.99-' ZERO.
```

Graphical mode:

```
REPORT GRAPHICAL WINDOWS ENGLISH MARGIN '1.000' '1.000' '1.000'
'1.000'
FONT 'Times New Roman' SIZE 10.00 COLOR 00000000
HEADING 1.02 1 ' ' ALIGN 0 FONT 'Arial' SIZE 10.00 BOLD 700 COLOR
00000000 3.06 'TOTAL' ALIGN 0 NEXT LINE 0.50 'Employee Name' ALIGN 0
2.76 'QTD Earnings '
DETAIL SUBTOTAL BREAK ON EMP-NAME FONT 'Times New Roman' SIZE 10.00
COLOR 00000000 0.00 EMP-NAME ALIGN 0 2.77
SUBTOTAL QTD-3-AMT-EE-1-30#1 FORMAT '9999999999.99-' ZERO ALIGN 1
TOTAL 2.77
TOTAL QTD-3-AMT-EE-1-30#1 FORMAT '9999999999.99-' ZERO BORDER HEIGHT
TEXT BOX SINGLE SOLID COLOR 07000000 SHADOW COLOR 07000000 ALIGN 1.
```

A

Comments

Comments on general report options are:

♦ Peachtree Report Writer looks for the HEADING, FOOTING, SUBHEADING, DETAIL, SUBTOTAL, and TOTAL keywords to identify the respective report areas. The REPORT command must define at least one of these report areas.

♦ The WIDTH and LENGTH options tell Peachtree Report Writer how to set the page size of the output for printed reports or reports sent to files. You can also use the WIDTH option to tell Peachtree Report Writer how wide to set the report width on the screen when you are using the Report Designer for editing the report procedure.

♦ The FOOTER option tells Peachtree Report Writer how many lines to reserve at the bottom of the page for the footer. (This is for character reports only.)

♦ The SUPPRESS option tells Peachtree Report Writer to print the column only on the first line after a subtotal area.

♦ The FORMAT option tells Peachtree Report Writer how to output the information. See the FORMAT command for more information on the options and features of this clause.

Comments on summary options:

♦ The DETACH option lets you print the subtotal area on a separate page. This may be convenient for printing subtotals from detailed information that may be confidential, such as paycheck amounts or customer credit balances. In addition, this feature is convenient if you have a large subtotal area or many subtotal breaks that would otherwise force Peachtree Report Writer to budget enough space for details and the complete subtotal area on a single page, thereby causing excessive white space at the bottom of report pages.

♦ The NEXT LINE option tells Peachtree Report Writer to start the definition of the report object on a new line.

♦ The SKIP *number* [LINES] tells Peachtree Report Writer to skip the specified number of lines and to start the definition of the report object on a new line.

♦ The NEW PAGE option tells Peachtree Report Writer to force a page break.

Comments on the report objects:

♦ The *position* option for an object tells Peachtree Report Writer where to print the object. This value is in characters if it is a character report, or in the unit of measure (metric or English) as specified in the REPORT command.

♦ The *repeat_count 'text'* option for an object tells Peachtree Report Writer to print the specified text string *repeat_count* times.

♦ The SIZE option for an object tells Peachtree Report Writer to use a specified column width for a character column rather than the column's default width. This value is in characters if it is a character report, or in the unit of measure (metric or English) as specified in the REPORT command.

CAUTION: If you specify a column that is too small for the information you are printing, Peachtree Report Writer will truncate the information.

♦ The TRIM option for an object tells Peachtree Report Writer to trim trailing blanks from the information in the column. Trimming may force the rest of the line to be adjusted to the left.

♦ The BLOCK option tells Peachtree Report Writer to create a rectangular block in the text column. The value of *width* times the value of *lines* must be greater than or equal to the total output size for the column. This value is in characters if it is a character report, or in the unit of measure (metric or English) as specified in the REPORT command.

♦ The PAGE-NO (or PAGE-NUMBER) option tells Peachtree Report Writer to print the current page number.

♦ The CURRENT-DATE, CURRENT-TIME, and CURRENT-DATETIME options tell Peachtree Report Writer to print the system date, time, or date and time when Peachtree Report Writer performs the procedure.

Comments on the *graphical-object-attributes*:

A

♦ The BORDER option for graphical objects tells Peachtree Report Writer where a box or border for an object begins.

♦ The HEIGHT option tells Peachtree Report Writer if left and right borders should be set according to the height of the graphical object or the height of the line the object appears on.

♦ The BOX, and the LEFT, RIGHT, TOP, and BOTTOM options tell Peachtree Report Writer whether to use a box or individual border lines around the object.

NOTE: You cannot use both the BOX and the LEFT, RIGHT, TOP, and BOTTOM options in the same object specifications.

♦ The *border-color* lets you specify a color (in hexadecimal notation) to use for the border. The border color code has the format *nnRRGGBB*, where RR, GG, and BB are the hexadecimal values for the red, green, and blue components of the colors, respectively. Values for each of these can be from 00 to FF. The smaller the value for the color component, the more color appears. For example, 01FF0000 would be a strong red and 010000FF would be a strong blue, whereas 01550000 would be a light red and 01000055 would be a light blue. Table A-5 shows the border color codes for the colors in the drop-down list on the REPORT windows.

You can specify custom colors by editing the color codes in the Edit Procedures window. The CONTROL.INI file in your Windows directory has the hexadecimal codes for the colors used in Windows.

NOTE: The codes for border colors are different from the codes for font colors.

♦ The SHADOW COLOR *border_color* tells Peachtree Report Writer to add a drop shadow. You can specify a color using the color codes shown in Table A-5.

Desired Border Color	Border Color Code
Red	01FF0000
Green	0200FF00
Blue	030000FF
Cyan	0400FFFF
Magenta	05FF00FF
Yellow	06FFFF00
Black	07000000
Dark Gray	08404040
Gray	09808080
Light Gray	0AC0C0C0
White	0B000000

Border Color Codes

Table A-5.

♦ The WIDTH option tells Peachtree Report Writer to set the container width for a graphical object. This value is in characters if it is a character report, or in the unit of measure (metric or English) as specified in the REPORT command.

♦ The ALIGN option tells Peachtree Report Writer how to align the text or column information in the container you have created. Entering 0 aligns the text to the left, 1 aligns the text to the right, and 2 centers the text.

♦ The SUBTOTAL, AVERAGE, MINIMUM, MAXIMUM, and COUNT options tell Peachtree Report Writer to print the information for the column. Using the ZERO AFTER option tells Peachtree Report Writer to reset this value after the information is printed. This has the effect of making the information apply only to this subtotal break rather than as a running calculation that applies to all the information that has been printed in the report so far.

♦ The PERCENT option tells Peachtree Report Writer to calculate the value of the subtotal as a percentage of the total value for the column (even if the total itself is not printed on the report).

♦ The HOURS option tells Peachtree Report Writer to calculate the column subtotal or total in an HH:MM format.

♦ The TOTAL option tells Peachtree Report Writer to calculate the total for the column.

♦ The *character-typestyle* can be bold, italic, and/or underlined.

Comments on graphical report options:

NOTE: Graphical reports can have font specifications in the report that relate to any of the objects appearing on the report, including columns, column headings, footers, page numbers, report date and time, titles, and so on. Peachtree Report Writer uses the default font until you enter a font specification in a REPORT command, whereupon Peachtree Report Writer will use this as the default font for the remainder of the REPORT command or until there is another font specification.

A

♦ *Font-name* is the font's typeface, such as Arial or Times New Roman.

♦ *Font-size* is the point size of the type. This must be in whole points; you cannot have a decimal point size such as 10.5.

♦ *Weight* is the degree of bolding to be used for the type, as shown in Table A-6.

Desired Font Weight	Value to Use
Thin	100
Ultra light	200
Light	300
Normal	400
Medium	500
Demi-bold	600
Bold	700
Ultra bold	800
Black	900

Table A-6. Font Weights

♦ *Font_color* lets you specify a color (in hexadecimal notation) to use for the font. The color code has the format 00*BBGGRR*, where BB, GG, and RR are the hexadecimal values for the blue, green, and red components of the colors, respectively. Values for each of these can be from 00 to FF. The smaller the value for the color component, the more color appears. For example, 01FF0000 would be a strong blue font color and 010000FF would be a strong red, whereas 01550000 would be a light blue and 01000055 would be a light red.

NOTE: The codes for font colors are different from the codes for chart colors, borders, and shadows.

SEARCH

The SEARCH command specifies criteria for evaluating rows for inclusion in a report.

Examples

```
SEARCH FOR ZIDX = 0 .

SEARCH FOR EMP-TYPE = 'SALES2'.
```

```
SEARCH FOR QTD-2-AMT-EE-1-30#2 > 1500.

SEARCH FOR QTD-2-AMT-EE-1-30 > 1500.
```

Comments

♦ You can use wildcards in comparison strings. The asterisk (*) represents zero or more characters of any type. The question mark (?) represents one character of any type. You can use the asterisk wildcard in equals or not equals comparisons only.

♦ You can combine AND and OR options within a condition, but you must use parentheses to establish which set of conditions is evaluated first. Peachtree Report Writer will evaluate the conditions in the innermost parentheses first, then work outwards through the conditions until all the conditions have been evaluated.

♦ To search for an apostrophe, you need to use two apostrophes to signify that Peachtree Report Writer should look for an apostrophe rather than interpret the apostrophe as the start of a text string.

♦ You can use mathematical symbols instead of the abbreviations shown in the condition syntax, as shown in Table A-7.

♦ The CASE option tells Peachtree Report Writer to do a case-sensitive comparison (for example, "abcde" would not be the same as "ABCDE"). The default is for Peachtree Report Writer to ignore case when doing comparisons.

♦ You can compare a date column to the CURRENT-DATE, a time column to the CURRENT-TIME. You can also compare dates and times to the CURRENT-DATETIME. All comparisons of date, time, or date-time columns must use the default Peachtree Report Writer date, time, or date-time format.

A

Mathematical Symbols Used in with IF commands
Table A-7.

Mathematical Symbol	Abbreviation	Meaning
=	EQ	Is A equal to B?
<>	NE	Is A not equal to B?
>	GT	Is A greater than B?
>=	GE	Is A greater than or equal to B?
<	LT	Is A less than B?
<=	LE	Is A less than or equal to B?

♦ To search for a single item in an array, specify the array element you want to search for, such as QTD-4-AMT-EE-1-30#6 for the sixth element in the QTD-4-AMT-EE-1-30 array. You can also search through an entire array by specifying the array without an element number. The SEARCH command will select the row if any array element matches the search criteria.

SORT

The SORT command sorts the rows into ascending or descending order based on the values in the specified column(s).

Examples

```
SORT ASCENDING EMP-NAME.

SORT DESCENDING EMP-TYPE ASCENDING EMP-ID.
```

Comment

♦ Peachtree Report Writer performs the sorts in the order they appear in the SORT command.

SUBSTRING

The SUBSTRING command extracts a portion of a column, such as the first few letters of an employee's last name, and puts the information into a temporary column.

Examples

```
SUBSTRING LAST-RAISE-DATE FORMAT MMM TO RAISE_MONTH.

SUBSTRING EMP-ID FROM 3 FOR 2 TO EMP-DEPT-CODE.
```

Comments

♦ The SUBSTRING command can be used in an IF command.
♦ You cannot extract information from time columns into date columns or date columns into time columns.

♦ The ALPHA option forces Peachtree Report Writer to create a text column for the result.

♦ If you are extracting a substring from a text column, Peachtree Report Writer will extract the *length* characters from the text column start at the character at *start-position*.

♦ If you are extracting a substring from a date column or a date-time column, Peachtree Report Writer will extract the month, day, or year characters to a numeric column.

♦ If you are extracting a substring from a time column or a date-time column, Peachtree Report Writer will extract the hours, minutes, or seconds characters to an interval column.

♦ If you are extracting a substring from a date-time column that is an entire date or time, Peachtree Report Writer will create a date or time temporary column. You can't use the ALPHA option when creating a date or time column.

SUBTRACT

The SUBTRACT command subtracts one numeric column, a temporary column, or a value from another numeric or temporary column, to produce a temporary column as the result. You can also subtract numeric, date, date-time, and interval columns and temporary columns.

Examples

```
SUBTRACT 500.00 FROM QTD-2-AMT-ER-1-30#5 GIVING ADJ-ER-INSURANCE-COST.
```

```
SUBTRACT CONTRACT-TOTAL-HOURS MINUS 08:00:00 GIVING RAW-OVERTIME.
```

Comments

♦ The SUBTRACT command can be used in an IF command.

♦ You can subtract using the system columns CURRENT-DATE, CURRENT-TIME, and CURRENT-DATETIME with the SUBTRACT command.

♦ If you subtract a temporary column from a date column, Peachtree Report Writer treats the temporary column as days. If you subtract a temporary column to a time, date-time, and interval columns, Peachtree Report Writer treats the temporary column as a quantity of seconds.

A

♦ The system columns CURRENT-DATE, CURRENT-TIME, and CURRENT-DATETIME may be used instead of a column.

♦ The ROUNDED and TRUNCATED options in the command let you round or truncate the result.

TITLE

The TITLE command tells Peachtree Report Writer to center the specified title in the first line of each page of the report. You can only use the TITLE command with the COLUMNAR, GRAPH, CHART, and MATRIX commands.

Examples

```
TITLE 'Employee Bonus Amounts'.

TITLE 'QTD Customer Revenue Summary'.
```

Comment

♦ *Title-text* can be up to 50 characters long. The title text can include any printable character and spaces.

Keywords

Table A-8 lists all the keywords in Peachtree Report Writer.

Although some of these keywords may be for features not implemented in this version of Peachtree Report Writer, Peachtree Report Writer may still give you an error if you attempt to use a keyword as a temporary column name.

3D	ADD	AFTER	ALIGN
ALPHA	AND	AREA	ARRANGE
ASCENDING	ASCII	ASCII_CSV	ASCII_FIXED
ASSOC	ASSOCIATE	ASSOCIATED	AUTHOR
AVERAGE	BACKGROUND	BAR	BARS
BITMAP	BLOCK	BOLD	BORDER
BOTTOM	BOX	BREAK	BTRIEVE
BY	CALCULATE	CASE	CENTIMETERS
CHANGE	CHARACTER	CHART	CLIP
CMS	COL-TOTAL	COLOR	COLUMNAR
COLUMNS	COMPUTE	CONCATENATE	CONVERT
COUNT	CURRENT-DATE	CURRENT-DATETIME	CURRENT-TIME
DASHED	DATA	DATE	DATETIME
DAYS	DBASE_2	DBASE_3	DELETE
DESCENDING	DETACH	DETAIL	DEVICE
DIAG	DICTIONARY	DIF	DISK
DIVIDE	DIVIDED-BY	DOTTED	DOUBLE
EDIT	ELSE	END	ENGLISH
EQ	EQUAL	EXCEL	EXECUTE
EXIT	FIELD	FILE	FIND
FIT	FONT	FOOTER	FOOTING
FOR	FOREGROUND	FORMAT	FROM
GE	GIVING	GRAND-TOTAL	GRAPHICAL
GREATER	GROUP	GROUPED-BY	GT
HEADING	HEIGHT	HORIZ_GRID	HOURS
HPITCH	IF	IN	INCHES
INITIALIZE	INTERVAL	INTERVALS	INTO
IS	ITALIC	ITEMS	KEY
LABEL	LABELS	LBLACROSS	LBLDOWN
LE	LEFT	LEGEND	LENGTH
LESS	LF	LIMIT	LINE
LINES	LIST	LISTPROC	LITERAL
LOCATION	LOTUS	LOTUS_123_1A	LOTUS_123_R2
LOTUS_123_R3	LT	MAILMERGE	MARGIN

Keywords
Used in
Peachtree
Report Writer
Table A-8.

A

MATRIX	MAXIMUM	ME	METRIC
MINIMUM	MINUS	MINUTES	MISSING
MISSING-DATA	MODIFY	MONO	MOTIF
MOVE	MP	MULTIPLAN	MULTIPLY
NE	NEW	NEXT	NO
NO-SPACE	NO-TRIM	NORMAL	NOSPACE
NOTRIM	NULL	NUMBER	NUMERIC
OF	OFFSET	ON	OR
ORGANIZE	OUTPUT	PAGE	PAGE-NO
PAGE-NUMBER	PARTTAB	PATTERN	PERCENT
PERFORM	PICK-COLUMN	PICK-PROCEDURE	PICKLIST
PIE	PLUS	POINTS	PRINT
PRINTED	PRINTER	PRIVATE	PROCEDURE
PROCESSED	PROMPT	QUIT	QUIZ
READ-ONLY	READ-WRITE	RECORD-DETAIL	RECORDS
REFERENCE	REPEAT	REPORT	RESTART
REVIEW	RIGHT	ROUND	ROUNDED
ROW-TOTAL	ROWS	SAVE	SCALE
SCATTER	SCREEN	SEARCH	SECONDS
SECURE	SELECTED	SHADOW	SHOW
SINGLE	SIZE	SKIP	SOLID
SORT	SPACE	SPACED	SQLSYNTAX
STACKED_BAR	STRIKEOUT	SUBHEADING	SUBSTRING
SUBTOTAL	SUBTRACT	SUMMARY	SUPPRESS
TABBED	TEXT	THAN	THE
THEN	TIME	TIMES	TITLE
TITLES	TO	TODAY	TODAYS-DATE
TOP	TRIM	TRUNCATE	TRUNCATED
UNDERLINE	UNIQUE	UNITS	UPDATE
USING	VALUES	VERSION	VERSUS
VERT_GRID	VIEW	VPITCH	VS
WIDTH	WINDOWS	WITH	WORDMARC
WORDPERFECT_42	WORDPERFECT_51	WORD_WIN	X_AXIS
X_TITLE	YES	Y_AXIS	Y_TITLE
ZERO			

Keywords
Used in
Peachtree
Report Writer
(*continued*)
Table A-8.

B

Online and Printed Resources

This appendix contains a selection of online and printed resources, including web sites, newsgroups, and books.

Online Resources

This section contains a listing of web URLs and newsgroups in the following categories:

Category	Description
HTML and Web Tutorials and References	Tutorials and references for HTML and related topics
Web Site Support	Sources for buttons, bars, graphics, and other information
Search Engines	Tools to get more information from the Web
Windows Resources	Web sites specific to Microsoft Windows topics
Shareware Resources	Places to look for shareware
Peachtree Products and Services	Web sites specifically devoted to Peachtree products
CD-ROM Web Sites	Web sites for products on the CD-ROM and products listed in Chapter 11, "Peachtree Accounting Add-ons and Other Software"
Finance and Business	Web sites on Finance- and business-related topics
Other Sites of Interest	A collection of other sites of interest to Windows 95 users and accounting professionals

URLs and online resources change frequently. As a result, some of the items listed in this chapter may no longer be valid when you try them. In addition to knowing how to use your browser to look up URLs, you should become familiar with using one or more web search engines (such as AltaVista and Yahoo) to update the information in this appendix as well as to find new listings. There is always another web site with something worthwhile.

TIP: You may encounter temporary problems accessing a web site due to heavy traffic, it being offline temporarily, or any of a number of other problems that may prevent access at that time. Some of the larger and more popular web sites are particularly prone to being overloaded when new versions of a program are released. If you cannot access a specific web site, try again. If you are still unable to access the web site, wait a while and try when it is not prime time (early morning hours are frequently the easiest times to get into busy web sites).

Although some of the sites in this appendix are listed as recommended (as particularly useful or appealing), all of the sites and newsgroups have a great deal to offer. You may want to check out the recommended sites first and then browse as many of the other sites as your schedule permits.

HTML and Web Tutorials and References

This section contains resources for tutorials and references for HTML and related topics.

Web Pages That Suck   *http://www.webpagesthatsuck.com*

An essential URL for every web developer! This web site illustrates many of the more grievous offenses commonly made by web developers and gives strategies for how to avoid committing them yourself. Their motto (shown in Figure B-1) says it all. **Recommended.**

Yahoo's WWW Information
http://www.yahoo.com/Computers/World_Wide_Web

General information on the Web and resources.

Microsoft Resources   *http://www.microsoft.com/workshop/author/default.asp*

A collection of FAQs, tips, and tutorials on web site development.

The Virtual Library   *http://www.stars.com*

An extraordinarily comprehensive selection of links, files, and information for web developers. The web page is shown in Figure B-2. **Recommended.**

B

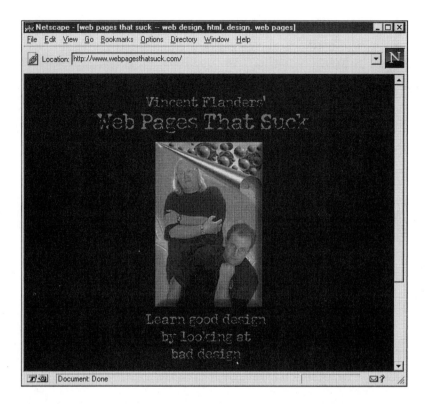

Web Pages
That Suck
Figure B-1.

WWW & HTML Developer's JumpStation
http://oneworld.wa.com/htmldev/devpage/dev-page.html

A site devoted primarily to HTML and the World Wide Web. There are dozens of HTML links for beginning, intermediate, and advanced HTML users.

Netscape's Open Network Environment Pages
http://developer.netscape.com/one/index.html

A section of the Netscape web site that provides information for developers. Look for information on HTML and Java here.

The Beginner's Guide to HTML
http://www.ncsa.uiuc.edu/General/Internet/WWW/HTMLPrimer.html

A FAQ for HTML from the National Center for Supercomputing Applications.

HTML: An Interactive Tutorial for Beginners
http://www.davesite.com/webstation/html

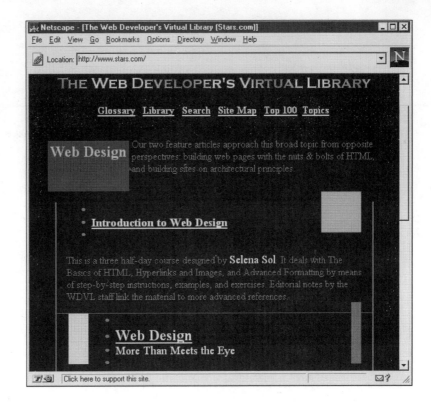

The Virtual
Library
Figure B-2.

A very good step-by-step online tutorial for learning HTML. The main page
is shown in Figure B-3.

The HyperNews Forum
http://union.ncsa.uiuc.edu/HyperNews/get/www/html/guides.html

The HyperNews Forum resources at the National Center for
Supercomputing Applications.

Composing Good HTML   *http://www.cs.cmu.edu/~tilt/cgh*

Tips and techniques on how to compose good HTML.

D.J. Quad's Ultimate HTML Site   *http://www.quadzilla.com*

Another really good site for HTML resources of all kinds. Figure B-4 shows
a list of main topics covered at this site. **Recommended.**

Beginning HTML Tutorials
http://www.devry-phx.edu/webresrc/webmstry/lrntutrl.htm

B

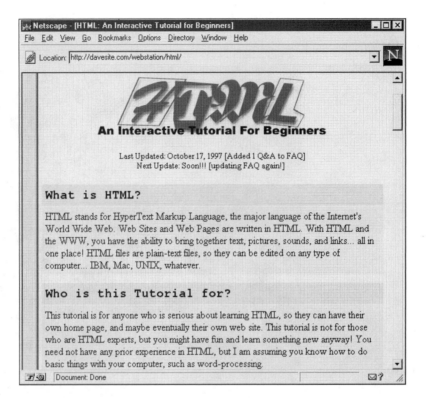

An Interactive
Tutorial for
Beginners
Figure B-3.

A collection of HTML tutorials for beginners.

HTML Table Tutorial   *http://www.charm.net/~lejeune/tables.html*

A tutorial specifically for information on creating tables in HTML.

In addition to the preceding URLs, the following newsgroups can provide current information on HTML as well as a venue for you to ask questions about HTML and building your web site:

comp.infosystems.www.authoring.html

comp.infosystems.www.authoring.misc

Web Site Support

This section contains information on where to find graphics (buttons, bars, and icons), site-visit counters, and instructions for listing your web page with various search engines.

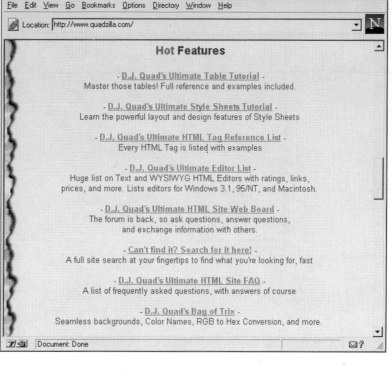

D.J. Quad's
Ultimate
HTML Site
Figure B-4.

Cool Graphics on the Web
http://www.geocities.com/SiliconValley/Heights/1272/index.html

One of the best graphics sites on the web! The site has several hundred free graphics and links to thousands of other clipart files on the web. **Recommended.**

Yahoo's Clipart
http://www.yahoo.com/Computers/Multimedia/Pictures/Clip_art

Dozens more links to clipart.

Hee Yun's Graphic Collection
http://soback.kornet.nm.kr/~pixeline/heeyun/graphics.html

A fine collection of graphics (a page of which appears in Figure B-5) you can use on your web site. **Recommended.**

The Graphics Station   *http://www.geocities.com/SiliconValley/6603/*

Graphics, wallpaper, and icons.

B

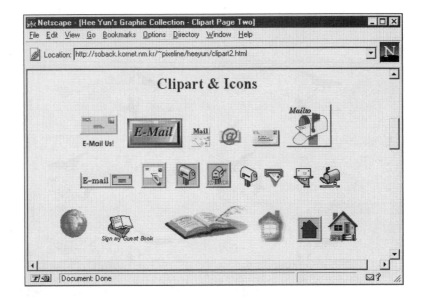

Hee Yun's
Graphic
Collection
Figure B-5.

Yahoo's GIFs
http://www.yahoo.com/Computers_and_Internet/Software/Graphics/

Links to information on graphics, viewers, and other utilities.

WebCounter Page   *www.digits.com*

One of the best-known site counters.

Fingers and Toes   *http://www.digitmania.holowww.com/*

Counters, clocks, and related fonts and graphics.

!Register-It!   *http://www.register-it.com*

A web site promotional tool (shown in Figure B-6) that lets you register your web site with a variety of different search engines. **Recommended.**

Submit It!: The Web Site Promotion Tool
http://free.submit-it.com/submit.htm

Another web site promotional tool for listing your web site with different search engines and search services.

Web Lint HTML Validator   *http://www.cen.uiuc.edu/cgi-bin/weblint*

A web page analysis tool that checks your web pages for places where the HTML code could be tightened up or clarified.

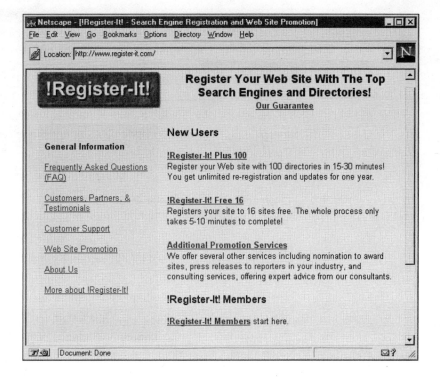

!Register-It!
Figure B-6.

Dr. HTML   *http://imagiware.com/RxHTML.cgi*

Another excellent web-page analysis tool.

In addition to the preceding URLs, the following newsgroups can provide information on graphics and clipart:

   comp.infosystems.www.authoring.images

   alt.binaries.clip-art

Search Engines

This section contains resources for tools to get more information from the Web.

AltaVista   *http://altavista.digital.com/*

AltaVista is the most popular search engine on the web today. Enter your search keywords and find almost anything you can think of. A typical AltaVista search for "Peachtree Accounting for Windows" appears in Figure B-7. **Recommended.**

B

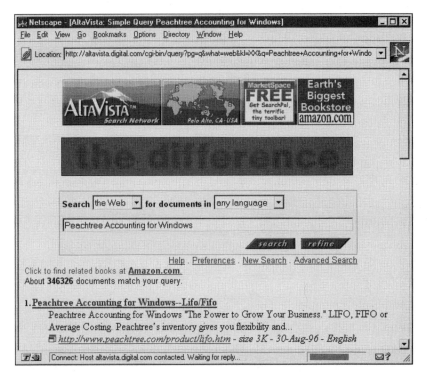

AltaVista
Figure B-7.

Yahoo! *http://www.yahoo.com*

Another extremely popular search engine, Yahoo! (shown in Figure B-8) uses a different search paradigm than AltaVista, making it frequently easier to find information for one of the many predefined categories. **Recommended.**

Lycos *http://www.lycos.com*

Another search engine that provides a number of predefined categories for quick reference.

WebCrawler *http://www.webcrawler.com*

A smaller search engine that also provides news and information.

Windows Resources

This section contains information on Microsoft Windows resources. (General shareware appears in the following section.)

Official Windows 95 Web Site *http://www.microsoft.com/windows*

The place to go for information about Windows 95.

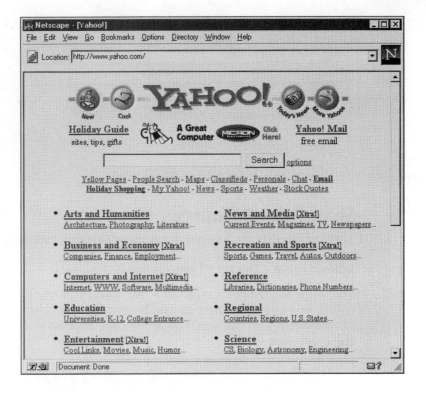

Yahoo!
Figure B-8.

Windows 95 Annoyances   *http://www.creativelement.com/win95ann/*

Tips, tricks, and workarounds for Windows 95.

Microsoft Windows 95 Service Packs
http://www.microsoft.com/windows95/info/service-packs.htm

This is the download site for Service Pack 1 for Microsoft Windows 95, which greatly reduces all kinds of problems. **Recommended.**

http://www.microsoft.com/windows95/info/krnlupd.htm

Fixes a memory "leak" that can cause you to run out of memory when running Internet applications over a long period of time in Windows 95. **Recommended.**

http://www.microsoft.com/typography/grayscal/smoother.htm

Here you'll find a font-smoothing utility for Windows 95, which makes text appear much better on the screen.

B

In addition to the preceding URLs, the following newsgroups can provide information about upcoming Windows 95 product announcements and Windows applications:

comp.os.ms-windows.announce

comp.os.ms-windows.apps.financial

comp.os.ms-windows.apps.misc

comp.os.ms-windows.apps.utilities.win95

Shareware Resources

This section lists places to look for shareware and freeware.

Walnut Creek CDROM   *http://www.cdrom.com/*

The home for Walnut Creek CDROM, maker of some of the best shareware collections available. Most of the shareware available on their CDs can be downloaded from this site. The home page appears in Figure B-9. **Recommended.**

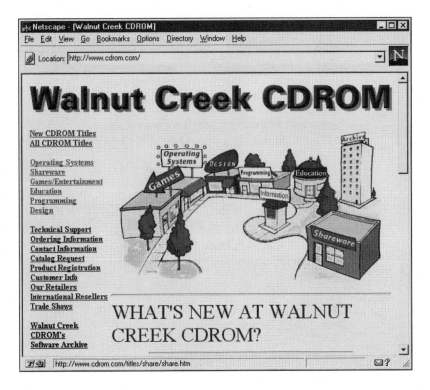

Walnut Creek
CD-ROM
Figure B-9.

Windows95.com   *www.windows95.com*

Windows 95 applications and information.

ZDNet Software Library   *http://www.hotfiles.com*

The ZDNet web page for Windows 95 and other software.

Stroud's CWSApps   *http://www.stroud.com/new.html*

A collection of Windows and Windows 95 applications. This is a very good site for tracking the latest interesting applications (shown in Figure B-10).

TUCOWS   *http://www.tucows.com*

The TUCOWS web site, a very extensive Internet software web site.

Randy's Windows 95 Resource Center   *http://pcwin.com*

Home site of Randy Burgess's PCWin Resource Center.

WIN95.COM   *http://www.win95.com*

A source for software and information specifically focused on Windows 95.

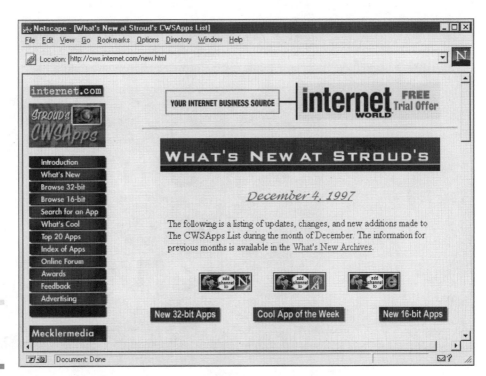

B

Stroud's
CWSApps
Figure B-10.

Thomas Leuthard's Fonts Page   *http://thomas.simplenet.com*

Excellent web page for downloadable fonts. A sample page of the fonts on this site appears in Figure B-11. **Recommended.**

Funduc   *http://home.sprynet.com/sprynet/funduc*

Some handy utilities for Windows 95.

Vector Development   *http://www.vecdev.com*

The Vector Development web site, home of DUNCE (the Dial-up Networking Connection Enhancement), an essential tool for Windows 95 Internet connection. **Recommended.**

Peachtree Products and Services

This section contains information on web sites and resources specifically devoted to Peachtree products.

Peachtree   *http://www.peachtree.com*

The main Peachtree web site, shown in Figure B-12.

http://www.peachtree.com/forms/html/psclist.htm

A list (by state) of local Peachtree Support Centers.

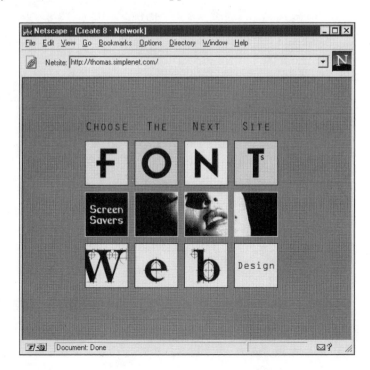

Thomas
Leuthard's
fonts page
Figure B-11.

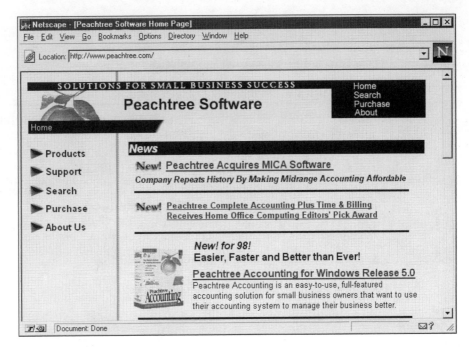

Main
Peachtree page
Figure B-12.

Perfect Systemss Inc.   *http://www.halcyon.com/psinc/*

A Peachtree Support Center located in Western Washington.

Wizard Business Solutions   *http://www.wizard-net.com*

Home site for Wizard Business Solutions, a Peachtree Support Center located in North Carolina.

In addition to the preceding URLs, the following newsgroups are excellent sources of information on accounting software:

alt.accounting

biz.comp.accounting

CD-ROM Web Sites

This section contains information on the web sites for the products on the CD-ROM and products listed in Chapter 11, "Peachtree Accounting Add-ons and Other Software."

Multiware, Inc.   *http://www.dcn.davis.ca.us/~walraven/pawet.htm*

Information on PAW/et.

B

Wizard Business Solutions   *http://www.wizard-net.com*

Home site for Wizard Business Solutions, makers of a wide variety of Peachtree add-ons (shown in Figure B-13).

Expert Software   *http://www.expertsoftware.com*

Home site for Expert Software, who produce multimedia training programs and collections of software and files on CD.

WinZip   *http://www.winzip.com/winzip/winzip_t.htm*

Nico Mak Computing, source for WinZip, one of the all-time best Windows utilities (shown in Figure B-14). **Recommended.**

Arachnophilia   *http://www.arachnoid.com/index.html*

Site for Arachnophilia, a first-rate HTML editor.

Eudora   *http://www.eudora.com*

Web site for the Eudora family of mail software.

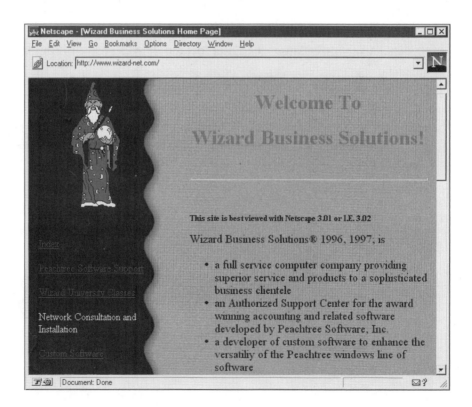

Wizard
Business
Solutions
Figure B-13.

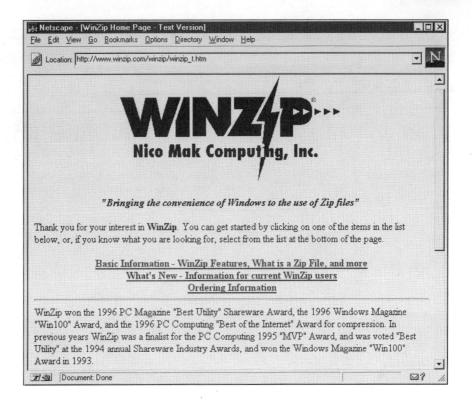

WinZip
home page
Figure B-14.

Free Agent   *http://www.forteinc.com*

Web site for Forté and the Free Agent newsreader.

WinCode   *http://www.winsite.com/info/pc/win3/util/wincode.zip*

Source of WinCode Internet decoding utility.

Visio   *http://www.visio.com/*

Web page for Visio charting tool (shown in Figure B-15).

Paint Shop Pro   *http://www.jasc.com*

Home page for JASC and Paint Shop Pro, an excellent paint and graphics program.

F-PROT   *http://www.datafellows.com/f-prot/*

Home page for the F-PROT virus scanner.

McAfee   *http://www.mcafee.com*

B

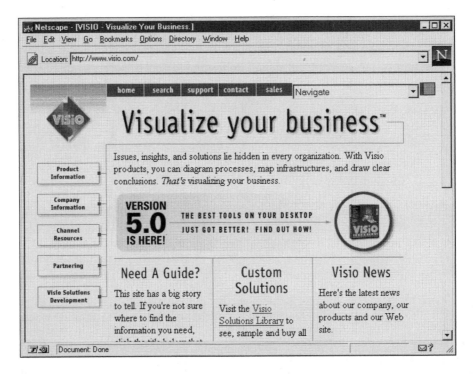

Visio
Figure B-15.

Home page for McAfee VirusScan for Windows 95.

Symantec   *http://www.symantec.com*

Home page for Symantec, Norton Desktop for Windows 95, and Norton AntiVirus.

Finance and Business

RCM Financial Group   *http://www.rcmfinancial.com*

A huge collection of stock and financial sites from RCM Financial Group LLC. The RCM Financial Site has over 1,200 pages and 80,000 links. **Recommended**.

DBC Online   *http://www.dbc.com*

Another good financial site, this one from Data Broadcasting Corporation (shown in Figure B-16).

Dogs of the Dow Online Magazine   *http://www.dogsofthedow.com*

A site for private investors. This site was selected "Best of the Web" by Money Magazine.

DBC Online
Figure B-16.

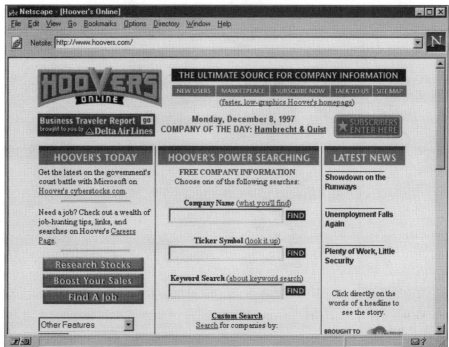

Hoover's
Online
Figure B-17.

B

Hoover's Online   *http://www.hoovers.com*

Curious about a company? Use this web site (shown in Figure B-17) to look up a company's background and financial information as well as track current news items mentioning the company.

NAIC Online   *http://www.better-investing.org/*

Resources for private investors. The National Association of Investors Corporation is a not-for-profit corporation focusing on providing assistance to the small investor. The home page appears in Figure B-18.

Silicon Investor Online   *http://www.techstocks.com/*

Information on high-tech stocks and businesses.

Financial Data Finder   *http://www.cob.ohio-state.edu/dept/fin/osudata.htm*

A first-rate site of financial resources run by Ohio State University and Fisher College of Business. Figure B-19 shows a sample page from this site. **Recommended.**

NAIC Online
Figure B-18.

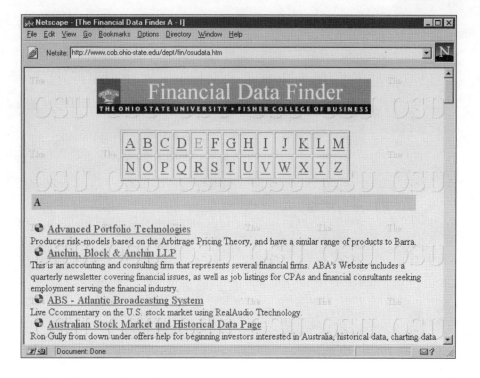

Financial
Data Finder
Figure B-19.

Other Sites of Interest

This section contains some other sites of interest to Windows 95 users and accounting professionals.

MTU-Speed Home Page *http://www.mjs.u-net.com/mtuspeed/mtuspeed.htm*

A useful utility for speeding up your Internet access by optimizing your connection to the Internet.

IRS Forms *http://www.irs.gov/forms_pubs/forms.html*

The source for IRS forms and filing instructions of all kinds.

Four-11 E-Mail Directory *http://www.Four11.com*

An online reference for e-mail, telephone, and address listings for the U.S. This site, which appears in Figure B-20, also has links to other national and global telephone listings.

MapQuest! Interactive Atlas *http://www.mapquest.com*

Invaluable for providing concise directions (with maps) from place to place. This site can provide maps and driving directions for most of the world.

B

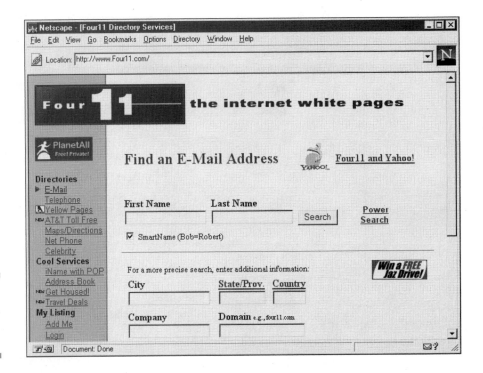

Four-11
E-Mail
Directory
Figure B-20.

Osborne/McGraw-Hill   *http://www.osborne.com/*

Use to order additional copies of this book or other books on Peachtree Accounting products. Figure B-21 shows a sample listing.

Sense Networking   *http://www.oz.net*

Home page for Sense Networking, the best ISP in Washington State.

CNET: The Computer Network   *www.cnet.com*

Home page for CNET, with news, reviews, and current information about the computer industry.

John Vernon Hedtke's Web Page   *http://www.oz.net/~jhedtke*

The author's web site. You can download forms for converting from other accounting systems to Peachtree Accounting. There is also information on other books of interest to Peachtree Accounting users.

My Desktop   *http://www.mydesktop.com*

Another source of current information and software.

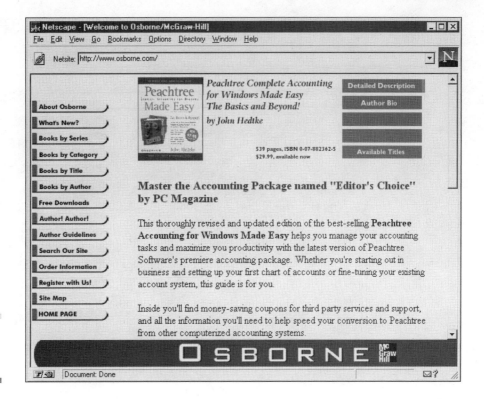

Osborne/
McGraw-Hill
Figure B-21.

Books A to Z *http://www.booksatoz.com*

An excellent source of links to online book services, publishers, and related services (shown in Figure B-22). While you're there, take a look at the page for Wit's End bookstore at http://www.booksatoz.com/witsend/index.htm.

Books

B

This section contains recommended books of interest on a variety of subjects.

♦ *The Non-Designer's Web Book* by Robin Williams and John Tollett (Peachpit Press, 1998). This book tells you everything you need to know about web basics, the elements of web-page design, technical information such as using graphics, fonts, and colors, and how to maintain and promote your web page. This book is particularly attractive in that it is printed in color, so you can clearly see the differences in choosing one combination over another.

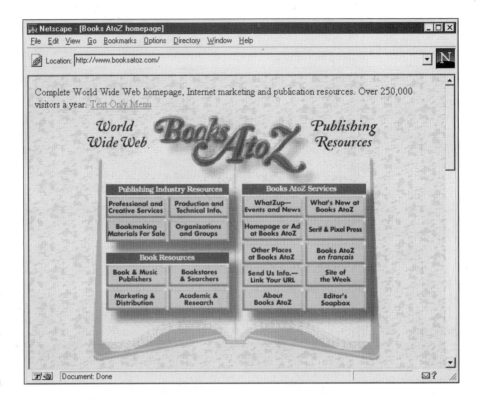

Books A to Z
Figure B-22.

♦ *Creating Commercial Web Pages* by Laura Lemay and Brian Murphy (SamsNet, 1996). This book provides information for the intermediate and advanced user on how to add technical features to your web pages. The book comes with a CD-ROM containing a variety of utilities, sample applications, and programs.

♦ *Web Marketing Cookbook* by Janice King, Paul Knight, and James H. Mason (Wiley and Sons, 1997). This book will help you adapt your sales and marketing material to the Web, generate publicity, and market your company's services online. The book comes with a CD-ROM containing a variety of templates, resources, and tools.

♦ *Webmaster Answers: Certified Tech Support* by Chris Ditto (Osborne/ McGraw-Hill, 1998). This handy troubleshooting guide is packed with answers to frequently asked questions about Web page creation and management, as well as solutions to common problems.

♦ *NetMarketing* by Bruce Judson (Wolff New Media, 1996). This book introduces you to the concepts of commercial web design by showing you commercial web sites for dozens of large corporations.

♦ *Getting Hits* by Don Sellers (Peachpit Press, 1997). This book focuses specifically on how to get more people to visit your web site by registering with search engines, using Internet newsgroups, and inspiring repeat business and recommendations from your customers.

♦ *Peachtree Complete Accounting for Windows Made Easy* by John Hedtke (Osborne/McGraw-Hill, 1997). This book gives you detailed information on how to use Peachtree Complete Accounting for Windows.

♦ *Peachtree Accounting for Windows Made Easy* by John Hedtke (Osborne/McGraw-Hill, 1995). This book gives you detailed information on how to use Peachtree Accounting for Windows. (Check the Osborne/McGraw-Hill web site at *http://www.osborne.com* for information on new and upcoming books on Peachtree Accounting for Windows and Peachtree Complete Accounting for Windows.)

♦ *Dynamic HTML in Action* by Michele Petrovsky (Osborne/McGraw-Hill, 1998) For the person who wants to explore what they can do with HTML, this book is a must. The Osborne/McGraw-Hill web site provides plenty of HTML code and a project template to supplement this book.

B

Index

I

N

O

P

W

Peachtree Support

Get the service you deserve from Peachtree's premier support center.

Whether you have a technical problem

or a quick question, need help setting up your system,

or want a local area network installed, PSI's Peachtree

certified staff is available to help you.

PSC
Authorized Peachtree
Support Center

Perfect Systems, Inc.
Helping you Build a Better Business
1-800-783-2399 or (206) 270-9080
Fax: (206) 324-2882
e-mail: psinc@halcyon.com
http://www.halcyon.com/psinc/

Software Business Products

Computer Checks, Forms and Envelopes

**25%
Discount**
(see below)

FOR INFORMATION AND ASSISTANCE
CALL TOLL FREE 1-800-553-6485
FAX FREE 1-800-245-1337
visit our Website at http://www.softwarebusprod.com

MAILING ADDRESS
Software Business Products
10150 Alliance Rd.
Cincinnati, OH 45242

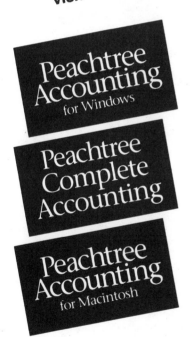

- **LOWEST FACTORY DIRECT PRICING**

- **WIDEST VARIETY OF PRODUCTS FOR YOUR PEACHTREE SOFTWARE**
  Continuous and laser checks, forms and envelopes for all versions.

- **100% GUARANTEED COMPATIBLE**
  – All checks, forms & envelopes for your Peachtree Software.

- **100% SATISFACTION GUARANTEED**
  If you are not satisfied with your order for any reason, within 30 days of delivery we will gladly correct or replace your order, or refund your money. NO HASSLE - GUARANTEED!

- **FAST, DEPENDABLE DELIVERY - COMPETITIVE TURNAROUND TIME**

- **TAX FORMS - A COMPLETE SELECTION THAT MEET IRS SPECIFICATIONS**

- **CUSTOM CHECKS, FORMS & ENVELOPES**
  For an enhanced professional image – Call 1-800-449-9599

- **STRONG DEALER PROGRAM WITH SUBSTANTIAL DISCOUNTS & PROMOTIONS**
  For More Information – Call 1-800-858-3676

$ SAVE MONEY $

25% DISCOUNT

On your next order of business forms, checks and envelopes for your Peachtree Software!
Please call for a free Brochure and Sample Kit.
Copy this coupon for your mail or fax orders. **Please use ad code CBTK** when placing orders.
CALL 800-553-6485 or FAX 800-245-1337
THANKS FOR CHOOSING Software Business Products

About the CD-ROM

The CD that accompanies this book has a wide selection of programs and utilities that will be of use to you when you use Peachtree Accounting for Windows, Peachtree Complete Accounting for Windows, and Windows 95.

For a complete list of the programs on the CD-ROM, do the following:

1. Insert the CD-ROM into your computer's CD-ROM drive.
2. Double-click the My Computer icon on the Windows 95 desktop. The My Computer windows appears.
3. Double-click the CD-ROM icon, shown here:

A standard contents window appears.

4. Double-click the README.TXT icon. Read the file for information on the programs and utilities on the CD-ROM.

NOTE: Most of the programs on the CD will have separate installation programs; however, some of them will be files that you copy to a directory on your computer. Check for a README.TXT file in each of the individual program directories for comments on installing specific programs or utilities.

WARNING: BEFORE OPENING THE DISC PACKAGE, CAREFULLY READ THE TERMS AND CONDITIONS OF THE FOLLOWING COPYRIGHT STATEMENT AND LIMITED CD-ROM WARRANTY.

Copyright Statement

This software is protected by both United States copyright law and international copyright treaty provision. Except as noted in the contents of the CD-ROM, you must treat this software just like a book. However, you may copy it into a computer to be used and you may make archival copies of the software for the sole purpose of backing up the software and protecting your investment from loss. By saying, "just like a book," The McGraw-Hill Companies, Inc. ("Osborne/McGraw-Hill") means, for example, that this software may be used by any number of people and may be freely moved from one computer location to another, so long as there is no possibility of its being used at one location or on one computer while it is being used at another. Just as a book cannot be read by two different people in two different places at the same time, neither can the software be used by two different people in two different places at the same time.

Limited Warranty

Osborne/McGraw-Hill warrants the physical compact disc enclosed herein to be free of defects in materials and workmanship for a period of sixty days from the purchase date. If the CD included in your book has defects in materials or workmanship, please call McGraw-Hill at 1-800-217-0059, 9:00 A.M. to 5:00 P.M., Monday through Friday, Eastern Standard Time, and McGraw-Hill will replace the defective disc.

The entire and exclusive liability and remedy for breach of this Limited Warranty shall be limited to replacement of the defective disc, and shall not include or extend to any claim for or right to cover any other damages, including but not limited to, loss of profit, data, or use of the software, or special incidental, or consequential damages or other similar claims, even if Osborne/McGraw-Hill has been specifically advised of the possibility of such damages. In no event will Osborne/McGraw-Hill's liability for any damages to you or any other person ever exceed the lower of the suggested list price or actual price paid for the license to use the software, regardless of any form of the claim.

OSBORNE/McGRAW-HILL SPECIFICALLY DISCLAIMS ALL OTHER WARRANTIES, EXPRESS OR IMPLIED, INCLUDING BUT NOT LIMITED TO, ANY IMPLIED WARRANTY OF MERCHANTABILITY OR FITNESS FOR A PARTICULAR PURPOSE. Specifically, Osborne/McGraw-Hill makes no representation or warranty that the software is fit for any particular purpose, and any implied warranty of merchantability is limited to the sixty-day duration of the Limited Warranty covering the physical disc only (and not the software), and is otherwise expressly and specifically disclaimed.

This limited warranty gives you specific legal rights; you may have others which may vary from state to state. Some states do not allow the exclusion of incidental or consequential damages, or the limitation on how long an implied warranty lasts, so some of the above may not apply to you.

This agreement constitutes the entire agreement between the parties relating to use of the Product. The terms of any purchase order shall have no effect on the terms of this Agreement. Failure of Osborne/McGraw-Hill to insist at any time on strict compliance with this Agreement shall not constitute a waiver of any rights under this Agreement. This Agreement shall be construed and governed in accordance with the laws of New York. If any provision of this Agreement is held to be contrary to law, that provision will be enforced to the maximum extent permissible, and the remaining provisions will remain in force and effect.

NO TECHNICAL SUPPORT IS PROVIDED WITH THIS CD-ROM.